ROOSEVELT UNIVERSITY LIBRARY
K5055.K381987
C001
KATZ, LEO
W9-BJS-365
3 3311 00068 643 8

BAD ACTS
AND GUILTY MINDS

Studies in Crime and Justice

BAD ACTS AND GUILTY MINDS

CONUNDRUMS of the CRIMINAL LAW

LEO KATZ

THE
UNIVERSITY OF CHICAGO PRESS
CHICAGO AND LONDON

Leo Katz is assistant professor of law at the University of Michigan.

THE UNIVERSITY OF CHICAGO PRESS, CHICAGO 60637
THE UNIVERSITY OF CHICAGO PRESS, LTD., LONDON

Printed in the United States of America
96 95 94 93 92 91 90 89 88 87   54321

Library of Congress Cataloging-in-Publication Data

Katz, Leo.
Bad acts and guilty minds.

(Studies in crime and justice)
Includes index.
1. Criminal act. 2. Criminal intent. 3. Criminal liability. 4. Criminal act—United States. 5. Criminal intent—United States. 6. Criminal liability—United States. I. Title. II. Series.
K5055.K38 1987   345′04   87-7035
ISBN 0-226-42591-6   342.54
ISBN 0-226-42592-4 (pbk.)

For Jana and Friedrich

According to the common law, each crime consists of two parts, one physical and one mental, the *actus reus* and the *mens rea,* the "bad act" and the "guilty mind"—in the case of murder, the act of killing and the malice aforethought.

Contents

Acknowledgments

I began thinking about this book while clerking for the Honorable Anthony M. Kennedy. My two co-clerks, Gregg Engles and Stephen Spitz, suffered through my first gropings and endured many a lunch-hour conversation about cannibalism, overcrowded lifeboats, the killing of ghosts, and the shooting of corpses. Actually, they didn't just endure. They willingly participated and revived my enthusiasm when it flagged.

Hans Zeisel was one of the book's chief sources of spiritual sustenance. He nurtured the project from its inception, if not earlier. He knew it was worthwhile even before I did. He read the manuscript-in-progress, and many a sentence is more graceful and many an argument more solid for his intervention. Those are only his most tangible contributions. The intangible ones, though even more important, are too wide-ranging for enumeration. Suffice it to say that but for him, I would probably not be a lawyer.

Norval Morris first taught me to love the criminal law. It was his first-year course at the University of Chicago that convinced me of the subject's intellectual excitement, philosophical richness, and literary possibilities. He also read through two drafts of the book and gave much encouragement and advice.

Michael Moore gave me an extraordinarily thorough, immeasurably helpful running commentary on the penultimate draft, exposing the weakness in some arguments and showing me ways to strengthen others—especially those having to do with the theory of direct reference, the difference between knowledge and intention, and the concept of cause-in-fact. If I failed to use Vittorio De Sica's *Bicycle Thief* to illustrate what the division of labor can achieve (as Moore suggested), it's because I haven't yet seen the movie.

Douglas Baird offered me moral support, when I had doubts that this was a feasible project, read through my most virgin draft, and helped me get started on a better second one.

Leonard Linsky read those portions of the manuscript leaning most heavily on the philosophy of language, saved me from an embarrassing howler involving Russell's theory of descriptions, and reassured me that it was all right for lawyers to have philosophical ideas.

Arthur Flemming, having taught me freshman composition in college, was willing to look at some of the remoter consequences of his work. In a detailed critique of the book's first two chapters, he showed me the need and the means for imposing discipline on a sprawling draft.

Sidney Hyman read the entire manuscript, and I was greatly buoyed by his enthusiastic interest and deft editorial touch.

Nadine Epstein and E. R. Shipp helped me choose between two competing versions of a chapter.

Robert Merton offered heartening words and a helping hand when they were most needed.

John Coatsworth wrote a painstaking review of chapter 4, which greatly improved my understanding of counterfactual history and the debate about the origins of the Second World War.

Peter Novick discussed with me at length the historians' view of causation and conspiracy.

Mirjan Damaška gave me some useful pointers on German law and George Bernard Shaw.

John Comaroff referred me to some good background sources in the African law and witchcraft literature.

Gary Friedman read and insightfully critiqued the first three chapters of an early draft.

Eli Seaman gave me my first nonlawyer, nonfamily reactions to the book. He rooted out many stylistic infelicities, haggled with me about how to handle the "he or she" problem, and refueled my enthusiasm for the final leg of this journey.

Russell Hardin allowed me to present chapters 3 and 4 to two of his public policy seminars at the University of Chicago, perhaps the most congenial group imaginable for this kind of book. Because Russell kept a written record of one of these discussions I am in fact able to credit many of its contributors: Cass Sunstein, Richard Helmholz, Michael Davis, Christine Korsgaard, Avner Cohen, Alan Gewirth, Paul Gomberg, an unnamed divinity student—and, of course, Russell himself.

Charles Silver gave me a detailed critique of chapter 3, helped me clarify my arguments on causation, and told me about Sherlock Holmes's "Adventure of the Blanched Soldier."

Stephen Schulhofer read the first chapter and suggested ways of tightening its argument.

Frank Zimring, having read chapter 3, reassured me that idiosyncracy is not a vice.

Richard Kimmel, one of the most inspiring teachers I ever had, awakened my interest in matters philosophical and first presented me with the puzzle of the forty logicians, which appears in chapter 1.

George Anastaplo read and richly annotated an earlier draft and convinced me, among other things, to name fewer of my hypothetical villains George.

Gerhard Casper read the penultimate draft, encouraged me to be less tentative in some of my conclusions, and, many years ago, told me the story of the two monks, which appears in chapter 3.

The late Ernest Nagel spent one extraordinary afternoon in October 1984 going over the entire book with me, section by section, providing me at one and the same time with a wealth of suggestions and criticisms, while also entertaining me with stories about the twentieth century's great philosophers.

Daniel Herwitz looked at the first three chapters. Discussions with him deepened my understanding of the causal theory of meaning and got me to sharpen my argument about the difference between acts and omissions.

Skip Bean argued through with me most of the major arguments in the book, in countless long-distance calls between Chicago and Philadelphia. He also supplied me with the book's best "unused footage"—a wonderful idea involving Socrates and the hemlock that would have required too elaborate a detour and was ultimately edited out. I am saving it for another project.

Maureen Whiteman saw the ideas of this book progress from half-baked to fresh-baked to rebaked. Although she encountered each idea at least three times—once before I wrote it up, once after I wrote it up, and once after I rewrote it—she greeted them enthusiastically at every turn and was full of good editorial suggestions.

Jacqueline Katz Oreglia was a fountain of philosophical advice and sisterly support. Her help in setting me straight on Gottlob Frege and the problem of substitutivity was especially important.

My parents, to whom this book is dedicated, managed to magically blend lots of helpful criticism with what psychotherapists call "unconditional positive regard."

It is customary to exonerate one's helpers of all complicity in the faults that remain. But as the reader will learn in chapter 5, complicity is not so readily avoided. For better or worse, all of the aforementioned are implicated in this enterprise. Let's hope it's for better rather than worse.

For Those Who Need to Look before They Leap

Some legal questions are instantly fascinating to the novice and perennially fascinating to the expert. This book is about such questions. I wrote it in the immodest hope that both lawyers and laymen would want to read it.

Most people think of the criminal law as something like the Ten Commandments, a long list of thou-shalt-nots, only much longer, duller, and more obscure. But the Ten Commandments would not do as a criminal code, and not only because there are just ten of them. As a criminal code, the Ten Commandments have serious shortcomings. In a sense, taking care of those shortcomings is what the criminal law (and this book) is all about. Of course, the shortcomings aren't so easily taken care of. What stands in the way are the "conundrums" of the title.

Chapter 1, "Necessity, the Mother of Invention," is about the first of these shortcomings: The Ten Commandments are absolute. "Thou shalt not kill." "Thou shalt not steal." "Thou shalt not bear false witness." None of these allow for exceptions. Obviously, the criminal law has to do better than that.

The criminal law should probably allow for cases of self-defense or insanity. But maybe it also has to allow for some less obvious cases—those that chapter 1 is really about: Is it a crime when a shipwrecked crew throws passengers out of an overburdened lifeboat? When a desperate citizen of a Communist country hijacks an airplane to freedom? When a Belfast Catholic drives a getaway car for some IRA assassins who threaten to kill him if he refuses? When American POWs collaborate with the enemy as a result of unrelenting indoctrination? What if the defendants were mistaken in their fears? What if they courted the predicament they're in? All of these are real cases. Do they have anything in common? Are there crucial differences between them? It is the aim of chapter 1 to cut a passage through this thicket; to make sense of our confused and conflicting intuitions about these situations; to probe notions like necessity and duress, threat and temptation, killing and letting die, coercion and authority, seduction and persuasion—in short, to find a just resolution.

Chapter 2, "Bad Acts," is about the second shortcoming of the Ten Commandments. The commandments give us a list of bad acts, but they do not define them. Again the criminal law has to do better.

It tries, for one, to define specific bad acts. The commandment says merely you shall not steal. The criminal law has to define theft, robbery, blackmail, plagiarism, criminal trespass, and burglary. The business of defining is a tricky one. Take a commonplace crime like theft. We call it theft when a man secretly absconds with another man's wallet. We also call it theft when a bank clerk keeps money entrusted to him, and we call it theft when a man dresses up as an Oxford don to get credit from a local tradesman. It's not obvious what these transactions have in common that they don't share with other dishonest transactions (like robbery, blackmail, plagiarism, criminal trespass, or burglary). Maybe they have nothing in common. Indeed, must they have something in common just because we call them by one common name? But if we can't be more specific, is the law against theft too elastic, vague, open-ended to be fair?

Take a more exotic crime like witchcraft. In 1899, the British colonial administration in Africa passed something called the Witchcraft Suppression Act. The act opened with a definition of witchcraft. Unfortunately, the drafters misdefined it; they weren't well-enough versed in the intricacies of the subject. It turned out that what the definition described was not witchcraft but some related ritual. That raised intriguing questions of statutory interpretation. What was a judge to do with defendants charged under the statute? They might have practiced witchcraft, but they hadn't done what the statute described as witchcraft. Under the conventional view, they should have been acquitted until the legislature rewrote the statute. Using insights from the modern philosophy of language, I will show why the conventional view is wrong. A statute doesn't have to mean what its drafters think it means.

It is not enough for the criminal law to define specific bad acts. Before we decide what type of crime (if any) the defendant's act amounts to, we have to decide whether it is an act at all. Often what looks like an act isn't really. At times, an act is devilishly hard to distinguish from something that happens to you, from an omission, or from a thought.

Fatma, a faith healer who treats people in a trance, wakes up one time to discover that she has brutally killed her patient. Fain, a sleepwalker, comes to on the hotel veranda to find he has shot the porter who tried to wake him. Decina, an epileptic, recovers from a seizure to notice that his Buick sedan has jumped the curb and killed four persons. Huey Newton, having been shot in the stomach, regains consciousness to learn that he has shot a policeman in an unconscious rage. H., after undergoing psychiatric treatment, realizes that he has been robbing banks under the posthypnotic suggestion of a friend. In each of these cases, the defendant ostensibly violated a criminal statute, and yet in none of them did he really act; rather he was acted on. He didn't do anything wrong; something went wrong with him. He didn't commit a crime; he underwent a crime. In short, there was no act, just a happening. Why is that? Why do the defendants' experiences in these cases count as happenings, not as acts?

In 1964, thirty-eight New Yorkers watched one of their neighbors, young Kitty Genovese, being murdered on the street. The assault lasted nearly half an hour. Yet during all that time no one called the police. If someone had, she probably would not have died. Although each of the witnesses had in some senses caused Kitty Genovese's death, we would not dream of charging them with murder. The witnesses, we would say, did not kill Kitty; they merely let her die. What makes for the difference? One is an act, the other an omission. How are acts and omissions conceptually different? Why does causing death sometimes get classified as an act, and sometimes as an omission? How are they different morally? Why should we feel one way about acts and another about omissions? How are they different psychologically? Why do we feel greater qualms about killing someone than letting him die unaided?

In 1979, some Arab sheiks approached Congressman Richard Kelly of New Jersey. They were interested in getting special help in immigration matters. They mentioned the possibility of sizable investments in his district as well as payoffs. Kelly was intrigued by the investments, but he wasn't willing to pledge any illegitimate help with immigration or to accept any payoffs. The sheiks kept pressuring him. They spread $25,000 in $100 bills on the table in front of him. They emphasized that if he did not cooperate, they would make their investments in other districts. Finally, Kelly gave in, stuffed the $25,000 into his pockets and left. The sheiks, it turned out, were not sheiks at all, but FBI agents scouting for corrupt congressmen. Kelly was charged with accepting bribes.

An act is different from a thought or disposition, but a case like this one raises the question of just how punishing an act differs from punishing a thought or disposition. True, the congressman had committed an act; he had accepted a bribe. But when a sting operation is used to bring to the surface a personal weakness that might never have surfaced otherwise, are we really punishing the criminal act or the criminal disposition?

The Ten Commandments don't mention states of mind. "Thou shalt not kill" reproves alike, it seems, the accidental killing, the negligent killing, and the intentional killing. It is this shortcoming that chapter 3, "Guilty Minds," is about.

The intentional killing of a human being is murder. When is a killing intentional? One dark night Muhamed, a Sudanese villager, is taking a stroll to visit his girlfriend in a village two miles away. The path between the two villages is reputed to be haunted. Suddenly, he sees before him a ghostlike figure wrapped in white sheets. He calls out to the creature, but gets no response. He becomes scared and runs his spear through the ghost. The ghost, it later turns out, was really an old man, perhaps a little hard of hearing. Has Muhamed intentionally killed a human being? Another villager kills his neighbor believing her a witch. Has he intentionally killed a human being? What about Bratton, who fires a bullet at a man, misses, and shoots the man's wife instead? Has he intentionally killed her? What about Rose who intends to shoot Schliebe but shoots Harnisch instead, whom he has mistaken for Schliebe? Has he intentionally killed him? And what of Clyde Griffiths, the protagonist of Theodore Dreiser's novel *An American Tragedy*, who takes his lover, Roberta, out on a lake to drown her? Somehow, not quite according to plan, the boat capsizes and she does drown. Has he intentionally killed her?

The negligent killing of a human being is manslaughter. But when is a killing negligent? When the defendant took an unreasonable risk. What is an unreasonable risk? Inevitably, that is a slightly subjective matter. We shouldn't be surprised or too worried when people occasionally differ in their judgments. We might be surprised and might be worried if the same person expresses radically different judgments depending on how the question is put to him. Yet that happens frequently. A group of doctors was asked: "Imagine that the U.S. is preparing for the outbreak of an unusual Asian disease, which is expected to kill 600 people. Two alternative programs to combat the disease have been proposed. Assume that the exact scientific estimate of the consequences of the programs is as follows: If program A is adopted, 200 lives will be saved. If program B is adopted, there is 1/3 probability that 600 people will be saved, and 2/3 probability that no people will be saved. Which of the two programs do you favor?'' The vast majority of the doctors, 72 percent of them, opted for program A.

Another group of doctors was given the same ''cover story'' as the first, but they were asked to choose among the following alternatives: ''If program C is adopted, 400 people will die. If program D is adopted, there is 1/3 probability that nobody will die, and 2/3 probability that 600 people will die. Which of the two programs do you favor?'' Only 22 percent of the doctors opted for C. The odd thing is that C is but a different way of phrasing A. If people's preferences among risks are so unreliable, is the notion of negligence workable?

The Ten Commandments don't discuss causation. To kill is to cause death. Whether the defendant caused his victim's death can be a genuine conundrum. The Ten Commandments don't address that question. Chapter 4, ''The Root of All Evil,'' is about how the criminal law copes with this particular shortcoming.

To say the defendant caused his victim's death seems to mean: But for what the defendant did, the victim would not have died. That's often a tricky determination to make. Josef and his brother Paul were bicycling down a dark country road one rainy and windy evening. Neither bike was equipped with the required headlight. Josef was ducking his head to avoid the elements and thus scarcely noticed oncoming traffic. As he passed an intersection, he collided head-on with K., another biker. K. suffered a severe skull fracture and died. Both Josef and Paul were charged with negligent homicide. The case against Josef was clear-cut and the trial court had no trouble convicting him. But the case against Paul was more complex. The prosecutor argued that Paul, like Josef, had been negligent in bicycling without a headlight. Had he had a headlight, it would have illuminated not only his own but also Josef's bike. K. would then have seen Josef, and the accident would never have happened. The trial court, however, did not think Paul's negligence had caused the accident. If Paul had not been negligent, it reasoned, he would not have been out riding without his headlight at all, and in that case K. would still not have noticed the oncoming Josef, and the accident would still have happened. Who is right?

To say the defendant caused the victim's death is to say more than that the victim wouldn't have died otherwise. John fires a bullet at Annie, intending to kill her. He misses; the bullet only penetrates her arm. She is brought to the hospital, where she contracts scarlet fever from a nurse and dies. Are we prepared to say that John caused Annie's death? It seems we aren't, even though we can say with confidence that but for what he did, she would not have died. What kind of connection does our intuition require between the defendant's deed and the victim's death before we will say that one caused the other? Many ingenious theories have been advanced to show what kind of connection is required. None of these theories works very well. I will show why none can ever be designed that works very well.

There remains the question: Why do we care about causation? Why do we make punishment contingent on whether or how it led to harm? John intended to kill Annie. She died shortly after he tried to kill her. Why do we insist on anything more? Why does it matter to us that John's misdeed and Annie's death are connected by such a circuitous route? An answer is suggested by a flourishing branch of psychology called attribution theory.

The Ten Commandments say nothing about those who help someone else break a commandment. This shortcoming is dealt with by the doctrines of complicity and conspiracy which are covered in chapter 5, "The Company You Keep."

Why do we need a doctrine of complicity? Why do we need a special rule that says that somebody who helps somebody else commit a crime is also a criminal? If A persuades B to kill C, couldn't we just convict A of murder for causing C's death? And couldn't we take care of every act of helping along these lines? In fact, we couldn't. The reason has to do with the economic principle of diminishing marginal returns.

Why do we need a doctrine of conspiracy? What makes groups so unusually dangerous that the law should intervene as soon as they have formed, regardless of how far along they are in their criminal enterprise? Social psychology permits us to be specific about these dangers, to show how it is that groups make better judgments, solve problems more effectively, and learn more quickly than individuals. Conspiracy raises a further question: How do we distinguish it from many other forms of social interaction that superficially resemble a conspiracy, but really aren't?

The sixth and final shortcoming of the Ten Commandments is that they don't bother with attempted crimes, crimes that failed. Chapter 6, "The Crime That Never Was," inquires into these doomed ventures.

It is concerned with but one problem: When an assassin aims to shoot the president but fails, it is clear he should be punished for attempted murder. When a pickpocket reaches into somebody's pocket and doesn't find anything, it is clear he should be punished for attempted theft. On the other hand, when a traveler smuggles some French lace past customs, and the lace is in fact duty-free, should he be punished for attempted smuggling? When a man has intercourse with his stepdaughter, thinking it's incest, should he be punished for attempted incest?

In style, this chapter is different from its predecessors. The first section takes the form of a fictitious judicial opinion, loosely based on the real case of the master forger Han van Meegeren, in which various views on the problem are aired. Next, I propose my own solution. Finally, as an aside, I include the astonishing and real story of Han van Meegeren.

I conclude with an epilogue, "Final Reckoning," in which I seek to convince the reader of the broader implications of what has been said about the criminal law. The concepts investigated (act, intention, cause, complicity, etc.) aren't unique to the criminal law, although the nature of the context forces one to scrutinize them with greater care than otherwise. Indeed, they are not unique to the law; they pervade the social sciences. What has been said about them may illuminate certain long-standing problems in other disciplines. I point to examples in literary criticism, psychology, history, and philosophy.

The reader can now see why the rules by which we judge criminals are more than a simple, lifeless list of proscriptions. They aren't simple because they employ concepts replete with philosophical and psychological complexities—which is what encouraged me to borrow extensively from analytical philosophy and experimental psychology. They aren't lifeless because they are forever subjected to litigation—which is what permitted me to illustrate even my most abstract arguments with an actual case or controversy. This last point bears repeating: Every argument in this book comes with a story. My hope is that where the argument isn't convincing, the story, at least, is enticing; that where the explanation isn't instructive, the case, at least, is intriguing; that where I fail to give knowledge, at least I give pleasure.

1 Necessity, the Mother of Invention

"O Oysters," said the Carpenter,
"You've had a pleasant run!
Shall we be trotting home again?"
But answer came there none—
And this was scarcely odd, because
They'd eaten everyone.

Lewis Carroll

The Speluncean Explorers

The murder case that came before the Supreme Court of Newgarth in the fall of the year 4300 presented problems that had not arisen within anyone's memory and for which not even the dustier volumes of the law reports offered any precedent. The four defendants had been tried and convicted in the Court of General Instances of the County of Stowfield for the murder of their traveling companion Roger Whetmore. In accordance with Newgarth's very succinct murder statute—"Whoever shall willfully take the life of another shall be punished by death" (N.C.S.A. [N.S.] Sec. 12-A)—they had been sentenced to death by hanging. They had appealed to the Supreme Court, and it was now up to the five justices to affirm or reverse the trial court.[1]

The four defendants and Roger Whetmore were all members of the Speluncean Society, a group of amateur cave explorers and archaeologists. In May 4299 the five set out to explore the interior of a limestone cavern located in the Central Plateau. While the five men were probing the remote inner reaches of the cave, a powerful landslide shook the area. A barrage of massive boulders rained down in front of the cave and blocked its only exit. Although physically unscathed, the five explorers found themselves hopelessly immured in the rubble, with little more than a meager supply of water, wine, and dates to last them through the indefinite future.

The absence of the five men was soon noticed. Their families grew alarmed and called on the secretary of the society to undertake a search. It turned out that the explorers had left at the society's headquarters fairly exact indications of their whereabouts, and a rescue party was immediately sent out for them. But freeing them proved far from easy. The society's rescue party was no match for the primordial boulders. Heavy machinery had to be moved in from far away. A whole army of workmen, engineers, geologists, and other experts had to be assembled. Fresh landslides repeatedly intervened to make working conditions hazardous and progress slow. Ten workmen ultimately died in the rescue effort.

As the days wore on, the rescuers grew increasingly anxious that starvation might kill the explorers long before a passageway could be cut through the detritus. Though considered hardy souls, the explorers were known to have taken only scant provisions along, and limestone caverns rarely, if ever, contain any nourishing vegetable or animal matter. On the twentieth day, however, the rescuers learned by accident that the explorers had with them a portable wireless machine capable of sending and receiving messages. A similar machine was installed in the rescue camp and communication established with the imprisoned men. The prisoners turned out to be unexpectedly alert and remarkably rational and detached about their predicament. Roger Whetmore, the most experienced among them, did most of the talking. He asked how long it would take to liberate them. The engineers estimated it would take at least ten more days, provided no new landslides occurred. Whetmore then asked whether any physicians were present and was immediately put in touch with a committee of medical experts. He described to them with precision what was left of the sparse rations they had taken with them into the cave. Taking turns, each of the prisoners then described his physical condition. Finally, Whetmore asked for a medical opinion whether they were likely to survive the next ten days. Despite some initial reluctance to answer, the committee chairman admitted that there was little likelihood of that. The wireless machine then remained silent for eight hours. Finally, Whetmore's voice reappeared; he asked to speak once more to the physicians. His voice unnaturally loud and quavering ever so slightly, he inquired of the chairman whether they would be able to survive if they ate the flesh of one of their number. The chairman refused to answer. When Whetmore continued to press him, he finally agreed that they probably would. Whetmore then asked whether it would be advisable for them to cast lots to determine who among them should be sacrificed. The chairman again refused to answer; this time he remained adamant. None of the other physicians were willing to respond either. Whetmore asked if there were among the party a judge or other government official who could answer his question. No one responded, not even the secretary of the society who was in fact a justice of the peace. Whetmore asked if there were a minister or priest who would answer his question but no one stepped forward, although a priest had only recently performed the last rites on a dying workman. The wireless machine then went dead, and it was assumed—erroneously, as it turned out—that the batteries had been exhausted.

Conscious that time was running out, the rescuers speeded up their efforts. They took risks they would ordinarily have avoided; as a result six more workmen were killed by another unexpected landslide. Eight days after the exchange with Whetmore, they finally laid bare the cave's exit. Four of the men were still alive, although close to expiration. The fifth, Roger Whetmore, was dead. His skeletal remains told most of the story, but the survivors made no secret of what had happened. On the twenty-third day of their captivity the defendants had killed and eaten their companion.

Ironically, Roger Whetmore had been the first to propose such a sacrifice. Not only would this ensure that at least some of them survived, he said, but even the victim had reason to be grateful for being spared the agony of a slow death by starvation. He for one, should the lot fall on him, would prefer it that way. Although at first repelled by the idea, his colleagues acquiesced in Whetmore's proposal when they heard the dire predictions of the medical experts. Whetmore happened to have a pair of dice with him, hence that was the method adopted for choosing the victim. But just before the dice were cast, Roger Whetmore had a change of heart and suggested that they wait another week before resorting to so awesome a remedy. The others disagreed. They charged him with a breach of faith and proceeded to roll the dice. When Whetmore's turn came, he refused to participate. Someone else rolled the dice in his behalf. They asked Whetmore if he had any objections to the fairness of the throw; he said he did not. The roll went against him.

The defendants were treated at length for malnutrition and shock and finally were put on trial. The trial was one of the least contentious in Newgarth's history, since there was little disagreement on the facts. Still, the jury deliberated for a long time. At one point, the foreman—as it happened, a lawyer—asked the court whether the jury might be allowed simply to issue a special verdict finding all the facts and leaving it to the trial judge to determine whether under those facts the defendants were guilty. Both sides agreed to this proposal; and the court acquiesced. Then, having examined the jury's rather unsurprising findings, he held the defendants guilty of murder and, as required, sentenced them to death. This done, he added his name to a petition drawn up by the defendants' supporters and carrying the signature of hundreds of citizens, including the twelve jurors, requesting the chief executive to pardon and release the defendants. The chief executive, however, let it be known that he would not consider the petition before the Newgarth Supreme Court—the honorable Chief Justice Truepenny and his brethren, Justices Keen, Foster, Tatting, and Handy—had passed on the defendants' appeal.

Hard Cases

The year 4300 has not yet arrived, and neither has the case of the Speluncean explorers. So far the case is only a hypothetical problem, invented in 1949 by the great Lon Fuller, professor at the Harvard Law School. Equally hypothetical is the State of Newgarth, the Newgarth Supreme Court, and the five justices who sit on it. Lon Fuller does not say how he would decide the case of the Speluncean explorers. Instead he writes out five imaginary opinions, one for each of his imaginary Supreme Court justices, explaining how they would resolve the case. Two of the justices, Chief Justice Truepenny and Justice Keen, vote to affirm the trial court's verdict. Two others, Justice Foster and Justice Handy, vote to reverse it. A fifth, Justice Tatting, feels so perplexed by the case that he declines to cast a vote. As far as the imaginary jurisdiction of Newgarth is concerned that settles the matter: The Supreme Court being evenly divided, the trial court's verdict is affirmed and, unless the chief executive chooses to pardon them, the spelunkers will be hanged. As far as we are concerned, the justices' opinions don't settle very much. Each of the five opinions develops some intriguing arguments, but none of them is very thorough or very persuasive. So the problem is still with us: How should the case of the Speluncean explorers be decided if it ever arises?

Could there be any reason not to affirm the guilty verdict? The statutory definition of murder is touchingly simple and pristine: the willful killing of another person. Roger Whetmore did not die of natural causes—he was killed. He was not killed accidentally either, but quite intentionally—willfully. Why even hesitate to brand the defendants murderers? Because we know on reflection that not every intended killing deserves to be called murder. Whether or not Newgarth's criminal code explicitly says so, the definition of murder must be subject to numerous exceptions, if it is not to lead to some absurd consequences. A man might kill in self-defense or because he has gone insane; in either case he is clearly not a murderer. The defendants, of course, did not act in self-defense; self-preservation, yes, but not self-defense. Nor did they go insane. In fact they bore their ordeal with remarkable equanimity, even fortitude. But perhaps the defendants should be exonerated on some related principle, one that makes allowance for the dire straits in which they found themselves, for the grim choices they faced, in short, for the extreme necessity that drove them to do what they did.

It seems that we would not hesitate to recognize such a principle in a large variety of more pedestrian settings. Imagine a fire in a prison. Threatened with almost certain death, the prisoners break out of their cells. Are they guilty of the crime of escape? Clearly not. Imagine a man who has just suffered a heart attack. Unless immediately given a dose of nitroglycerine, he might die. A druggist administers the drug to him without prescription, because there is no time to fetch a doctor. Is the druggist guilty of the crime of selling a prescription drug without a prescription? We need not make up such examples. Courts occasionally encounter such cases. In 1810, the United States Congress imposed an embargo on the West Indies. While sailing from Alexandria to Boston, a heavy storm forced the *William Gray* to put in at the harbor of Antigua in the West Indies. The West Indies governor compelled the captain to sell his cargo and only then allowed him to leave. Was the ship guilty of a criminal violation of the embargo statute? The court held that it was not. The court admitted that the embargo statute was not qualified by an explicit exception for ships caught in stormy weather. But this statute like all statutes, the court reasoned, was subject to the "principle of necessity" as recognized "from time immemorial."[2]

New Hampshire, like many other states, has a statute making school attendance compulsory. A parent who keeps his child out of school commits a criminal offense. Samuel Jackson's daughter was in very feeble health; he feared for her life and did not dare send her to school. In fact he never even applied to the school board for a special exemption or dispensation. Had he acted criminally? The court again appealed to the idea of necessity: "A parent cannot be required to imperil the life of his child by delays incident to an application to the school board, before he can lawfully do what is apparently reasonably necessary for its protection."[3]

Texas, like most other states, requires that anyone in a car accident stop and wait for the police to arrive at the scene. Elmer Woods had a collision with another car. As a result of the accident, "a lady companion who was riding in the car with him" suffered some serious cuts and bruises, and Woods immediately sped off to drive her home.[4] The hit-and-run statute allowed for no exceptions. But the court held that Woods should be acquitted "if in the collision his companion was injured to such an extent as in his opinion rendered it necessary that she receive treatment."[5]

The *Merrimack*, a sailing ship, set out in 1834 from Boston for Rio de Janeiro. She was leaky to begin with. Several days out of harbor she met with a ferocious gale that further worsened her condition. The crew insisted on taking her back, but the captain turned a deaf ear. The crew eventually refused to go farther and the captain had no choice but to go back. In Boston the crew members were charged with mutiny. Invoking the idea of necessity, the court held they should be acquitted if they reasonably thought the ship unseaworthy and a serious hazard to life.[6]

Having seen the necessity principle at work in cases that run the gamut from car accidents to mutiny on the high seas, we may feel reasonably confident applying it to run-of-the-mill situations, although, obviously, no necessity case is ever entirely "run-of-the-mill." Perhaps we should be content to leave it at that, to rest happy with being able to do justice in most cases that are likely ever to confront us. In other words, we may be tempted just to dismiss the issue: Why bother with cases like that of the Speluncean explorers, which are evidently nothing more than the fiendish product of a law professor's frenzied imagination? Why agonize over a hypothetical that was invented for the sake of agony? Why cross bridges we may never get to?

In fact, there is much to be said for considering seriously such unlikely scenarios as the case of the Speluncean explorers. Whatever this "principle of necessity" is, the run-of-the-mill cases have not forced us to do more than vaguely articulate it. To the extent that we can put our finger on it, the principle appears to say: In situations of necessity, criminal laws may be broken. That sounds as simple and satisfactory as any one of the Ten Commandments, the archetypes of our criminal laws. But are we really serious about living with such a principle?

Consider its application to the Speluncean explorers. It would make the case trivially easy to decide and would lead us to acquit the defendants instantly. But does that not show that there is something amiss with the principle? Even if inclined to acquit, one must feel eerie qualms about doing so, a gnawing unease. Why those qualms, why that unease? Let us try to identify slowly, deliberately, one-by-one, the sources of our discomfort.

First, we may be troubled that "necessity" should serve to sanction a breach of the most fundamental prohibition of our criminal law: Thou shalt not kill. Do the most basic provisions of the criminal law cease to apply to someone when he finds himself in sufficiently dire straits?

Second, we may question whether the sacrifice of Whetmore was even necessary to save the lives of the four. The rescue team made its final penetration two days earlier than expected. Perhaps all five could have survived until then.

Third, we may speculate whether the cave explorers did not have reason to know of the risk that faced them when they embarked on their expeditions. And if they deliberately courted the chance of finding themselves in such a situation of necessity, should they be permitted freely "to take advantage" of it when it occurred?

Fourth, we may be of two minds whether even Roger Whetmore's consent to being killed could have served to exonerate the defendants. The Newgarth legislature, let us suppose, at one point expressly considered sanctioning euthanasia but declined to do so. Would Roger Whetmore's consent have been any different from that of a cancer patient who asks for and receives a lethal injection of morphine?

Fifth, we may be uncertain whether casting lots was clearly the appropriate way of determining who should be sacrificed. Weren't there other criteria available too? Who was the most valuable to society? Who valued life the most? Who was willing to pay the most to the others for the privilege of staying alive? Who had the larger family to support?

These questions are no idle concerns. Although less obvious, similar questions lurk behind the simplest of the run-of-the-mill cases. Recall the case of mutiny at high sea. What if the *Merrimack* had been a navy ship steaming toward some distant battleground? Are we still willing to put it in the hands of the crew to turn the ship back because it seems unlikely to survive the next storm? Remember that ship that violated the embargo. What if the captain of the *William Gray* left Alexandria knowing full well that the weather would be foul and might force him to put in at the West Indies? Think again of the druggist who administers nitroglycerine to a heart patient. What if the FDA had not yet approved use of the drug, if in fact there were significant risks associated with giving it which only a doctor could fully appreciate?

These questions, to which only the extreme case of the Speluncean explorers alerted us, cast a new light on the "simple" cases as well. They show that our original formulation of the principle of necessity ("In situations of necessity, criminal laws may be broken") will not do. A correct formulation will have to provide an answer to all those troubling questions.

Contemplating the predicament of the Speluncean explorers may help us arrive at such a principle.

Contrary to the popular adage, hard cases do not make bad law. Law schools spend most of their time confronting their students with hard cases—absurd hypotheticals like that of the Speluncean explorers. Are they teaching them bad law? No, they use hard cases to show up bad law: good law makes sense not only in the easy case but in the hard one. Hard cases reveal the shortcomings of superficially appealing rules.

The law of criminal attempts provides an especially illuminating example of how a cleverly constructed hard case can serve to bring out the hidden inadequacies of a seemingly sensible principle. It is probably clear on short reflection that a person can be liable for a criminal act even though he never succeeds in completing the intended crime. Just because the assassin misses his target, he must not go scot-free. He is guilty of attempted murder. Anyone who seriously attempts to put into practice a criminal plan is guilty of a criminal attempt. Having decided to punish attempted crimes, one is quickly led to the intriguing question of how one should deal with attempts that are doomed from the very outset, crimes that could never succeed, in other words, crimes that are *impossible* to execute. Suppose a thief reaches into a man's pocket but does not know that the pocket is empty. Suppose a man attempts to poison his wife but mistakenly assumes that a milligram of strichnine will do the trick. Or suppose two men furtively engage in homosexual intercourse, but erroneously think they are violating a state law. Finally, suppose a traveler tries to smuggle into the country some French lace that he believes is subject to a high tariff; alas, he never learned that the tariff has been lifted. All of these persons are attempting to commit a crime. All of them are doomed to fail, because what they attempt to do is impossible. Which of them should be acquitted, which of them should be convicted of the crime of attempt? Most peoples' instincts, I suspect, give a fairly clear answer to these cases: convict the pickpocket and the poisoner, acquit the homosexuals and the smuggler.

Can we articulate a principle that makes explicit what our instincts tell us? Judges faced with this question focused intently on examples just like the ones given, seeking to divine what attribute cases like the first two shared that cases like the second two lacked. Finally, they thought they had spotted the crucial difference between the two kinds of cases. The first two cases involved situations in which the *facts* simply weren't right for what the defendants intended—the picked pocket happened to be empty and the poisoned human immunological system stronger than expected. The second two cases involved situations in which the *law* wasn't right for what the defendants intended—homosexual intercourse happened to be legal and French lace duty-free. The first two attempts thus were dubbed "factually impossible," the second two "legally impossible." The rule courts adopted ran: Legal impossibility exonerates, factual impossibility does not.

The principle seemed satisfactory at first, indeed compelling: you can sensibly charge a frustrated pickpocket with attempted theft, but what do you charge the French-lace smuggler with—attempted import of a duty-free product without paying duty? But then two legal scholars, Sanford Kadish and Monrad Paulsen, proposed this ingenious hypothetical scenario: "Two friends, Mr. Law and Mr. Fact, go hunting in the morning of October 15 in the fields of the state of Dakota, whose law makes it a misdemeanor to hunt any time other than from October 1 to November 30. Both kill deer on their first day out, October 15. Mr. Fact, however, was under the erroneous belief that the date was September 15; and Mr. Law was under the erroneous belief that the hunting season was confined to the month of November, as it was the previous year."[7] Mr. Fact has attempted to do the "factually impossible." His attempt to hunt deer out of season failed only because of the purely adventitious fact that the date was October 15 and not September 15. Hence he will be convicted. Mr. Law, however, has attempted the "legally impossible." His attempt failed because of a purely adventitious feature in the game law extending the hunting season that year by an extra month. He will be acquitted. But is there any meaningful distinction between Mr. Law and Mr. Fact? Is a criminal law defensible that punishes one and not the other? The example suggests that the proposed principle is seriously deficient, that whatever it is that separates the first two cases from the next two cases has not been captured by it.

The story of Mr. Law and Mr. Fact is as contrived and absurd a concoction as the tale of the Speluncean explorers. But in law, as elsewhere, it is our encounter with the "absurd" that lets us understand the "normal," by making us feel as though we saw it for the first time. Christian Morgenstern, a German poet (brilliantly translated by Max Knight), captured this experience in a trenchant little quatrain:

> The heath sheep glares at me with frightened awe
> as though I were the first of men it saw.

Contagious glare! We stand as though asleep;
it seems the first time that I see a sheep.

He entitled the verse "Birth of Philosophy."[8]

Appalling Precedents

Lon Fuller did not invent the case of the Speluncean explorers out of whole cloth. Cases very much like it have actually occurred. Few cases, even imaginary ones, are bizarre enough never to have happened before. Do these cases give us any guidance?

In March 1841, the *William Brown*, a seasoned but rickety sailing ship, left Liverpool. She was bound for Philadelphia and carrying on board sixty-five Irish and Scottish immigrants. From the start her voyage was marred by uncommonly vicious squalls. Rain, sleet, and cold winds whipped several of her sails to shreds. When she neared Newfoundland, a heavy fog set in. Finally, disaster struck; she hit an iceberg. The damage was beyond repair: the leak too wide to be plugged, the inrushing torrent too strong for pumps to keep at bay. The captain saw no choice but to abandon ship.[9]

There were only two lifeboats. The larger one, the longboat (despite its name only a modest 22 1/2 feet long), was quickly crowded far beyond capacity. It now held forty-one passengers but was meant for only a fraction of that number. Its gunwale was perilously close to the water, its seams were strained near bursting, and its bottom had a poorly plugged hole. The captain, his two officers, and six of his crew took the jolly boat, which was even smaller than the longboat and meant to hold six or seven at best. Some thirty passengers, most of them children and none of them crew, were left behind on the main ship, when the sea finally swallowed it up. There had been no room for them in the lifeboats. "Poor souls," the ship's mate consoled them from afar as they went under, "you are only going a little before us."[10]

The captain then ordered his mate to take charge of the longboat. "Captain, that boat can't live," the mate protested on being asked to leave the jolly boat, "she will never see land." "Nevertheless, you must try," the captain insisted.[11] There was no one else on her who knew navigation. He gave the mate a compass, a chart, a quadrant, and a watch and suggested that he follow the jolly boat to the Newfoundland coast. But the mate knew that without sails, his only hope was to be picked up by another boat. But how long could the longboat hold out? Their supplies were relatively plentiful, but the ship was seriously overcrowded and could be sunk by the slightest squall. As the jolly boat was about to depart, the mate called out, loud enough for everyone to hear: "Captain, we shall have to draw lots. The boat is overcrowded and she leaks." "I know what you mean," the captain replied. "You understand we shall have to draw lots?" the mate persisted. "Say no more about it," shouted the captain. "I know what you will have to do. Let it be the last resort." The jolly boat left.[12]

The jolly boat, equipped with both sails and oars, made for the Newfoundland coast. A hundred and fifty miles from shore, just as their supplies had dwindled to the vanishing point, a fishing lugger sighted them, picked them up, and brought them to the nearest port town, St. Peter. All but one sailor recuperated from the ordeal.

The longboat did less well. It carried substantial amounts of water, meat, oatmeal, and bread—enough to last its forty-two occupants six or seven days. But it was leaking both from its strained seams and ill-fitting plug. They were still surrounded by icebergs, although most were hidden behind a dense fog. The sky was too cloudy for the mate to determine their position; and they spent their first day drifting aimlessly. On the second day the wind grew stronger and the sea wilder. Worse yet, a new hole, 4 by 8 inches, was discovered. Water was now both leaking in from below and pouring in from above. The men were bailing frantically, but toward midnight the situation grew unmanageable. Several powerful waves had dashed over the side, the plug seemed to have jumped out of place, and the ship appeared to be sinking. "God help me, this won't do," the mate exclaimed. "Men, fall to work, the boat must be lightened, or we all will be lost." For several moments there was no response. "Fall to work, or we perish," the mate cried out again. This time there was a reaction.[13]

Although the mate was formally in charge, the boat's most commanding presence was Holmes, a mere sailor. Tall, sturdy, and handsome, Holmes was, as one contemporary described him, "an artist's model for decision and strength."[14] He had always been trusted by his superiors, respected by the crew, and well-liked by the passengers. Many felt indebted to him. A sick young Scottish woman whom he had carried off the sinking ship at great personal risk owed her life to him. Others had benefitted from more minor acts of generosity: several women wore pieces of his clothing which he had given them when he saw them shiver. The panic that seized everyone else when the boat was about to sink seemed to have left him unperturbed. But when the mate called out to the sailors to lighten the boat, Holmes was the first to respond.

He got up, motioned to another sailor to join him, and walked over to Owen Riley, a married man whose wife was awaiting him in Philadelphia. "Stand up, Riley," he quietly intoned. But the man did not move. Holmes and the other sailor then took hold of him. "Help me, Isabel," the man cried out to the young Scottish woman whose life Holmes had saved, thinking perhaps that she had some special influence with him. "For the love of God, tell them to spare me," he yelled to another. "You Judy, help me," he appealed to a third. She was the only person who dared respond. "What is the man crying for? Are they going to throw him out?" "Yes, they are," a sailor shouted, "and you will all go after him." "No, they won't," Holmes declared immediately, "we'll save the women, if we have to throw all the men overboard."[15] With that they tossed the struggling Riley into the sea. The Scotsman James Todd was the next to go. The third victim, James McAvoy, pleaded for five minutes to pray. These granted, he, too, was ejected. A woman implored them: "Holmes, you aren't going to throw me out, or any of the girls, are you?" "No, we won't," he repeated, "we will go ourselves first."[16] Then came Frank Askins, to whom his two sisters were clinging in desperation. When Holmes reached for him, the man offered fierce resistance. "I'll not go out, you know I wrought well all the time. I'll work like a man till morning, and do what I can to keep the boat clear of water; I have five sovereigns, and I'll give it for my life till morning, and when morning comes if God does not help us we will cast lots, and I'll go out like a man if it is my turn."[17] "I don't want your money," Holmes said, lifted him up at last and dropped him into the sea.[18] The other sailors threw out his sisters after him. The next few to go scarcely protested. When it was James Black's turn, the mate told them to leave him alone, because he had family on board. "You must not part man and wife."[19] They came to Charley Conlin, whose fourteen relatives had already gone down with the *William Brown*. "Holmes, dear, you will not put me out," he said. "Yes, Charles, you'll go, too," Holmes answered and he, too, was thrown over.[20] The sailors at first overlooked two men who were hiding. They found them in the morning and sacrificed them also. Holmes, by this time, was no longer part of the manhunt.

When it was all over Holmes was more visibly in command than ever. The mate had become very passive and quiet. Holmes was the one who distributed food and water, tried to cheer up the rest, and suggested that they not head for the Newfoundland coast, which they were unlikely to reach, but away from the icebergs where they stood a chance of being picked up. Just as Holmes was about to improvise a sail with the help of an oar and a man's quilt, he saw a vessel on the horizon. He told the passengers, "Lie down, every soul of you, and lie still. If they make out so many of us on board, they will steer off another way, and pretend they have not seen us."[21] He fastened a woman's shawl to a boathook and began waving it wildly. The ship saw them, and they were saved.

When they arrived in Le Havre several weeks later, the news of their misadventure had preceded them and public sentiment had already crystallized against the crew. Whereas the passengers were received with open arms, the crewmen were immediately put under arrest. They were released, however, when the British and American consuls in Le Havre assured the authorities that in their opinion the crew had behaved blamelessly.

The passengers and crewmen who some months later finally made it to America found the reaction there to be nearly the same. Newspapers were unanimous in demanding a public investigation. The *New York Commercial Advertiser* commented: "We have emigrant ships sailing every week, and if it is held as law that 'might is right' and that the crew are justified under extremities in throwing overboard whom and as many as they think right, without casting lots, or making other choice than their will it had better be declared so. It might well be considered under what flag emigrants will trust themselves; I scarcely think it will be the flag of that nation which so declares the law to be."[22] The *Public Ledger of Philadelphia* demanded that "the mate and sailors of the *William Brown*, who threw the passengers overboard to save themselves, should be put upon their trial for murder." "Let a court decide," it said "how far imperious circumstances warranted or extenuated their conduct. Thus much is due wounded humanity."[23] The *Boston Courier*, the most vehement of all, even excoriated the American consul in Havre who had found no fault with the sailors' conduct. "The consul at Havre who gave the exculpatory opinion disgraced the name of man," it declared, and it expressed the hope that the government "would not lose a moment in discharging from its employment such a disgrace to humanity."[24]

Some of the longboat's passengers sought out the district attorney of Philadelphia and signed a complaint against Holmes, who, as it happened, was the only crew member then in the city. Holmes was arrested and charged with murder. The grand jury, however, refused to indict him for murder, and ultimately he was put on trial for the voluntary manslaughter of Frank Askins, the young man who had offered Holmes five sovereigns if he would let him stay on board for the night.

The case was tried by an illustrious assembly of lawyers. The presiding judge was Henry Baldwin, a United States Supreme Court justice who was doing double duty as a trial judge. Baldwin was a respected jurist whose chief fault was said to be "excessive smoking"—a "great fault in a lawyer," wrote one contemporary, "and much greater in a judge, [for a] confirmed smoker or opium eater becomes nervously irritable when deprived of his indulgence. Of course a judge cannot smoke on the bench, and he is rendered uneasy, inattentive and sometimes petulant."[25] At Baldwin's side was Judge Randall, less prominent and erudite, but known as a man of "abundant good sense" and "calm judgment."[26] The prosecution rested in the hands of William Morris Meredith, later secretary of the treasury, and George Mifflin Dallas, later vice-president of the United States. Holmes himself had been taken under the wing of the Female Seamen's Friend Society. They made him sign a temperance pledge and then secured him the best criminal defense attorney in the city: David Paul Brown, a somewhat theatrical figure given to frequent literary allusions and irrepressible hyperbole.

The trial attracted enormous attention, but it did not hold the suspense of the usual murder trial. There were no surprising twists and turns, no scathing cross-examination, no unexpected disclosures, no involuntary confessions. There was little mystery about what had happened. The various witnesses produced by the prosecution and the defense, all of them passengers of the longboat, merely served to add color to the already well-known tale relayed by the newspapers. The prosecution and defense disagreed on very few issues of fact. True, the prosecution insisted that catastrophe was not as imminent as the defense made it out and that the sacrifice was premature. The defense insisted that not a minute was to be lost if anyone in that boat was to be saved. But the issue that really separated the two sides, the issue that had moved the newspapers to editorialize so extensively, the issue that caused the public at large to follow the case with proverbially baited breath, was one of principle: Even if the circumstances were as compelling as the defense made them out to be, did Holmes's actions cease to be criminal?

Yes, argued the defense. In situations of necessity, it contended, conventional law ceases to operate, and gives way instead to "natural law," by which it meant "the law of self-preservation." The defense tried to make the "law of self-preservation" sound as obvious and compelling as the "law of self-defense." The theatrical David Paul Brown never tired of reminding the jurors: "You sit here, the sworn twelve . . . reposing amidst the comfort and delights of sacred homes . . . to decide upon the impulses and motives of the prisoner at bar, launched upon the bosom of the perilous ocean—surrounded by a thousand deaths in their most hideous forms, with but one plank between him and destruction."[27] The prosecutor, in turn, insisted that, however imminent the hazard that faced the longboat, "full and distinct notice of the danger should have been given to all on board," and "lots should have been cast, before the sacrifice of any for the safety of the rest would become justifiable."[28]

Justice Baldwin in his instructions to the jury sided with the prosecution. He acknowledged that "on a kindred principle of self-defense, the law overlooks the taking of life under circumstances of imperious necessity, of a character similar to those which are now in evidence before you."[29] However, he added, when it comes to selecting the victims, passengers take precedence over sailors. If there are more sailors than are necessary to operate the boat, "the residue have no right to call for the sacrifice of a passenger for their protection."[30] And if more sacrifices yet are called for, lots must be cast.

In a sense these instructions all but sealed Holmes's fate. No sailors had been sacrificed, only passengers. And among them no lots had been cast. But Holmes could still hope for an acquittal by a sympathetic jury "in the teeth of the law." For nothing prevents a jury from disregarding the instructions the judge issues and acquitting a defendant purely on a whim. In fact that rarely happens, and it did not happen here. Holmes was convicted and sentenced to six months in prison and a $20 fine.

A presidential pardon ultimately relieved Holmes of his fine, but he did serve his entire sentence. When he was released, he went back to the sea, as had the rest of the crew, none of whom had been tried for their part in the *malheur*. Even the longboat was refurbished and sent out to serve as lifeboat in another voyage.

Forty years later there occurred another sea adventure, even more similar to the case of the Speluncean explorers. A wealthy Australian barrister had purchased a yacht, the *Mignonette,* in Essex. Although the ship was not the sturdiest, the owner decided to have a crew sail it to Sydney for him, rather than send it as deck cargo. He hired Thomas Dudley as captain, and Dudley recruited Edwin Stephens as mate, Edmund Brooks as able seaman, and a seventeen-year-old boy, Richard

Parker, as ordinary seaman. They left in late May and experienced several weeks of smooth sailing. Later the weather turned foul, and Dudley decided to turn off the main trade route. The winds, however, dogged them. Then suddenly, in the late afternoon of July 5, a heavy wave smashed against the stern of the ship and sprang loose its plankings. The *Mignonette* sank in less than five minutes. The four seamen just barely managed to get into their lifeboat, a 13-foot open dinghy. Unfortunately, they salvaged very little else. The emergency barrico of water they had hastily thrown overboard next to the dinghy was swept away by the waves. Only Dudley brought anything with him into the dinghy, two tins of turnips and a sextant.[31]

Sixteen thousand miles away from the closest shore their only hope was to get on the main trade route and be picked up by another ship. However parsimoniously rationed, the two tins of turnips were quickly consumed. Occasional rainfall permitted the men to collect some unsalted water in their oilskins. Parker, far sicker than the rest, immediately devoured his rations; the rest were able to hold out longer. On the fourth day they spotted a turtle asleep on the water, hauled it overboard, and fed on it for nearly a week, even eating the bones and chewing on its leathery skin. They tried to catch some fish, but with no success. Their lips and tongues parched and blackened from thirst, they took to drinking their urine. Eventually Parker and Stephens resorted to drinking seawater, then thought to be certain poison.

On the nineteenth day, feeling more dead than alive, Dudley proposed that one of them, to be chosen by lots, be killed for the rest to feed on. Brooks would not hear of it; Stephens was hesitant, and the idea was temporarily abandoned. Dudley next tried to persuade Stephens. He no longer talked about drawing lots. Parker evidently was the sickest, and he had no wife or children; it only seemed fair, Dudley reasoned, that he be the one killed. Finally, Stephens agreed. Dudley walked over to where Parker lay at the bottom of the boat, his face buried in his arms. "Richard," he said in a trembling voice, "your hour has come." "What? Me, sir?" mumbled the only half-conscious boy, uncomprehending. "Yes, my boy," Dudley repeated and then plunged his knife into Parker's neck.[32] The boy emitted a brief scream and then subsided. Dudley fetched a baler and drained off the blood that was spurting from Parker's neck. For the next four days all three, including Brooks who had objected to the killing, fed on the young boy's body, even drinking his blood. On the twenty-fourth day of their odyssey they were sighted by a German bark, the *Montezuma*, heading home from South America. (According to one author, the ship saw them only because the captain had deviated from the main trade route in hopes of finding mermaids.)[33] Of the three men, only Brooks was able to clamber aboard; the rest had to be carried. Parker's remains, still in the dinghy, left no doubt about what had happened, and both Dudley and Stephens completed the tale as soon as they had recovered sufficiently. The German crew, however, continued to treat them with the utmost kindness.

On 6 September 1884, the *Montezuma* sailed into Falmouth. The survivors were taken to the Customs House and closely questioned. It did not occur to them that they had done anything criminal. Dudley told of their adventure with something resembling gusto and even insisted on keeping the penknife with which he had killed Richard Parker as a memento. They were stunned when they were put under arrest and charged with murder. The upright Dudley immediately insisted that he was the ringleader and that Brooks was completely innocent. Brooks was indeed quickly discharged and became the prosecution's chief witness.

Throughout the trial and the preparations preceding it, public sympathy was almost entirely on the side of the "cannibals." When Dudley traveled from Falmouth to London to meet his wife at Paddington Station, men took their hats off as he passed. The trial judge described Dudley as a man of "exemplary courage."[34] The mayor of Falmouth was threatened with murder for having arranged the men's arrest. The prosecutor was similarly threatened, if he obtained a conviction. And, most remarkably, Daniel Parker, Richard Parker's eldest brother, forgave Dudley in open court, and shook hands with him. Parker's family planted a tombstone on Richard's grave that read:

> Though he slay me, yet I will trust him.
> (Job, xiii, 15)
> Lord, lay not this sin to their charge.[35]

The jury in the case was not permitted to render a verdict, for fear it would simply acquit the defendants, but was merely allowed to determine the facts. Nor did the trial judge render a verdict. Instead, by way of a highly unorthodox procedure, the case was brought before a five-judge tribunal, presided over by Lord Chief Justice Lord Coleridge, who rendered the opinion for the court: guilty as charged. He prefaced his opinion by expressing doubt whether a situation of necessity had truly existed. The defendants, he noted, "might possibly have been picked up the next day by a passing ship; they might possibly not have been picked up at all. In either case it is obvious that the killing of the boy would have been an unnecessary and profitless act.''[36] Even if necessity existed, he went on, that could not possibly justify killing another human being. For one, there was no judicial authority to support such a bold proposition. The only similar case was *United States v. Holmes*, and Coleridge merely scoffed at the American idea of gambling for one's life. Coleridge refused to recognize self-preservation as an all-justifying end. ''To preserve one's life is generally speaking a duty,'' he conceded, but added, ''it may be the plainest and the highest duty to sacrifice it. War is full of instances in which it is a man's duty not to live, but to die. The duty in case of shipwreck, of a captain to his crew, of the crew to the passengers, of soldiers to women and children. . . . these duties impose on men the moral necessity, not of preservation, but of the sacrifice of their lives for others. . . . It is not correct, therefore, to say there is any absolute or unqualified necessity to preserve one's life.''[37]

A rule permitting killing someone in situations of necessity, he finally remarked, would be virtually unworkable. ''Who is to be the judge of this sort of necessity?'' he asked. ''By what measure is the comparative value of lives to be measured?'' he continued. ''Is it to be strength, or intellect, or what?'' The court then sentenced the defendants to death.[38]

For all its fervent rhetoric, the court did not want to be taken too seriously. A pardon by the home secretary had been arranged well in advance, and when it came to pronouncing the death sentence, the judges did not even wear the black hoods customary on such occasions.

The defendants were released from prison six months later. Brooks had already gone back to the sea, but neither Dudley nor Stephens were enamored of the idea. Stephens settled down near Southampton and apparently supported himself through odd jobs. He continued to be absorbed by the events on the dinghy and over time went quietly mad. Thomas Dudley emigrated to Sydney, Australia, where he opened a chandler's shop and for a long time managed to keep his past history a secret. He, too, however, was haunted by memories of the dinghy, which, according to one author, he tried to relieve through great quantities of opium. He died as the first victim of the bubonic plague that hit Australia in 1900. ''His corpse was then subjected to indignities as gross as any that befell poor Richard Parker. Bathed in diluted sulphuric acid, and wrapped in many layers of sail cloth, it was taken by water for burial in grave 48 in the Quarantine Station on the South Heads of Sydney harbor. The family regarded it all as divine retribution."[39]

The Principle of Necessity

The *Holmes* court thought necessity could be a defense for murder. The *Dudley* court did not think it could. Lon Fuller's imaginary Supreme Court was badly splintered. So the weight of authority cannot decide. We have to look at the arguments and make up our own minds about the spelunkers.

Clemency

For many people and for many courts the solution offered by the *Dudley* court—convicting the defendants but arranging for an executive clemency—is enormously, if not irresistibly, tempting. It suggests that we do not need to make up our minds on the defendants' guilt after all: we can at one and the same time satisfy the impulse to convict and the impulse to acquit, the impulse to punish and the impulse to forgive. Chief Justice Truepenny is absolutely beguiled by this idea. Our murder statute, he regretfully declares, "permits of no exception applicable to this case, however [much] our sympathies may incline us to make allowance for the tragic situation in which [the defendants] found themselves."

Nevertheless, he gleefully goes on to say, "In a case like this the principle of executive clemency seems admirably suited to mitigate the rigors of the law, and I propose to my colleagues that we follow the example of the jury and the trial judge by joining in the communications they have addressed to the Chief Executive. There is every reason to believe that these requests for clemency will be heeded, coming as they do from those who have studied the case and had an opportunity to become thoroughly acquainted with all its circumstances.

"If this is done," he triumphantly concludes, "then justice will be accomplished without impairing either the letter or the spirit of our statutes and without offering any encouragement for the disregard of the law."[40]

Unfortunately, this solution is an illusory one. It merely cuts the Gordian knot it purports to disentangle. A pardon is *not* a substitute for an acquittal. The chief justice conveniently glosses over the fact that a pardon is not in the court's power to bestow. Accordingly, Justice Handy takes the chief justice to task for disguising from the public

> the most crucial fact in this case, a fact known to all of us on this Court, though one that my brothers have seen

> fit to keep under the judicial robes. This is the frightening likelihood that if the matter is left to him, the Chief Executive will refuse to pardon these men or commute their sentence. As we all know, the Chief Executive is a man now well advanced in years and of very stiff notions. Public clamor usually operates on him with the reverse of the effect intended. As I have told my brothers, it happens that my wife's niece is an intimate friend of his secretary. I have learned in this indirect, but I think, wholly reliable way, that he is fairly determined not to commute the sentence if these men are found to have violated the law.[41]

There is, however, a much more fundamental flaw in Chief Justice Truepenny's approach than the possibility that the clemency is denied. Even a conviction unaccompanied by a tangible penalty constitutes punishment. For it is not the penalty per se that makes a criminal sentence "punishing." People often suffer penalties that we would not consider punishments: parking tickets, sackings, flunkings, disqualifications, and so on. But what is it that makes some deprivations mere penalties and others punishments? What is it that a punishment has and a penalty lacks? Perhaps the difference is simply the degree of severity: penalties generally are light, punishments are harsh. Clearly, however, that is frequently not true. The loss of one's driver's license is a penalty. A day in jail is punishment. Yet the former is for many people significantly harsher than the latter.[42]

Perhaps the difference is a more elusive one: penalties are meant to be mere "price tags" for engaging in certain activities, punishments generally are meant to absolutely deter such activities. That distinction seems to explain why we view a cigarette or liquor tax as merely a penalty on smoking and drinking, not as our punishment for doing so. The tax is meant to discourage smoking and drinking—and incidentally to raise some revenues—but not to prohibit them. Thus a criminal who persists in repeating his criminal offense every time he is released will find himself subjected to ever harsher sentences until he stops. A smoker who cheerfully persists in smoking his daily pack will not find himself subjected to an ever mounting tax penalty until he quits. But not every penalty can be explained as a price tag on some disfavored activity. It would be hard to see someone who is fired for being surly, demoted for being incompetent, or flunked for doing poorly on an exam as "paying the price" for indulging in some undesired pasttime. Yet clearly he has suffered a penalty.[43]

What separates a punishment from a mere penalty is something else: the punishment condemns, the penalty does not. Unlike the penalty, punishment is designed to express a community's attitude of resentment, indignation, and outrage. Indeed there are many situations where we do not much care about the tangible deprivations and discomforts that go with punishment but solely for the punishment's symbolic significance.[44] In 1978 three girls driving a Ford Pinto died in a car accident. They had parked on the side of a highway. A van ran into the rear of their car, and a fire broke out that consumed all three girls. The state of Indiana indicted the Ford Motor Company for reckless homicide. It claimed that but for the criminal negligence with which Ford engineers had designed the Pinto model the fire would not have occurred and the girls would not have died. The Ford company faced a comparatively small monetary penalty. (Corporations, after all, cannot be sent to jail!) Nevertheless, it spent a multiple of that sum defending itself to avoid the symbolic tarbrush of a criminal conviction. (Ford was acquitted.)[45]

In 1925 in Dayton, Tennessee, William Jennings Bryan took on the prosecution and Clarence Darrow the defense of John Thomas Scopes, the school teacher who insisted on teaching evolution in defiance of the law that forbade it. The tangible stakes were no more than a fine of $500. The real stakes were symbolic: the right of Christian fundamentalists to regulate the dissemination of scientific knowledge.[46]

The novel *To Kill a Mockingbird* tells the story of a white girl who tries to seduce a black man, suffers remorse, and charges the man with rape. She, too, understands the symbolic significance of punishment: if the man is convicted of rape, this will absolve her of all complicity in what he did.[47]

Many otherwise forgiving people are offended by the law's tolerance of paramour killings. Why? Have they turned vengeful on this delicate point? Do they really believe that harsh punishment is the best way of preventing such incidents? No, what they desire is not the suffering of the killer, but a symbolic denunciation of what he or she did. They want the state to dispel all suspicion that it acquiesces in the practice.[48]

When people call for a "punishment that fits the crime," they implicitly understand and acknowledge the symbolic function of punishment. Few think that the only punishment that fits the crime is one that exacts an eye for an eye and a tooth for a tooth. As Blackstone observed long ago, "theft cannot be punished by theft, defamation by defamation, forgery by forgery, adultery by adultery." And while death may be punished by death, he quaintly added, "the execution of a needy and decrepit assassin is a poor satisfaction for the murder of a nobleman in the bloom of his youth and full enjoyment of his friends, his honors, and his fortune."[49] Rather what people mean by punishment that fits the crime is simply one that adequately expresses the community's disapproval, one that condemns more harshly the more heartily the community disapproves.[50]

This difference between punishments and penalties, although intangible, is far from tenuous. The United States Constitution takes it very seriously. The Bill of Rights provides special safeguards to all who are threatened by punishment: the right to confront witnesses against them, the right to a trial by jury, and so on. The person who is threatened by a mere penalty—a deportation, a suspension of his driver's license, or a surcharge for the late payment of his income tax—is protected by no such safeguards.[51]

It will not do, then, to convict and pardon. Conviction means punishment. And punishment means not just a penalty but condemnation. A pardon would merely wipe out the penalty, not the condemnation. There is no escaping the question whether the defendants are truly guilty and deserving of punishment.

We have to face head-on the question; Is there any way to justify what the spelunkers did? To justify is to show that some overriding social interest makes what was done rightful, good, desirable, or at least tolerable. Although neither the Sixth Commandment ("Thou shalt not kill") nor the Newgarth murder statute make mention of this, some killings are clearly justifiable. The soldier who shoots a man in the field is eligible for a medal. The citizen who kills some would-be burglars could in past centuries be knighted for this feat, as was Mr. Purcell, a septuagenarian, who in 1811 killed four burglars with a butcher knife.[52] The woman who drives an ice pick through the skull of her rapist assailant will be similarly commended today, as was Joan Little, who thus killed a prison guard trying to rape her.[53]

Self-Defense

The most obvious instance of a justifiable killing continues to be self-defense. The attorneys representing Holmes, Dudley, and Stephens repeatedly invoked self-defense as an analogy. But the analogy does not work. It is easy to see how society can sanction the killing of an evil-minded aggressor to save the life of his innocent victim. (And even here the law keeps the victim's privilege very narrow: he may not fling a knife after a departing assailant who has just stabbed him and left him bleeding in the gutter.) The killing of an innocent to save one's life is obviously very different. Obviously? Well, perhaps not entirely. Picture the following scenario. It is midnight. The defendant, who lives on the first floor atop the store he owns, is fast asleep. He is awakened by rioters demanding to be let in. The defendant grabs a gun and shoots in it the air several times to scare off the rioters. The shots attract a police officer who passes through the crowd and starts to walk up to the defendant. The defendant, however, mistakes him for one of the rioters and shoots at him, wounding him badly. Was the defendant justified? Yes, for his mistake, although regrettable, was reasonable. Thus at times, it seems, one is justified in killing an innocent to protect one's life. But the analogy to the spelunkers' case is still not very close. The defendant did in fact shoot an innocent man, but he did not know him to be innocent. In the case of the Speluncean explorers the defendants killed a man they knew to be innocent.[54]

Natural Law

The defense in *Holmes* and *Dudley* raised another argument as well. They contended that somehow the circumstances in which the defendants found themselves were so extreme as to plunge them into a "state of nature" in which society's "positive law" (in those times called "municipal law") ceased to apply. The argument has a great deal of intuitive appeal. Somehow what goes on in the spacious, soft-carpeted, high-ceilinged courtrooms of civilization seems to have little bearing on what men do to each other under circumstances as extraordinary as those in which the sailors and the spelunkers found themselves. Justice Foster of the Supreme Court of Newgarth endorses this argument and gropes to make it coherent and plausible. "I take the view," he says, "that the enacted or positive law of this Commonwealth, including all of its statutes and precedents, is inapplicable to this case, and that the case is governed instead by what ancient writers in Europe and America called 'the law of nature.' " His explanation runs as follows: "Our positive law is predicated on the possibility of men's coexistence in society. When a situation arises in which the coexistence of men becomes impossible, then a condition that underlies all of our precedents and statutes has ceased to exist. When that condition disappears, then it is my opinion that the force of our positive law disappears with it . . . *Cessante ratione legis, cessat et ipsa lex*. [When the reason for a law disappears, so must the law itself.]"[55]

In short, he says, when men agreed to enter into the social contract out of which society was formed, they did so on condition that that would improve the situation of each or at least ensure the survival of each. When it is no longer capable of doing that, there is no reason for any man to abide by the contract: the precondition for its formation having failed, the contract ceases to be binding. Thus the courts of Newgarth, according to Justice Foster, were stripped of their jurisdiction over the spelunkers just as though the incident had occurred in a faraway country. "If we look to the purposes of law and government, and to the premises underlying our positive law, these men when they made their fateful decision were as remote from our legal order as if they had been a thousand miles beyond our boundaries. Even in a physical sense, their underground prison was separated from our courts and writ-servers by a solid curtain of rock that could be removed only after the most extraordinary expenditures of time and effort."[56]

Justice Foster's colleagues sense that his argument is preposterous, but they are not very good at rebutting it. So, for instance, Justice Tatting complains that Justice Foster's proposed principle has no clearly defined boundaries. "If these men passed from the jurisdiction of our law to that of 'the law of nature,' at what moment did this occur? Was it when the entrance to the cave was blocked, or when the threat of starvation reached a certain undefined degree of intensity, or when the agreement for the throwing of the dice was made?"[57] But Justice Tatting is being too hasty. Socrates used to insist that no one had the right to maintain a thesis unless he was prepared to give an unequivocal definition of its key terms that would leave no doubtful or marginal cases. As a rhetorical device this demand was quite successful; it flustered his opponents because it seemed to suggest that they did not know what they were talking about. In fact the demand was quite unreasonable, as a burlesque of the Socratic style quickly shows: "What is life? Can we define the moment of death? Can we, moreover, define the difference between actually killing and just failing to preserve life? And what is a baby? Would fine healthy puppy dogs brought forth by a human mother count as babies? If you can't answer these questions, you have no right to say with any confidence that it's wrong to kill babies, since you don't know what you mean by 'killing' or 'baby.' "[58] We may not always be able to tell whether something should be classified as a horse or a mule, but that does not mean that we don't know what a horse or a mule is. Similarly, just because it has a blurry borderline, Justice Foster's principle need not be invalid.

But it does have its problems. It rests on a fiction—a fictitious precondition to a semifictitious social contract. It is similar to another fiction courts and philosophers have occasionally flirted with, the notion that an immoral law is no law at all. In 1944, a woman denounced her husband to the authorities for making insulting remarks about Hitler. (She had lovers and wanted to be rid of him.) The husband was arrested and sentenced to death pursuant to a law that made such statements a crime. He was not actually executed but was sent to the front. In 1949, a West German court convicted the woman for an offense akin to false imprisonment, punishable under the German Criminal Code of 1871, which had remained in force continuously. The court reasoned that the woman had illegally procured her husband's imprisonment, because her conduct, although pursuant to a law, was too immoral to be lawful. The court's argument was clearly a fiction. However immoral, the Nazi law was a law, and the woman's conduct lawful.[59]

Clinging to such a fiction has unfortunate consequences. Through its use, the German court deprived itself of the much more persuasive argument that certain immoral laws, laws though they be, are too immoral to follow. Similarly, Justice Foster deprives himself of the much more persuasive argument that applying certain laws, under any and all circumstances, laws though they be, is undesirable.[60] The fiction has another unfortunate consequence. If the woman's conduct wasn't lawful, neither, it seems, was the conduct of the policeman who arrested her husband, the prosecutor who indicted him, the judge who sentenced him, or even the army officer who took charge of him. But shouldn't each of these cases be tackled separately rather than with one undiscriminating blow? (In fact, the court made a feeble, unconvincing attempt to weasel out of these implications.) Justice Foster's analysis produces a similar result. It suggests that even if the killing had been performed completely gratuitously, with no intention to feed on the victim's flesh, it would still not be punishable, since it took place in a "natural state" and outside the jurisdiction of a court constituted under positive law.

The Argument of Numbers

The most straightforward argument in behalf of the spelunkers is suggested by the *Holmes* court. The *Holmes* court agreed that if a lifeboat is likely to sink unless lightened, some passengers may be jettisoned so long as they are selected fairly. The court evidently thought that it is worth slightly accelerating the death of a few to save the lives of many.

To some this rationale is instantly compelling, to others it is anathema. Supreme Court Justice Benjamin Cardozo abhorred the idea of such forced sacrifice.

> Where two or more are overtaken by a common disaster, there is no right on the part of one to save the lives of some by the killing of another. There is no rule of human jettison. Men there will often be who, when told that their going will be the salvation of the remnant, will choose the nobler part and will make the plunge into the waters. In that supreme moment the darkness for them will be illumined by the thought that those behind will ride to safety. If none of such mold are found aboard the boat, or too few to save the others, the human freight must be left to meet the chances of the waters. Who shall choose in such an hour between the victims and saved? Who shall know when the masts and sails of rescue may emerge out of the fog?[61]

Echoing these sentiments, another jurist, Edmund Cahn, wrote,

> I am driven to conclude that otherwise—that is, if none sacrifice themselves of free will to spare the others—they must all wait and die together. For where all have become congeners, pure and simple, no one can save himself by killing another. In such a setting and at such a price, he has no moral individuality left to save. Under the terms of the moral constitution it will be *wholly* himself that he kills in his vain effort to preserve himself. The "morals of the last days" leave him a generic creature, only; in such a setting, so remote from the differentiations of mortal existence, every person in the boat embodies the entire genus. Whoever saves one, saves the whole human race; whoever kills one, kills mankind.[62]

More whimsically, the philosopher Anthony Kenny has stated that he, for one, would rather be in a lifeboat with companions who accepted the rule of *Dudley and Stephens* "than in company with lawyers who accepted necessity as a defence to murder."[63]

The high moral tone of these reprobations makes the other side, the "argument of numbers," seem coarse and unfeeling. But is it? The position of thinkers like Cardozo, Cahn, and Kenny reduces to this: Where one has the choice between killing a few and letting many die, it is better to let many die. Is killing really so much more offensive than letting die? Consider this conundrum:

> Edward is the driver of a trolley, whose brakes have failed. On the track ahead of him are five people; the banks are so steep that they will not be able to get off the track in time. The track has a spur leading off to the right, and Edward can turn the trolley onto it. Unfortunately, there is one person on the right hand track. Edward can turn the trolley, killing the one; or he can refrain from turning the trolley."[64]

If Edward does nothing he is letting five die. If he turns the trolley he is killing one. Is that a decisive reason for not turning the trolley?

In its rocket attacks on London during World War II, Germany relied extensively on the reports of London spies to find out how accurately it was hitting its targets. The spy ring was headed by a British double agent. Somebody suggested that to reduce the number of casualties the double agent should tell his German superiors that the rockets had fallen north of London, though in fact they hadn't. That would lead the Germans to aim their rockets farther south. The rockets would then fall on Kent, Surrey, or Sussex and kill far fewer people than if they fell on London. If letting die is so much better than killing, regardless of the numbers involved, such a proposal should be out of the question. As a matter of fact it was rejected. But wisely so?[65]

Undoubtedly there is a moral difference between killing and letting die. After all we wouldn't generally convict someone of murder for letting someone else die. But the difference is not so very large. Compare the following two scenarios. (1) Alfred hates Alfrieda and wants her dead. He puts cleaning fluid in her coffee, and she dies. (2) Bert hates Berta and wants her dead. She inadvertently puts cleaning fluid in her coffee, mistaking it for cream. Bert happens to have the antidote to cleaning fluid, but does not tell her. She dies. Alfred *killed* Alfrieda. But Bert merely *let* Berta die. Yet there isn't much to choose between the two men. Everything else being the same, letting die is not *intrinsically* much better than killing.[66]

The "argument of numbers" is appealing for another reason. We constantly impose risks of harm on others, and the law finds nothing wrong with that. When we drive a car, we risk harm to pedestrians. When we build a factory, we risk harm to neighbors. So long as the benefits to the majority (drivers, workers, consumers) outweigh the risks to the minority (pedestrians, neighbors), the law will not interfere with such activities.

(Of course, if the benefit doesn't outweigh the risk, the activity is deemed reckless.) Well, if it is all right to risk harm to a few to help the many, why isn't it all right, sometimes at least, to harm a few to help the many?

What makes the argument of numbers seem especially attractive is that, unlike the arguments from self-defense and natural law, it can easily be generalized to account for other cases of necessity. What it generalizes to is the proposition that where following a law does more harm than good, it should be broken. In this generalized form the argument explains effortlessly our intuitions about the easy cases. If we feel that a prisoner is justified in breaking out of his burning cell, a druggist in giving a heart attack victim unprescribed nitroglycerine, and a father in keeping his daughter out of school, that's because following the law in these cases would do more harm than good. Most states have in fact accepted the necessity argument in this form. The Model Penal Code, an illustrative penal code on which most states draw in drafting their criminal statutes, puts it thus: "Conduct that the actor believes to be necessary to avoid a harm or evil to himself or to another is justifiable, provided that: . . . the harm or evil sought to be avoided by such conduct is greater than that sought to be prevented by the law defining the offense charged."[67]

I mustn't oversell the argument of numbers. It has to be qualified. It would be wrong to say that a person is free to kill whenever he brings about a net saving of lives. Suppose a doctor has five patients who need organ transplants. Two of them need a lung; two need a kidney; the fifth needs a heart. A patient walks into the doctor's office for his annual check-up. The doctor, a zealous advocate of the argument of numbers, kills the man, gives his lungs to the first two patients, his kidneys to the other two, and his heart to the fifth, thus saving five lives at the cost of one.[68] Is that all right? The argument of numbers suggests that it is. Yet clearly, it is not, even though it would be hard to say just how this case is different from, say, the case of the trolley driver. Fortunately, the principle of necessity is more flexible than the argument of numbers out of which it grew: Applying that principle, we would probably conclude that in this case "the harm or evil sought to be avoided" is not "greater than that sought to be prevented by the law defining the offense charged."

Despite this qualification, the principle of necessity—the generalized argument of numbers—seems like the last best hope of defendants like the Speluncean explorers. It strongly suggests that the spelunkers were in the right. Or does it? In its generalized form, the principle is awfully vague. It doesn't really tell us whether the harm of eating one spelunker is outweighed by the good of saving many more spelunkers. It tells us to weigh the two acts against each other, but it doesn't tell us what weights to assign to each. Nevertheless, I suspect that at least in this particular case most people won't have trouble carrying out the weighing process. But what about the infinitude of cases in which the good and the harm resulting from breaking a law are so different as to seem beyond comparison? How does the weighing process work then?

An example of this problem is the case brought recently against an East German fugitive named Hans Detlev Alexander Tiede, who had diverted a Polish airliner bound for East Berlin to West Berlin.[69]

Hans Tiede was a waiter in East Berlin, with a Polish wife and two children (one of them named John, after John F. Kennedy). He wanted to "go West," but, not surprisingly, was denied permission the twelve times he applied. His wife, being Polish, was able to move, took the children with her, and left it to Tiede to find his way there.

Ingrid Ruske was a waitress in East Berlin, divorced, with a small daughter, and in love with a West German engineer. They had planned to escape to West Berlin by boarding a Polish cruise ship in Gdansk with fake Western ID's. Ingrid, somewhat fearful, wanted someone else to try the strategy first. She remembered her former boyfriend, Hans Tiede, who was delighted to play guinea pig.

Hans and Ingrid flew to Gdansk to wait for the engineer to bring them their ID's. He never came. East German agents had gotten wind of his efforts through their underground network in West Berlin and arrested him when he reentered East Berlin. The would-be fugitives guessed what had happened. What to do now? Their own arrests could not be too far off, since the photographs on the engineer's fake ID's would clearly give them away. They couldn't stay in Poland much longer, since they had no money left. In fact, their only assets were the return tickets to Berlin, which they had bought merely to avoid arousing suspicion. Hans suggested hijacking the plane to West Berlin. Unfortunately, he had no weapon. As they all aimlessly wandered the streets of Gdansk, Ingrid's daughter drew their attention to a toy gun in a shop window. It looked real enough, Hans thought. He sold some of his clothing and bought the gun.

They got on the plane quite easily, by putting the gun into the child's luggage. Airport security in fact searched their bags and found it, but thought nothing of it when they saw it was a toy. The moment of truth came when the pilot announced the plane's impending landing in East Berlin's Schoenefeld Airport. Ingrid was having second thoughts. Wouldn't the Gdansk control tower tell the pilot the gun was toy? Hans brushed aside her reservations, stormed into the cockpit, gun in hand, and ordered the crew to take him to West Berlin. Everyone reacted calmly. The pilot checked with the East Berlin airport, then with the West Berlin airport and within a few minutes the plane had landed in West Berlin. By this time, Hans's relationship with the crew was almost cordial. He had told them why he did what he did, had passed around pictures of his wife and children, and by the time police led him away the captain even flashed him a thumbs-up sign. (In fact, it seemed to Hans the captain had known all along he was carrying only a toy gun.) Before the plane took off again, eight other East Germans had decided to stay in the West as well.

West Germany, East Germany, Poland, and the United States are all party to an international agreement to prosecute hijackers. But West German authorities did not at all relish the idea of prosecuting Tiede. The West German constitution makes all Germans, including East Germans, West German citizens and gives them a "protected right" to enter West Germany. West Germany does not recognize the validity of East German travel restrictions. In fact, an East German border guard who shoots a fleeing East German under West German law has committed murder. There is a celebrated case in which an East German border guard was indeed brought to justice in West Germany. The West German way out of this distasteful dilemma was to remind the Americans that they continued to exercise the powers of an occupation force in West Berlin and to ask them to convene an American court to try the hijackers. The Americans obliged. They set up a special United States District Court of Berlin and installed Judge Herbert Stern of the United States District Court of New Jersey to preside over it.

Ingrid Ruske was never brought to trial. Her part in the hijacking was evidently very minor. The only proof of her involvement was a statement she had made to an interrogator. The judge ruled that the statement had been improperly elicited from her and ordered it suppressed. Stripped of its evidence, the prosecution withdrew the charge against her.

The case against Hans Tiede went ahead. He was charged with hijacking, taking a hostage, depriving other persons of liberty, and doing bodily injury to a stewardess. The case was tried before a jury of West Berliners. Tiede raised the defense of necessity. He pointed out that he had not diverted the plane for profit or for some political cause. He was simply asserting his rights under the West German constitution. He pointed out that both he and Ingrid Ruske were faced with imminent arrest if they returned to East Berlin. Finally, he pointed out that his act had secured not only his own and Ingrid Ruske's freedom, but that of eight other East Germans who had leapt at the opportunity to defect. That was the "harm avoided" by his illegal conduct.

What about the "harm sought to be prevented by the law defining the offense"? Tiede, the prosecution contended, had "endangered the lives and safety of 68 innocent people," the passengers of LOT flight 165.[70] The captain had had to land on an unfamiliar airfield that was highly unsuitable for planes of this size. Tiede, the prosecution added, had also caused mortal anguish to an innocent stewardess. What the prosecution didn't mention, though perhaps should have (had the judge permitted it), was the risk that the East bloc countries might cease to abide by the antihijacking agreements should men like Tiede go free.

The jurors deliberated for two days. Their verdict: not guilty of hijacking, depriving other persons of liberty, and inflicting bodily injury, guilty of taking a hostage. How could they find necessity justified the former three, but not the latter? The verdict was obviously the product of compromise. But it's the jury's prerogative to be inconsistent.

The interests weighed in *United States v. Tiede* were as diverse as could be. Does the necessity principle really give the jury any guidance as to how the balance between them should be struck? How does one weigh the fugitive's interest in liberty against the passengers' interest in safety? Does the principle do any more than tell the jurors, Do as you please? In short, is the necessity principle as we stated it really helpful in this case?

When a scientist chooses between two competing scientific theories, he is told to weigh them according to a variety of considerations: What is the explanatory power of each? How well does each fit with the data? How broad and diverse is the evidence supporting each? How testable is each? How simple is each? How well does each fit with other accepted theories? There may be no formula integrating all these questions into a straightforward test. It may be hard in a given case to choose between a theory that is simple and broad and one that fits well with the data and is very testable. That doesn't make the choice between them a matter of whim. It doesn't make the rule that we should weigh these considerations against each other empty or useless. The same goes for the principle of necessity.[71]

False Alarms

The Speluncean explorers were rescued two days earlier than anticipated. This raised doubts in people's minds whether Whetmore's sacrifice had really been necessary after all. Considering that the spelunkers could not reasonably have anticipated such a breakthrough, should it matter to their guilt or innocence?

Jack Mayer was a third-year medical student who participated in an antiwar demonstration in May 1968. He happened to notice that police tried to arrest a man who appeared to have suffered a severe spinal injury. He implored the officers not to move the man without a stretcher since that would greatly aggravate the injury. When the officers ignored him, he tried to stop them. He was charged with disorderly conduct and interfering with police officers in the performance of their duty. He defended his actions on the grounds of necessity: resisting the officers was illegal, but it prevented a much more grievous injury to the prostrate man. Unfortunately, the man turned out not to have suffered a spinal cord injury after all. The fact was that moving the man would not have harmed him in the least. Nevertheless, it was held that Mayer should be acquitted if he reasonably believed the man had suffered a spinal cord injury.[72]

Most states take this position. The Model Penal Code, quoted earlier, goes even further. It acquits the defendant whenever he believes himself to be in a situation of necessity, whether that belief is reasonable or not. But not all states subscribe to such a lenient view. The New York penal code requires that the defendant's conduct actually be "necessary as an emergency measure to avoid an imminent public or private injury."[73] Jack Mayer would be convicted in New York. So would the spelunkers. Is the New York rule unjustly harsh? Perhaps not. The following case came before the High Court of Southern Rhodesia in September 1961. The two defendants, Pange and Matini, had lived all their life in a secluded reserve belonging to the primitive Kalanga tribe and had never had any dealings with the European community. In times of drought, when crops might be inadequate, it was customary among the Kalanga to call on their witch doctors "to prepare a medicine called *dupa*, which is mixed with the seeds before planting so the crops will be plentiful. A person is killed and his body taken to the witchdoctor; normally the witchdoctor requests that a relative of the person who is asking for the medicine be killed. He will want the toes, fingers, the inside portion from the stomach, and some fat for the *dupa*. The head of the victim is also removed and placed in a hidden place until dry; then the seeds are placed inside the skull before planting.''[74]

A drought had settled over the region and the threat of starvation hung ominously over the reserve. While having a drink with a local witch doctor, Pange and Matini, both women, voiced their fears about the impending harvest. ''You must be fools,'' the witch doctor replied. ''Why don't you find some *muti* [a magic portion] so that you get plenty of crops?'' He promised to find them some *muti*. Just as the rainy season began, he returned with a bag of caterpillars, which he referred to as *muti*, but declared that he needed something else to make it work. ''You must kill a human being and bring the body to me. You must kill a child so that you will be able to carry the body and bring it to me.'' Pange said that she had no children, but the witch doctor pointed to some children playing about the kraal and asked: ''What about these children?'' Two nights later the two women brought the witch doctor a cardboard box containing the body of Matini's two-year-old cousin, one of the children who had been playing in the kraal. The women were charged with murder. Yet the object of their heinous deed was eminently honorable. Given where they grew up, it was entirely reasonable for them to believe the sacrifice of a child was called for to save the community. Should they be acquitted by reason of necessity?[75]

The trial court did not think that the belief in witchcraft tended to ''lessen the magnitude of the offence of murdering an innocent child, even if the motive was to avoid a crop failure and so starvation.'' It found the defendants guilty of murder, refused to recognize their misguided beliefs as even an extenuating circumstance, and sentenced them to death. The appeals court expressed concern over the fact that ''these women in these circumstances could hardly have offered effective opposition to the appalling suggestion made to them. [One may] regard them as little more than automata, acting under compulsion of pressures which they could not possibly resist.'' Nonetheless, it affirmed the trial court's verdict. The governor ultimately commuted their sentences to life imprisonment.[76]

Under most states' necessity principle the defendants would have been acquitted, since they reasonably believed themselves in a situation of necessity. That's not necessarily for the best. The natives are subject to all kinds of imagined threats that can only be averted through the most extraordinary remedies. Are we to encourage the use of such remedies?

What goes for the African native may also go for the trapped spelunker or the shipwrecked sailor. Calamitous predicaments tend to impair one's judgment. They make even reasonable people subject to imagined threats that can only be averted through the most extraordinary remedies. If we exonerate such tragic, albeit reasonable, misjudgments, we are likely to encourage them.

We may have to deny ourselves liberal use of the necessity defense, the way Odysseus denied himself the power of command when passing by the Sirens. (Because he knew that sailors were apt to be seduced by the song of the sirens so that their ship crashed into the cliff, he ordered his crew to stop their ears with wax. But because he wanted to hear the song, he had himself tied to a mast, and told the crew to ignore his orders until they had passed the cliff.)[77] Interestingly, this strategy of dealing with one's own weakness of will is not original with the wily Odysseus. Even animals sometimes use it. In one pigeon experiment, things had been set up so that if the pigeon pecked a key when it lit up red, it got two pellets, but if it didn't peck the key, it got four pellets. Under these circumstances, the pigeons will persist in pecking, even though not pecking would yield more pellets. They behave as though they realized that pecking is rewarded with food, but do not realize that *not* pecking is rewarded with even more food. In a variation of the experiment, however, the red key lit up green a few seconds before lighting up red. If the pigeons pecked the key when it was green, it never lit up red, and the pigeons ended up with four pellets. Very soon the pigeons started to peck the key when it lit up green. In effect, they were pecking the key when it lit up green to prevent themselves from pecking it when it lit up red. To cope with their weakness of will the pigeons were playing Odysseus.[78]

Ultimately, our decision whether to treat the mistake of the spelunkers' like that of Jack Mayer or that of Pange and Matini should turn on how severely we think calamities impair people's judgments. We should convict them if we think that situations of necessity tend to turn people into Pange and Matini. We should acquit them if we think that, on balance, judgment calls like theirs, even if occasionally mistaken, are for the better.

Courting Disaster

Reflecting on the predicament of the Speluncean explorers, one is haunted by the suspicion that the defendants may not have been entirely blameless in bringing it about. Experienced amateurs that they were, they should perhaps have been a bit more alert to the rumbling of rocks or the swaying of walls or other signals of an impending landslide. Perhaps they were just a bit reckless in not keeping a hawkeyed watch for such warnings.

But what if they were just a bit reckless—does that make their necessity defense any less convincing? There is an argument to be made that it does. Think of the playboy who races his Jaguar down a narrow alleyway. Suddenly he sees a group of people. It is too late to stop. He can avoid them only by swerving into the adjacent bookshop, where the owner is just in the process of rearranging the window display. The driver resolves to kill the owner rather than run into the group and turns his car into the shop window, killing the man instantly. He is charged with voluntary manslaughter and defends by pleading necessity. If he had not driven into the bookshop, he argues, he would undoubtedly have killed many more people. The defense seems preposterous. It was the defendant's recklessness that put him into the position of having to make such a Hobson's choice.

Bearing examples like that of our playboy in mind, many courts consider it axiomatic that unless the defendant's hands are utterly "clean," he may not raise the necessity defense. By "clean" they often mean immaculate. The defendant in *Butterfield v. Texas* had been out drinking with one of his companions. He had had a great deal to drink and his companions had to carry him home to his garage apartment in the early hours of the morning.[79] As the defendant entered his bedroom, somebody whacked him on the head, and he passed out. When he awoke, he found himself in a pool of blood. He realized that he was still bleeding and needed immediate medical help. He had no telephone, and he lived alone. He got into his car and drove himself to the hospital. On his way there he caused a minor traffic accident, was arrested, and charged with drunk driving. He tried to plead necessity, but the court rejected the defense. Why? It thought the defense so patently frivolous it did not bother to give a reason. The court was only slightly more loquacious in *Sansom v. Texas*. There the defendant was merely a passenger in a friend's car.[80] The defendant was drunk, but his friend, the driver, even more so. When a police officer noticed the wobbling car, he signalled them to stop. The driver ignored the signal. The defendant thereupon seized the wheel from him, drove the car onto the street shoulder, and brought it to a stop. Then the incredible happened: he was charged with drunken driving. The court refused to instruct the jury that the defendant should be acquitted if he only took the wheel to park the car. "If appellant is found in a predicament," it reasoned, "it is of his own doing, and he may not by such conduct claim the benefit of a defense to which he is not entitled."[81]

The notion that a defendant must be blameless before he can invoke necessity is even more popular with writers of fiction than courts of law.

The Caine Mutiny, both a novel and a play by Herman Wouk, climaxes in the court martial of a naval officer, Stephen Merrick, who had the audacity to relieve a mad captain of his command when the captain's irrational orders in the middle of a storm threatened to run the ship aground. Merrick is acquitted. But when the trial is over his own lawyer tells him that he believes him morally guilty. If Merrick and the crew had only been more cooperative and understanding from the outset, the lawyer explains, Captain Queeg would never have gotten close to the brink of insanity and would never have had to be relieved of his command.[82]

Everyone's intuition seems to be that the blameworthy defendant forfeits his right to invoke necessity. But why is that? At the root of this intuition seems to be the idea that the blameworthy defendant "voluntarily assumed the risk" of a mishap, a terrible predicament, a choice-of-evils befalling him. Having assumed that risk at the outset, he is not entitled to escape it by invoking "necessity" when it materializes.

In law, one runs into this concept of a "voluntarily assumed risk" all the time. But does it make any sense? Has the person living next to a nuclear plant voluntarily assumed the risk of radioactive poisoning? He didn't want the nuclear plant where it is. That makes the risk seem involuntary. He could have moved away. That makes it seem voluntary. Has a window washer voluntarily assumed the risk that his ropes may break? He has a large family to support and couldn't find an equally well-paying job for a man with his skills. That makes the risk seem involuntary. He could have taken a lower-paying job all the same. That makes it seem voluntary. If it didn't cost us anything, we would not expose ourselves to the risk of any mishap. That makes the risk of any mishap seem involuntary. If we made a large enough sacrifice, we could avoid the risk of any mishap. That makes it seem voluntary. Whether we call a risk voluntary or involuntary depends mostly, it seems, on whether we like to call the cup half empty or half full.[83]

If we yield to our intuition and deny the blameworthy defendant the necessity defense, this could have manifestly unjust consequences. Think of the backpacker who recklessly takes along too little to survive his long trek through the wilderness and finally decides to break into an empty weekend cabin for food. Should he be deemed guilty of burglary?

If we deny the blameworthy defendant the necessity defense, that could also produce some very undesirable behavior. The Jaguar-driving playboy might decide to smash into that group of people (killing many) instead of swerving into the bookshop (killing one). Had he smashed into the group, he would only have committed involuntary manslaughter. By crashing into the bookshop, he committed voluntary manslaughter, possibly even murder.

Our false intuition about denying the blameworthy defendant his necessity defense is so persistent because we mistakenly believe that the defendant will otherwise get completely off the hook. Since he was blameworthy and brought about some harm, we are naturally loath to permit that. But usually he wouldn't get off the hook! The Jaguar-driving playboy may be acquitted of the charge of murder or manslaughter for turning his car into the bookshop, but he can still be convicted of manslaughter for driving recklessly in the first place, which recklessness ultimately eventuated in somebody's death. The spelunkers will be treated the same. They will be acquitted of the charge of murder for killing Roger Whetmore, but they might still be convicted of his manslaughter for recklessly venturing into the cave without adequate supplies, which recklessness ultimately eventuated in his death. (If indeed they were reckless!) Whether any of the other defendants could be convicted of anything would depend on whether they recklessly risked the creation of a choice-of-evil situation and whether the harm that came of it, combined with the initial recklessness, corresponds to some crime (such as manslaughter). The reckless backpacker probably couldn't be convicted of anything. He was reckless, and his recklessness resulted in an act of misappropriation. But reckless acts of misappropriation aren't crimes, only intentional ones are.[84]

Necessity and the Rule of Law

When Roger Whetmore first proposed cannibalism as an alternative to starvation, he argued: "Even the person who is killed is better off than he would otherwise have been. I, for one, prefer quick merciful death to the agony of prolonged starvation." Let us assume for the moment that Roger Whetmore did not back out of the arrangement he proposed but gratefully submitted to his execution. Even if the survival of four does not outweigh the killing of one, the defendants might nevertheless argue that the agony of starvation outweighed the harm of killing even for the victim himself. In other words, the defendants could seek to justify their action as a form of euthanasia—mercy killing.

As it happens, the issue of euthanasia is not a new one for the Newgarth legislature (let us suppose). Only some years earlier someone proposed a bill that would have legalized euthanasia in some circumstances. Its advocates urged the need to bring clarity into what had for too long been a cloudy and unsettled area. They noted that the case against euthanasia was basically a religious one and should thus be consigned to the consciences of the persons involved, not the courts. Above all, they dwelt on the misery and suffering that euthanasia would help to eradicate. The bills' opponents were no less vocal. Any attempt to legalize euthanasia, they argued, would be vulnerable to tremendous abuse. A doctor's diagnosis of the patient's predicament and his chances of a recovery could be wrong. The patient, filled with sedative drugs, might be in no position to evaluate his own situation competently and to decide whether life was worth living any longer. And how is one to treat those who are never able to consent competently to euthanasia—the retarded and the insane? Even if the availability of euthanasia were confined to terminal diseases, as some advocates of the bills offered, that raises troubling definitional questions: what is a terminal disease? Anything that makes for a short life expectancy, even old age? And how short a life expectancy is that—five months, two years? The floor debate was fierce and tortuous. When the dust settled, the issue had been handed over to a committee for further study. There it still rests.[85]

The spelunkers are essentially trying to make an end run around this legislative deadlock. There is no express provision sanctioning euthanasia, they concede, but the rule of necessity, they claim, implicitly sanctions euthanasia in some circumstances. This effort has precedent. On 10 July 1970, around midnight, two young men broke into the Selective Service Office in Little Falls, Minnesota, carrying with them a screwdriver, hammer, crowbar, glass cutter, flashlights, and other equipment. They forced open several of the file drawers, removed some of the draft registration cards and placed them in a plastic garbage bag intending to burn them. Fifteen minutes after the defendants had come in, the FBI, which had been tipped off to the entry, arrested them. They searched the men and found on them some letters disclosing a plan to destroy all I-A files for that county. Charged with "wilfully and knowingly attempting to hinder and interfere with the administration of the Military Selective Service Act of 1967 by force and violence," the protestors raised the defense of necessity.[86] They produced numerous witnesses who testified as to the perniciousness of the Vietnam War: "the damage to Vietnamese society caused by the war; the impact of the war on Cambodia; the extent of civilian casualties in Vietnam and Cambodia; the impact of an act of civil disobedience in bringing the war to an end; the ecological damage to Vietnam; the extent to which draftees carry the burden of the war; the effect of domestic protests and acts of civil disobedience on the decision-making of high government officials; and the probability that the war [would] continue unless there [was] domestic opposition to it.'' They then requested that the judge instruct the jury to acquit, if it found, consonant with the necessity rule, ''that the evils sought to be avoided by the defendants were far greater than those sought to be prevented by the law defining the offense.''[87]

A similar situation developed eight years later in New Hampshire over the issue of nuclear power. Here some protestors were arrested during a mass occupation of the construction site of the Seabrook Nuclear Power Plant. They were charged with criminal trespass. One of them invoked the necessity defense, seeking to prove that the evil of nuclear power outweighed the harm done by his trespass.[88]

If you happen to believe that even a miserable life is too precious a thing to be deliberately extinguished, that the Vietnam War was a good thing, or that nuclear power is the solution to our energy problems, none of those cases will present much of a problem to you: the necessity rule, you will say, just doesn't apply; so go ahead and convict those fellows. But suppose you happen to agree with the defendants that mercy killing sometimes is the better of two grim alternatives, that the Vietnam War was evil, or that nuclear power plants are a threat to mankind and that what the defendants did will go a long way toward eliminating these evils. Are you prepared to acquit them on that ground? Or is there something that makes you hesitate? And if there is, can you identify the source of that hesitation?

We frequently describe our system of government by using two pet phrases: ''law and order'' and ''rule of law.'' When we refer to ours as a system of ''law and order,'' we mean that it is for the legislature (or courts) to make (or interpret) the laws and for citizens to obey them. Once the legislature has passed a statute, it is not for the citizen to judge whether it is wise and deserves to be followed or unwise and deserves to be flouted. He is free to denounce the law and seek to change it through the political process, but while the law stands, he must comply. We say that ours is a government ruled by laws and not by men to indicate that not just ordinary citizens but officials as well are subject to the rules laid down by the legislature. The official, as one book puts it, is just ''a wheel in the machine; he may never be its ghost.''[89] If we give citizens and officials free reign to disobey the law where they reasonably think it does more harm than good, it seems that we are undercutting the very foundation of our system of law—the obligation of every citizen to abide by the rules passed by the legislature whether he likes them or not. Cases like that of the Speluncean explorers, the antiwar protesters, and the nuclear power protesters dramatize a contradiction that seems inherent in every application of the necessity principle. The legislature has made a rule, yet we permit the citizen to disregard it if he thinks it is for the better. Such a principle seems inherently incompatible with a well-functioning system of law.

Strangely enough, the law is full of provisions—quite apart from the rule of necessity—that seem to confer on citizens and officials the power to disregard a rule they think unwise. The most interesting and dramatic example of this is the jury. The jury is a group of twelve laymen that listens to the facts of a case as presented by the lawyers and their witnesses under the supervision of the trial judge. When the trial is over, the judge instructs them in the pertinent rules of law. Then they find their verdict. What is there to ensure that they faithfully apply the rules given to them by the trial judge? What guarantees that they will not find a verdict "in the teeth of the law"? What prevents them from acquitting the defendant because he is poor, handsome, or orphaned, although he is clearly guilty? Nothing. The jury's acquittal is beyond challenge or reproach. If a jury does not like a law, it is in effect free to disregard it and to acquit the defendant who is charged with violating it.

Why do we give the jury such latitude? It is not impossible to discipline the jury or to control its inclination to disregard the law. In the sixteenth century it was common practice to "allow the party that had lost a case to assemble a larger jury to find the facts anew; if the larger jury found contrary to the first, it could attaint the members of the first, which meant loss of lands, fine, or imprisonment, and reverse their judgment."[90] We have gotten away from that. We now pride ourselves on the jury's ability to disregard the law when it chooses. Judicial decisions abound with Te Deums to the jury's power to nullify the law. They hold up as shining examples the case of Peter Zenger, an eighteenth-century American journalist, whom a colonial jury acquitted of the charge of seditious libel in the face of overwhelming evidence, and the cases of Northern Abolitionists, whom Northern juries habitually acquitted of the charge of helping fugitive slaves in the face of equally overwhelming evidence. Moreover, judges are well aware, and rarely offended, that nullification is not confined to such spectacular instances. It is very much a part of the everyday functioning of juries. In about one fifth of all cases the jury acquits a defendant whom a judge would have convicted, often because it disagrees with some aspect of the law under which he is charged.[91]

But how is one to reconcile the idea that the jury can "remake" a law it does not like with the idea that it is for the legislature to make laws and the courts to apply them? The issue was neatly forced in a case involving Vietnam War protesters who wanted to tell the jury that tried them about its right to "nullify." The defendants had broken into the Washington offices of the Dow Chemical Company, vandalized office furniture and equipment, and defaced the walls with a bloodlike substance—all this to protest Dow's production of napalm. The defendants' guilt was open-and-shut since they had summoned newsmen to film their actions. Their only hope was that a war-weary jury would acquit them out of sympathy with their cause—at least, if told that they could disregard the law if they chose.[92]

The court denied the defendants' request. It explained, "We know that a posted speed limit of 60 m.p.h. produces factual speeds 10 or 15 miles greater, with an understanding all around that some tolerance is acceptable to authorities, assuming conditions warrant. But can it be supposed that the speeds would stay substantially the same if the speed limit were put: Drive as fast as you think it is appropriate without the posted limit as an anchor, a point of departure!"[93] Similarly, the court asked, could one expect that the jury would continue to practice restraint before nullifying the law if it were told outright that it was free to do so?

The court's answer suggests the proper way to understand jury nullification. Juries should faithfully heed the law unless there are extremely weighty reasons for departing from it. To ensure that juries disregard the law only in the rare, the unusual, the worthy case, we put numerous hurdles in the way of such departure. We subject jurors to an oath, repeatedly exhort them to follow the law, and don't permit any of the lawyers to tell them otherwise. But what is a "worthy" case? Why do we ever want the jury to depart from the strict letter of the law? However meticulous the draftsman of a rule is, he cannot foresee all contingencies, all circumstances in which the rule will be applied. There are bound to be numerous circumstances that he failed to foresee in which he would not want to see his rule applied. In these circumstances it is expected that the jury will make use of its prerogative to nullify.

The citizen's right to disobey where necessity requires can be explained the same way as the right of the jury to disobey its instructions. Ordinarily, what the legislature says goes. But contingencies may arise which the legislature failed to foresee, situations in which the basic purpose of the law is better served by a departure from than submission to its literal terms. It is only when such weighty reasons for disobedience materialize that a citizen is permitted to invoke necessity.[94]

But why shouldn't one expect the meticulous draftsman to foresee all, or nearly all, contingencies. Are there really so many? There are indeed, as the organization theorist Herbert Simon points out in a striking example. It could hardly have occurred to the British Parliament that when it passed the law on marriage bonuses, it might be affecting the country's clover crop. Yet a British statistician discovered a remarkable correlation between the number of spinsters and the size of the clover crop in English counties. He even found the reason: Spinsters keep cats. Cats eat mice. Mice eat bumblebees. Bumblebees flower clover. Hence more spinsters mean more cats, fewer mice, more bumblebees, and more clover. Higher marriage bonuses thus mean less clover.[95]

Even if the meticulous draftsman could think of all contingencies, he couldn't articulate them all—and not just because he would run out of paper. The problem goes deeper. Much of what we know we cannot say. For instance, we can pick a familiar face out of a crowd but could not say how we recognized it. We can ride a bicycle but could not explain the intuitive knowledge of physics that goes into it. Often judges know what the right decision in a case is but cannot explain it. (The law takes account of that by giving more precedential weight to the facts and the outcome of a case than to the reasoning that connects them.) The inarticulable nature of much of our knowledge—the philosopher Michael Polanyi has dubbed it "tacit knowledge"—severely limits our ability to provide for the future with explicit rules.[96]

Necessity and jury nullification are in fact just a few of the many mechanisms society has evolved to cope with the draftsman's limited foresight and tacit knowledge. Only recently economists recognized that entire institutions, like corporations, exist mostly to cope with these limitations. A corporation consists of several divisions each of which produces some component of the corporation's final product. Economists used to wonder, Why do these divisions interact as members of the same organization? Why don't they exist as separate firms and interact across the market? Put differently, if division B gets its components from division A and turns them into the final product, why doesn't division A just operate as a separate firm and sell its components to B? The answer, argues the economist Oliver Williamson, hinges on limited foresight and tacit knowledge—and the resulting impossibility of drawing up rules for the future. If A and B were separate companies, but dealt with each other frequently, each would come to occupy a somewhat monopolistic position vis-à-vis the other. Sure, A wouldn't be B's only possible supplier. But having traded with A for a long time, B would find it very uncomfortable to switch. That means A gains a lot of leverage over B. Similarly, although B isn't A's only possible buyer, A would find it very uncomfortable to switch, having traded with B for so long. That means B gains a lot of leverage over A. The result of all this mutual leverage could be a lot of time-consuming and expensive bargaining over the lifetime of the A-and-B relationship. Now, A and B could avoid all this if they could only write up a detailed contract in advance (before they have become dependent on each other, before there is this mutual leverage, before there is this haggling problem). But they can't. The contract requires an ability to foresee and articulate we just noted no one possesses. The only way out of their dilemma is to merge into one organization.[97]

In sum, there are limits to the rule of law. Necessity is meant to accommodate those limits. Having recognized that as its function, we are now in a position to dispose of the troublesome cases with which we began this section. Those cases are different from the run-of-the-mill necessity case. None of them dealt with situations that the legislature failed to foresee. Rather they dealt with situations in which the defendants disagreed with the legislature. The Vietnam War and the building of nuclear power plants were not unforeseen contingencies. They had been expressly authorized by the legislature. Invoking the necessity rule here would not serve its basic purpose. Clearly, then, the necessity principle should be revised to exempt such cases from its sway. That is precisely what the Model Penal Code does. It states that the necessity defense is available only if "a legislative purpose to exclude [it] does not otherwise plainly appear." In the case of Vietnam and the nuclear power plants such a purpose did "plainly appear."[98]

Unfortunately, this proviso will not always be easy to apply, as is illustrated by the case of the Speluncean explorers. The Newgarth legislature never adopted a clear stance with respect to euthanasia (unlike the United States Congress with respect to the Vietnam War and nuclear power). The failure to assent to an express euthanasia statute arguably means that it rejects the idea, arguably it means that it leaves the law where it was to begin with. So can we say that "a legislative purpose to exclude the [necessity defense] plainly appears"?

The Fair Way to Die

The necessity rule as we have laid it out so far does not yet answer Roger Whetmore's initial question to the medical experts: If someone is to die for the sake of the others, should he be chosen by lot?

That is the method the *Holmes* court recommended. Yet it is far from self-evident that whenever a tragic choice of this kind is called for, the proper selection mechanism is the lottery. There used to be fewer kidney dialysis machines than there were people who needed them. We did not roll dice to determine who could be hooked up to such a machine. Even in wartime, the army often needs only a fraction of the nation's eligible youth. We do not rely on the lottery, to the exclusion of everything else, to decide who is to be conscripted. Instead we turn such decision over to certain political bodies—medical committees, draft boards—who will take into consideration a great number of factors a lottery ignores—the likely ineffectiveness of a dialysis machine for a specific patient, for instance, or the hardship of forcing a student to interrupt his schooling to serve in the army. And we use neither the lottery nor a political body to decide which of many critically ill patients shall receive the attention of a certain world famous heart surgeon or how extensive a search to mount for the occupant of a vanished airplane. Such matters are, for the most part, decided by the market, that is, the pocketbook of the victim or his family. If the ailing patient is wealthy, he will be able to fly in a South African heart surgeon someone poorer could not afford. And if the occupant of a vanished plane happened to be a multimillionaire, his family will be able to mount a much more extensive rescue effort than if it had to rely on the resources of the police. Each method of selection has its own set of virtues and vices. Let us explore the vices of each. The virtues are then easy enough to see—they are the vices that only the other methods have.[99]

The Lottery

The first problem with the lottery is that it doesn't discriminate. It treats all participants as equals. That may be all right when allocating places in a lifeboat, but what about the right to a scarce university spot, a heart transplant, or a seat on the last helicopter out of an embattled Saigon? Here we would probably want to give priority to the most promising student, the most suitable patient, the most endangered Vietnamese.

The second problem with the lottery is that it highlights society's stinginess. It highlights the fact that society has chosen not to provide enough for all. Were we to allocate kidney machines by lottery, we would make it painfully obvious that we deliberately chose to sacrifice some lives to save money. That may not be wrong, but it is hard to face up to.

The third, and most interesting, problem with the lottery is that it makes us feel impotent. We have no control over the outcome. Psychologists have found that a painful event will seem much less painful, if we feel we can reduce the pain whenever we choose—even if we never take advantage of the option. A group of experimental subjects was asked to work on a variety of puzzles, problem sets, and proofreading chores against the background of a loud, unpleasant noise. Some of the subjects were told that they could stop this noise if they wanted to by pushing a certain button, although the experimenter would prefer it if they didn't. Although none of the subjects with the button option actually used it, they proved to be much less bothered by the noise than those without the option: they reported less annoyance and they did much better in their assignments.[100] In a more practical version of the same experiment, dental patients who were given a button to press if the discomfort became unbearable were able to tolerate much greater levels of pain than others. Evidently, more control means less suffering.[101]

A sense of control is such a comforting feeling that people will often grossly delude themselves into thinking they have control even when they clearly don't. Such self-deception is most evident in games of chance. Psychologists have observed, that gamblers will roll the die softly when they want a low number, but hard when they want a high number; that they are willing to bet larger amounts before the die is cast than afterwards (but before the outcome is disclosed); that they will take greater risks against shy, submissive opponents, than against brash, domineering ones; that they will value lottery tickets they selected themselves more highly than tickets assigned them. In short, people behave as though luck were a matter of skill and fortitude. They pretend that they can roll a die well rather than poorly, that they can influence the outcome just as long as the die isn't cast yet, that they can outwit a weak opponent, that they can select the right ticket. They yearn for a sense of control.[102]

Despite these possibilities of pretense, lotteries largely destroy one's sense of control. A tragic choice inevitably inflicts pain, at least on some. But that pain is especially hard to bear when administered according to chance.

The Committee

In most settings other than the lifeboat the faults of the lottery loom too large to ignore. The most favored recourse is to delegate all tragic decisions to a committee—whether it be called jury, agency, board or commission. Unlike the lottery, the committee *does* discriminate: it makes reasoned choices. Unlike the lottery, it doesn't highlight society's stinginess: it will make it appear as though anyone who lives up to its standards will receive a spot. (Any student "good enough" can get into the university.) Unlike the lottery, it doesn't make us feel impotent: we can argue, convince, implore, in sum, plead our case.

The paragon of such institutions is the Seattle God Committee, a group of seven anonymous laymen—a lawyer, housewife, banker, surgeon, labor leader, state official, and minister—put to the task of selecting patients for kidney dialysis. For a long time the Swedish Hospital in Seattle was virtually the only American hospital offering such treatment and represented for many patients their only hope of survival. Given its limited resources, the hospital was able to accommodate only fifty of the hundreds of kidney patients who each year faced imminent death without such help. Once the physicians had decided who was medically and psychiatrically suitable for the limited number of dialysis beds available in the artificial kidney center, they left it up to the committee, guided only by their consciences, to decide who should receive treatment. How did the committee make its decisions? By and large, in great secrecy. In 1962, however, the record of a typical committee meeting appeared in the pages of *Life* magazine. The committee had just been asked to choose two patients from a group of five to fill the center's two new vacancies. The deliberations make for eerie reading. The committee is agonizingly conscientious. Few things in a patient's medical or personal history escape its attention. Patient number four, observes the minister, is an aircraft worker with six children whom his death would leave unprovided for. The patient seems too ill to work anyhow, counters the state official. No, injects the labor leader, the man's employer is doing everything possible to help rehabilitate him. What about patients one and two, inquires the housewife; they are an accountant and a chemist, respectively, and if the committee is looking for the men with the highest potential of service to society, then it should consider that the chemist and the accountant have the finest educational background of all five candidates. How about the small businessman, patient number three, asks the surgeon. The man is active in church affairs, which shows great moral strength. That certainly would help him conform to the demands of the treatment, adds the housewife. But that would also help him endure death more easily, objects the lawyer. They could rule out the chemist and the accountant on economic grounds, suggests the banker, since both have substantial net worth. The lawyer agrees, for it means that neither family would be a burden on the state. The state official objects: That would seem to be placing a penalty on the very people who have perhaps been most provident. The labor leader returns to the topic of children: For the children's sake, he says, the committee should reckon with the surviving parent's opportunity to remarry, and a woman with three children has a better chance of finding a new husband than a young widow with six. In the end they settle on the small businessman and the aircraft worker.[103]

The Seattle God Committee's deliberations bring out the chief faults of this approach. To begin with, it humiliates the loser. He is not just left wanting; he is found wanting. He has, in some sense, been pronounced inferior to someone else. He hasn't just lost at roulette; he has lost at chess. The committee can try to keep the nature of his inferiority a secret by not giving any reason for its decision. But over time, a pattern will emerge, as it did in the case of the Seattle God Committee. "On the basis of the past year's record," wrote Shana Alexander in her *Life* magazine article, only half-facetiously, "a candidate who plans to come before this committee would seem well-advised to father a great many children, then to throw away all his money, and finally to fall ill in a season when there will be a minimum of competition from other men dying of the same disease."[104]

In addition, the committee approach says aloud what society would rather leave unsaid. An egalitarian society is loath to admit openly its preference for the wealthy over the poor, the young over the old, the bright over the dull (or maybe the other way around). These are open secrets, treasured hypocrisies. But what harm does it do to reveal such secrets, to expose such hypocrisies? How can the statement of something everyone knows possibly make a difference?

It can indeed. The point is best made through a somewhat esoteric brain teaser: There lives in Africa the wild tribe of logicians. As their name suggests, these are people with razor-sharp minds. The tribe has a savage custom. If any man ever learns that his wife has cheated on him, he must behead her the night after he finds out. It so happens that every tribesman is very well informed about every other man's wife—whether she has been faithful or not—but knows nothing about his own wife. Moreover, no one ever talks to him about her. As a result, decapitations never actually occur. One day, the chieftain convenes the tribe and makes an announcement: "There has been infidelity in this tribe, on the part of women. I will not say whether one or more." For a while, nothing happens. But in the fortieth night after the chieftain's announcement, forty tribesmen behead their forty wives. Why?[105]

This is a very hard nut to crack. What makes it so hard is that at first glance the story seems incomplete. It seems that some necessary information has been left out. If forty tribesmen kill their forty wives, presumably each knew all along that thirty-nine wives had cheated on their husbands. But in that case, the chieftain's announcement did not tell them anything new. How then could the announcement of something everyone knew precipitate such grave consequences?

The way to solve the puzzle is to simplify it radically. Suppose the puzzle were just as I told it, except that less than forty nights elapse and less than forty wives are killed. Suppose rather that the first night after the chieftain's announcements, one man kills his wife. You would have no trouble accounting for this event. Evidently only that man's wife was cheating. When the chieftain made his announcement, the man looked around, saw no other unfaithful woman, and concluded that the chieftain must have been talking about his own wife. Hence he kills her the very night after the announcement.

Now suppose that nothing happens during the first night, but during the second night two men kill their wives. Evidently what occurs is this: When the chieftain makes his announcement, each of the two cuckolds is aware that at least one woman in the tribe (the other cuckold's wife) is being unfaithful. He assumes the chieftain is referring to her. Assuming she is the only unfaithful woman in the tribe, he expects the cuckold to kill her the night after the announcement. In fact, no such thing happens, for the other man thinks the chieftain is referring to the first man's unfaithful wife. Thus both men are driven to conclude after one night has elapsed uneventfully that there is more than one unfaithful woman in the tribe. Since they see but one, they conclude the second must be their wife. So they kill her the second night after the announcement.

Now try a third, yet more complex variation of the puzzle. This time three men kill their three wives on the third night. Why? Evidently each is aware of the only two other unfaithful wives. Therefore he expects a bloodbath during the second night. When it doesn't happen, he concludes that there are more than two unfaithful wives in the tribe. Since he sees no others, he concludes, his wife must be the third. The process can be carried on till we get to forty.

Even after solving the puzzle, we are left with a question. How can the chieftain's announcement of something each man knows precipitate the ultimate massacre? He must be imparting new information, and yet his statement doesn't seem to contain any new information. Again, simplify. Think of the case of two executions during the second night. That case makes it clear that the chieftain is indirectly telling each cuckold something new: Beforehand each cuckold only knew that there was infidelity in the tribe. But he didn't know whether the other cuckold also knew there was infidelity in the tribe. The chieftain's announcement tells him the other cuckold now knows there is infidelity in the tribe. His knowing that the other cuckold knows permits him to deduce after an uneventful first night that his own wife is cheating as well. In the case of forty, the chieftain's announcement tells each cuckold something far more complex: it tells him what others know that others know that others know that others know. . . . And it is this knowledge combined with the uneventful first thirty-nine nights that permits him to deduce his wife's infidelity.

The case of the logicians is extreme. But something like this goes on in real life. Often the announcement of something obvious will impart information in the same indirect way. Think of the fairy tale about the emperor's new clothes. Why does the child's announcement of what everybody is thinking have such devastating consequences for the emperor? Because before the child's announcement, no one knew that others were thinking the same thing. After the child's exclamation and the failure of others to reprimand him, it begins to dawn on everyone that no one else thinks the emperor is wearing any clothes.[106]

It is in this way that the committee's announcement of what everybody knows can have real consequences. The open assertion of something obvious permits others to know that others know and that others know that others know, and that. . . . It is thus that it saps society's treasured hypocrisies of their strength and may do serious damage to the social peace.

The Market

The market approach discriminates, hides social stinginess, preserves our sense of control, doesn't publicly humiliate, and expresses no open preferences. No wonder it is often used or recommended for making tragic choices. Kenneth Boulding thinks it should be used for limiting population growth. He suggests allocating to each family the right to have two children and letting them sell that right if they choose. In effect, he favors a market in baby rights.[107] During the Civil War, the market was used to recruit soldiers; although soldiers were initially picked by draft, each had a right to "buy" a substitute. (Among the people taking advantage of this was the young Grover Cleveland, who paid an illiterate Polish immigrant $150 to take his place. Twenty-one years later, in the 1884 presidential election, Cleveland's opponent James G. Blaine tried to exploit this fact—until it turned out that he had done the same.)[108]

The market is used more often than people realize. Even when something is allocated on a first come, first served basis, the market is being used—not the market in money but the market in time. One tends to forget that waiting time is a "price." Recall the so-called Oregon plan, popular at the height of the energy crisis, when government regulation kept the price of gas below the market-clearing level and produced long queues at the gas pump. It was suggested that the lines might be shortened by restricting cars with odd-numbered license plates to odd-numbered days, and cars with even-numbered license plates to even-numbered days. The proposal did not work. It was doomed from the outset. The amount of gasoline was fixed. There was only one market-clearing price, which had to be charged either in monetary or nonmonetary form. Since the monetary component of the price was pegged too low, the nonmonetary component, waiting time, had to make up the slack. However hard the administrators tried, the inconvenience of waiting time could not be eliminated as long as it was necessary to clear the market.[109]

The most obvious shortcoming of the market is, of course, that it favors the rich over the poor. The rich will buy substitutes, the poor will serve. The rich will buy baby rights, the poor will abstain. (If the market is in time, it will favor the rich-in-time over the poor-in-time.) The bias in favor of the rich becomes especially hard to bear in tragic situations, in which everyone engages in "desperation bidding," offering everything he has to stay alive. Where something less basic is at stake, one can always argue that it isn't wealth, it is greater desire that is reflected in the successful bidder's greater willingness to pay. In tragic situations, everyone's desire is equally desperate. What differentiates them is solely their ability to back that desire up with resources.

Another serious shortcoming is that the market approach puts a price tag on things better left unpriced—life, liberty, and happiness. The economist will deride this objection. There is no danger in putting a price tag on something as long as that price tag isn't taken to mean the wrong thing: The fact that a baby right costs $300 doesn't mean a baby can be killed if that brings a profit of more than $300. But it is far from clear when one is interpreting such prices properly and when one isn't. What's most alarming is that the economists themselves all too often seem to read more meaning into prices than they have.

The most extreme example of this I know is the so-called efficient market hypothesis, which says that a stock is worth no more and no less than what it happens to be selling for on the market. The current price of a stock, it says, is the best available estimate of its value. If someone were to offer me the gift of a $2 share or a $10 share, on condition that I hold on to it for five years, the hypothesis claims that I would be foolish to opt for the $2 share on the ground that the first company strikes me as more promising. Unless I have some insider information the rest of the market doesn't have, the best judgment about the two companies' respective worth is already reflected in the stock price, and I am irrational to quibble with that judgment.[110]

This claim strikes me as doubtful. Suppose the two companies in question are biotechnology firms (like Genentech). We won't know whether they are successful for at least five years. They will be successful if the scientific theories on which they are based pan out. Let us suppose also that the two companies happen to be based on competing theories, the A theory and the B theory. Only one of them will prove right. The bulk of the experts seem to favor the A theory, but some very reputable people advocate the B theory. In fact, A stock happens to be selling for $10 and B stock for $2, reflecting the greater confidence inspired by the A theory. The choice between scientific theories, as we have learned, is no hard-and-fast matter. One certainly isn't irrational in opting for a minority view. Often the scientist's preference of one theory over another is no more firmly grounded than a literary critic's preference of Henry James over H. G. Wells. One wouldn't be irrational for subscribing to a minority view, just as one wouldn't be irrational (merely odd) for ranking Wells above James. But if I am not foolish or irrational for preferring the B theory to the A theory, why am I foolish for believing the B stock more valuable than the A stock? Yet the efficient market hypothesis asserts that I am. It dramatizes a dangerous tendency one might call "price worship."

The Cop-out

Sometimes none of the three allocation mechanisms makes us content. Sometimes the allocation is just too painful. We decide instead to provide enough for all. Of course, the feeling that now we are providing enough for all rests partly on self-delusion. More kidney machines mean fewer hospital beds for heart patients or less emergency care for accident victims. More university students mean fewer mineworkers and firemen. But it is easy to put those facts out of one's mind, to compartmentalize one's thinking, as it were, to think only of the cancer patients saved and not of the MS patients sacrificed.

But how do some categories of suffering get singled out for such royal no-holds-barred treatment? Why do limited-allocation mechanisms work less well for some categories than others? Sometimes no more is involved than that some affliction has quite adventitiously seized the popular imagination. More money was spent on poliomyelitis than most other afflictions of equivalent risk. The fact that Franklin Delano Roosevelt was one of its victims probably had something to do with it. Often the reasons go deeper, though. An extra million dollars channeled into kidney machines may save a specific number of lives next year, and there may be only that many victims in the country who will need such treatment. An extra million dollars channeled into heart transplants may save many more lives next year, but there are a great many more whom it will not help. We may well choose to devote the money to kidney machines, just to avoid the agony of choice.

Occasionally, the reasons for providing enough for all seem nearly unfathomable. Sometimes a mining enterprise will spend vast sums to rescue a few men in a mining shaft but would not dream of spending equivalent sums on safety precautions that would prevent such accidents in the first place and in the long run save more lives. Why? A hospital with limited space may discharge its appendectomy patients one day earlier than desirable to make room for a few heart surgery patients who require many weeks of hospitalization—even though it could save more lives if it simply turned the heart patients away, with the certain knowledge that they would soon die without surgery. Why? Developing nations occasionally devote substantial sums to general medical facilities, although a few simple public health measures would reduce the death rate much more efficiently. Why? It has been suggested that when we take precautions against future mining accidents, we are merely protecting statistical ciphers, whereas when we embark on a rescue mission for some stranded miners we have in mind specific flesh-and-blood individuals. But the stranded miners are strangers for most of us. Moreover, the rescue mission often imperils the lives of other known flesh-and-blood individuals. To put the point differently: the appendectomy patient is no more of a cipher than the heart patient. Yet we sacrifice one group to the other. Why?

It seems to most of us an inconceivably harsh fate to have to look forward to one's certain death at an appointed time in the very near future. However much we generally desire certainty, we do not want to know in advance the hour of our death.[111] By avoiding such knowledge, we preserve an illusion of immortality. We become like the man in the Thursday hanging paradox, who is told on Sunday that he will be hanged on one of the next seven noons, but that it will come as a surprise. He reasons that he can't be hanged next Sunday because he would know on Saturday afternoon and thus not be surprised. He can't be hanged next Saturday because he would know on Friday afternoon, Sunday already being out. He can't be hanged on Friday because he would know Thursday afternoon, Sunday and Saturday already being out. By the same reasoning, he can't be hanged on Wednesday, or Tuesday, or Monday. He concludes that he can't be hanged at all. He is mighty surprised when the hangman appears at his door at 11:55 A.M. on Thursday. We want everyone to be thus surprised and are willing to pay dearly to make it so.[112]

Let us take stock of our argument so far. We began with what looked like a contrived piece of science fiction, the case of the Speluncean explorers. But the case turned out not to be so contrived after all. The annals of the law harbor some real cases no less exotic. And the issues raised are genuine and important: has a person who breaks the law out of "necessity" committed a crime? Does necessity warrant breaking even the most sacrosanct rules?

The question can't be evaded by convicting the offender and pardoning him afterwards. Either a conviction with a pardon is tantamount to an acquittal, in which case we might as well acquit him, or it isn't, in which case we have to consider whether he deserves to be punished. Nor can the question be evaded by fitting the offender within some well-recognized exception, such as self-defense or insanity, because by assumption and design, none applies. Nor, finally, can it be evaded by saying that in cases like that of the Speluncean explorers, the positive law ceases to apply because natural law has taken over. Such a view only obscures the real dilemma: should a rule be obeyed under any and all circumstances? Such a view also implies that anything a person does in this natural state is beyond reproach. And such a view doesn't help us with cases less extreme than that of the spelunkers: Is it all right to break the speed limit on the way to the hospital, because the natural law has taken over?

The proposed solution was that any and all laws are subject to a great exception: they may justifiably be broken if obeying them would do more harm than good. This rule may ask us to weigh things that seem incommensurable at first: the lives of a few here against the lives of many there, the freedom of an East German refugee against the safety of air traffic. But it turns out that respectable people—not lawyers or judges, but scientists—are weighing such incommensurables all the time. Nor can we overlook the fact that the person who declines to weigh such incommensurables is striking a balance between things that are even less commensurable. He is saying, in effect, that it is always better, under any and all circumstances, to obey a certain law than to disobey it. He is balancing the virtue of following the law against the undifferentiated mass of reasons for not following it and deciding that the former always outweighs the latter. (His position recalls the Austrian literary critic Karl Kraus, who used to say, "Given the choice between two evils, I choose neither.")

Having recognized the necessity defense in principle, we run into several snags as we try to apply it to some special circumstances. Each of these special circumstances again calls into question the general wisdom and workability of the rule. How does the rule apply to people who fancy themselves in a situation of necessity when they aren't? If we acquit them, so long as they act reasonably, aren't we giving them broad license to do some horrendous things? Recall Pange and Matini. And if we convict them, aren't we punishing them because a reasonable guess turned out to be unlucky? Maybe so. But it is crucial not to make the necessity defense available in situations where people are known to make poor judgments.

And there is another snag: How does the rule apply to people who "invited" the emergency in which they find themselves? That proved to be irrelevant. Somebody who recklessly or intentionally brings about an emergency that results in someone else's death may be liable for that, but he should be free to invoke necessity to defend actions he takes during an emergency.

We encountered next a difficulty that was far more than a snag. It made us wonder whether the necessity defense was even compatible with a system of "law and order" (understood in its classic sense). Aren't we constituting every citizen a superlegislature, entitled to disobey a law he dislikes so long as he can convince the court that the law is, on balance, unwise? To avoid this unfortunate result, we had to amend the rule to make it clear that it applies only to situations the legislature didn't contemplate when it drafted the law. As to those, the citizen really does act like a superlegislature, but so does the jury. Even without the necessity defense, ours never was a system of "law and order," in which citizens and law enforcement officials are bound to abide by the letter of the law, come hell or high water. That doesn't mean we live in anarchy.

Finally, there remained that special group of cases where necessity called for the choice of a sacrificial lamb. How is that choice to be made? We make tragic choices all the time, and the methods we use are disparate: lottery, committee, market, and admixtures of all three. Each has its own drawbacks, but among the less obvious ones, lotteries destroy our sense of control; committees publicize harmful, though well-known, truths; markets create misleading price tags. We again face a choice of evils in choosing among them.

More Hard Cases

The cases we shall take up next at first glance look like cases of necessity, but they aren't. That's what makes our reaction to them so puzzling. Like the necessity cases, they involve people who face grim choices and whose plight enlists our deepest sympathy. But unlike those cases, they don't involve situations where the law clearly should have been broken. In fact, we feel the defendants shouldn't have done what they did. Still, we want to acquit them. Why do we want to, and how can we?

The question is posed vividly in *Lynch v. Director of Public Prosecutions*, a case that confronted the British House of Lords.[113] The defendant, Lynch, was charged as an accomplice in the assassination of a Belfast constable. But the way Lynch told the story he had no choice in the matter. One day Sean Meehan, a notoriously ruthless gunman for the Irish Republican Army, had called on Lynch and ordered him to accompany Mailey, another IRA gunman, on a car theft. Later on, a third man joined them. The three gunmen then put on combat jackets and woolen helmets and commanded Lynch to drive them to a certain garage. He asked Meehan what he was planning to do. "Bates knows a policeman," was the reply.[114] The three got out of the car, told Lynch to stay put, and ran toward the constable they had spotted across from the garage. They fired a few shots which felled the man, ran back to the car, and had Lynch drive them home. Indicted as an accomplice, Lynch stood to be punished no less severely than the three men who had fired the shots. The gist of his defense was: I *had* to do it.

Master Sergeant William Olsen was captured during the Korean war by the Communist forces in late 1950 and taken to the Kangye prisoner of war camp.[115] There the Chinese who ran the camp set out to educate him and his fellow prisoners as to the "true" nature of the war, namely, "that they [the prisoners] were the victims of the warmongers and were the aggressors in Korea."[116] The education was in no way haphazard. It was systematic and relentless, involving countless hours of lecturing, group discussion, and interrogation. The Chinese called this treatment of the POWs "lenient policy," because it was short on threats and long on "persuasion." Over the course of the war, it proved remarkably successful. It got American POWs to do things the Germans had never gotten them to do. They informed on each other, frustrated each other's escape attempts, and in one way or another almost all collaborated with the enemy.[117]

The capstone of the Chinese strategy was "start small and build," which the psychologist Robert Cialdini describes thus:

> Prisoners were frequently asked to make statements so mildly anti-American or pro-Communist as to seem inconsequential. ("The United States is not perfect." "In a Communist country, unemployment is not a problem.") But once these minor requests were complied with, the men found themselves pushed to submit to related yet more substantive requests. A man who had just agreed with his Chinese interrogator that the United States is not perfect might then be asked to make a list of these "problems with America" and to sign his name to it. Later he might be asked to read his list in a discussion group with other prisoners. "After all, it's what you believe, isn't it?" Still later, he might be asked to write an essay expanding on his list and discussing these problems in greater detail.
>
> The Chinese might then use his name and his essay in an anti-American radio broadcast beamed not only to the entire camp but to other POW camps in North Korea as well as to American forces in South Korea. Suddenly he would find himself a "collaborator," having given aid and comfort to the enemy. Aware that he had written the essay without any strong threats or coercion, many times a man would change his image of himself to be consistent with the deed and with the new "collaborator" label, often resulting in even more extensive acts of collaboration.[118]

On Christmas day 1950 Olsen and his fellow prisoners were assembled for a Christmas party and bullied into making some speeches. Olsen was one of those who spoke. He noted that the Communists were treating their prisoners better than the Germans did theirs during World War II. He also said that the Korean war was a "millionaire's war and that the prisoners had innocent blood on their hands."[119] Later Olsen and some other prisoners were moved to a camp for newly arrived POWs. Olsen would greet the new arrivals by telling them "how to get along with" the Communists, "that escape was impossible, that the Chinese were not guards but were there to protect the prisoners from the Koreans, and [that] they, the prisoners, had been cannon fodder for the imperialists and warmongers." He contributed articles to some POW publications, lauding the Communists' treatment of POWs and saying that America "was engaged in an imperialistic war to fatten certain capitalists and that the blood of innocent victims was on the hands of Americans."[120] After the war, Olsen was charged with aiding the enemy. His main defense: They made me do it, I wasn't myself.

Should either of these defendants be convicted?

The Principle of Duress

A feeling in our stomach tells us no. What they did may have been undesirable—the harm avoided did not clearly exceed the harm done—but we feel, if anything, *less* inclined to convict them than the defendants in many of the previous cases. Few can picture themselves plunging a knife into a half-conscious boy of seventeen, or tossing overboard fourteen living, screaming, kicking human beings. But many who hear of the plight of Lynch and Olsen might have at least a fleeting feeling that "There but for the grace of God go I." We are disinclined to convict because we sympathize with their predicament.

But is our sympathy grounds enough for acquitting them, even if we don't like what they did? The House of Lords in the *Lynch* case thought that it was. Its explanation is not to be improved upon. "If then someone is really threatened with death or serious injury unless he does what he is told to do," the court asked, "is the law to pay no heed to the miserable, agonizing plight of such a person? For the law to understand not only how the timid but the stalwart may in a moment of crisis behave is not to make the law weak but to make it just. In the calm of the courtroom, measures of fortitude or of heroic behavior are surely not to be demanded when they could not in moments for decision reasonably have been expected even of the resolute and the well-disposed."[121]

The principle here adumbrated has found expression in most criminal codes and judicial opinions addressing this point. It is usually referred to as the principle of duress. The Model Penal Code formulates it thus: "It is an affirmative defense that the actor engaged in the conduct charged to constitute an offense because he was coerced to do so by the use of, or threat to use, unlawful force against his person or the person of another, that a person of reasonable firmness in his situation would have been unable to resist."[122]

The principle of duress is fundamentally different from the principle of necessity, although often confused with it because cases of duress resemble cases of necessity. Why are they fundamentally different? To acquit someone on grounds of necessity is to approve, support, applaud what he did. It is to find his actions *justified*. To acquit him on grounds of duress is merely to sympathize, understand, commiserate with what he did. It is to find his actions *excused*. Does the difference matter? Is it important that we know whether we acquit someone on the basis of one or the other? He gets off either way, of course, but it may be important. A great deal may follow if we acquit because we approve, not because we sympathize. We approve of the man who drives his stricken mother to the hospital speeding along at nearly 70 m.p.h. Hence we not only find him innocent of any crime, but we will not hold as an accomplice the neighbor who lent him his Jaguar. And we might very well hold criminally liable the policeman who stopped the man for speeding knowing full well why the man was doing it. By contrast, we may sympathize with Lynch for having to drive the IRA assassins' car, but we don't approve of his doing it. Hence, although we may find him innocent of any crime, we are not prepared to acquit his accomplices, and we wouldn't charge anyone with a crime who tried to prevent Lynch's car from reaching its destination. In sum, when the defendant's act is justified (worthy of approval), everyone may help him, and no one may hinder him. When the defendant's act is excused (worthy of sympathy, but not approval), no one may help him and everyone may hinder him.[123]

I hasten to add that the difference between justification and excuse is not the hard-and-fast, cut-and-dried, open-and-shut issue I just made it appear. All justifications have elements of excuse, and all excuses have elements of justification. With only a little verbal legerdemain, you can turn any justification into an excuse (and vice versa). It's done like this:

Step One. Observe that certain cases of mistake straddle the fence between justifications and excuses. Take, for instance, the defendant who has misjudged a situation to be one of necessity when it really isn't (arguably the spelunkers were in this situation). The misjudgment may have been entirely reasonable. Given the information he had, the defendant may have acted the way we would want anyone to act under the circumstances. That makes it sound like a justification. But then again, we do regret the misjudgment. We would rather it hadn't occurred. That makes it sound like an excuse.[124]

Step Two. Every case of justification can be interpreted as one of mistake. If the defendant had correctly anticipated the predicament he was going to find himself in, he could have prevented it from ever arising. In a sense, therefore, the harm he did to prevent greater harm was the consequence of an earlier mistake. And mistakes, we saw in step one, could be classified as excuses.

Step Three. Somebody might object that this legerdemain only works because of the misguided conclusion that mistakes are excuses. He might contend that really the first of the two arguments in step one is better than the second, and therefore (reasonable) mistakes are really justifications, not excuses. But I would challenge that: Why is a mistaken decision justified? Because it was appropriate in light of the information available to the defendant. But why did the defendant not gather more information? Presumably, because he had information indicating that the information he had was sufficient. But why did he not gather more information on whether the information he had was sufficient? Presumably, because he had information indicating that the information he had indicating that the information he had was sufficient was sufficient. But why . . . . and so on ad infinitum. But at some point the defendant has to stop. He has to admit that he had no information permitting him to conclude that certain other information he had (about certain other information about certain other information . . .) was sufficient. At that point he just leapt to a conclusion. That leap was not justified (because it wasn't based on any information) but excusable. So at bottom, every justified mistake is really an excused mistake.

All this fanciful arguing is not meant to deny that there is a tremendous difference between a justification and an excuse, one that's a lot more profound than most others the law hangs its hat on. It's just meant to show that the difference isn't quite like water-versus-wine, more like water-versus-ice.

Let's return to duress. The principle of duress may seem like something the criminal law has to have, like the principle of necessity. But that's far from clear. Despite our "gut reactions," we should have second thoughts about acquitting someone merely because other men of reasonable firmness would have behaved no better. A British court was forced to have such second thoughts by the case of *Abbot v. The Queen*, that arose shortly after the House of Lord's decision in Lynch's favor.[125]

"The story starts in May 1971," the court's fact summary laconically opens, "when a man named Malik bought and gave [Abbot] a return ticket from Trinidad to London with orders to carry out certain commissions for him in London and to return to Trinidad immediately on receipt of instructions from Malik to do so. When [Abbot] expressed his resentment at being ordered about, Malik threatened to kill [Abbot's] mother unless his instructions were obeyed. [Abbot] regarded Malik as a very dangerous man—no doubt with good reason. Malik has since been hanged for murder." Shortly thereafter, Malik summoned Abbot back to Trinidad. He insisted that Abbot join a commune over which he presided consisting of Malik's own and several other families. One of the inmates of the commune had an American mistress named Gale Benson. Malik despised Benson. One day he convened the commune while Benson and her lover were gone and announced point-blank that he wanted Benson killed. She was causing her lover too much "mental strain," he explained. Abbot suggested that they send her back to America, but "Malik said he wanted blood." Abbot later explained that "if he had gone to the police that night and told them of the plot to kill the girl, he did not think that they would have believed him because of Malik's cloak of respectability created by his luxurious home and the famous people who had visited him there. He said that he did not believe that the police would have given him or his mother protection." The next morning Malik ordered Abbot and some others to dig a grave for Benson. Just as the grave was completed she arrived in a jeep. Abbot, on Malik's instructions, invited her to look at the hole.

> She went to its edge and asked what it was for. [Abbot] replied that it was for her and thereupon flung his arm around her neck and jumped into the hole with her. [A] hired assassin named Kidogo then jumped into the hole after them. Whilst [Abbot] held her, Kidogo attempted to stab her to death with a cutlass. The girl struggled frantically and perhaps because of her struggles and the confined space in which Kidogo and [Abbot] were operating, she only received a number of comparatively minor stab wounds; when it seemed impossible for the coup de grace

> to be administered by Kidogo, [Abbot] called for help. [Another man] then jumped into the hole, seized the cutlass from Kidogo, placed the tip of the cutlass's blade against the girl's neck with one hand and with the other struck a blow on the end of the cutlass handle driving the blade down through the girl's lung. She collapsed, dying but not dead. Four of the men including [Abbot] then buried her while she was still alive."[126]

Abbot claimed duress. The court agonized. The case was a lot like *Lynch*. True, Lynch had only driven the killers' getaway car, whereas Abbot had actually wielded a weapon. But that was hardly a major difference.[127] Yet most of the judges were loath to decide in Abbot's favor. To acquit Abbot, they feared would give

> a charter to terrorists, gangleaders and kidnappers. A terrorist of notorious violence might, e.g., threaten death to A and his family unless A obeys his instructions to put a bomb with a time fuse set by A in a certain passenger aircraft and/or in a thronged market, railway station or the like. A, under duress, does obey his instructions and as a result, hundreds of men, women and children are killed or mangled. Should the contentions made on behalf of [Abbot] be correct, A would have a complete defence and, if charged, would have to be acquitted and set at liberty. Having now gained some real experience and expertise, he might again be approached by the terrorist who would make the same threats and exercise the same duress under which A would then give a repeat performance, killing even more men, women and children. Is there no limit to the number of people you may kill to save your life and that of your family?[128]

Other judges, however, continued to ask: How can we punish someone for falling short of sainthood, for failing to do what few men would manage to do? To which others yet replied: Why not?

> It is true that to resist duress . . . may call for heroism. It does not follow that it is morally permissible to do anything else. Most of us most of the time can steer a middle course between wickedness and heroism, but in tragic circumstances—as for instance in concentration camps or in natural disaster—we may be faced with a

> stark choice between the two. If the law punishes immoral actions done under duress . . . then it is not being unjust or enforcing anything beyond minimum standards of morality. . . .
>
> It is a very great misfortune to be placed in a situation where one must kill and suffer the consequences, or be killed oneself: any man must pray never to be thus placed between the devil and the deep blue sea. But if the law takes away the deep blue sea, a man will go wherever the devil drives.[129]

Is it sanctimonious or insincere to call for the punishment of those who behaved less than heroically? Then think of it this way: Punishing a duress killer now surely will deter some duress killers in the future. In deciding on the fate of an Abbot, the law must in effect make a terrible choice between inflicting pain on the person who behaved less than heroically under duress and inflicting pain on his innocent victims (whom the law might deter him from killing). Given that choice, isn't it better to inflict pain on the killer?

But if we convict Abbot, we might as well do away with the principle of duress. All duress cases are like *Abbot*. In all of them the defendant is faced with terrible pressures and decides to do something far worse, like murder or treason. (If it weren't worse, we could acquit him on grounds of necessity.) Yet few want to own up to that. Abbot was hanged. His conviction met with general approval. The duress defense, however, is still alive and well.

Duress without Threats

Let's assume the principle of duress is a good idea. Most scholars continue to think it is. Let's worry instead whether the principle as it is usually understood does what it sets out to do—acquit people who commit crimes under undue pressure. Unfortunately, it doesn't. It will have to be changed quite a bit before it does.

To begin with, the principle only protects those who are threatened by another human being. What about the person who is threatened by nature? What about the starving, shipwrecked sailor who eats the only other survivor? If we have a principle of duress, it should protect him too, even though he is threatened with death not from a human but a natural source.[130]

Why is the principle of duress usually limited to human threats? How is the shipwrecked sailor different from Lynch?[131] Probably because it seems he merely yielded to temptation, whereas Lynch yielded to a threat. We perceive it as much less immoral to yield to a threat than a temptation. A recent psychological experiment at the University of California at Los Angeles has borne this out. The experimenters told different groups of students different versions of a story and asked them to judge how immorally the story's protagonist had behaved. The story was about one Jerry C., an American graduate student about to compete in the Olympic decathlon. To secure a position as assistant business manager in a sports equipment firm, Hubbex, Inc., Jerry promises to use only Hubbex equipment. This violates the Olympic code of amateurship. As told to one group, Jerry has been assistant business manager for some time. Then Hubbex gets a new manager who fires several employees including Jerry. But the new manager lets Jerry know that he would keep him if he would promise to use Hubbex equipment on the decathlon. As told to another group, Jerry is just applying for the job, and it is he who thinks of the idea of using only Hubbex equipment. The second group judged Jerry more harshly than the first. The experimenters concluded: According to popular perception, a person committing an immoral act to get what he does not already have, especially if he thinks of the idea himself, yields to temptation and is very immoral. By contrast, a person committing an immoral act to retain what he already has, especially if someone else pushes the act upon him, merely yields to a threat and is much less despicable.[132]

Yielding to threats looks less immoral than yielding to temptations because threats look more coercive than temptations. But that is probably an illusion. Often a slight change in perspective will convert what looked like a threat into a temptation and vice versa. When I *threaten* to kill you if you don't do what I tell you, am I not *tempting* you with your life to do what I tell you?[133]

That the principle of duress is limited to *human* threats seems like a minor shortcoming. What's more disturbing is that it is limited to *threats*.[134] William Olsen was never much threatened by the Chinese; yet it seems he acted under duress. Threats are not the only way to pressure someone into doing something he doesn't want to do. Other techniques can be just as effective. In the past few decades, psychologists have made great strides demonstrating the awesome power of such techniques. In skillful hands, these amount to nothing short of brainwashing. The principal three techniques involve the use of authority, peer pressure, and seduction.

Authority

Perhaps the most famous of these "brainwashing" experiments was conducted by Stanley Milgram. Milgram advertised throughout New Haven, Connecticut, for subjects for a psychological experiment in learning. Eventually several hundred people from all walks of life—students, clerks, high-school teachers, salesmen, engineers, and laborers—submitted to the experiment. When the subjects arrived in the laboratory, usually in pairs, they discovered that the purpose of the experiment was to study the effect of punishment on learning. One of the subjects, it was explained to them, would be playing the role of "teacher," the other that of "learner." The learner was strapped into an electric chair apparatus, and the experimenters then asked the teacher to read him certain word pairs. Thereafter they asked the teacher to read the learner individual words again, followed by long series of words, from which the learner was to pick out the one with which the initial word had been paired. They told the teacher to administer an electric shock whenever the learner made a mistake. The teacher was seated in front of an instrument panel consisting of switches with thirty levels of intensity, ranging from 45 to 450 volts. The switches were labeled seriatim "Slight Shock," "Extreme Intensity Shock," and "Danger: Severe Shock." The switches beyond that designation were simply marked "XXX." With every mistake, the teacher was to increase slightly the shock level. The experimenters made it a point to explain that the electric shocks could do no tissue damage.[135]

The real object of the experiment, however, was not to study the effect of punishment on learning, but to see how far the teachers were willing to go in administering shocks to their victims. Unbeknownst to the teacher, the learner was in fact an accomplice of the experimenters. Although the subjects had drawn lots to determine who would teach and who would learn, the lottery had been rigged, so that the real subject of the experiment would always end up being the teacher. Moreover, the learner did not in fact receive any shocks, but only pretended to. He would take the first few levels of shock in stride, but as the levels increased would gradually begin to protest more and more vehemently and finally ask to be let out. At 75 volts he would register a grunt. At 90 volts he would shout that the shocks were becoming painful. At 135 volts he would emit painful groans. At 150 volts he would cry, "Experimenter, let me out of here. I won't be in the experiment anymore! I refuse to go on." At 180 volts he would cry out, "I can't stand the pain." And at 270 volts he would shout in desperation that he would no longer provide any answers. But whenever the teacher hesitated to go on with the experiment, the experimenter would forcefully urge him to continue.

Whenever Milgram lectured a group of students, colleagues, or laymen about the experiment he would ask them to predict its outcome, before disclosing the actual outcome. Almost everyone agreed that most subjects would not go beyond the tenth shock level (150 volts, when the victim makes his first demand to be freed), that a few would reach the twentieth shock level, and that about one in a thousand would administer the highest shock level on the board. As it happens almost everyone was wrong; 65 percent of all subjects obeyed the experimenter to the very end, and most of the rest stopped not very far short of that.

It wasn't that people enjoyed hurting another human being. They got terribly anxious about what they were doing and cheated whenever the experimenters gave them an opportunity. But they felt compelled to do what the voice of authority (the experimenters) told them to do.

More benign forms of this excessive deference to authority are part of everyday life. When someone is introduced with a title like "professor" or "doctor," people tend to think him taller than he is. (A visitor was introduced to five classes of an Australian college: to the first as a student, to the second as a demonstrator, to the third as a lecturer, to the fourth as a senior lecturer, to the fifth as a professor. His estimated height grew by a half-inch with each "promotion." The "professor" was two and a half inches taller than the "student.")[136] When someone drives a prestige car, people are less likely to honk at him if he lingers at a green light than when he drives an economy model. (An experimenter driving an economy model provoked nearly universal honking; two cars even rammed him in the rear. The same man driving a prestige car was left alone much longer, and in the end only honked at by half the cars.)[137] When doctors give their nurses absurd-sounding orders, they will observe them to the letter, unquestioningly. (One doctor, meaning to prescribe ear drops for the right ear of a patient suffering from an infection there, wrote: "Place in R. ear." The nurse dutifully administered the required number of drops to the man's anus.)[138]

Peer Pressure

Almost as celebrated as Stanley Milgram's experiment was one conducted by Solomon Asch in the 1950s. Asch asked his subjects to tell him which of three lines was equal in length to a fourth one. The task was trivially easy. But there was a catch. The experiment was conducted with a group of about nine people. Of these nine people, all but one were "stooges," accomplices of the experimenter pretending to be subjects. All of them were asked to say which two lines were the same length. All of the stooges, however, when asked, gave an obviously wrong answer. And then a funny thing happened. Most subjects would repeatedly go along with that. Yielding to peer judgment, they too would give the obviously wrong answer.[139]

Juries display the same phenomenon. They are required to reach a unanimous verdict. That seems like a tough requirement to meet. But they generally meet it. Yet when the first ballot is taken, right after the trial and before deliberations, most juries are split. They become unanimous because in nine out of ten cases the first ballot minority yields to the majority.[140]

In several recent parliamentary elections German pollsters observed an odd phenomenon. Up until election day, the voters were evenly split between the Socialist party and the conservative Christian Democrat–Christian Socialist party. However, when people were asked to predict who would win, a significant majority usually predicted the win of one or the other party. In the end, the election wouldn't even be close. Rather, the party the majority thought was going to win won. The reason? A sort of bandwagon effect. Bowing to the perceived peer judgment, many people voted not for the party they preferred but the party they thought was going to win.[141]

In the aftermath of a well-publicized suicide, the number of suicides and accidents goes up. It's not that what causes one person to commit suicide causes others to commit suicide and have accidents as well; the increase occurs only when the suicide is well-publicized. It's not that the suicide so saddens people that they start killing themselves intentionally or inadvertently; only certain kinds of suicides and accidents go up. If the initial suicide was a shooting, shooting suicides go up. If it was a car crash, car crashes go up. If it was a teenage death, teenage deaths go up. The answer seems inescapable: Here, too, people yield to peer pressure, by imitating the suicides of their peers. (Sometimes truly en masse, as in Jonestown.)[142]

Such instances of collective folly shouldn't really surprise us much. History is full of them: speculative fevers, patriotic frenzy, religious zealotry. In the mid-nineteenth century, a lawyer, Charles Mackay, composed a fat tome recounting with loving care the most amazing of these. It is called *Extraordinary Popular Delusions and the Madness of Crowds* (1841). In his preface, Mackay marvels at how often

> whole communities [will] fix their minds upon one object, and go mad in its pursuit; [how millions of people can become] simultaneously impressed with one delusion, and run after it, till their attention is caught by some new folly more captivating than the first. We see one nation suddenly seized, from its highest to its lowest members, with a fierce desire of military glory; another as suddenly becoming crazed upon a religious scruple; and neither of them recovering its senses until it has shed rivers of blood and sowed a harvest of groans and tears, to be repeated by its posterity. At an early age in the annals of Europe its population lost their wits about the sepulchre of Jesus, and crowded in frenzied multitudes to the Holy Land; another age went mad for fear of the devil, and offered up hundreds of thousands of victims to the delusion of witchcraft. At another time, the many became crazed on the subject of the philosopher's stone, and committed follies till then unheard of in the pursuit. It was once thought a venial offence, in very many countries of Europe, to destroy an enemy by slow poison. Persons who would have revolted at the idea of stabbing a man to the heart, drugged his potage without scruple. Ladies of gentle birth and manners caught the contagion of murder, until poisoning, under their auspices, became quite fashionable. . . .
>
> . . . Men, it has been well said, think in herds; it will be seen that they go mad in herds, while they only recover their senses slowly, and one by one.[143]

Seduction

Less well known than the Milgram and Asch experiments, but equally worthy of attention is one conducted by Scott Fraser and Jonathan Freedman. The two psychologists sent researchers around some residential neighborhoods in California, asking homeowners to put a large, ungainly, poorly lettered billboard reading, "Drive carefully" on their front lawn. To give them an idea of what the arrangement would look like, the researchers showed them a photograph in which the unattractive sign all but obliterated the view of the house behind it. Not surprisingly, nearly all residents (83%) refused.

The researchers then went to some different neighborhoods. This time their approach was different. They merely asked people to display a three-inch-square sign that read, "Be a safe driver." The request was so trifling, nearly everyone went along. Two weeks later the researchers returned. This time they asked people to put up the large billboard. The result? Seventy-six percent of all residents agreed to do it. Why? It seems that many people, having made a commitment to drivers' safety by displaying the small sign, could not in good conscience refuse a request that, in principle, was no different—putting up the billboard.[144]

The researchers then went to yet another neighborhood to try a third approach. This time they asked people to sign a petition for "keeping California beautiful." That being no more controversial than motherhood and apple pie, nearly everyone signed. Two weeks later they asked the same group to put up the large billboard. About half complied. Again, having made a commitment to being "public spirited," people could not in good conscience refuse a request that, in principle, was no different.

The lesson of this experiment is perhaps no less scary than those of Milgram and Asch. Writes one psychologist:

> It scares me enough that I am rarely willing to sign a petition anymore, even for a position I support. Such an action has the potential to influence not only my future behavior but also my self-image in ways I may not want. And once a person's self-image is altered, all sorts of subtle advantages become available to someone who wants to exploit that new image.
>
> Who among Freedman and Fraser's homeowners would have thought that the "volunteer worker" who asked them to sign a state beautification petition was really interested in having them display a safe-driving billboard two weeks later? And who among them could have suspected that their decision to display the billboard was largely due to the act of signing the petition? No one, I'd guess. If there were any regrets after the billboard went up, who could they conceivably hold responsible but *themselves* and their own damnably strong civic spirit? They probably never considered the guy with the "keeping California beautiful" petition. . . ."[145]

At last we understand why governments are so insistent on loyalty oaths, allegiance pledges, and flag salutes, and why others, equally insistently, resist them. Both sides probably understand intuitively what Fraser and Freedman demonstrated experimentally: Token gestures have more than token consequences.

Brainwashing and Paradox

It is hard to accept these experiments at their face value. We have always known that we like to please authority, be part of the group, and act consistently. What's hard to believe is that we would carry these desires to such absurd lengths. How do we manage to survive in the world if our instinctual attachment to authority, peer judgment, and self-consistency is so intense and so crude? It is well to have misgivings. The success of experiments like Milgram's is attributible, I think, less to our irrational attachment to certain values than to the clever way in which these experiments (and situations like it) lead us to commit certain *logical* fallacies. It is in combination with these logical fallacies that our attachment to certain values results in absurd behavior. What are those fallacies and how do they work their charm?

Seduction and the Paradox of the Heaps

The paradox of the heaps originates with the ancient Greeks and it goes like this: There are no heaps of sand. Why? If a collection of grains isn't yet a heap, adding another grain won't make it a heap. Clearly one grain makes no heap. Therefore two grains make no heap. Therefore three grains make no heap. Therefore. . . . Therefore there are no heaps of sand.[146]

A modern version of this is Wang's paradox: All numbers are small. Why? Well, if a number is small, then its successor is also small. Clearly "one" is small. Therefore "two" is small. Therefore "three" is small. Therefore. . . . Therefore all numbers are small.

Another version comes from the philosopher Max Black: A 7′ man is short. Why? If a man is short, adding a quarter inch to his height won't make him tall. A 4′ man is short. Therefore a 4′ 1/4″ man is short. Therefore a 4′ 1/2″ man is short. Therefore a 4′ 3/4″ man is short. Therefore. . . . Therefore a 7′ man is short.[147]

Those California homeowners who were seduced into exhibiting a billboard because they had already agreed to display a small square sign were falling victim to the paradox of the heaps. Implicitly, they reasoned: If something is worth doing for drivers' safety, something only slightly harder is also worth doing. Displaying a small square sign is worth doing. Therefore displaying a slightly larger sign is worth doing. Therefore displaying a yet larger sign is worth doing. Therefore. . . . Therefore displaying a big billboard is worth doing.

Authority and the Dollar Auction

The game theorist Martin Shubik has invented a weird sort of game called a "dollar auction." Someone puts up a dollar. Others get to bid for it. However, the person who enters the second highest bid also has to pay whatever he bid, even though he doesn't get the prize.[148]

At first this looks like a game everyone should like to play: Who wouldn't want to get a dollar for less than a dollar? There is only one thing one wonders about: Who in his right mind would want to put up his dollar for auction? But first impressions deceive.

Howard Raiffa, another game theorist, describes playing the game with two of his Harvard Business School colleagues. Raiffa put up the dollar. He reports:

> The opener bid 10 cents; the follower responded hesitatingly with 20 cents; and they continued, still somewhat hesitatingly with 50 cents and 60 cents. There was laughter when the players realized that already I, as the auctioneer, was making money. In quick succession came 70 cents, 80 cents, 90 cents. There was a pause, and the follower said, "one dollar" with a note of triumphant finality to it. The starter then wanted to clarify a point: "Could I bid $1.10?" I said there was no reason why not.
>
> Rather quickly the bids escalated to $1.60. Another pause for clarification. "Must we pay with the money we have in our pockets?" I assured them, to their amusement, that I trusted them and would take a check.
>
> The bidding resumed. At $2.50 there was another pause for clarification. "Is this for real?"
>
> "Of course!" I answered. "Wouldn't you have taken my dollar if you had won with a bid of 30 cents?"
>
> The bidding continued with a perceptible change in mood: the players were angry. The dollar bill had become the least of their objectives; each was now intent on winning out over the other.
>
> When the bidding reached $3.10, I became uncomfortable and intervened, persuading them that the game had gone far enough and that I'd be satisfied with collecting $2.00 from each of them. They agreed, with a

> certain amount of annoyance. It wasn't that they minded losing $4.00 to me—but they were irked that I hadn't let them finish the game.[149]

Why would you ever bid more than a dollar for a dollar? Well, suppose you have already bid 90 cents and your opponent raises his bid to $1.00. If you stop now, you are 90 cents poorer. If you go up to $1.10 and he doesn't stop you, you get the dollar for $1.10 and you are 10 cents poorer. It is clear now that the game can easily get out of hand—to the delight of the auctioneer and the chagrin of the players. It's become known as the "escalation game."

Many real world situations are like an escalation game. Wars, for example. When a war is over, both sides—winner and loser—often find that they sacrificed much more than the prize for which they fought was worth. Why? In a war each side is "bidding" with arms and men for the coveted prize. The side that bids the most may win, but the loser won't get back what he bid. The sacrifice in arms and men is irretrievable. At any point in time, each side will not consider whether the prize is worth what it has already spent on it (that's "water under the bridge," a "sunk cost"), but only whether it is worth another incremental expenditure. In this way both sides can "lose" a war, and there isn't even an auctioneer to benefit from their woe. Strikes, litigation, contract talks, in fact most conflicts, are escalation games, too.

The escalation game helps explain the behavior of Stanley Milgram's docile subjects. It helps clear up a paradox that surrounds that experiment. We know that the subjects behaved as they did out of their great deference for authority, out of their inordinate desire to win the approval of the experimenters (the authority figures). Yet we are also convinced, rightly, I suspect, that if the subjects had been asked from the very outset to inflict the amount of pain and suffering on the learner they ultimately inflicted just to please the experimenters, they would probably have said, "No way." They only did what they did because the experimenters managed to involve them in an escalation game. The prize in this escalation game was the approval (or goodwill) of the experimenter. The two bidders are the subject (or teacher) and the experimenter. The teacher makes his bid by pressing a lever whenever the learner makes a wrong response. The experimenters make their bid by having the learner give the wrong response. That forces the teacher either to raise his bid by pressing the next lever or to lose the prize, the experimenters' approval. Whenever the teacher thinks about whether to press the next lever, he doesn't ask himself whether retaining the experimenters' approval is worth inflicting all that pain on the learner, because much of that pain has already been inflicted. It is "water under the bridge," a "sunk cost," something that can't be undone. All he asks himself is whether the experimenters' approval is worth inflicting *just a bit more* pain. It is thus that he ends up making a monstrous sacrifice by committing an act of inhuman brutality for a trivial prize—the experimenters' approval.

Peer Pressure and the Efficient Market

It is an implication of the efficient market hypothesis discussed earlier than the investor who carefully picks and chooses his stocks will do no better than the investor who selects his stocks randomly. That's because there are no "bargain" stocks. If there were, the advocates of the hypothesis argue, somebody would already have bid up the price to the point where it ceased to be a bargain. This kind of argument is frequent in economics and often makes a lot of sense. But it is easily overextended. The story is told of a finance professor strolling down the street with some students, when one of them sees a $10 bill lying on the pavement. The student is about to reach for it, but the professor tells him: "Don't bother; if it were real, somebody would already have picked it up."[150] The subjects of Solomon Asch's experiment are committing the same kind of mistake.

The Chinese running the Korean POW camps were apparently adept at all of these techniques. In fact, interviews with returning POWs showed them to have been true masters. Keenly appreciating the force of authority, they made sure that all sources of authority but their own were eliminated. Noncommissioned officers, for instance, who could have contended with the Chinese for the minds of their prisoners, were segregated from the rest of the men. To emphasize to everyone the irrelevance of old lines of authority, the Chinese often appointed the youngest and most inept member of a squad its leader.[151]

Acutely aware of the power of peer pressure, the Chinese made sure that *perceived* peer pressure ran in their favor. A pervasive network of spies and *agents provocateur* kept the men from ever voicing anything but collaborationist opinions to each other. The only sources of information were Chinese, Russian, Polish, and Czechoslovak newspapers and broadcasts, as well as *The Daily Worker*. Even the mail was heavily controlled: The Chinese preferred only to transmit to the prisoners letters that were short on general information and long on depressing personal news.[152]

Well versed in the art of seduction, the Chinese approached the task of producing collaboration with infinite patience. To get a man from voicing the mildest of anti-American sentiments to broadcasting ferociously anti-American propaganda, they were willing to have him take the tiniest steps.[153]

Finally, the Chinese realized that not everyone was equally susceptible to these techniques, and they went out of their way to detect the most vulnerable. All prisoners were interrogated at length about their personal history. Some men tried to lie, making up fictional characters when they filled out their forms. The Chinese had a simple way of coping with this. They repeated the same procedure several times over. The prisoner usually could not remember everything he had previously said. He would then be confronted with the discrepancies and forced into the fatiguing task of inventing justification after justification to resolve them. Once they had a reasonably accurate life history in hand, the Chinese would examine it with the prisoner, seeking to show him "that he or his parents had been ruthless capitalists exploiting workers, yet had really received only meager benefits from such exploitation." "Whenever possible any setbacks that a man had experienced economically or socially were searchingly analyzed, and the blame was laid on the capitalistic system." In the process, the Chinese would learn whether the prisoner was a promising brainwashing prospect.[154]

All of this took place against a background of extreme deprivation: starvation and disease. Collaboration was rewarded with favors large enough to give significant relief, but not so large as to seem like the reason for collaboration. The Chinese wanted the collaborator to be motivated from "within," not "without."[155] Chances are that William Olsen was one of the prisoners singled out for a special dose of "lenient policy." If we are going to have a duress defense, the likes of Olsen should probably be acquitted. In any event, it seems parochial to exclude brainwashing from the concept of duress.

Necessity and duress are the basic complement of defenses available to a criminal defendant. That may sound strange. They are not defenses one ever hears about in the news, in the papers, in books, or in movies. What one hears about instead are self-defense, defense of another, defense of property, arrest of a felon, insanity, diminished capacity, provocation. In fact, these defenses are carved out of the basic complement of necessity and duress. If we find that a man is justified in breaking a law in self-defense, in defense of someone else, in defense of his property, or to arrest a felon that is because we think on balance it is for the better. If we think he is excused because he is insane, of diminished capacity, or subject to provocation, that is because he is the victim of extraordinary pressures—internal or external. These subcategories of necessity and duress are so frequent that they have acquired separate names. Only the unusual, the rare, the residual case wears the label "necessity" or "duress." That shouldn't obscure the fact that necessity and duress underlie all of these other, more humdrum defenses. To understand necessity and duress is to understand why anyone is ever justified or excused in breaking the law.[156]

The "commandments" of the criminal law, then, are not absolute. They are subject to broad exceptions. This chapter we spent examining those exceptions. The rest of the book we will spend examining the commandments themselves. As was noted earlier, according to the common law, each criminal offense has two parts, a physical part and a mental part. The former is called the actus reus, the bad act or forbidden deed; the latter is called the mens rea, the guilty mind or forbidden state of mind. In murder, if it is defined as an intentional killing, the actus reus is the killing, the mens rea the intent to kill. Many of the problems that arise in determining criminal guilt can be roughly divided into two groups: those involved in finding whether a bad act has occurred and those involved in finding whether the bad act was performed with the requisite guilty mind. The next two chapters take up each of these two groups in turn.

The next chapter inquires into the meaning of "bad act." The inquiry has two parts. We ask first, What makes what the defendant did bad? We ask next, What makes it an act?

What makes it bad? By that I mean: Is the defendant's act within the range of conduct the statute was meant to forbid? Sometimes that's easy to tell, but often it isn't. It often isn't because the legislature misdescribed what it meant to forbid or because it contradicted some of its earlier pronouncements. Why do such misdescriptions and self-contradictions happen, and how do we cope with them?

What makes it an act? Not all criminal statutes punish acts. Many punish omissions, and a few have tried to punish thoughts or mere conditions. But the typical criminal statute aims to punish acts. Because some conduct seems to fall within the language of a statute without being an act, we must understand the nature of an act, if we want to effectuate the statute's intent to punish acts. Otherwise, without wanting to, we may find ourselves punishing someone not for what he did, but for something that happened to him or for something he failed to do or for something he merely thought about doing.

2 Bad Acts

The Definition of Witchcraft

"I have nothing to say. I deny it."[1] But by being stubborn and taciturn, the woman only strengthened the prosecution's case against her. Puna was an African native, a member of the Shona tribe, who had been charged with violating Southern Rhodesia's Witchcraft Suppression Act, first passed in 1899 but still actively enforced in 1948, the year of her trial. Contrary to its name, the act was not intended to punish witches. It was intended to punish those who engaged in witch-hunts or those who invited witch-hunts by pretending to be witches. Puna was in the former category.

The case against Puna was formidable. Mazinyana, Puna's neighbor, had testified that Puna had publicly denounced her as a witch and caused her to leave the local kraal: "Last year the accused had eye-sickness. She consulted a diviner . . . , who visited our kraal. I was not present. Next day she said I was a witch (*Muroyi*) as the diviner had said I was the cause of her eye-sickness. She said if I did not believe her I could go to another diviner and that I was to leave the kraal." In fact, Mazinyana and her family did consult a diviner of their own. "We threw the bones," she proudly testified, "and all of us were cleared." Still, she felt compelled to leave the kraal. Puna's own daughter-in-law, Tizirayi, confirmed Mazinyana's account: "A diviner . . . spent a night with us at tax time. Accused asked him to divine the cause of her illness. He said it was witchcraft (*Uroyi*) and caused by Mazinyana, who was not present. Next day accused told Mazinyana she was a witch (*Muroyi*) . . . . She left the kraal."[2] The prosecutor was confident of a conviction.

When the British came to Africa, they were outraged by the natives' custom of blaming most of their misfortunes—from a back ailment to a crop failure to the death of a baby—on witchcraft and of killing or ostracizing those of their neighbors they believed had bewitched them. The Witchcraft Suppression Act was a very comprehensive statute designed to eradicate such customs.[3] The statute punished a variety of related practices: the imputation of witchcraft, especially by a professional witch doctor or diviner; the hiring of a witch doctor or diviner to "smoke out witches"; trial by ordeal of suspected witches; and the practice of witchcraft itself, whether intended to injure an enemy or help a friend. The specific provision under which Puna had been indicted provided that "whoever names or indicates any other person as being a wizard or witch shall be guilty of an offence and liable for a fine not exceeding one hundred pounds or to imprisonment not exceeding three years, or to corporal punishment not exceeding twenty lashes or to any two or more of such punishments." The drafters of the act thought the term witchcraft somewhat vague and prefaced the substantive portions of the statute with a definition that read: "In this Act 'witchcraft' includes the 'throwing of bones', the use of charms and any other means or devices adopted in the practice of sorcery." Unfortunately, the drafters knew very little about the customs they were seeking to eradicate. They did not know, for instance, that the "throwing of bones," a ritual the British had frequently seen witch doctors engage in, was not a means of bewitching someone, but a means of detecting witches. Nor did they know that the natives drew a sharp distinction between witchcraft and sorcery. Witchcraft, the natives believed, was the use of malevolent psychic powers. Only a woman possessed by an evil ancestral spirit could practice it. It was largely an inherited skill. Sorcery was a much less serious affair. Although used to harm others, it was much less awe-inspiring. It merely required the performance of some ritual acts; almost anyone could learn it.[4] The Witchcraft Suppression Act thus completely misdescribed the phenomenon it sought to root out.

The drafters' misapprehension of the nature of witchcraft beliefs was understandable. But it had the potential of stultifying the purpose of the statute. Puna was accused of calling Mazinyana a witch. But the statute says a witch is someone who throws bones or practices sorcery. Puna had charged Mazinyana with neither. What was a conscientious judge to do? Throw his hands up and say: It is for me to apply, not make, the law. The legislature blundered. But I must do what they say. And what they say is—punish those who have accused others of sorcery or throwing bones. Hence I acquit Puna. Or should he just ignore the definition—

which is what the judges of Southern Rhodesia did? If he did, would he be faithful to the purpose of his office which is to interpret a statute according to its plain meaning?

What is the plain meaning of a word like "witchcraft" in a statute like the Witchcraft Suppression Act? Is it really what the drafters say it is? That's how the traditional conception of meaning would have it.[5] But is the traditional conception right?

If a biologist were asked the meaning of "tyrannosaur," he might say that it is a giant flesh-eating, two-legged reptile that lived in the Mesozoic era. According to the traditional conception of meaning, if that's what the biologist thinks of when he says "tyrannosaur," then that's what he's referring to. Such a view has strange consequences. It's conceivable that much of our knowledge about tyrannosaurs will turn out to be wrong. Tyrannosaurs might turn out to be plant-eating and four-legged, for instance. Yet under the traditional view that's absurd: a plant-eating four-legged tyrannosaur wouldn't be a tyrannosaur, just as a married bachelor wouldn't be a bachelor. *But it doesn't seem absurd.* It's also conceivable that under the appropriate environmental pressures tyrannosaurs could have evolved into plant-eaters. Again, under the traditional view that's absurd—for the same reason. *But it doesn't seem absurd.* Finally, it's conceivable that there exists somewhere a group of animals that look just like tyrannosaurs, but evolved by an entirely different route (say from mammals). A biologist would deny that these are tyrannosaurs. Again, under the traditional view, that's absurd.[6] *But it doesn't seem absurd.*

Another example. If someone were asked the meaning of "Shakespeare," he might say that it refers to a sixteenth-century playwright who wrote *Hamlet, Macbeth,* and *Romeo and Juliet.* According to the traditional view, "Shakespeare" to this speaker is synonymous with "a sixteenth-century playwright who wrote *Hamlet, Macbeth,* and *Romeo and Juliet.*" It's conceivable that Shakespeare didn't write any of the plays attributed to him. Yet, under the traditional view, that's absurd. (If Shakespeare didn't write those plays, he wouldn't be Shakespeare.) It's also conceivable that if Shakespeare hadn't become a playwright, he would have gone into law. Yet again, under the traditional view, that's absurd. (If Shakespeare hadn't become a playwright, he wouldn't be Shakespeare.) Finally, it's conceivable that the celebrated William Shakespeare didn't really write those plays, but had an unknown ghostwriter by the same name who wrote them. Nevertheless, when people speak of Shakespeare, they appear to be referring to the celebrity, not the ghostwriter. Under the traditional view, that's absurd. ("Shakespeare" refers to the playwright, not a *poseur*.) *But none of this seems absurd.*

The traditional conception of meaning has another strange consequence. It makes scientific discourse incomprehensible. Early scientists believed that atoms were the basic building blocks of matter. Later it was discovered that even smaller particles existed. They described this by saying: We have discovered new things about the atom; they consist of even smaller particles. According to the traditional view, this perfectly natural statement must seem eccentric. If by atoms scientists mean the basic building blocks of nature, they could not possibly discover that something else was the basic building block of matter (just as one cannot discover that not all bachelors are unmarried, after all). They could only discover that some things they thought were atoms are not in fact atoms because they are made up of even smaller particles.[7]

What is amiss with the traditional view? How can it be remedied? Another example will show us. Gerald attends a cocktail party with his wife. In a faraway corner he notices his boss, whom his wife has never yet met. Gesturing toward the corner, he whispers to her: "The man in the Brooks Brothers suit, the Yves St. Laurent tie, and the Gucci shoes is my boss." As it happens, he didn't get it quite right. The man is indeed his boss, but his suit is not from Brooks Brothers but the Marshall Fields Department Store, the tie isn't Yves St. Laurent but Pierre Cardin, the shoes aren't Gucci but Florsheim. According to the traditional view, "the man in the Brooks Brothers suit, the Yves St. Laurent tie, and the Gucci shoes" means just what it seems to mean: a man in a Brooks Brothers suit, an Yves St. Laurent tie, and Gucci shoes. Under this view we would have to say that Gerald's statement is wrong. There is no man wearing a Brooks Brothers suit, Yves St. Laurent tie, and Gucci shoes who is also his boss. Yet the statement seems true. What the traditional view overlooks is that "the man in the Brooks Brothers suit," etc., is here merely used *referentially*. It is used to pick out a certain man of whom it is then asserted that he is Gerald's boss. As long as the man whom the "Brooks Brothers" phrase picks out really is Gerald's boss, it should be considered true.[8]

At first it may seem that we only use such referential expressions very sparingly. After all, usually when we refer to someone, he isn't present for us to point him out as we misdescribe him. And if he isn't present, how would anyone know whom we meant if we misdescribed him? But suppose I want to make a statement about Lee Harvey Oswald. Unable to recall his name I speak of him as "Kennedy's murderer." Let us assume, arguendo, that Oswald is innocent. Clearly my misdescription of Oswald does not prevent your knowing who I mean even though Oswald is not in the same room with us for me to point him out and even though I have misdescribed him. The reason my misdescription works is that you understand "Kennedy's murderer" to refer to the same person that journalists mean when they speak of "Kennedy's murderer," and journalists mean Oswald.

What these examples show is that very often we use nouns not as shorthand expressions for certain properties the speaker associates with them, but referentially, as a way of picking out a particular object. The person who says "Shakespeare" is not using it as a shorthand for "sixteenth-century playwright who wrote *Hamlet, Macbeth,* and *Romeo and Juliet.*" He is using it to refer to whomever the person who introduced him to the name was referring. And who was that person referring to? Whomever the person who introduced *him* to the name was referring to. And so on down the line to the persons who actually knew Shakespeare and used the name to refer to that particular person. It now becomes clear why the statement "Shakespeare did not write *Hamlet, Macbeth,*" etc., is not absurd. When we finally discover the person to whom the name Shakespeare was applied by those who knew the man, it might well turn out that he did not write the plays attributed to him. Similarly, the biologist who says "tyrannosaur" is not using it as a shorthand for "giant, flesh-eating, two-legged reptile," etc. He is using it to refer to animals like those the person who introduced him to the term was referring to. And so on down the line to the archaeologists who first unearthed the bones of a tyrannosaur. That is, by "tyrannosaur" the biologist is referring to animals of the same species as the one whose bones the archaeologists discovered at a certain spot. It might well turn out that that animal wasn't a flesh-eater or two-legged. We can now dispel the air of paradox surrounding scientific discourse. The early scientists who said that atoms are not the smallest particles of matter were simply stating that certain specific entities they had encountered and dubbed "atoms" are not in fact the smallest particles there are.[9]

It is a startling consequence of this new view that people do not necessarily mean what they think they mean. People think that when they say Shakespeare they mean a certain playwright who lived in the sixteenth century and wrote certain plays. Any of these facts may turn out to be wrong. On closer reflection, this ceases to be startling. There is a rule in the law of wills known as the doctrine of incorporation by reference.[10] The rule permits a testator to make reference in his will to documents not attached to the will itself. The testator might, for instance, bequeath all properties listed in a certain document to his son. The list, let us say, contains a valuable lamp. Did the testator mean to bequeath the lamp to his son? Quite clearly. Did he know that he was bequeathing the lamp to this son? Not necessarily. Conceivably he even thought that the lamp was listed in a separate document whose contents he bequeathed to his wife. There is nothing very surprising about the fact that the testator means something different from what he thinks he means. Our new view of meaning maintains, in essence, that every speaker is like a testator who in using a certain word incorporates by reference whatever it is that that word meant to the persons who first introduced it.

What does the new theory of meaning imply about our witchcraft statute? Again, remember Gerald, who attends a cocktail party given by his boss. He might tell his wife: "Would you please talk to the man over there with the Brooks Brothers suit, the Yves St. Laurent tie, and the Gucci shoes. He is my boss." She complies with his request. Later on the man discovers that his boss is not wearing a Brooks Brothers suit, an Yves St. Laurent tie, or Gucci shoes. Would he be entitled to complain to his wife: "Darling, you did not comply with my request. I asked you to talk to a man with a Brooks Brothers suit, an Yves St. Laurent tie, and Gucci shoes and you did not!" The legislature's law can be construed in a similar fashion. The drafters (or the people they relied on to supply them with relevant information) had observed a certain set of practices among the natives. They pointed their finger toward these practices and said "Stop that!" Of course, unless they were personally present and pointing no one would know what "that" meant. So they tried to describe what "that" was, just like the man who tried to describe his boss to his wife. The fact that they slightly misdescribed "that" does not mean that their order cannot be complied with. It is complied with by punishing that which they were pointing to as opposed to that which their misdescription conjured up! Clearly, then, by witchcraft the legislature meant something other than throwing bones and sorcery, even though what it thought it meant was throwing bones and sorcery.

I may seem to have made too much of what is after all only a minor glitch in a rather exotic statute. But it is not atypical. Some kind of misdescription is virtually inevitable in a comprehensive statute seeking to regulate a complex reality. Judges are fond of taking the legislature severely to task for such glitches. Yet they rarely do much better themselves when asked to formulate rules of a quasi-legislative nature. Think of the Supreme Court's attempts to produce a reasonably clear definition of obscenity. What stands in the way of such a definition is not just that the Justices differ in their value judgments but that they are unable to put into words what they agree on. In *Roth v. United States,* the court defined obscenity as something whose "dominant theme" the "average person, applying contemporary community standards" would find "taken as a whole, appeals to the prurient interest."[11] Shortly after this pronouncement the Supreme Court was embarrassed by the case of someone who published books depicting sadomasochism, fetishism, and homosexuality. He argued quite correctly that under the court's definition such books are not obscene because they do not appeal to the prurient interest of the average person. The court replied lamely that the definition should not be so narrowly construed.[12]

The Trouble with Definitions

Why is accurate description so difficult? Conversely, why is misdescription such a common pitfall? The main reason is that the legislature will often need to refer to things whose underlying nature (or "deep structure," as philosophers like to say) neither the drafters nor anyone else understands yet. The legislature may need to regulate the export of gold even before its molecular structure is understood. It may need to quarantine leprosy victims even before the responsible virus has been identified. But any definition of gold or leprosy without such knowledge will be inaccurate. An appearance-based definition of gold is likely to include fool's gold and exclude white gold. A symptom-based definition of leprosy is likely to include many cases of fungal infection (or ichthyosis, as happened in Sherlock Holmes's celebrated "Adventure of the Blanched Soldier") and exclude many atypical leprosy cases with initial symptoms resembling altogether different diseases, like tuberculosis of the skin. Fortunately, not everything has a "deep structure." Gold and leprosy do. Bachelors, pens, and garbage pails don't. Their meaning is conveyed by simple dictionary definitions. Philosophers call something with a "deep structure" a "natural kind."

The judge in *Regina v. Puna* proceeded as though he understood all this. To begin with, he didn't dismiss the case just because the witchcraft definition was inaccurate. He realized that a correct reading of the statute required him to ignore the misdefinition of witchcraft and focus on that concept's "deep structure." But he didn't stop there. Puna was charged with witchcraft imputation. The judge realized that the meaning of "imputation" in this context would not be conveyed by a simple dictionary definition either. "Imputation" in this context is really a "natural kind" term.

The judge knew that there was but one authoritative procedure for ferreting out witches:

> The procedure was for all adult members of a kraal to be called together suddenly to form a *gumbgwa* [divination party] to visit the *nganga* [diviner]. Those who could not join the party sent [some personal effects instead]. The *gumbgwa* having assembled, the *nganga* threw the bones to reveal the reasons for the visit, or the type of misfortune, several further throws might indicate the cause of the trouble, such as irritation of an ancestral spirit through neglect of some old tribal law. That was as far as the *nganga* [could] go; at this point he could show what had caused the trouble.[13]

Even if he diagnosed witchcraft as the source of a problem, the diviner was still not in a position to "name" the witch. That required the witch's active cooperation. "Each member of the party had to throw bones, and the *nganga* would identify the witch by returning to the thrower the object which he had brought to the *nganga*. Such manual tradition was the traditional affirmation that this particular thrower was a witch."[14] In Puna's case, the correct procedure had never been followed. To be sure, on some literal reading of the term "imputation," she had in fact imputed witchcraft to someone. But "witchcraft imputation" in this context functioned as a "natural kind." It referred to a certain set of rituals that rendered a verdict of witchcraft authoritative. Those rituals not having been performed, there had been no witchcraft imputation. The judge acquitted her.[15]

Misdescription can have another reason altogether. Even terms that don't refer to "natural kinds" may be diabolically hard to define. Not all such terms are like "pen" and "bachelor," which can be captured in a pithy phrase like "ink-dispensing writing utensil" or "unmarried male." "Pen" and "bachelor" are easy to define because the objects they refer to all have something obvious in common. It is tempting to think that all terms are like that. After all, why would the same label be applied to some potpourri of objects unless they all had something in common? But consider a word like "game." As the philosopher Ludwig Wittgenstein observed in a classic passage, there are

> board-games, card-games, ball-games, Olympic games, and so on. What is common to them all?—Don't say: "There *must* be something common, or they would not be called games"—but *look* and *see* whether there is anything common to all.—For if you look at them you will not see something that is common to *all,* but similarities, relationships, and a whole series of them at that. To repeat, don't think, but look!—Look for example at board-games, with their multifarious relationships. Now pass to card-games; here you find many correspondences with the first group, but many common features drop out, and others appear. When we pass next to ball-games, much that is common is retained, but much is lost.—Are they all "amusing"? Compare chess with naughts and crosses. Or is there always winning and losing, or competition among the players? Think of patience. In ball games there is winning and losing; but when a child throws his ball at the wall and catches it again, this feature has disappeared. Look at the parts played by skill and luck; and at the difference between skill in chess and skill in tennis. Think now of games like ring-a-ring-a-roses; here is the element of amusement, but how many other characteristic features have disappeared! And we can go through the many, many other groups of games in the same way; can see how similarities crop up and disappear.
>
> And the result of this examination is: we see a complicated network of similarities overlapping and criss-crossing: sometimes overall similarities, sometimes similarities of detail.
>
> I can think of no better expression to characterize these similarities than "family resemblances"; for the various resemblances between members of a family: build, features, colour of eyes, gait, temperament, etc. etc. overlap and criss-cross in the same way.—And I shall say: "games" form a family.[16]

In other words, the sundry items that are referred to by a single word may have nothing in common at all, save the label. Any two or three of them will have a lot in common, of course, but not the group. They are like the members of the Habsburg dynasty: each reigning monarch greatly resembled his predecessor. But there is no trait all Habsburgs shared—

not even the famous Habsburg lip. Such "family resemblance" terms resist pithy definition.

The law has its share of family resemblance terms, and they have caused their share of trouble. There is no obvious unifying trait that all transactions labeled "theft" share. Take the following three:

1. *Y* has tied his horse to a pole and is making some purchases in the general store. *X* stealthily approaches, unties the horse, and rides off into the sunset.
2. *A*, who is *B*'s trustee, secretly sells *B*'s land to a third person and keeps the money.
3. *O*, an oil prospector, persuades *P* to sell him a valuable oil property for a pittance by telling him (falsely) that a soon-to-be built highway will lower its value dramatically.

By what elements could we characterize theft so as to capture all three transactions? We can say that all three are crimes against property. But so is arson, which surely does not qualify as a variety of theft. We can say that they are all involuntary transfers of property. But so is the foreclosure of a mortgage, again not a variety of theft. We can say that they are all involuntary transfers of property, not pursuant to prior agreement (so as to eliminate foreclosures). But so are robbery, blackmail, and bad checks, not generally classed as varieties of theft either. There are some further similarities between the first and second actions. They both involve the stealthy appropriation of another man's property. That of course is not true of the third. The second and third actions both involve an ostensibly voluntary property transfer under a misapprehension, and in both that property is immovable real estate. The first is without even the owner's apparent consent and involves movable personal property. The first and third both involve an intent to strip the rightful owner of his property at the time the commodity is acquired. In the second action that intent ripens much later. In short, there are no elements common to all three transactions.

Given the difficulty of defining one offense to capture all three transactions, the common law not surprisingly viewed each as a separate offense. The first was called larceny ("the trespassory taking and carrying away of personal property of another with intent to steal it"); the second embezzlement ("the fraudulent conversion of the property of another by one who is already in lawful possession of it"); and the third false pretenses ("a false representation of a material present or past fact which causes the victim to pass title to his property to the wrongdoer who knows his presentation to be false and intends thereby to defraud the victim.")[17]

But the three offenses were not, of course, unrelated. They were all parts of the same "family." That gave rise to some familial tensions, as shown in 1867 by the case of *Commonwealth v. O'Malley.*[18] Bridget McDonald "was a servant in a family residing in Boston, and received from her employer, in payment of her wages, thirty-eight dollars in bank-bills." The defendant, Martin O'Malley (his relationship to Bridget is never explained) "asked her to let him take the money and count it, she not being able to read or write." He "counted it several times over in her presence, and then, upon her asking that he should return it to her refused to do so." Bridget then locked the door to keep him from escaping, but O'Malley "threatened to jump out of the window or to burn the bills, in consequence of which she opened the door; and . . . he went off with the money." O'Malley was caught and prosecuted for larceny. The trial court, however, seemed to feel that he was guilty of embezzlement, not larceny, since he hadn't actually taken the property away from Bridget but merely kept it against her will, and it acquitted O'Malley. The state then prosecuted O'Malley for embezzlement. This time a jury convicted him. O'Malley, however, appealed the case, arguing that a jury could not possibly find him guilty of embezzlement, since what he had done clearly amounted to larceny. The appeals court agreed: When a person turns her property over to another for some brief, limited task, such as counting the bills, she has never actually divested herself of possession. But absconding with something in somebody else's possession is larceny, not embezzlement, and so the court acquitted O'Malley of the embezzlement charge. It appears that O'Malley went free.

To put an end to such injustices, many legislatures eventually consolidated larceny, embezzlement, and false pretenses into a single offense called "theft." But how do you define theft? You can't just define it as the "dishonest appropriation of another's property." That begs the question. What is "dishonest"? Since there is no central attribute that all theft offenses share, legislatures typically define theft as larceny–embezzlement–false pretenses.[19] It is not clear how that solves anything. Under the common law, fairness was thought to require that the defendant be told whether he was charged with larceny, embezzlement, or false pretenses and that he be convicted only if the jury could agree which of the three he had committed. Why doesn't fairness now require that he be told which kind of theft he is charged with and that he be convicted only if the jury can agree which kind he has committed?

There is a third reason for misdescription: the drafter's irrepressible impulse to overdescribe. The "orgy of statute making" inaugurated by the New Deal helped bring into fashion a style of drafting aimed at "unearthly and superhuman precision."[20] The common law—that is, the judge-made rules that made up the bulk of the law for most of the last and much of the present century—had been a paragon of seeming imprecision: full of elastic phrases like "reasonable," "good faith," or "relevant." The newly active legislatures wouldn't rely on such slippery concepts unless they had first been defined. Otherwise who was to know what "reasonable," "good faith," or "relevant" meant? The Securities Act of 1933 says that under certain circumstances the underwriter of securities is not liable for misstatements he reasonably believes to be true.[21] The regulations following the act then painstakingly explain that whether the issuer's belief is "reasonable" depends on "(a) the type of issuer; (b) the type of security; (c) the type of person; (d) the office held when the person is an officer"; and so on.[22] The Uniform Commercial Code scrupulously defines "good faith" as "honest in fact in the conduct or transaction concerned."[23] And the Federal Rules of Evidence with equal seriousness spell out the meaning of relevance: " 'Relevant evidence' means evidence having any tendency to make the existence of any fact that is of consequence to the determination of the action more probable or less probable than it would be without the evidence."[24] In the same spirit, the Securities Act of 1933 opens with an interminable, thirteen-part definitional section seeking to supply exhaustive definitions for all of the act's basic terms, from "security" ("any note, stock, treasury stock, bond, debenture, evidence of indebtedness, certificate of interest or participation in any profit-sharing agreement, collateral-trust certificate . . ." etc.), to "person" ("an individual, a corporation, a partnership, an association, a joint-stock company, a trust," etc.).[25] The Uniform Commercial Code opens with a similar forty-six-part section defining everything from "aggrieved party" ("party entitled to resort to a remedy") to "fault" (a "wrongful act, omission or breach").[26]

What the drafters of these acts appear afflicted with is a malaise known in philosophical circles as "Wittgenstein's paradox on rules." What they are haunted by is the fear that many imposingly formulated and long-hallowed rules of law are so flexible as to be void of all content—in fact, not rules at all, but empty formulas, invoked to rationalize rather than justify. It was Wittgenstein's contention that, *in a certain sense,* all rules are "empty." Take a rule as ironclad and lucid as addition:

> Let us suppose, for example, that 68 + 57 is a computation that I have never performed before. . . . I per-

form the computation, obtaining, of course, the answer 125. I am confident, perhaps after checking my work, that 125 is the correct answer. It is correct in the . . . sense that "plus," as I intended to use that word in the past, denoted a function which, when applied to the numbers I called "68" and "57," yields the value 125. Now suppose I encounter a bizarre sceptic. This sceptic questions my certainty about my answer. . . . After all, he says, if I am now so confident that, as I used the symbol "+," my intention was that "68 + 57" should turn out to denote 125, this cannot be because I explicitly gave myself instructions that 125 is the result of performing the addition in this particular instance. By hypothesis, I did no such thing. But of course the idea is that, in this new instance, I should apply the very same function or rule that I applied so many times in the past. But who is to say what that function was? In the past I gave myself only a finite number of examples instantiating this function. All, we have supposed, involved numbers smaller than 57. So perhaps in the past I used "plus" and "=" to denote a function which I will call "quus" and symbolize by *. It is defined by:

$$x \oplus y = x + y, \text{ if } x, y < 57$$
$$= 5, \text{ otherwise}$$

Who is to say that this is not the function I previously meant by "+"?

The sceptic claims (or feigns to claim) that I am now misinterpreting my own previous usage. By "plus," he says, I *always meant* quus; now, under the influence of some insane frenzy, or a bout of LSD, I have come to misinterpret my own previous usage.

Ridiculous and fantastic though it is, the sceptic's hypothesis is not logically impossible. To see this, assume the common sense hypothesis that by "+" I *did* mean addition. Then it would be *possible,* though surprising, that under the influence of a momentary "high," I should misinterpret all my past uses of the plus as symbolizing the quus function, and proceed, in conflict with my previous linguistic intentions, to compute 68 plus 57 as 5. . . . The sceptic is proposing that I have made a mistake precisely of this kind, but with plus and quus reversed.[27]

If Wittgenstein's argument still seems obscure, here is another way of making it. Suppose a lab technician is charged with murder because he has destroyed a frozen human embryo. The judge must decide whether a frozen embryo, conceived in a test tube, is a human being. The judge's aim is to decide the question consistent with previous usage of the term "human being." Whatever the judge decides, we will not be able to prove him wrong. Since the drafters of the murder statute never thought about frozen embryos, *as a matter of logic,* any decision by the judge is consistent with their usage of the term "human being." Now suppose that John Doe is charged with murdering Jane Doe, his wife. Wittgenstein would argue that the judge in this case is no more compelled, as a matter of logic, to classify Jane Doe as a "human being" than the frozen embryo. After all, the drafters of the murder statute never thought about Jane Doe. If the judge decides Jane was not a human being, we could not prove him wrong. We could not prove that his usage of the term human being is inconsistent with that of the drafters.[28]

The meticulous draftsman who realizes that many familiar rules of law don't logically compel a judge to do anything is onto Wittgenstein's discovery that no rule ever logically compels anyone to do anything. Of course, he fails to realize that if Wittgenstein is right, it won't help to draft rules more scrupulously and to define vague terms more precisely. According to Wittgenstein, even a detailed rule, meticulously defining each of its terms, fails logically to compel those who purport to follow it to do anything.

If Wittgenstein is right, if rules logically don't ever compel us to do anything, why have rules? Whether or not a rule logically compels the answer to a certain question, most people will agree what the right answer is, in other words, what answer accords with the rule. That alone is enough to make the concept of rule a useful one. We may have no logical grounds for disputing that the person who says 68 + 57 is 5 is not following the rule of addition as it was hitherto understood (assuming for a moment that that particular sum had not yet been computed by anyone ever). But the answer "feels wrong" to most others who consider themselves part of the community of adders. Saying that 68 + 57 = 5 fails to conform to the rule of addition is a convenient way of saying that it feels wrong to most adders. We may have no logical grounds for saying that Jane Doe is a human being. But any other answer feels wrong to most other people. Saying that past usage demands that the judge classify Jane Doe as a human being is a convenient way of saying that it feels right to most people.

We now have our reply for the meticulous draftsman who scowls at loose terms like "reasonable" and "good faith." Such terms may seem vacuous; they may seem compatible with any decision. In fact people tend to agree quite closely that they correctly apply to some situations and not to others. There may be no objective way of verifying whether a criminal's guilt has been proved beyond a reasonable doubt, but as long as most men looking at the evidence in most cases can agree that there was or was not reasonable doubt present, the concept remains useful. "Superhuman precision" in defining it is not only unattainable but pointless, and, given the risks of misdescription, counterproductive as well.

When psychologists in the middle of the century began to develop personality tests designed to measure traits like extraversion and introversion, skeptics of the same school as the meticulous draftsman complained that the questions on these tests were too vague. "Do you prefer the company of books to that of people?" a test might ask. Or, "Do you like to go on long walks by yourself?" It seems that anyone could in good conscience give almost any answer to these questions he liked. The most introverted character sometimes prefers the company of *some* people to the company of *some* books. The most extraverted person *some*times likes to go on walks by himself. How did psychologists reply to the criticism? Exactly as Wittgenstein would have them. They admitted the questions were vague, ambiguous, logically indeterminate. Perhaps anyone could in good conscience answer them any way he liked. But in fact the extravert will tend to answer them in one way and the introvert in another. Thus even if the questions are devoid of content they are nevertheless useful.[29]

When Statutes Collide

The Witchcraft Suppression Act prohibits calling someone a witch. It also prohibits the practice of witchcraft. Each of these provisions, taken alone, makes sense. Together they produce an odd result. Although a person may witness somebody practicing witchcraft, he is prohibited from reporting him to the authorities, since the act prohibits calling someone a witch.

Here is a similar absurdity in more modern garb. Unlike most other states, California limits its duress defense to defendants who committed a crime while faced with the threat of death. We may think this rule too conservative—there are arguments pro and con, as the last chapter showed—but it is not absurd. California defines rape as intercourse without the victim's consent. If a woman acquiesces only under threat of serious bodily harm, her consent does not count. There is nothing absurd about that rule either. Finally, California prohibits various forms of deviant sexual conduct, such as sodomy. Even this rule, though perhaps anathema to followers of John Stuart Mill, is not patently absurd. What is patently absurd is the result that all these rules can produce when put together. If a man forces a woman to engage in sodomy under threat of serious bodily harm, she can, of course, press rape charges against him. Her forced submission will not count as consent. But she herself is vulnerable to a charge of sodomy. Now her forced submission will count as consent. She cannot claim to have consented under duress, since duress in California requires a threat of death.[30]

What these examples show is that misdescription is not the only mishap a new statute can run into. Incompatibility is another. A statute does not stand on its own; it is grafted onto an existing body of law. And that body may not be ready for the new implant. Several rules of law, each of which, taken alone, looks eminently sensible, may produce an absurdity when allowed to interact. In fact, misdescription is just a special case of such unfortunate interaction: An approximately correct definition interacts with a perfectly sensible prohibition so as to render it pointless or silly. But misdescription can be cured by adopting a sensible theory of meaning. Many forms of interaction, like the aforementioned, are much more troublesome. They really can't be cured in any other way than an amendment.

One form of interaction is especially troublesome because it is so frequent. Almost every criminal statute overlaps a little with every other criminal statute. Such overlap of two statutes is very easy to find—all one need do is think up a way of violating them both at the same time. Overlaps are disturbing. They make it look as though the defendant is being brought to book twice for a single misdeed. That seems to offend fairness; indeed, it seems to offend the Constitution, which says that no one should be punished twice for the same act. (Literally: No one "shall be subject for the same offense to be twice put in jeopardy of life or limb.")

We are facing an interesting question: Is the person who manages to break two statutes in one fell swoop being punished twice for the same act? Suppose a storeowner sells a fifteen-year-old boy a bottle of Johnny Walker on Sunday. Is it wrong to charge him with selling liquor to a minor *and* with selling liquor on Sunday? Suppose a university official misappropriates government subsidies? Is it wrong to charge him with defrauding the government *and* with misusing government funds? Suppose a man rapes his daughter? Is it wrong to charge him with rape *and* with incest? Suppose a man threatens you with a gun. Is it wrong to charge him with assault with a deadly weapon *and* with possession of an unregistered handgun?

There are compelling arguments on both sides. Let's hear them, as presented in a dialogue between the philosopher's favorite interlocutors, Salviati and Simplicio.

SALVIATI: I have no qualms punishing the defendant for each statute he violated. Why should it matter whether he killed two birds with one stone or with two?

SIMPLICIO: Let's not get entangled in secondary issues. The central question is: Has the defendant, who breaks several statutes at once, committed one or more criminal acts? To me the answer seems clear—just one act. In all of those cases about the liquor store owner, the thief of government funds, the rapist, and the mugger, the defendant has done just one bad thing, which different statutes in their roundabout way say he shouldn't have done. Whether we call it rape or incest, isn't it still the same act of intercourse? Whether we call it fraud or misuse, isn't it still the same money being misappropriated? Whether we call it sale to a minor or sale on Sunday, isn't it the same bottle of Johnny Walker changing hands?

SALVIATI: All right, let's stick to the question whether the defendant has committed one or more acts. But let's be exact about it. The German philosopher Leibniz several centuries ago made the following unremarkable, but helpful and unassailable observation: Two things are identical if they have all of the same properties. Under this criterion of identity, it becomes clear that the person who breaks several statutes simultaneously is committing several acts, not one.[31]

Consider the man who rapes his daughter. The problem with saying the rape and the incest are the same act is that they have different properties. To begin with, they have different causes. The rape would not have happened if the daughter had welcomed her father's advances. The incest would still have happened. So the daughter's resistance is a cause of the rape, but not of the incest. The two acts are also different in the ease with which they can be proved. Incest is easy to prove, requiring only evidence of intercourse. Rape is hard to prove, requiring evidence of nonconsent.

I can see, though, why you made the mistake of thinking the rape and the incest the same act. You are yielding to a certain alluring, but false intuition. When two physical objects occupy the same space at the same time, we know they are identical. We know they share all of the same properties. One's first intuition is that the same is true of events: If two events occupy the same place at the same time, they should be the same; they should share all of their properties. But that's not so. Just think of a rainfall in Chicago and a nightfall in Chicago, both taking place between 8:00 and 8:15 P.M. They happen in the same place at the same time but are quite distinct. Acts are events. The rape and the incest are two events that occupy the same space at the same time. Hence we are inclined to say they are the same act—until we notice that different events can occupy the same place at the same time.

Incidentally, there is a shortcut for deciding whether two events are the same. We don't always have to ask whether the two events share all of their properties, just as we don't always need to ask whether two physical objects share all of their properties before we know they are identical.

To determine whether two physical objects are the same, we need only ask whether they occupy the same place at the same time. The analogous shortcut for events is whether they *necessarily* occupy the same space at the same time. The event of a Chicago nightfall and the event of a Chicago rainfall do not necessarily coincide. By contrast, the event of a rain in Chicago and the event of precipitation in the Windy City necessarily do.

SIMPLICIO: All this metaphysical talk about intangible events occupying space and time is leaving me quite dizzy.

SALVIATI: Now don't start being evasive. We talk about events occupying space and time all the time. Jurisdictional rules turn on *where* events like murders, contracts, and nuisances occur. Statutes of limitation turn on *when* they occur.

SIMPLICIO: Okay, okay. But I don't think your principle of identity, or Leibniz's I should say, makes much sense, however appealing it sounds at first. There's a story by Jorge Luis Borges that will show you how absurd it is.[32]

The story is about the French writer Pierre Menard, who reproduces word-for-word certain portions of Cervantes's *Don Quixote* and then claims to have created an original work of art. The notion strikes us as preposterous, but Borges manages to make a plausible case for it. He points out that the "new" *Don Quixote* is in many respects quite different from, indeed "more subtle" than the "old" *Don Quixote*. Cervantes's book was a contemporary novel; Menard's was a historical novel. Cervantes's book was written in the author's native tongue; Menard's was written in a tongue foreign to its author. Cervantes's book was very much a product of the seventeenth century; Menard's, with its rich allusions to Gustave Flaubert's *Salammbô* and William James's pragmatism, was very much one of the late nineteenth.

This whole story is, of course, nothing but a parody on Leibniz's silly criterion of identity. Because according to that criterion the two *Don Quixotes* really are different.

SALVIATI: Is that really such a silly conclusion? Why not say the two *Don Quixotes* are different? If Andy Warhol places a soup can on a pedestal, we consider it an original work of art, even though it could for decades have been found in any supermarket.

SIMPLICIO: You *are* persistent. Let me make my point in a different way. Do you see that cat sitting on that mat over there? It's called Tibbles. Well, have a good look at Tibbles. When you're done, have another look at Tibbles; but this time focus on everything except one of her hairs. Note that what you are focusing on is still a cat, but according to your Leibniz criterion a different cat. It's not the same as the original Tibbles because it doesn't share all of its properties—it's missing one of Tibbles's hairs. Let's call this second cat "Tibbles the Second." Well, have another look at Tibbles. This time look at everything except some other of its hairs. You are still looking at a cat, but one that is different from both Tibbles and Tibbles the Second, because it doesn't have some of the hairs they have. We could go on and on . . . till we have arrived at Tibbles the One Thousand and First. Would you really insist that there are one thousand and one cats sitting on that mat? But that's what your Leibniz criterion implies.[33]

Indeed, take any act of murder and you run into the same problem. Suppose a man kills his wife with three ax-blows to the head. Let's call this the "three-blow murder." Now focus on everything about his actions except the third blow. What you are focusing on also constitutes a murder. Let's call this the "two-blow murder." Now focus on everything about the murder except the last two blows. What you are focusing on is also a murder. Let's call this the "one-blow murder." According to the Leibniz criterion, those are three different murders. Are you really going to maintain that the defendant has committed three different murders?

SALVIATI: I have to think about that.

SIMPLICIO: While you do, consider this further problem with your position. If you are right, the double jeopardy clause becomes trivial. It loses its bite. It would only apply if the legislature first passed a statute prohibiting, say, intentional killings and then another one prohibiting willful homicides. In other words, only if the legislature happens to rephrase rather precisely a statute already on the books, would it be deemed to punish twice for the same act. And why would it ever do that?

Salviati: Not so fast, Simplicio. That last argument really doesn't work. Even under my approach the double jeopardy clause has plenty of bite. It doesn't just come into play when a new statute rather obviously rephrases an existing one. Let me give you an example.

Suppose a disease breaks out, called the X syndrome. It is falsely reputed to be highly infectious, and victims begin to be fired from their jobs. The government passes a law making it criminal for employers to discriminate against victims of the X syndrome. A little later another disease breaks out, the Y syndrome. It, too, is falsely reputed to be highly infectious, and victims begin to be fired from their jobs. Again, the government makes it criminal for employers to discriminate against Y-syndrome victims. Suppose now an employer fires someone who has been diagnosed as suffering from both the X syndrome and the Y syndrome. It seems, according to our analysis, that he is not being prosecuted for the same act twice, but for two different acts, discriminating against an X-syndrome victim and discriminating against a Y-syndrome victim. But by the time the case goes to trial, scientists discover that the X syndrome and the Y syndrome are really the same disease, the X-Y syndrome, as it comes to be called. It's just that the disease first surfaced among young adults and later among the elderly, and it so happens that the disease's older victims show different symptoms than its younger victims. The two discrimination statutes now turn out to refer to the same disease. If we proceeded to punish the defendant for both violations, we would indeed be punishing him for the same act twice. In this case, the determination that the two statutes cover identical offenses is far from trivial.

Neither Salviati nor Simplicio is really wrong in what he says. It's just that each is arguing for a different notion of identity. One is arguing for logical identity, the other for numerical identity. When we say the morning star is the same as the evening star, we are speaking of logical identity. The two stars are identical in the strict, Leibnizian sense. They share all of their properties. When we say that a certain baby today is identical with a certain man ninety years from now, we are speaking of numerical identity. We do not mean that they share all of their properties—they clearly do not. (These by no means exhaust all notions of identity used in everyday life. There is for instance "qualitative identity," according to which two separate copies of a book are identical, and a harder-to-name form of identity, according to which *Anna Karenina*'s Levin is identical with Tolstoy.) Which kind of identity is relevant to the double jeopardy clause and related questions? It's quite unclear. American law has been very uncertain which notion to endorse. The leading Supreme Court case on the subject, *Blockburger v. United States,* bespeaks this uncertainty.[34]

The Harrison Narcotics Act, a federal statute seeking indirectly to regulate the sale of narcotics, made it an offense to sell certain drugs except in a federally stamped package. It also made it an offense to sell such drugs except "in pursuance to a written order of the person to whom such article is sold . . . on forms to be issued in blank for that purpose by the Commissioner of Internal Revenue."[35] Blockburger was charged with selling drugs that hadn't been stamped and hadn't been ordered through a government form. He complained that he was being punished twice for the same act. The court disagreed: "Each of the offenses created requires proof of a different element. The applicable rule is that where the same act or transaction constitutes a violation of two distinct statutory provisions, the test to be applied to determine whether there are two offenses or only one, is whether each provision requires proof of a fact which the other does not."[36] The test is very close to the Leibniz criterion. Lots of closely overlapping acts will be deemed to be different. On the other hand, it doesn't totally adopt that criterion. For instance, an attempted murder and a murder (defined as an intentional killing) would be deemed the same act under *Blockburger,* but not under the Leibniz criterion.

This problem of how to count, distinguish, or, as the philosophers say, "individuate" acts isn't unique to the double jeopardy clause. It only happens to be more sharply focused there. It recurs throughout the law, whether we try to make sure that the "same" contract breach is only tried once, or that the "same" tort injury is only compensated once, or that the "same" invention is only patented once, or that the "same" sale is only taxed once. Each of these cases raises a puzzle as to the appropriate criterion of "sameness."

The problem of "act individuation" makes for an inevitable clash between statutes. But the clash would not be eliminated if there were only one statute. That statute might still "clash with itself," in the sense that it would often be hard to say whether the defendant's conduct amounts to one or several violations of that statute.

The drafters are apt to misdescribe what they want to forbid. Not necessarily because they're sloppy. They may not know what they mean to forbid well enough to describe it; all they know is that it's harmful. They may think that because the conduct in question is denoted by one word, they can get away with a short, succinct definition; they overlook the fact that a single word often subsumes a vast range of loosely related activities without a single common attribute. They may have tried too hard to be precise; they don't realize that all rules can be willfully misunderstood, that the test of a good rule is that most people acting in good faith will in most situations understand it similarly.

Misdescription tends to render a statute toothless, although it often shouldn't. Courts will apply the statute to the situations it ostensibly describes—sometimes nonexistent—and decline to apply it to those it was really intended to cover. They do so on the basis of a dubious theory of meaning: that what a rule means is always what its drafters think it means. I have tried to show why a judge is not unfaithful to the meaning of a rule when he applies it not to the situations it ostensibly describes but to those it was intended to describe.

The other great drafting mishap is self-contradiction, which may lead to rules that are either outrightly incompatible with each other or at least coexist in tension. A certain amount of tension is inevitable, because statutes are bound to overlap—for no other reason than that it is usually possible to think of a way of violating any two statutes at once. What makes that tension hard to resolve is that there are several competing, seemingly legitimate criteria for individuating criminal acts.

Forgive and Forget

The accused, Fatma Hussein El Bakheit, a twenty-five-year-old woman who lived in the Sudanese village of Un Labona, was renowned far and wide for her healing powers. "It was the belief of the natives of the locality," the Major Court of Sudan explained, "that she was possessed of [a] 'kugur' that diagnosed and cured illness; and that the said 'kugur' was some spirit which enters and possesses accused's body for a while during which accused's body would be a tool obeying the commands of the said spirit towards curing the patients. In order that the spirit possesses her, the accused used to burn and inhale 'Bukhur'—smoky perfume.''[37] The accused herself testified: ''When I am overridden by the 'kugur' I lose realization of anything—it is the 'kugur' who overtakes curing the patients—I [am merely] the medium. I know what happened from attendants after I wake up.'' A man from a neighboring village had brought his wife to see Fatma because she was suffering from stomach pains. As was her custom, Fatma inhaled the Bukhur, lapsed into her trancelike state, and did as the ''kugur'' spirit moved her. When she woke she discovered that she had seized a razor blade and cut the woman's stomach open. The woman had bled to death. Fatma was charged with murder.

Is Fatma a murderer? Let us try to articulate the many dimly felt reasons that might make us hesitate to say so. The most striking aspect of Fatma's story is that she does not remember any of it and, when told about it, is horrified. That alone might make us feel that when we are punishing Fatma, we are not really punishing the person who committed the heinous deed. There is no denying, of course, that that person and Fatma share the same body, but are they the same person? After all, suppose we transplanted person A's brain into person B's body, and vice versa. Who now is the real person A, the one with A's body or the one with A's brain? Surely the latter. A proof of this assertion might run like this: Before we ever switch brains, we announce to A that later on either the A body or the B body would have to suffer some very painful form of torture. Which of the two bodies would A slate to be subjected to this? What if A designated the B body? After the operation is performed, we begin to subject the B body to torture. The B body would probably exclaim, ''Oh, how I regret now telling you to torture the B-body.'' What would happen if A slated the A body to receive the treatment? Now the B body would probably exclaim, ''I sure am glad I told you to torture the A body.'' Such a thought experiment strongly supports the view that personal identity attaches to our brains, not our bodies. The mere fact that Fatma shares a body with the person who killed the woman does not prove that she is identical with that person.[38]

But don't Fatma and the killer share the same brain? True enough, but even that may not guarantee that they are one and the same person. Some recent split-brain experiments have conjured up the possibility that more than one mind may inhabit a single brain. As is well known, the brain divides into two hemispheres. By and large, the left hemisphere is in charge of the right side of the body, the right hemisphere is in charge of the left side. Tactile stimuli picked up by the right side are transmitted to the left hemisphere, those picked up by the left side are transmitted to the right one. Things seen on the right side of one's visual field are registered by the left hemisphere, things seen on the left side are registered by the right one. (Smells and sounds are the exception: they are transmitted ipsilaterally.) The two hemispheres communicate with each other primarily through a large transverse band of nerve fibers called the corpus callosum and some smaller pathways.

The function of the corpus callosum was not appreciated until the late 1950s. Before that time surgeons had severed the corpus callosum of a number of patients as a way of treating epilepsy. At first the incision seemed not to have affected the patient's behavior at all. Laboratory experiments proved this an illusion. In one experiment the word "hat" was flashed to the left half of a patient's visual field. Asked whether he had seen anything, the patient would report that he had seen nothing. But asked to pick out from a table full of objects what he had just seen, his right hand would dutifully retrieve a hat. What had happened? Only the right hemisphere had registered the image. But speech is confined to the left hemisphere. Thus the left hemisphere would verbally deny having perceived anything, while the right hemisphere would nonverbally communicate what it had seen. In a more colorful version of this same experiment the patient was shown the picture of a nude woman on the left half of his visual field. Again the patient would verbally deny seeing anything. Nevertheless, he would begin to giggle, grin, blush, and exclaim something highly inappropriate like: "Wow, that's quite a machine." The right hemisphere evidently fully registered the image. Since the right hemisphere is in charge of emotions, the patient's emotional responses were entirely in keeping with the subject matter. The left hemisphere did not register anything at all, except some scraps of information, sent its way through some secondary pathways. The patient's verbal reactions were correspondingly inappropriate. In other experiments yet, the patient's right nostril was presented with an unpleasant odor. Verbally, the patient would deny smelling anything. Nevertheless, he would make aversive grunts and exclaim "Phew" in evident disgust.[39]

The reason these pecularities remain hidden in ordinary life is that most stimuli present themselves simultaneously to both hemispheres. Yet even in everyday life the brain's bisected nature occasionally manifests itself. When a brain-bisected monkey gets hold of a nut, his two hands, controlled by separate hemispheres, may begin to fight each other for it. And one human patient reported that his left hand appeared to be somewhat hostile to his wife. One might thus well be inclined to describe these brain-bisected patients as really having two minds—two minds occupying the brain space ordinarily inhabited by one. They control different parts of the body; they are ignorant of each other; they have different objectives and different reactions. The same might be said of Fatma. Her brain and body, too, seem to house two creatures, only indirectly aware of each other, never present at the same time, and occasionally at loggerheads.[40]

For these and similar reasons, many philosophers believe that personal identity has nothing to do with physiological continuity: the sameness of the body or the sameness of the brain is only tangential evidence of the sameness of the person. Personal identity, they believe, rests on psychological continuity. John Locke argued that a person today is identical with a person yesterday, if he remembers having the experiences of that person.[41] That formula is a little too crude. Thomas Reid, a near-contemporary of Locke, pinpointed its most glaring shortcoming.

> Suppose a brave officer to have been flogged when a boy at school, for robbing an orchard, to have taken a standard from the enemy in his first campaign, and to have been made a general in advanced life: suppose also, which must be admitted to be possible, that, when he took the standard, he was conscious of his having been flogged at school, and that when made a general he was conscious of his taking the standard, but had absolutely lost the consciousness of his flogging.
>
> These things being supposed, it follows from Mr. Locke's doctrine, that he who was flogged at school is the same person who took the standard, and that he who took the standard is the same person as he who was made a general. Whence it follows, if there be truth in logic, that the general is same person with him who was flogged at school. But the general's consciousness does not reach so far back as his flogging—therefore, according to Mr. Locke's doctrine, he is not the person who was flogged. Therefore the general is, and at the same time is not, the same person with him who was flogged at school.[42]

But one can easily modify the formula to avoid this problem. Personal identity merely requires, one might say, that in the series of experiences that make up a person's history later sections always contain some experiences that are memories of earlier experiences. The gist of this new test is that even if X cannot remember experiencing event E, as long as he remembers a time when he did remember E, E is part of his personal history and he is identical with the person who experienced E.

But what happens when a period is completely blocked out of a person's life? While it lasts, the person cannot remember anything that happened before, and when it is over, he cannot remember anything that happened during it. Fatma experienced just such a blackout, but it was relatively short. Would such a period cease to be part of one's life and become the life of a different person? To appreciate the difficulty of the question, one has to envision much more extended periods of blackout.

They do occur. William James's *Principles of Psychology* describes a number of such cases, the most noteworthy, perhaps, being that of Mary Reynolds, a "dull and melancholy young woman, inhabiting the Pennsylvania wilderness in 1811." She "was found one morning, long after her habitual time for rising, in a profound sleep from which it was impossible to arouse her. After eighteen or twenty hours of sleeping she awakened, but in a state of unnatural consciousness. Memory had fled. To all intents and purposes she was as a being for the first time ushered into the world. All of the past that remained to her was the faculty of pronouncing a few words, and this seems to have been as purely instinctive as the wailings of an infant." She did not recognize her family.[43]

She quickly reacquired the ability to speak, read, and write, but not her memories—and not her personality. "Instead of being melancholy she was now cheerful to extremity. Instead of being reserved she was buoyant and social. Formerly taciturn and retiring, she was now merry and jocose."

This lasted for five weeks, when after another extended sleep she became her former self, with no memory of the intervening period. Over the next few years, she alternated several times between the two states, with continuous memories only within each state. Finally, at age thirty-six, she lapsed into the second state and remained in it for the remaining twenty-five years of her life. On the day of her death, at age sixty-one, she "rose in the morning in her usual health, ate her breakfast, and superintended household duties. While thus employed, she suddenly raised her hands to her head and exclaimed 'Oh! I wonder what is the matter with my head!' and immediately fell to the floor. When carried to a sofa, she gasped once or twice and died."

James Hilton wove a novel, *Random Harvest*, around a case just like this.[44] A man wakes up in a military hospital in Germany. He knows that he is a British prisoner-of-war, and he recalls being blown up by a shell;

he can remember no more. So when he returns to Britain, he starts life afresh. He takes the name Smith, embarks on a promising career in journalism, and marries a sprightly girl named Paula. But, one rainy day in Liverpool, on his way to a job interview, as he hurries across the pavement, he takes a fall.

When he comes to, he suddenly remembers his past. He remembers that he is Charles Rainier, scion of a large manufacturing dynasty, that he has led his regiment into a valiant but hopeless battle, that he was rocked by a violent explosion. But thereafter he remembers nothing.

He goes home to resume his prior exalted position in life and eventually takes over the family business. But he is only partly happy. The mental gap of those forgotten years is a perennial source of discomfort to him. He has a brief, unsatisfying dalliance with his niece, a woman he feels to be "almost right" for him, but not quite. She reminds him of someone he cannot remember. Ultimately, he marries his secretary, a Miss Hanson, more as a matter of default, it seems, than love. Miss Hanson makes Charles an even greater social success. She entertains lavishly, helps him make valuable contacts, and is instrumental in his election to Parliament. He would now be happy, but for the fact that his memory gap continues to nag, haunt, obsess him.

Then suddenly, one day something jogs his memory: he sees a play he last saw in his shell-shocked state. Suddenly he is able to remember his life as Smith, his career as a journalist, and his marriage to Paula. Quite distraught, he launches a search for Paula—only to discover that she and Miss Hanson are one and the same.

An amnesia of this kind very nearly became an issue in the prosecution of Rudolf Hess, one of the defendants at the Nuremberg war crimes trial.[45] Hess was one of Hitler's earliest and most faithful followers, the man to whom he dictated *Mein Kampf*. When Hitler assumed power in 1933, he appointed Hess deputy führer, second in line only to Goering.

Shortly thereafter, Hess's career stagnated. He apparently fell prey to numerous psychosomatic "superstitions and obsessions." He suffered from various psychosomatically induced ailments: colitis, imaginary gall and kidney stones, and angina. He had a pervasive fear of cancer and had many teeth pulled as a precaution against it. He never ate out without bringing along his own supply of "biologically dynamic" ingredients. Unhappy with his doctors, he surrounded himself with soothsayers and astrologers.

In 1941, he decided to stake his life on one great deed. Hitler, he knew, was preparing to attack Russia. Yet the war with England was dangerously unfinished. Hess thought he was the man to finish it. One fine spring day, Hess climbed into one of his airplanes, and without bothering to ask Hitler, flew to England to negotiate peace, that is, to persuade the British to accept the terms of Hitler's peace proposals. Instead of accepting, the British arrested him, and Hess spent the rest of the war on a tightly guarded country estate.

There he grew stranger by the day. He suspected the world of trying to poison him, would in the course of meals demand to exchange plates with other officers dining with him, and would squirrel away food for later chemical analysis. His breaking point came, when he heard about the attempt on Hitler's life, in which his closest friend in Germany had participated and died. He claimed to be unable to recall most of his past and grew amnesic even from day to day.

Uncertain of his mental status, the British nonetheless decided to join him as a defendant at Nuremberg. He continued to plead amnesia. An American interrogator, Colonel Amen, convinced he was shamming, questioned him closely the morning of his arrival:

> "Do you remember that you used to be in Germany?" Amen addressed Hess, who was clad in the same flying jacket and flying boots he had worn to England and refused to discard.
>
> "Well I think that is self-understood, because I have been told so repeatedly, but I don't remember. It has all disappeared. It is gone." . . .
>
> "But don't you know what the proceeding is for?"
>
> "I have no idea."

Later on Amen confronted Hess with old acquaintances like Goering, in an effort to jolt his memory, but to no apparent avail.

> "Don't you know me?" Goering asked.
>
> "Who are you?" Hess was startled.
>
> . . . .
>
> "Listen, Hess, I was the supreme commander of the Luftwaffe, and you flew to England in one of my planes." Goering was irritated that he could not elicit the proper acknowledgment of his own importance from Hess. "Don't you remember I was the supreme commander of

> the Luftwaffe? First, I was a field marshal, and later a Reichsmarshal! Don't you remember?''
>
> ''No.''
>
> ''Do you remember that the Fuehrer at a meeting of the Reichstag announced that if something happened to him that I would be his successor and if something happened to me you were to be the successor. Don't you remember that?''
>
> ''No.''

A little later Goering asked him if he remembered Hitler.

> ''Well, I know what he looks like. I had a picture in my room.''
>
> ''Do you remember his manner of speech?''
>
> ''His picture didn't speak, so I don't remember his speech.''

The Nuremberg tribunal never actually had to address the potentially troublesome issue of whether or not a defendant could be convicted in the face of such complete and extensive amnesia. Hess was told by an American psychologist that he would probably be ruled incompetent to defend himself and would thus be separated from his codefendants and no longer allowed to attend the trial. Having been in an alien country for several years, he apparently found the thought of being isolated from his compatriots intolerable. He got up and, reading a barely coherent statement from a slip of paper, announced that he had merely simulated amnesia and wanted to stand trial next to his comrades. The tribunal accepted the statement at face value and Hess's amnesia never actually became an issue.

Yet it is far from certain that Hess was indeed shamming. Throughout the trial he continued to exhibit shocking lapses of memory from day to day. His behavior became ever more bizarre. When his sentence was read to him, he did not even bother to put on his earphones. He left the courtroom under the erroneous impression that, like most of the other defendants, he had been sentenced to death.

The three stories show both why it is tempting and why it is troubling to say that Fatma-the-woman and Fatma-the-healer were two different creatures inhabiting the same body and that Fatma-the-woman should not be blamed for the misdeeds of Fatma-the-healer. It is tempting because, as the three stories illustrate, it is possible for the same physical entity to lead two very separate lives. It is troubling for several reasons.

1. Although Charles Rainier and Rudolph Hess were severely amnesic, unlike Miss Reynolds, they showed substantial continuity of character. Can one speak of two persons when there aren't even two personalities?

2. None of the three amnesiacs showed complete amnesia. Charles Rainier and Rudolph Hess retained most of their basic skills. And while Mary Reynolds forgot how to read or write, surely she retained some rudimentary skills, and a subliminal grasp of some not-so-rudimentary skills. How else could she relearn reading and writing so quickly? In fact, amnesia usually only affects "episodic" memories. But are episodic memories the crucial, identity-determining ones? Besides, is there even a meaningful distinction between episodic and nonepisodic memories?

3. What are we to do when the person living one life remembers his other life? Do the two identities suddenly merge? That is, did Smith and Rainier suddenly become one person again?

4. If someone were to tell you that he would subject you tomorrow to some terrible pain, but that he would first induce in you complete amnesia about who you were, would that put your fears to rest? Would Charles Rainier not have feared injury on the battlefield, if he had been told that it would be accompanied by amnesia? Would the young Rudolf Hess not have minded the prospect of a war crimes trial, if he had been told that by the time he went to trial he would not remember his past? Put differently, would they have felt about these things the way one feels about indignities one's corpse might suffer?[46]

5. Whether a person is sufficiently amnesic for certain earlier experiences not to count as *his* experiences seems a matter of degree. If we decide that Smith and Charles Rainier are different persons, surely we aren't going to change our mind, if it turns out that Charles Rainier has one tiny recollection relating to Smith's life. How substantial a recollection is required to make us change our mind? That's hard to say. We only know that the more substantial the recollection, the more disinclined we will be to view Smith and Rainier as different persons.

That gives rise to a problem. If somebody asks you whether the person who inherits your eyes (via a transplant, say) after the rest of your body has ceased functioning is "you," you would say no. If somebody asks you whether the person who inherits your brain (via some futuristic transplant, say) after the rest of your body has ceased functioning is "you,"

you would say yes. Indeed, whenever somebody confronts you with some scenario and asks you whether the person in that scenario is "you," whether his pain is your pain, whether his death will be your death, you will have some precise answer for him—yes or no. It will never be a matter of degree. You will never say, "Somewhat." But if personal identity is not a matter of degree, how can amnesia, which is a matter of degree, be the key to it?[47]

None of these objections is fatal. One might reply to the first that psychological continuity short of memory isn't enough for personal identity. Otherwise we might be justified in punishing one twin brother for the deeds of the other. One might reply to the second that psychologists have discovered the distinction between episodic and nonepisodic memory to have a firm physiological basis. So it's not such an abstruse distinction.[48] To the third, fourth and fifth one might reply that just because the thesis has some counterintuitive implications doesn't prove it's wrong.[49] (To be persuasive, of course, all of this requires elaboration.)

Some philosophers, like Ludwig Wittgenstein, would insist that questions such as whether Fatma-the-woman and Fatma-the-healer are the same person just don't have an answer. "Our actual use of the phrase 'the same person' and of the name of a person," he observes, "is based on the fact that many characteristics which we use as the criteria for identity coincide in the vast majority of cases."[50] It is based on the fact that ordinarily sameness of body goes along with sameness of brain and continuity of memory. In cases like that of Mary Reynolds, Charles Rainier, Rudolf Hess, or Fatma El Bakheit that does not hold true. Wittgenstein constructed his own example. "Imagine a man whose memories on the even days of his life comprise the events of all these days, skipping entirely what happened on odd days. On the other hand, he remembers on an odd day what happened on previous odd days, but his memory then skips the even days without a feeling of discontinuity. If we like we can also assume that he has alternating appearances and characteristics on odd and even days." Wittgenstein then asks, "Are we bound to say that here two persons are inhabiting the same body? That is, is it right to say that there are, and wrong to say that there aren't?" Wittgenstein's answer is "Neither." The concept was simply not designed to answer such questions. Its application presupposes that the various hallmarks of identity—sameness of body, sameness of brain, continuity of memory—all coalesce. When they don't, we cannot say that we are or that we are not dealing with the same person.

The fact is that extraordinary circumstances like those epitomized by the cases of Mary Reynolds, Charles Rainier, and Rudolf Hess occur very rarely, if at all. What occurs more frequently are occasional blackouts. These don't call for anything more than a slight straining of our ordinary concept of personal identity. Hence, not surprisingly the judicial consensus has been that amnesia, by itself, does not negate a defendant's responsibility. And yet several courts have been sufficiently disturbed by the phenomenon to declare that a defendant who cannot remember his crime is therefore unfit to stand trial until he can.[51]

Those Who Know Not What They Do

If we hesitate to punish Fatma, it is not merely because of her amnesia. We hesitate because she seemed "possessed." Am I suggesting that the kugur spirit possessed her and is to blame for the murder? Astonishingly enough, there are cases in which the defendants did try to blame supernatural forces for their misdeeds. *Regina v. Matengula* is one such case. The defendants, four African natives of the Lamba tribe, were pallbearers at a funeral. As the victim approached the coffin, it began to move, rammed him three times, and knocked him dead. The defendants introduced evidence of a Lamba belief that this was the way in which a deceased avenged himself on the person responsible for his death. They steadfastly maintained that although they had been carrying the coffin at the time the blows were struck, it was the coffin itself which had by some supernatural means done the act complained of. The judge, needless to say, brushed this defense aside. I am not suggesting that this is what happened to Fatma.[52]

What I am suggesting is that Fatma's case is but one of a motley variety of cases in which courts have acquitted defendants because they acted in a state of unconsciousness. A classic pronouncement of this kind is found in a century-old Kentucky case called *Fain v. Commonwealth*.[53] The defendant, Fain, and his friend, Welch, "went to the Veranda Hotel after dark on an evening in February. The weather was cold, and there was snow upon the ground. They sat down in the public room and went to sleep." Welch awoke a short time later, and, seeing the hotel porter in the barbershop next door asked him for a bed for Fain and himself. He tried to awaken Fain but failed to rouse him. He then turned to the porter and asked him to try to awaken his friend. The man walked up to Fain, seized him by his coat lapels, and started to shake him. Fain did not react. At Welch's suggestion he shook Fain harder and harder. Finally, Fain seemed to be coming to. He grumbled that he wanted to be left alone. The porter protested that "it was getting late, and he wanted to close the house." Then, suddenly, while the porter was still holding him by his coat lapels, Fain leaped up from his chair and drew a pistol from his pocket. A bystander screamed "Don't shoot." "But without noticing or giving any sign that he had heard what was said," Fain fired at the porter. The "porter instantly grappled him to prevent him from shooting again, but a second shot was fired almost immediately, and a third soon followed." After the third shot was fired, the porter managed to throw Fain down. Fain "hallooed hoo-wee very loud two or three times and called for Welch. He asked the [porter] to let him get up; but [the man] said 'If I do, you will shoot me again.' [Fain] said he would not, and [the man] released his hold and allowed him to get up. Upon getting up [Fain] went out of the room with the pistol in his hand. His manner was that of a frightened man. He said to a witness: 'Take my pistol and defend me'; said he had shot someone, but did not know who it was, and upon being told who it was, expressed sorrow for what he had done." Shortly thereafter the porter died of his wounds.

At his trial Fain "offered to prove that he had been a sleepwalker from his infancy; that he had to be watched to prevent injury to himself; that he was put to sleep in a lower room, near that of his parents, and a servant-man required to sleep in the room to watch him; that frequently when aroused from sleep, he seemed frightened, and attempted violence as if resisting an assault, and for some minutes seemed unconscious of what he did or what went on around him; that sometimes when partly asleep, he resisted the servant who slept in the room with him; as if he supposed the servant was assaulting him." By 1879, there existed, surprisingly enough, already a wealth of medical authority attesting to the genuineness of a sleepwalking defense. The authorities acknowledged that a subject in a state of somnambulism—defined as the "lapping over of a profound sleep into the domain of apparent wakefulness"—enjoys "not only the power of locomotion . . . , as the etymology of the term signifies, but the voluntary muscles are capable of executing motions of the most delicate kind. Thus, the somnambulist will walk securely on the edge of a precipice, saddle his horse, and ride off at gallop; walk on stilts over a swollen torrent; practice airs on a musical instrument; in short, he may read, write, run, leap, climb, and swim, as well as, and sometimes even better than, when fully awake." But though seemingly awake and alert, they added, the subject is in fact in a state of "involuntary intoxication, which for the time destroys moral agency." They concluded: "As the somnambulist does not enjoy the free and rational exercise of his understanding, and is more or less unconscious of his outward relations, none of his acts during the paroxysms can rightfully be imputed to him as crimes." The court agreed. "It is one of the fundamental principles of the criminal law," the court explained, "that there can be no criminality in the absence of criminal intentions." If the jury found that Fain "was . . . unconscious when he fired the first shot, or the first and second, . . . and regained consciousness before he fired the second or third shot . . . [but] believed in good faith that he was in danger of losing his life or of sustaining great bodily injury," it was to acquit him.

An even more spectacular example of a sleepwalking crime occurred more recently in Canada.[54] Mrs. Cogdon had a nineteen-year-old daughter, Pat, who was still living at home. One evening during the Korean War, while her husband was out, Mrs. Cogdon had a dream that "the war was all around the house, that soldiers were in Pat's room, and that one soldier was on the bed attacking Pat." This was the only point of the dream she could later remember. The next thing she remembered—no longer part of the dream—was running from Pat's room, out of the house to the house of her sister next door. "When her sister opened the front door Mrs. Cogdon fell into her arms crying, 'I think I've hurt Patti.' " What in fact had happened was that Mrs. Cogdon, still asleep, had gotten up, fetched an axe from the woodpile, entered Pat's room, and with two well-aimed blows on the head with the axe blade killed her almost instantly. Mrs. Cogdon had a history of turbulent dreams and sleepwalking. She was acquitted.

Nor is sleepwalking the only recognized form of unconscious, and therefore innocent, "criminal" behavior. Huey Newton, the well-known Black Panther leader, was stopped one night by a policeman. An altercation ensued.[55] Newton drew a gun, and soon he and the policeman, John Frey, were locked in a scuffle for its possession. In the course of the struggle the gun went off and wounded another policeman, Heanes, standing nearby. Heanes fired back and shot Newton in the stomach. The wound sent Newton into a near-frenzy. He succeeded in wresting the gun away from Frey, then fired several shots at him point-blank, and ran away. Shortly afterwards Newton turned up at a hospital emergency room. He was arrested and charged with the voluntary manslaughter of John Frey.

At his trial, Newton testified that he had carried no gun. According to his account, the struggle began when Frey drew a revolver. Shortly thereafter, he felt a

> "sensation like . . . boiling hot soup had been spilled on my stomach," and heard an "explosion," then a "volley of shots." He remembered a "crawling . . . moving sensation," but nothing else until he found himself at the entrance of Kaiser Hospital with no knowledge of how he arrived there. He expressly testified that he was "unconscious or semiconscious" during this interval, that he was "still only semiconscious" at the hospital entrance, and that—after recalling some events at Kaiser Hospital—he later "regained consciousness" at another hospital.[56]

The defense produced an expert witness, a doctor, who explained that a "gunshot wound which penetrates in a body cavity, the abdominal cavity or the thoracic cavity is very likely to produce a profound reflex reaction, that is quite different than a gunshot wound which penetrates only skin and muscle and it is not at all uncommon for a person shot in the abdomen to lose consciousness and go into this reflex shock condition for short periods of time up to half an hour or so." The court agreed that if the jury found Newton to have been in such an unconscious state, he should be acquitted.

The case that attracted the greatest amount of popular attention to the subject of unconscious crimes was the trial of Jack Ruby, the assassin of Lee Harvey Oswald. The Dallas police department was in the process of transferring Oswald from his jail in the Dallas Police and Courts Building to the Dallas County Jail, where he would await trial. It had taken extensive measures for Oswald's protection. An armored truck, ostensibly intended to afford Oswald maximum protection on his fifteen-block trip to the county jail, was being used as a decoy. A heavily manned police convoy was in charge of the actual transport. The basement garage through which Oswald would be led had been emptied of all cars. At 11:20 A.M. a handcuffed Oswald, flanked by two detectives, emerged from the jail office and began his short walk toward the convoy. He was staring fixedly ahead, ignoring all onlookers. Just as he passed in front of the television cameras, an unremarkable looking man in a conservative business suit and dark felt hat lunged toward him, shouted, "You son of a bitch," and fired a single fatal shot at him. Jack Ruby had killed Oswald in full view of the television cameras.[57]

Ruby's defense was handled by Melvin Belli, then America's most renowned trial lawyer. It was Belli's contention that his client was suffering from epilepsy, that the emotional stress of Oswald's appearance had triggered in him an epileptic seizure, in the course of which—utterly unconscious of what he was doing—he had killed Oswald. A battery of psychological and neurological tests strongly supported a finding of some organic brain damage, which, at least in the opinion of some of the experts who testified, suggested epilepsy. Myriads of witnesses also supported the view that Ruby, a Dallas nightclub owner, had, to say the least, a somewhat eccentric personality. He had an almost pathological attachment to his dogs, a homosexual attraction to President Kennedy, and was given to fixed stares and emotional outbursts. It was also clear that he had not been planning to kill Oswald. Ruby always carried a gun with him. The precise time of Oswald's transfer was known to no one in advance, and only a couple of minutes before Oswald's appearance, Ruby had wired a money order from a telegraph office nearby. His presence at Oswald's transfer was thus clearly fortuitous.

Unfortunately for Belli's defense, Ruby had never before suffered an epileptic seizure. Nor did Ruby's conduct during the incident seem in any way trancelike. The most Belli was able to establish was that Ruby was holding the gun a little awkwardly, in particular that he had squeezed the trigger with his middle rather than index finger, which seemed a very clumsy way to shoot. In fact, a forensic expert testified that experienced shots know that firing at close range is best done with one's middle finger. What undid Ruby's defense was the testimony of the two detectives flanking Oswald. According to them, Ruby had shouted, just as he had been wrestled to the ground, "I hope the son of a bitch dies." And a little later he had complained that the police had moved too fast—he had meant to shoot three times, but could only get off one shot. These remarks directly contradicted Ruby's claim that he had been unconscious of what he was doing. However many psychiatric experts the defense was able to summon, it could not overcome those facts. The jury deliberated only a little over two hours, before it found Ruby guilty and sentenced him to death.

We have no difficulty analogizing Fatma's state of "possession" to Mrs. Cogdon's somnambulism, Huey Newton's shock-induced frenzy, or Jack Ruby's putative epileptic fit. We have a bit more difficulty explaining the character of that state. Courts have tended to say very casually that the defendant here is unconscious. More than one critic has found that description thoughtless and potentially pernicious. Surely, the philosopher Irving Thalberg has pointed out, Mrs. Cogdon was conscious "to the extent that she had enough perceptual contact with her surroundings to get an ax and reach her daughter's room. Moreover, would she report that she had hurt her daughter if she was totally unaware of what transpired? No, and thus her report is evidence of some form of consciousness."[58] Not that Mrs. Cogdon was in a normal, waking, conscious state, but she was not in an unconscious state either, Thalberg argues.

Has Thalberg correctly characterized consciousness? He is, in effect, suggesting that consciousness is a matter of being in better or worse "perceptual contact" with one's surroundings. That doesn't seem right. We can be in very poor perceptual contact with our surroundings, yet totally conscious: Suppose you are blindfolded, gagged, and chained, and have no idea where you are. Suppose further you are amnesic and have no idea who you are. You may be out of touch with your surroundings, but hardly unconscious.

Conversely, we can be in excellent perceptual contact with our surroundings, yet quite unconscious of what we are doing. In fact, almost anything we do, however skillful, we do in part unconsciously. Suppose I showed you two superficially similar photographs, one of a person you've never seen, the other of a close friend. You would instantly identify your friend, but would you be able to say how the two faces are different?[59] You may be an expert typist, but can you say straightaway what finger you use to type a *q*—without first consciously going through the motions? Imagine you look in the rear-view mirror of your car and you see a truck approaching. Do you first consciously reason: The truck seems to be approaching me from the front, but this is a mirror, hence it must really be coming up from behind? No, you never consciously draw any inference. You just realize that the truck is coming up from behind. You could do none of these things—recognize a face, type a *q*, locate an approaching car—without being in perceptual touch with your environment, and yet you do them for the most part unconsciously.

When we are most in touch with our environment, we are often least conscious of what we are doing. Ask someone to sit down with you and say as many words as he can think of, stopping after every one for a few seconds, so you can take them down. Every time he utters a noun, tell him "good" or "right" or "mm-hm," or repeat the word in a pleasant manner—in other words, imperceptibly show your approval. Within a short time the number of nouns uttered will rise dramatically. Question the subject, and you'll find that he has no idea of what he was doing. Although supersensitive to your approval or disapproval, he never realized that he was catering to it.[60]

Everyday examples of this phenomenon abound. The psychology professor at a girl's college asked his students to compliment any girl wearing red. Within a week the cafeteria was a blaze of red, yet none of the girls was aware of being influenced. A class at the University of Minnesota tried the method on their psychology professor. They laughed and paid rapt attention whenever he moved toward the exit. Within no time they had very nearly conditioned him out of the door.[61] The behaviorist B. F. Skinner tried the method on his adversary, the psychoanalyst Erich Fromm. Fromm was giving a lecture at an academic symposium attended by Skinner. Fromm, Skinner wrote,

> proved to have something to say about almost everything, but with little enlightenment. When he began to argue that people were not pigeons, I decided that something had to be done. On a scrap of paper I wrote "Watch Fromm's left hand. I am going to shape a chopping motion" and passed it down the table to [a colleague]. Fromm was sitting directly across from the table and speaking mainly to me. I turned my chair slightly so that I could see him out of the corner of my eye. He gesticulated a great deal as he talked, and whenever his left arm came up, I looked straight at him. If he brought the hand down, I nodded and smiled. Within five minutes he was chopping the air so vigorously that his wristwatch kept slipping out over his hand.[62]

Even when we think long and hard about our environment, we may do so unconsciously, as shown by Norman Maier's ingenious two-string experiment. Maier hung two strings from the ceiling of his laboratory. He asked his subjects to tie the two strings together. The problem was that the strings were very far apart. While holding on to one string a person couldn't reach the other. The trick to solving the problem was to attach a weight to one string, make it swing, and catch it while holding on to the other string. Few of the subjects thought of this. Then Maier tried dropping a hint. He brushed past one of the strings and set it swinging. Soon the subjects were on to the solution. On questioning, however, only a third of them identified the swinging as the clue. They were obviously scrutinizing their environment attentively for any clue it might offer, but they did so unconsciously.[63]

In sum, consciousness seems dispensable for the execution of most tasks. Julian Jaynes, a Princeton psychologist, has even speculated that for most of his history man has survived without consciousness altogether and survived quite well. It is no accident, Jaynes believes, that the Iliad, the Odyssey, the Gilgamesh Epic, and early portions of the Old Testament never so much as hint at the inner life of their human protagonists. They are action flicks in a purer and more thoroughgoing way than even a Mickey Spillane thriller. They show their heroes performing all kinds of valiant deeds, but they never show them engaged in any sort of conscious reflection. According to Jaynes, that's because as recently as four thousand years ago the human brain looked different from today. It did not, he says, permit conscious thought.[64]

If consciousness is not simply awareness of one's surroundings, what is it? What do sleepwalkers, epileptics, or frenzy-killers lack that makes us call them unconscious? Let's begin with the simpler case of a person who isn't unconscious but who is doing certain things unconsciously: the person who unconsciously increases the number of nouns he utters or the person who unconsciously solves a puzzle. In what sense are they acting unconsciously? They are acting unconsciously not because they aren't aware of their surroundings—they are all too aware of them, reacting to the subtlest signs of approval and the gentlest of clues—but because they aren't aware just how aware they are of their surroundings. They are wide awake to their outer environment; they are only dimly awake to their inner environment: they notice certain things, but they don't notice that they notice. The person who is unconscious in the more general sense exhibits this disability on a grander scale. The sleepwalker is unaware not just of a specific aspect of his inner environment, he's unaware of most of it; he is unaware not only of having picked up little hints, he is unaware of having picked up a rock. He may see, hear, touch, believe, or think certain things, but he doesn't realize that he is seeing, hearing, touching, believing, or thinking anything. He's aware of everything except himself.[65]

That may sound very paradoxical. How can a person have sensations but not know that he has those sensations? Can we have pain and not notice it? Can we see something and not know it? Can we taste something and not realize it? As a matter of fact, we can do each of these things. It's possible to have pain and not notice. In a recent movie, the waiter pours some coffee, laced with lye, into a mafioso's cup. The mafioso's face is suffused with a relaxed smile as he languidly takes a few sips from the cup. The relaxed smile gives way to surprise, the surprise to puzzlement, the puzzlement to panic, the panic to anger. So surprised is he by the assault that it takes him what seems to the spectator like an eternity before he realizes the pain he is in. There is a moment in time, then, when he has pain, but does not notice it. Not so, you might object. He doesn't have the pain until he notices it. But that doesn't square with what he would tell you. He would say: "I drank the cup, felt this strange sensation, and then, ohmygod, I realized what that sensation was—it was like my mouth was on fire." Undoubtedly, you've had similar experiences yourself—experiences where you bumped your shin against a sharp corner and only realized moments later that the piercing sensation you felt was pain. It is also possible to see something and not know it. Certain kinds of brain damaged persons profess to be blind even though their visual apparatus is unimpaired. Moreover, they are able to "guess" where an object is with nearly perfect accuracy. It seems appropriate of them to say that they can see the object, but they do not know they see it.[66] Finally, it's possible to taste something and not realize that you tasted it. Lime sherbet tastes very similar to orange sherbet. In blindfold experiments people will frequently misclassify a lime as orange sherbet. But if they are given a real orange sherbet afterwards they will immediately retract their identification. Evidently, they are having the taste sensation of lime, but they aren't aware that that's what it is. Nor could it be through self-suggestion that they made themselves experience the taste sensation of orange, because then they wouldn't revise their judgment after tasting real orange sherbet.[67]

Of course the idea is counterintuitive, but it isn't illogical. To see if you have grasped it, test your wits against this ingenious brain teaser invented by the logician Raymond Smullyan.

> Inspector Craig of Scotland Yard was called over to France to investigate eleven insane asylums where it was suspected that something was wrong. In each of these asylums, the only inhabitants were patients and doctors—the doctors constituted the entire staff. Each inhabitant of each asylum, patient or doctor, was either sane or insane. Moreover, the sane ones were totally sane and a hundred percent accurate in all their beliefs; all true propositions they knew to be true and all false propositions

> they knew to be false. The insane ones were totally inaccurate in their beliefs; all true propositions they believed to be false and all false propositions they believed to be true. It is to be assumed also that all the inhabitants were always honest—whatever they said, they really believed.[68]

Craig visits one such asylum and asks an inhabitant: "Are you a patient?" The man replies "Yes." Is there anything wrong with this asylum? Pause, reflect, then read on. There is indeed. If this is a patient who said yes, then he must be sane. Insane patients don't believe that they are patients. If this is a doctor, then he must be insane. Sane doctors know they are doctors. In either case there is something wrong with the asylum. Later Inspector Craig tries the question on the inhabitant of another asylum. He again asks the man: "Are you a patient?" This time the patient replies: "I believe so." Is there anything wrong with *this* asylum? Pause, reflect, then read on. It may seem that this is the same puzzle I just gave, all over again. But it isn't. There is nothing necessarily wrong with this asylum. An insane patient could perfectly well respond, "I believe so." If he is a patient, he will not believe he is a patient. *But if he does not believe he is a patient, he will also believe that he does believe he is a patient.* (Insane people always believe the opposite of what is true.) Hence he might say, "I believe so." The puzzle is hard because it seems so utterly counterintuitive to suppose of anyone that he can believe something, yet not believe that he believes it. It's counterintuitive, but not impossible. Think again of the person with blind sight. Of him we can say that he believed an object to be located at a certain spot, but he didn't believe that he believed that.

Caught in the Act

Just why is it that Fatma's unconsciousness is grounds for acquitting her of responsibility for an act she so evidently committed? Are cases like hers simply *sui generis,* and does her innocence rest on no more general a principle than that unconscious acts should not be punished? The courts that have passed on such cases rest their decision on a broader principle: The quintessential requirement for criminal liability is that the defendant have committed a criminal act. An unconscious act, they say, is no act at all.

How can that be? If Mrs. Cogdon raises her ax, takes careful aim, and severs her daughter's head, she has done precisely what the statute proscribes. Isn't that a criminal act? Not necessarily. It clearly is possible to seem to run afoul of a criminal statute and yet not commit an act. *Martin v. State* is an obvious instance of such a case.[69] An Alabama statute provided that "any person who, while intoxicated or drunk, appears in any public place where one or more persons are present . . . and manifests a drunken condition by boisterous or indecent conduct, or loud and profane discourse, shall, on conviction, be fined." For reasons not revealed in the case, Martin was arrested in his house. He had been drinking. On his way to the police station he apparently let fly a profanity or two. He was prosecuted under the Alabama statute for "manifesting a drunken condition." The court acquitted him. True, Martin was drunk. True also, he had uttered some profanities. But he had not, the court noted, appeared in public of his own free will. He was "involuntarily and forcibly carried to that place by the arresting officers." Though ostensibly in violation of the statute, the defendant had not actually performed an *act*. And without a criminal act he could not be convicted.

A similar case is that of Miss Larsonneur. Article 18(1)(b) of Britain's Aliens Order made it a criminal offense for a alien to be "found" in the United Kingdom without permission. As one commentator elegantly sums up the case, "Miss Larsonneur was a French woman who, it is said, worked more by night than by day. She decided to come to England, possibly in an endeavour to acquire a sufficient dowry to return to a happy Continental marriage. She was given permission to land in England. Later, the propriety of her means of livelihood being doubted, she was required to leave. Anxious not to commit an offense she promptly traveled to the Irish Free State. Far from being welcomed there, she was arrested and handed back in custody to the English police. She was then, by skilful detection, 'found' in the United Kingdom—in a cell."[70] She was prosecuted for violating Article 18(1)(b) of the Aliens Order. The British Court of Criminal Appeals was less perspicacious than the Alabama Court of Appeals and convicted her. But the commentators are virtually unanimous that although in violation of the literal terms of the statute, Miss Larsonneur should have been acquitted because she never committed a criminal act. As in the case of Martin, things happened to her that put her in violation of the statute. She did not actually do anything to violate it. To convict Miss Larsonneur suggests, one writer observed, that "an alien without leave to land might have been held liable even if he had parachuted into the United Kingdom from an aeroplane against his will."[71]

Cases where one is physically manipulated into violating a statute are not the only ones where one has failed to act. A California criminal statute used to make it a criminal offense for a person to "be addicted to the use of narcotics.''[72] The statute, as the Supreme Court observed in a case called *Robinson v. California* ''is not one which punishes a person for the use of narcotics, for their purchase, sale, or possession or for antisocial or disorderly behavior resulting from their administration.'' It is rather like a statute making it a criminal offense to be ''mentally ill, or a leper, or to be afflicted with a venereal disease.'' It punishes a condition—one which is often involuntarily acquired—not an act. To punish for a condition rather than an act amounts to cruel and unusual punishment.

The case is not as obvious as the court suggests. It's not so easy to accept the court's analogy between leprosy and addiction. Addiction can be avoided, leprosy cannot. If one does accept the analogy, it is improper not only to punish a man for being an addict but for using drugs. After all, the compulsive use of drugs is only a symptom of the addiction. In fact, this very argument was urged before the court in the follow-up case *Powell v. Texas*.[73] This time the disease involved was not narcotics addiction, but alcoholism. The statute in question, passed by the Texas legislature, did not make alcoholism per se an offense. That would clearly be unconstitutional under *Robinson*. It merely punished ''whoever shall get drunk or be found in a state of intoxication in any public place, or at any private house, except his own.'' Leroy Powell, charged under the statute, argued that he was ''afflicted with the disease of chronic alcoholism,'' ''that his appearance in public was not of his own volition,'' and that, under *Robinson,* it would be cruel and unusual to punish him. The court was badly splintered over the merits of this argument. A minority of four thought the argument irrebuttable. A majority of five proceeded to rebut it. Justice White conceded that it made no sense to distinguish between punishing someone for being an alcoholic and punishing him for yielding to the irresistible urge to drink. ''Distinguishing between the two crimes,'' he said, ''is like forbidding criminal conviction for being sick with flue or epilepsy but permitting punishment for running a fever or having a convulsion.'' But the Texas statute, he pointed out, did not punish getting drunk per se but getting drunk outside one's own house. ''The sober chronic alcoholic has no compulsion to be on the public streets, many chronic alcoholics drink at home and are never seen drunk in public.''[74] He concluded: ''On such facts the alcoholic is like a person with smallpox who could be convicted for being on the street but not for being ill, or like the epileptic, punishable for driving a car but not for his disease.'' Some of the justices sought to escape the dilemma by asserting, somewhat implausibly, that there was no proof that alcoholism produced an irresistible urge to drink. Justice Black, finally, thought that it was not necessarily cruel and unusual to punish the defendant for conduct he could not control.

So more is required of a criminal than offending the literal words of a statute. He must commit an act. What is an act? In what way did Martin, Miss Larsonneur, perhaps even Robinson and Powell, and the unconscious killers fail to act? An act, nineteenth-century judges and philosophers of the common law used to explain, is a movement, a contraction of one's muscles, preceded by a volition, a desire to execute the movement. Spasmodic, somnambulistic, compelled, or compulsive movements are not produced by such volitions, hence they are involuntary movements, therefore not acts at all. The notion of volitions has been rightly disdained. Do our actions typically consist of muscle contractions preceded by volitions? Simple introspection, observes H. L. A. Hart, tells us that "a desire to contract our muscles is a very rare occurrence." Only in some very special situations is it quite right to say that we are contracting our muscles in response to a specific desire to do so. When the gym instructor says "Lift your right hand and contract the muscles of your upper arm," it is appropriate to say we desired to and did contract our muscles. When the door handle will not turn and we clench it so that we are actually conscious of the muscles we must contract, we might also say this. Ordinarily, however, "when we shut a door, or we hit someone, or when we fire a gun at a bird, these things are done without any previous thought of the muscular movements involved and without any desire to contract the muscles."[75]

In German law, a different theory has gained prominence, pioneered by Hans Welzel.[76] Welzel approached the problem like this: When a cloud causes lightning to strike a farmer working in the field, he observed, that's *not* an act, but when a man causes a bullet to hit his adversary that *is* an act. In both cases, we have one thing causing another thing to happen. Why doesn't the first case constitute an act, whereas the second does? Well, most obviously because in the first case the causal trigger isn't human, whereas in the second case it is. But why does that matter? Because without a human being, there is no sense of purpose behind the causal chain. With a human being there is. Or as Welzel puts it: In the first case, causation is "blind," in the second it is "goal-directed." What fundamentally distinguishes acts from mere "happenings," he concludes, is that they are "goal-directed," or as we might put it more conventionally, that they are intentional.

At first blush that seems pretty persuasive. Martin did not intentionally manifest his drunkenness in public, Miss Larsonneur did not intentionally have herself found in Britain, and Robinson was not intentionally in a state of addiction. Welzel's test quite properly flunks all of these instances of nonaction. Unfortunately, it flunks quite a number of others as well. Suppose someone drives vastly in excess of the speed limit, loses control of his car, crashes into a bungalow, kills two people, and sets off an explosion. The loss of control, the crash, the deaths, the explosion are all unintended. Welzel's test would then imply that bringing them about could not be deemed actions. Welzel admits that we will often want to punish the driver in cases like these, but says that we are really punishing him for the act of driving above the speed limit, not the *non*acts of causing a crash, some deaths, and an explosion. But on this Welzel just seems wrong. The driver's bringing about a crash, some deaths, and an explosion—all of these are acts, albeit unintentional ones. Welzel seems to wrongly deny the existence of unintentional acts, yet they clearly abound. They abound because of a fundamental property of acts, which Welzel ignores, and which modern philosophers have called the "accordion effect,"[77] that is, if something is an act, then, *generally speaking,* the bringing about of any consequences by that act, however unintended they may be, is also an act. If someone's driving is an act, then his (unintentionally) bringing about an accident thereby has got to be an act as well.

Despite their shortcomings, both of these theories contain more than a grain of truth, which with a bit of work one can extract. When Hans Welzel insists that human action is inextricably bound up with intention, he is onto something. Although it is not true that every act is intentional, something very similar *is* true: every genuine act, even if it is unintentional, can be "redescribed" as an intentional one. Take Oedipus' marrying his mother. We can "redescribe" this unintentional act as the intentional act of Oedipus marrying Jocasta. Take Gavrilo Princip's starting World War I (by killing the Archduke Franz Ferdinand). Again, we can "redescribe" the unintentional act of starting the war as the intentional act of killing the archduke. Take the driver's act of causing the death of those two bungalow dwellers. We can "redescribe" this unintentional act as the intentional act of driving above the speed limit. At this point you may wonder: What do I mean by "redescribe"? To redescribe an act is to refer to the same underlying set of bodily movements but to incorporate into that description (or else to delete from that description) various surrounding circumstances, background facts, and consequences (as long as they are not too remote or far-fetched). For instance, we redescribed "Oedipus married his mother" as "Oedipus married Jocasta" by adding the fact that Jocasta was his mother. We redescribed "Gavrilo Princip started World War I" as "Gavrilo Princip killed the archduke" by leaving out the further consequences of that killing. And we redescribed "The driver caused the death of two bungalow dwellers" as "The driver drove above the speed limit" by leaving out the further consequences of his speeding.[78]

The volition theory, for all its superficial silliness, also contains a valuable insight. What makes a bodily movement into an act is not perhaps the fact that it is preceded by a "volition," but that it is accompanied by a very characteristic experience, which for lack of a better word, we may call the experience of acting. The two are genuinely separate things. One can occur in the absence of the other. When someone else physically seizes my arm and lifts it up and even when a physiologist applies an electrode to my motor cortex, my arm will rise, but unaccompanied by the characteristic experience of acting. Conversely, when my arm has been anesthetized and I am asked to raise it, I will have the distinct experience of raising it, yet when I look at it, I will discover that it has not moved. The bodily movement of my arm, then, is as separate from my experience of raising the arm as a perceived object is from the experience of perceiving it. The object may exist without being perceived and the perception can exist without there being an object to trigger it—in which case we speak of a hallucination. We can say more. The insights we drew from Welzel's theory and from the volition theory are linked. If we redescribe an act (like Gavrilo Princip's starting World War I) so that it becomes intentional ("Gavrilo Princip pulled the trigger of his gun"), we can see that the experience of acting is simply the intent to perform the redescribed act.

The upshot of all this is that we may call something an act if under some (re)description it can be decomposed into a bodily movement accompanied by the intent to perform that bodily movement, that is, the experience of acting. This definition disposes handily of Martin and Miss Larsonneur: There was perhaps a bodily movement there, but as they were physically expelled into the area where they were then found to be offenders, they did not have the experience of acting. It also disposes of the unconscious "criminal": Unconscious "criminals" do not have the experience of acting because they lack self-awareness. Finally, it disposes of cases like *Robinson*: Being an addict does not entail a physical movement, except perhaps trembling and shaking, and those are clearly not accompanied by the experience of acting—so being an addict is not an act. Of course, if *being* an addict isn't an act, *becoming* an addict is. To punish someone for being an addict could thus be defended as essentially punishing him for the act of becoming an addict. Still, technically the *Robinson* statute does not refer to that act, but to the state of being addicted. Taken literally, it would cover even the congenitally addicted offspring of an addict—even if the addiction were incurable.

But our definition of an act is not yet complete. There is a category of cases where the defendant looks as though he is acting (he is performing bodily movements), inwardly feels as though he is acting (he is having the requisite experience of acting), and yet probably is not acting at all.[80]

Those Who Can't Help Themselves

One day in the early 1930s a young German woman was taking the train from her hometown to the nearby metropolis of Heidelberg.[81] She was suffering from stomach pains and went to seek treatment from a specialist in Heidelberg. On the train she made the acquaintance of one Dr. Bergen, a self-described "nature healer." He thought hers was just the kind of illness he could treat very well. They stepped out of the train together at Graben and had a cup of coffee. From that moment on the young woman became Dr. Bergen's patient.

His treatment turned out to be hypnosis. Unfortunately, it did not seem to do much good. After numerous visits with Dr. Bergen, her ailments, rather than waning, multiplied; she grew more anxious and irritable and made several suicide attempts. When Dr. Bergen's fees reached the stately sum of 3000 marks the woman's husband complained to the police. Dr. Bergen, he claimed, was a fraud.

The police investigated. One of Germany's finest clinical hypnotists, Dr. Ludwig Mayer, became interested in the case and examined Mrs. E, as the young woman came to be known in the annals. He determined that she had no identifiable organic illness. When he asked her about Dr. Bergen, she was unable to remember anything about him—not even what he looked like—evidently the result of certain "locking suggestions" Dr. Bergen had given her. When Mayer put her under hypnosis, she vaguely recalled Bergen's hairstyle, his clothes, and some white turkish towels with blue stripes that hung in his bathroom. The police had recently arrested a con man named Franz Speyer for, among other things, posing as a doctor. He fit Mrs. E's description, as did the towels in his apartment. Of course, he denied knowing Mrs. E, and she could not positively identify him. It took almost two more years of hypnosis for her to break through Bergen's locking suggestions and recall the events of those years of treatment with Dr. Bergen.

What finally came to light showed Dr. Bergen's power over her to have been more extensive than anyone suspected. He had induced her to have intercourse with him and some of his friends. When Mrs. E's husband grew suspicious, Bergen ordered her to kill him. Once he told her to poison him with clover salts, and another time he told her to shoot him. He tried six times. He failed not because Mrs. E refused—she went along with every suggestion—but because she bungled the attempts. The day she was to buy clover salts, her husband happened to prohibit her from going out. The day she was to shoot him, the gun was unexpectedly empty. Remarkably, the husband had no inkling of his narrow escapes, and Mrs. E lapsed into instant amnesia about her misdeeds. When Dr. Bergen thought Mr. E on the verge of putting the police on his tracks, he told her to commit suicide. Mrs. E made two such attempts, but both times changed her mind at the last minute. Dr. Bergen's last ploy came when Dr. Mayer's investigation had already started. He sent an accomplice, who approached Mrs. E disguised as a detective, merely uttered one of Dr. Bergen's magical hypnotic phrases ("Filofi") and was able to put her into an immediate trance. He then fed her information designed to confuse and mislead the authorities. Alas, Dr. Mayer ultimately gained such complete control over Mrs. E that he was able to ascertain the identity of the accomplice. Thereafter, the investigation could quickly be wound up. Franz Walter alias Franz Speyer alias Dr. Bergen was brought to trial and condemned to ten years' imprisonment, his accomplice to four years'.

Mrs. E was never actually charged with committing any crimes. The authorities only learned of her crimes through her own hypnotic confession. The case of Mr. Z, another German tale, is one where the hypnotic subject was actually brought to trial for the crimes which his hypnotist had led him to commit.[82] Mr. Z was a young school teacher in a small village in Thuringia. He is described as having been "a model student, intelligent, fond of sports, well-liked by his fellow students . . . helpful and good-natured," but also "slightly uncritical in his choice of friends." When Z's father died, he left his son a small house and a general store belonging to it, in a market town some forty miles away. Z's new neighbor there was a thirty-eight-year-old worker, A, coarse and uneducated, but full of guile. A took an immediate interest in his more refined neighbor and proceeded to insinuate himself into his good graces with various small services. He would frequently visit Z and shower him for hours on end with his war adventures. Z frequently fell asleep. On one such occasion, A, who had a passing acquaintance with hypnosis, discovered that it was very easy to transport the sleeping Z into a deep hypnotic trance. In the next few weeks, he induced Z to make him lavish gifts, first of wine and cigars, later of money. To test the full extent of his powers, he gave Z the posthypnotic suggestion that on receipt of a certain cue ("Don't be foolish!"), Z was to hurry home, take his gun, and shoot himself in the left arm. As always, he told Z to forget everything that had happened during the seance. Ten days later, he ran into Z on a Sunday stroll with his sweetheart. He uttered the cue. Z promptly went home, ostensibly to change, took out the gun, and shot himself in the arm. Later he rationalized what had happened by saying a cramp in his hand had caused him to pull the trigger. He survived the incident with a permanently stiff elbow.

A's next move was to set Z up for a crime—an insurance swindle. Under hypnosis, he made him draw up false inventories, told him to leave for a while so he could break into the store, and ordered him to submit the false inventories when the time came to file the insurance claim. Things went without a hitch, and A collected most of the insurance proceeds. Then A started to be careless, and the authorities grew suspicious. In another seance, A told Z that if ever during the inquiry he said to him "It's no use any longer—tell them everything" he was to confess immediately to being the instigator of the crime.

Shortly thereafter, Z was arrested. The police told him A had confessed and named him as an instigator. The astonished Z denied the charge. Then he was confronted with A. As soon as A had spat out "It's no use any longer—tell them everything," Z confessed.

A few days later, the bewildered Z learned from his guards that A had claimed to have been put up to his crimes through hypnotic suggestion by Z. Suddenly Z began to suspect the truth. Odd incidents—clocks jumping forward in time by several hours, meetings at which A had emptied Z's wallet—began to fall into place. But Z was unable to convince the court. He was sentenced to thirteen months in jail.

When his term was up, he turned to a well-known hypnotist. He underwent a series of seances that helped him retrieve his hidden memories.

Z's attorney sought to reopen the case, but the court considered the matter moot, since Z had served his term.

Seventeen years later, Z's mishap came to haunt him a second time. The hypnotist who had helped him published Z's story. But hypnotized or not, Z's conduct so scandalized the school board, he was fired from his teaching job.

In September 1946, a Danish court sentenced H, a twenty-two-year-old toolmaker, to fourteen years of prison for collaborating with the Nazis.[83] H, though honest and upright, was something of a dreamer and had felt a mystical attraction for the Nazi invaders. He joined the German auxiliary police corps, but soon regretted his decision. He tried to get out of it by shooting himself in the foot, but the injury wasn't serious enough.

In jail, he became friends with N, another collaborator and a fairly sinister character. N had been convicted of a long array of offenses that included being a Nazi informer, blackmailing businessmen by pretending to belong to the Resistance, and simple robbery. What caught H's attention was N's extensive knowledge of yoga, mysticism, the occult—and hypnosis. N purported to teach H hypnosis, by alternately hypnotizing H or undergoing hypnosis at H's hands. N discovered that H was a "natural," capable of deep somnambulistic trances. (N never actually let H hypnotize him, although occasionally he pretended to.) N quickly realized what vast opportunities this opened up for him. He inculcated in H a blind obedience to his every wish and he tightened his hold by appealing to H's deep-seated mystical proclivities. He invented a guardian angel, X, to whom H had to swear an oath of fealty. He explained to H that he, N, was X's representative on earth and that by following his orders, he would become the savior of Scandinavia. To disguise what he had done from any potential intruder, he fed H the usual locking suggestions.

He then took full advantage of his powers. He periodically suggested to H the need to fast, so that he could get H's meal rations. He suggested the need to free oneself of all material attachments, so that he could get H's watch and accordion. One day, H who was an intelligent fellow, made an invention, a slot machine for selling newspapers that would replace kiosks. At N's behest, he signed all profits over to him.

They were both set free a few years later, but that did not end N's domination. In fact, it extended it. N ordered H to break with his family, to marry a woman N had selected for him, to permit the woman to sleep with him, N, whenever he felt the desire, and to turn most of his earnings over to him. He also began to prepare him for criminal tasks. During his hypnotic seances he had him rehearse crime scenarios of increasing depravity. He began with stealing small sums from the kitchen table and moved on to closed drawers, locked safes, and a poor old woman's money box. Eventually, he had H imagine himself calmly committing murder—first, only of a randomly selected stranger, later of his mother.

Finally, he asked H to commit an actual bank robbery. He made this request, of course, during a hypnotic session, deepened beyond its usual level through the inhalation of ether. He embedded the request in a fanciful tale about the guardian angel, the threat of a Russian invasion of Scandinavia, and the need for an emergency fund to evacuate Denmark's intelligentsia. In August 1950, H broke into a suburban branch of a Copenhagen bank and collected about 1075 pounds without further incident.

Emboldened by this success, N planned another bank robbery only a few months later. Again he made the request during an ether-deepened trance, embedded it in another preposterous tale about a utopian community which the money would be used to set up. In March 1951, H, wearing sunglasses, strode into a Copenhagen bank and pulled out his gun. The clerks were uncooperative. H calmly shot two of them. Then his self-assurance failed him. His guardian angel, he felt, had abandoned him. He made a token attempt to flee, but was quickly arrested. At the police station he earnestly explained that he had been ordered to perpetrate the robbery by his guardian angel to create a utopian society.

Psychiatrists pronounced him insane but had a hard time classifying his insanity. The head of a psychiatric ward, Dr. Paul Reiter, an expert hypnotist, was intrigued by the case. At first it proved impossible to hypnotize H, but with the help of trance-inducing drugs, Reiter eventually broke through N's locking suggestions. Thereafter, H proved the excellent hypnotic subject he had always been. During his trance, he recalled in detail his relationship with N. At Reiter's posthypnotic suggestion, he prepared a written record of his life since entering prison. It was thus that his story eventually came to light.

In evaluating the significance of N's hypnotic influence for H's life, Reiter ran into an extraordinary piece of luck. H happened to have a twin brother. As children and teenagers, the two had been inseparable. Indeed their early histories up to H's encounter with N were identical. (H's brother also had collaborated.) When Reiter examined H's brother, he found him not the least bit psychopathic, in no way "psychically unusual," but rather a "normal member of society."

Despite Dr. Reiter's testimony, H was convicted but was sentenced to a much lighter term than N and sent to the Institute of Psychopaths. Ironically, the trial and its aftermath once more dramatized the extent of N's hold over H. After having been reexposed to N during the trial, H began to claim (when it was all over) that he had been lying to Dr. Reiter, that he had only pretended to be hypnotized by him, that N was completely innocent. While confined at the institute, he inherited 500 pounds from his father. He persuaded another inmate to flee with the money and use it to organize a wildly fantastical escape for him and N, which was to culminate in the shooting of the institute's chief and the minister of justice. The friend was captured and confessed everything. The man's interrogation revealed that he had recently occupied a cell next to N and been given orders to pass on to H.

A word of caution about these cases: they are based on the hypnotists' account of what happened. Critics frequently object that the doctors have not heard the other party's version of the story, that the subjects might have been using hypnosis from the very beginning as a way of disclaiming responsibility for their actions. One cannot rebut these criticisms; one can only bear them in mind. What takes some of their edge off, however, is that in a variety of experimental settings, hypnotists were able to induce upstanding citizens to commit criminal acts.

Why is a crime performed on a posthypnotic suggestion not an act? It certainly looks like an act to the outside world and it feels like an act to the defendant. What the hypnosis cases show, I believe, is that we are wrong to seek a definition of an act that is wholly intrinsic to the actor, one that depends exclusively on *his* feelings and *his* state of mind. It is a tempting mistake, and one that has been made before, when trying to define concepts like knowledge, meaning, and identity.

Knowledge. To say that somebody knows something sounds like a statement about his mind, and nothing but his mind. It is tempting to think that one can define what it means for someone to know something by looking solely at the person that's doing the knowing. But there's a strange thing about knowing: one can't know anything that is wrong; whatever one knows *perforce* is right. Does that mean that the knowing state of mind is some weirdly sublime state of mind in which one is incapable of mistakes? Of course not. It just means that for someone to know something, it is necessary, first, that he believe it and, second, that it be right. To see whether it's right we have to look outside his mind, at the world at large. Only then do we know that what he believes he also knows.

Meaning. When somebody says X, it seems that what he means depends solely on what he is thinking of when he says X. It's tempting to think that one can define what the speaker means by X by focusing only on the speaker. We have already seen why that's wrong. A speaker often means something different from what he thinks he means. What he means we find out by looking at the world, not just his mind.

Identity. Consider the old story about the ship of Theseus. One-by-one the ship's planks are exchanged. When they have all been replaced, do we still have the same ship? It would seem that way. After all, a person's cells all get replaced over the course of a lifetime (several times, in fact) and that does not change his identity. But suppose you were to learn that the old planks had not been discarded but reassembled according to the original design. We now have two identical-looking ships: the planks of one old, those of the other new. Which of these is the original ship of Theseus? I should think the one with the old planks. Both are descended from the same ship. Both have the original design. But one has even more—it has the original planks. Thus to determine whether a certain ship today is identical with a certain ship in the past, it will not do just to focus on the history of that particular ship. We have to look at other ships as well: perhaps their history links them even more closely to that original ship.

The concept of an act, I believe, is like that of knowledge, meaning, or identity. It may look as though a person has performed an act. It may feel to him as though he has performed an act. But some other person may be much closer to the act than the ostensible actor. The conduct may mesh much more closely with *his* plans and desires than those of the ostensible actor. Such is the case with hypnosis. The hypnotic subject's act reflects much more closely the will of hypnotist than of subject. The subject's act is thus the *hypnotist's* and only the hypnotist's act, not the subject's. To be sure, if some nonhuman outside influence had induced the same conduct in the subject—if a full moon, for instance, were for some people tantamount to a posthypnotic suggestion to rob the bank—we would call the act his, even though "intrinsically" there is nothing different about him. To decide whether someone is acting one needs to look beyond him, at the world around him. Only if his conduct links up more closely with his own motivations than those of someone else, is it he that has acted. (The idea about the full moon isn't altogether fanciful.

There are studies showing correlations between mood swings and planetary, especially lunar, movements. "Lunacy," "mercurial temper," and "saturnine disposition" might prove to be surprisingly apt labels.)[84]

What have the drafters of the criminal codes done about this hoary problem of distinguishing between acts and things that happen to you? They have acknowledged that sometimes a defendant who seems to run afoul of a statute may not be acting, but undergoing something, and should be acquitted. But they have avoided trying to articulate just what it is about the faith healer in a trance, the epileptic, the frenzy killer, the sleepwalker, the subject of a posthypnotic suggestion that renders their conduct involuntary and prevents it from being an act. They don't try to explain what makes certain conduct unconscious, how a voluntary act is an intentional act under a certain description, how it can be decomposed into a bodily movement and a certain experience characteristic of acting, and why certain bodily movements accompanied by that experience of acting—posthypnotic conduct—still don't count as acts. The Model Penal Code simply says that a defendant cannot be convicted unless he has acted voluntarily and then describes a voluntary act, in language of majestic generality, as "a bodily movement that otherwise is not a product of the effort or determination of the actor, either conscious or habitual." Recognizing that description to be vague, the drafters included a list of cases they felt sure should not qualify as voluntary acts: "a reflex or convulsion," "a bodily movement during unconsciousness or sleep," and "conduct during hypnosis or resulting from posthypnotic suggestion." Given the philosophical difficulties involved, it's not surprising the drafters steered clear of trying to say more.[85]

Crimes of Omission

In the wee hours one spring morning in 1964 a young woman, Catherine Genovese—Kitty to those who knew her—was making her way home to her apartment in Queens, New York City.[86] She was the manager at a bar in the Hollis district and so the late hour was not unusual for her. She parked her red Fiat in a parking lot no more than a hundred feet from the door of her apartment house, a respectable-looking tudor building with a storefront on the first floor and apartments on the second. As she shut the door of her car, she noticed a man at the far end of the lot, near another seven-story apartment house. She headed in the opposite direction and straight toward a call box to the 102d Police Precinct in nearby

Richmond Hill. But before she could reach the call box the man was upon her. She screamed. Lights went on in a nearby apartment house, facing the place where she had been assaulted. There was a sound of windows sliding open and of muffled voices. Kitty shouted: "Oh my god, he stabbed me! Please help me!" A man from one of the upper stories called down: "Let that girl alone." The assailant looked up, shrugged, and began to saunter away toward a white sedan parked a couple of yards away. Kitty tried to get up.

Then the lights went out again. The man turned around and walked back toward Kitty who had managed to get up and tried to drag herself toward the apartment house entrance. He stabbed her again. She emitted a piercing shriek: "I'm dying . . . I'm dying." The lights went on again. The assailant walked toward his car and drove away.

Several minutes later he returned. Kitty had again tried to crawl toward an apartment house door. The man did not see her at first, scouted about, finally spotted her prostrate at the bottom of a staircase. He stabbed her again—and she died.

It was almost half an hour after the first assault that the police received a call from a reluctant neighbor who had witnessed the incident from his window. There was nothing they could do for Kitty. But they investigated. They had some unusual luck and actually found Kitty Genovese's murderer, one Winston Mosely, a twenty-nine-year-old business machine operator. The man confessed to killing Kitty, but more than that, he confessed to two other murders. What initially attracted the attention of the newspapers was the fact that he confessed to a murder to which another man had already confessed. But as a *New York Times* journalist began to look into the case, he discovered something much more unusual and gripping about this otherwise humdrum urban slaying. The whole incident had been witnessed by no less than thirty-eight neighbors. Only one of them had bothered to call the police—after talking the matter over at length with a friend in Nassau County and after a half-hour delay.

The publication of the story by the *New York Times* caused an uproar. What these thirty-eight seemingly upright citizens had done—or rather, failed to do—seemed beyond the pale, urban callousness at its incomprehensible worst. "I feel it is the duty of *The New York Times* to try to obtain the names of the witnesses involved and to publish the list," one woman wrote. "These people should be held up for public ridicule, since they cannot be held responsible for their inaction. . . . Apparently these thirty-seven people feel no moral obligation to their fellow men. Therefore constant reminders in the newspapers are necessary to show them the contempt in which other morally responsible citizens hold them.'' That, however, was much too mild for another letter writer, the wife of a professor: ''The implications of their silence—and of the cowardice and indifference it revealed—are staggering. If the laws of New York State do not prescribe some form of punishment, then we believe your newspaper should pressure the state legislature for an amendment of those laws.'' In short, what the woman had in mind was a law making it a legal duty for bystanders, in some fashion, to help the victim of an assault—on pain of criminal punishment.

At first blush, it may seem preposterous to punish a person for doing nothing at all. To make a crime out of an omission seems like making a dish out of the holes of a cheese. But what about prosecuting the thirty-eight silent witnesses for murder? Had not their silence caused Kitty Genovese's death? They had not, of course, themselves committed any act of violence against Kitty. But the common law has long recognized that no actual violence is necessary to render someone liable for murder. There is a sixteenth-century case about a harlot who hid her baby in an orchard under a pile of leaves where a kite swooped down and killed it, another one about a son who carried his sick father from town to town in a frost until he died, and another one about two overseers who, to avoid a bastard child's becoming a burden on their respective parishes, sent it to and fro between the parishes until it died—in all of these cases the defendants were found guilty of homicide, notwithstanding the absence of any violence. But the witnesses of Kitty Genovese's murder are different from any of those defendants. They had not done anything to or with Kitty Genovese. They had merely failed to help (or call for help). Their sin was one of omission, not commission.[87]

Even then, however, the common law has often recognized liability. In 1776, Steven Self, an artisan, was convicted of manslaughter. His apprentice had returned from a brief stay at the local prison ''in a lousy and distempered condition.'' The master refused him his bed ''on account of the vermin'' and only allowed him to ''lie on [some] boards . . . without covering and without common medical care.''[88] As a consequence the already sick boy died. It was critical for the court, however, that Self and his apprentice were not strangers. ''Anyone who, assuming to take care of another, refuses the necessary subsistence, or by any other severity though not of a nature to produce immediate death, as by putting the party in such a situation as may possibly be dangerous to life or health, if death actually and clearly ensues in consequence of it, it is murder.''[89] Since then courts have rigidly adhered to the rule that in the absence of some special relationship between victim and bystander, sins of omission are never crimes. In the absence of such a special relationship, a passerby may with impunity fail to pull a drowning baby out of the water or to rescue an unconscious person stretched across the railroad tracks, however trivial the effort required. Despite such apparently gruesome consequences, most early common law judges and commentators considered this rule the only sensible one. The alternative, they reasoned, was patently absurd. ''It will hardly be maintained,'' wrote Macaulay,

> that a man should be punished as a murderer because he omitted to relieve a beggar, even though there might be the clearest proof that the death of the beggar was the effect of this omission, and that the man who omitted to give the alms knew that the death of the beggar was likely to be the effect of the omission. It will hardly be maintained that a surgeon ought to be treated as a murderer for refusing to go from Calcutta to Meerut to perform an operation, although it should be absolutely certain this surgeon was the only person in India who could perform it, and that if it were not performed the person who required it would die.[90]

The circumstances giving rise to a special duty to aid are varied but limited. Courts have frequently relied on the existence of a certain close personal relationship between bystander and victim. A father who failed to call a doctor for his sick child, a mother who failed to prevent her lover from flogging her child to death, a husband who left his intoxicated wife out in the snow, all were found guilty of homicide. But the relationship has to be quite close to generate such a duty. That is the lesson of a case called *People v. Beardsley*.[91] Beardsley was a clerk at the Columbia Hotel in Pontiac, Michigan. While his wife was out of town one weekend, he invited to his home a woman from another hotel with whom he had been entertaining a casual affair for quite some time. When the woman arrived, as the court primly sums it up, ''they at once began to drink, and continued to drink steadily, and remained together, day and night, from that time until the afternoon of the Monday following.'' When it came time to leave, the woman had a suicidal fit and swallowed several pills of morphine.

Anxious to hide her presence from his wife, Beardsley hid her in the basement of the house. He never bothered to call a doctor. The woman died. He was charged with manslaughter. But did Beardsley owe the woman a duty? The court did not think so and acquitted him:

> The fact that this woman was in [defendant's] house created no such legal duty as exists in law and is due from a husband towards his wife. . . . Such an inference would be very repugnant to our moral sense. [Defendant] had assumed either in fact or by implication no case or control over his companion. Had this been a case where two men under like circumstances had voluntarily gone on a debauch together, no one would claim that this doctrine of legal duty could be invoked to hold the other criminally responsible for omitting to make an effort to rescue his companion. How can the fact that one of the partners was a woman change the principle of law applicable to it.

If the bystander has a contract with some third party to help potential victims, that too can create a duty under the criminal law. "A lifeguard employed to watch over swimmers at the beach, and a railroad gateman hired to safeguard motorists from approaching trains, have a duty, to the public they are employed to protect, to take affirmative action in appropriate circumstances."[92] But those contracts are often very narrowly construed. So, for instance, a brakeman was found to have no duty to signal the engineer to stop the train when he sighted a child on the tracks. That, after all, was not what he was hired to do.[93]

A duty can also arise out of the fact that the defendant himself quite innocently created the peril in which the victim finds himself. One who accidentally sets a fire, however innocently, is no longer free to take off without concern for persons still trapped in the burning buildings. This rule as well is often applied very conservatively. The Kentucky case of *King v. Commonwealth* is a good example.[94] Davis had attacked King's father. King, in justifiable defense of his father, had shot Davis in the leg. Davis collapsed. King was very lackadaisical about securing medical assistance for Davis. Davis died. King was charged with manslaughter. The court acquitted him, and though it did not clearly explain why, the court probably thought that one owed no duty to an aggressor who had brought on his own injury.

If omissions are treated so much more leniently than acts, that makes it important to be able to distinguish the two. Some cases are easily classified. To fail to help Kitty Genovese is an omission; to stab Kitty Genovese is an act. But a disconcertingly large number of cases dumbfound one's intuitions. A man is riding his spring cart. Instead of holding the horse's reins in his hands, he lets them rest on its back. As the horse is trotting down a hill, a child passes in front of it, is knocked down, and dies. Had the man held the reins, he could have pulled the horse up. Did the passing cart's careless driver kill the child or merely fail to prevent its death? A pharmacist repeatedly sells a patient some highly toxic medication. The first time the patient has a prescription, on subsequent occasions he does not. The patient dies. Is the pharmacist guilty of an act or an omission? A manufacturer permits unsterilized chinese goathair to be worked into cloth as a result of which several employees die of an infection. Act or omission? A man picks up his inebriated friend at a local tavern. They have a quarrel, and the man abandons his friend at some dangerous spot, so that in attempting to make it home on his own he stumbles into a pond and drowns. Act or omission? A child, chased by a wild dog, runs toward the open door of a nearby villa. The malicious owner slams the door in his face, and the dog tears the child to pieces. Act or omission?

The need to distinguish between acts and omissions is not confined to the criminal law and neither is the difficulty in articulating the distinctions. Among the most pivotal Supreme Court decisions of recent times is *Immigration and Naturalization Service v. Chadha.*[95] At issue was one of the most basic provisions of the Constitution, the requirement that every law be passed by both houses of Congress and not disapproved by the president (unless Congress overrides his veto). Beginning in the 1930s Congress saw the need to create more and more administrative agencies to oversee the implementation of increasingly complex pieces of legislation: that is how the Immigration and Naturalization Service, the Internal Revenue Service, the Federal Trade Commission, and the Environmental Protection Agency were born. Congress soon discovered that it could not possibly anticipate the infinitude of problems these agencies would have to address and as a result drafted its laws very loosely, giving the agencies extensive power to "fill them out" with more specific rules and regulations of their own. Then it began to have second thoughts. What if it disapproved of some of the regulations passed by the agencies? Would it have to amend the law formally so as to nullify regulations it did not like? That seemed terribly cumbersome. Instead Congress gave the agencies only a conditional grant of power. They were free within very broad limits to pass the regulations they saw fit. These regulations would become effective within a specified amount of time unless one of the houses of Congress found them abhorrent, in which case it could just veto the regulation by a simple majority vote, and it would never become effective.

Chadha argued that this scheme was unconstitutional. The merits of his case hinged on the distinction between acts and omissions. Chadha pointed out that under the congressional scheme one house of Congress could all by itself act to overturn a regulation and thereby remake the law without getting the approval of the other house or the president.

But there is another way to look at the congressional scheme. One might view the house's veto as an *omission* rather than an *act*. By vetoing the regulation, one might argue, the house is not really *acting* to change the law but *omitting* to change the law: After all, it is keeping a new regulation off the books. And when a house is omitting to change the law rather than acting to change it, clearly the approval of the other house or the president is not required. That, of course, raises the question: If the new regulation is itself a change in the law, why isn't the president, like the two houses, free to veto it? But, in fact, he is. As head of the executive branch of government, he can simply tell the administrative agency not to propose the regulation in the first place. Alas, the Supreme Court did not see things this way. It decided the "one-house veto" was an act rather than an omission and held it unconstitutional. But whether the Court was right is far from obvious.

These many hard cases are alarming. True, any distinction has its borderline cases. But are these merely borderline cases or do they betoken the lack of any analytical substance to the distinction between acts and omissions? A man in Brazil is committing suicide. Were we to fly to Brazil and try to dissuade him, he would not kill himself. We view this as a clear-cut case of omission. King fires a bullet into Davis's chest. We view this as a clear-cut case of an act. Nevertheless: But for our staying in America and minding our own business, the man in Brazil would still be alive. But for King's firing a bullet into Davis's chest, he would still be alive. Thus presented, the two cases seem virtually identical. Why are we so sure that they exemplify two very different concepts?

Some have suggested that acts involve bodily movements and omissions do not. But the man who stays in America and busies himself with his own affairs instead of setting out for Brazil is a paragon of physical agitation. He is nonetheless guilty of no more than an omission.

More intriguing is a suggestion made by the philosopher Jonathan Bennet.[96] Bennet was confronted by the need to develop a basis for the distinction between act and omission in the course of investigating the following hypothetical: "A woman in labor will certainly die unless an operation is performed in which the head of her unborn child is crushed or dissected, while if it is not performed, the child can be delivered, alive, by post-mortem caesarean section." Unless the obstetrician operates and crushes the baby's skull, the mother will die. Many people in this context, a group Bennet dubs "the conservatives," would rigidly adhere to the credo: It is always wrong to kill an innocent human, whatever the consequences of not doing so. They would prohibit the doctor from operating. In this case, Bennet pointed out, not killing one human being seems to involve killing another human being. Why do "conservatives" not see it that way? Why do they see the mother's death as the consequence of an act? Why do they not call the doctor who sits down to write up his medical report instead of crushing the baby's skull to save the mother a killer, but do so label the doctor who chooses to save the mother? Bennet can only see one reason. The doctor who writes up his lab notes is taking one of many possible actions that would result in the mother's death. The doctor who crushes the baby's skull is taking the only action that would result in the baby's death. In short, the difference between death-producing omissions and death-producing acts is that in the former the actor engages in one of many death-producing activities whereas in the latter he engages in one out of a very few death-producing activities. Bennet concludes that this distinction is morally irrelevant. Others have thought it highly relevant. It shows, they point out, that our "reluctance to penalize omissions is justified by the fact that to prohibit an act . . . leaves the subject free to do many, many alternative acts; prohibiting an omission leaves him free to do only one act, the act which he is forbidden to omit. This is a more severe burden to place on the citizen than if he is merely forbidden to perform the act."[97]

The validity of Bennet's test has been seriously questioned. Suppose Cooper stands surrounded by a lynch mob. Miller gives him the coup de grace. But it is clear that if not Miller, someone else would certainly have killed him. According to Bennet's criterion, Miller is merely guilty of an omission. Our intuition tells us he is guilty of an act. Or suppose "Jones and Smith are spies who have been captured by the enemy. They have been wired to each other so that a movement by one would electrocute the other. Jones moves and kills Smith.''[98] Here all of Jones's actions but one—sitting still—would have resulted in Smith's death. Jones took one of those actions. Under Bennet's criterion he is guilty merely of an omission. According to our intuition that's far from clear.

The true test for whether something is an act or an omission I believe to be the following: If the defendant did not exist, would the harmful outcome in question still have occurred in the way it did? This test certainly gives us the right answer to our easy cases. If the witnesses to Kitty Genovese's murder had not existed, she would still have died. But if her assailant had not existed, she would not have died. If you did not exist, the man in Brazil would still have committed suicide. But if Miller had not trampled Cooper to death, his death would have occurred in a somewhat different manner: someone other than Miller would have finished Cooper off. The test helps us to treat satisfactorily some cases where our intuition hesitated. It would pronounce the man who rode his spring cart so recklessly guilty of an act. It is evidence, however, that the test captures our intuitions well, that it yields equivocal results in the very cases that cause our intuitions to equivocate most strongly. What would have happened if the pharmacist who refilled the patient's outdated prescription had not existed? Are we to assume another pharmacist would have filled his prescription the first time around? Are we to assume that pharmacist to be careful or negligent? We can't tell. What would have happened if the manufacturer who permitted the use of unsterilized goathair had not existed? Would his factory exist? Would somebody more or less careful run it? We can't tell. What if the man who picked up his inebriated friend at the tavern did not exist? Would the drunk then have awaited sobriety before he left the tavern and not drowned in the pond? We can't tell. What if the owner who slammed the door in the fleeing child's face had not existed? Would a more benevolent owner occupy his place? Would the villa exist at all? We can't tell.

It is a problem of many counterfactual assumptions that they are inherently ambiguous. Because of this ambiguity contradictory results can often be deduced from them. Assume for a moment that New York City is located in Georgia. What follows from that? Arguably it follows that New York is located south of the Mason-Dixon line. Arguably it follows that Georgia extends north of the Mason-Dixon line. The source of the problem is this. There are three true facts: (1) New York City is not located in Georgia. (2) Georgia lies south of the Mason-Dixon line. (3)

New York is north of the Mason-Dixon line. We are asked to assume the opposite of 1. To be in a consistent world we now have to assume the opposite of either 2 or 3. If we assume the opposite of 2, we conclude that Georgia extends north of the Mason-Dixon line. If we assume the opposite of 3, we conclude that New York is south of the Mason-Dixon line. But the counterfactual assumption does not tell us whether 2 or 3 is to be negated. Hence a question based on the assumption is unavoidably ambiguous. This same problem plagues the counterfactual question: Would X have occurred in the same manner if the defendant had not existed? It lies at the heart of our hitherto mysterious inability to classify some occurrences as acts or omissions.[99]

Having settled the nature of omissions, the question remains: Why do omissions strike us as morally less offensive than acts? Why do we loathe the indifferent onlookers of Kitty Genovese's stabbing less than her assailant?

Many of our reasons for not prosecuting the callous bystander are practical rather than moral. A law requiring bystanders to help is very difficult to draft. What is such a law to do, for instance, with the wealthy man who refuses to give alms to the starving beggar? Is he obligated to give away his money to starving beggars until he has no more to give? One statutory proposal seeks to avoid this undesirable possibility by providing: "The circumstances placing a person in a position to act [must be] purely fortuitous."[100] Under this rule the wealthy man need not give any money to the starving beggar because the beggar is without funds. "If the rich man [passing by the beggar] had food with him, he might be required to share it, for the presence of food would be purely fortuitous. But he is not required to share his money, because a man's wealth is not a fortuity." Unfortunately, this restriction rests on the hazy concept of fortuity. Why isn't a man's wealth a fortuity? What if he just won it in the lottery?

Another practical reason for not prosecuting callous bystanders is that such prosecutions might be counterproductive. Many people might stay away from places where they could be called upon to help. Others would be less willing to help, because help has become mandatory rather than voluntary.[101]

Yet another practical reason for not prosecuting bystanders is that the consequences of an omission are generally less certain than those of an act. Holding somebody's head under water is more likely to kill him than not throwing him a life vest.[102]

But there is a deeper, moral, reason why killing-by-omission offends us less than killing-by-commission. Compare these two situations. (1) Bert will die unless Berta gives him one of her kidneys. Berta is ailing and doesn't want to risk an operation. So she lets Bert die. (2) Berta will die unless Bert gives her his only kidney. She kills Bert and takes his kidney. In both 1 and 2 Berta brings about Bert's death to assure her own survival; in 1 she does it by an omission, in 2 by an act. Why are we less offended by her conduct in 1 than in 2? Because in 1 she simply holds on to her own kidney, whereas in 2 she appropriates somebody else's kidney. We value personal autonomy and Berta's conduct in 2 offends against that value, while her conduct in 1 doesn't. Our sentiments about every other case of omission can be understood by analogizing it to these two cases. The person who fails to prevent harm that would occur even if he didn't exist simply fails to give away something he owns. The person who brings about harm that wouldn't occur if he didn't exist takes away something owned by someone else. Both persons may be callous, but only the latter offends our sense of personal autonomy.[103]

Live and Let Die

The case of Kitty Genovese is not an altogether isolated incident. In its wake newspapers across the nation unearthed several more such episodes. Andrew Mormille, reports a New York paper, is stabbed in the stomach while taking the A train home to Manhattan. Eleven people witness the attack. Not one intervenes. The assailants leave. And then the truly shocking thing happens: Not one of the witnesses comes to his aid. He eventually bleeds to death. Another incident involves an 18-year-old switchboard operator who, while alone in her office in the Bronx, is raped and beaten. "Escaping momentarily, she runs naked and bleeding to the street, screaming for help. A crowd of 40 passersby gathers and watches as, in broad daylight, the rapist tries to drag her back upstairs; no one interferes. Finally, two policemen happen by and arrest her assailant."[104]

What accounts for this phenomenon? Because we value personal autonomy highly, we consider letting someone die less blameworthy than killing him. But we don't consider it praiseworthy either. Why then do we so often fail to help? "Apathy!" "Indifference!" "Lack of concern for our fellow men!" "The Cold Society!" Most explanations tend to run in that vein. But they ring both facile and false. Asked for the time, for directions to Time Square, or for change for a dollar bill, few of the onlookers would have refused.[105] And many of them probably contribute to charities to help people they have never met. Those are not the actions of apathetic people. In fact not even their actions at the scene of the crime were those of apathetic people. Darley and Latane, two psychologists who have investigated the problem, commented:

> Although it is unquestionably true that the witnesses in these incidents did nothing to save the victim, "apathy," "indifference," and "unconcern" are not entirely accurate descriptions of their reactions. The 38 witnesses of Kitty Genovese's murder did not merely look at the scene once and then ignore it. Instead they continued to stare out of their windows at what was going on. Caught, fascinated, distressed, unwilling to act but unable to turn away, their behavior was neither helpful nor heroic; but it was not indifferent or apathetic either.

Their behavior in fact was very much like crowd behavior generally. "Car accidents, drownings, fires, and attempted suicides," Darley and Latane point out, "all attract substantial numbers of people who watch the drama in helpless fascination without getting directly involved in the action. Are these people alienated and indifferent?" they ask. "Are the rest of us? We think not. . . . But why, then, don't we act?"[106]

Darley and Latane constructed an ingenious series of experiments to find out. A randomly selected sample of Columbia University students were invited to visit with some psychologists, ostensibly to be interviewed about the problems of urban life. When the student arrived at the waiting room, he or she was left alone in a room and given some preliminary forms to fill out. After the student had worked on the forms for a little while, some smoke would begin to enter the room through a vent in the wall. "For the entire experimental period, or until the subject took action, the smoke continued to flow into the room in irregular puffs. By the end of four minutes, enough smoke had filtered into the room to obscure vision, produce a mildly acrid odor, and interfere with breathing." The reaction of the students was entirely predictable. Typically,

> the subject would glance up from his questionnaire and notice the smoke (perhaps from the corner of his eye). He would show a slight but noticeable startle reaction and then undergo a brief period of indecision, perhaps returning briefly to his questionnaire, before again staring at the smoke. Soon, most subjects would get up from

> their chairs, walk over to the vent, and investigate it closely, sniffing the smoke, waving their hands in it, and feeling for temperature changes. Gaining little enlightenment from this investigation, the usual subject would show several more signs of hesitation, but finally walk out of the room. Finding somebody in the hall who looked as if he belonged there, he would calmly report to him the presence of the smoke.[107]

About 75 percent of all subjects eventually reported the smoke; the rest took no action.

Then the experimenters varied the experiments slightly. Three subjects were led into the waiting room at the same time, and all three were busily filling out their questionnaires when the smoke began to seep in. We know now that 75 percent of all students are "responsive bystanders" when left alone. That means that there is a probability of 98 percent that a group of three will contain at least one person who, if left by himself, would have reported the fire. The remarkable thing was that in only 30 percent of the cases did anyone bother to report the smoke. What the experiment suggests is that people's reluctance to help is not a matter of individual apathy but an aspect of crowd behavior.

Darley and Latane followed this up with an experiment replicating the typical emergency situation even more closely. Again Columbia undergraduates were telephoned and asked to participate, for a small fee, in a survey conducted by the Consumer Testing Bureau, a market research organization interested in testing the appeal of a number of adult games and puzzles.

> When the subject arrived for his appointment, he was met by an attractive and vivacious young woman who introduced herself as the market research representative and showed him to the testing room. The small room was separated by a collapsible cloth folding curtain wall from the "Consumer Testing Bureau Office" next door. The testing room was furnished with a table and several chairs and a number of adult games were scattered about. A large sign giving preliminary instructions covered most of the one-way window in the room. In the office next door, whose door was open, the subject could see a desk, chairs, and a large rather ramshackle bookcase with stacks of paper and equipment arrayed precariously on the bookshelf.

The market research representative explained the purpose of the research survey, gave the subjects some forms to fill out, and disappeared behind the curtain. As they were working on their forms, if they listened closely, the subjects could hear the woman climb up on a chair to get a book from the top shelf. Then, suddenly, they would hear a loud crash and a woman's screams as the chair fell over. "Oh, my God, my foot," the woman would be heard to cry. "I. . . . I. . . .can't move . . . it. Oh, my ankle. I can't . . . can't . . . . get . . . this thing off . . . me."[108] She moaned and cried for about a minute longer.

Again the first round of the experiment involved merely one subject at a time. Not a single subject failed to respond to the woman's screams. All rushed to her help. The second round of experiments involved two strangers at a time, both listening to the agonized screams of the woman. And the remarkable thing happened again: In only 70 percent of such cases did the woman receive any help.

Darley and Latane's explanation for what happened is persuasive:

> In public, people tend to feel constrained from expressing too much emotion or from making fools of themselves. These constraints may themselves tend to inhibit action by individuals in a group, but in conjunction with the processes of social influence, they may be expected to have especially powerful effects. As each person in an ambiguous and potentially dangerous situation looks to others to gauge their reactions, each may be falsely led to believe that the others are not concerned and consequently to be less concerned himself. This state of pluralistic ignorance may make each member of a group less likely to act than he would have been had he witnessed the emergency alone.[109]

This, then, goes a long way toward explaining the reaction of those witnesses who stood by while Andrew Mormille bled to death and of the crowd of forty who passively watched as the switchboard operator was chased by her assailant. It does not, however, explain the reaction of those people who from the privacy of their homes witnessed the murder of Kitty Genovese. They did not have to fear public embarrassment or humiliation. They could call the police and remain anonymous to their neighbors. Yet they did not do so. Another experiment by Darley and Latane sheds light on their reasons.

This time students in an introductory psychology class were asked to participate in an experiment. The subjects were led into a room and asked to put on a set of headphones. The experiment's ostensible purpose was to have a group of students, each located in a separate room, to preserve anonymity, talk to each other about the problems of living in a high-pressure, urban environment. Each subject would be able to talk for about two minutes at a time, at which point a mechanical switching device would turn off his microphone and turn on the microphone of another student. Thus at any given time only one subject could be heard over the network. The discussion was opened by some remarks which an accomplice of the experimenter had dictated into a tape recorder. The accomplice pretended, of course, to be one of the subjects participating in the study. He described his difficulties in getting adjusted to New York and to university life. Then, very hesitantly and with obvious embarrassment, he would mention that he was prone to seizures, particularly when studying or taking exams. Other people then took their turn and described similar problems. When it again became the first subject's turn, something strange happened. He made a few calm comments, then grew very loud and incoherent and finally began to stammer:

> I-er-um-I think I-I need-er-if-if could-er-er-somebody er-er-er-er-er-er-er give me a little-er-give me a little help here because-er-I-er-I'm-er-er-h-h-having a-a-a real problem-er-right now and I-er-if somebody could help me out it would-it would-er-er s-s-sure be-sure be good . . . because-er-there-er-er-a cause I-er-I-uh-I've got a-a one of the-er-sei——er-er-things coming on and-and-and I could really-er-use some help so if somebody would-er give me a little h-help-uh-er-er-er-er c-could somebody-er-er-help-er-uh-uh-uh (choking sounds). . . . I'm gonna die-er-er-I'm . . . gonna die-er-help-er-er-seizure-er (chokes, then quiet).[110]

The experiment was conducted with three kinds of groups: a group consisting solely of the one subject and the tape recorder, a group including two subjects and the tape recorder, and a six-person group. The results: 85 percent of the people who thought themselves alone with the victim responded. Only 62 percent of the people who thought there were five other people around responded. What happened? Darley and Latane explain it thus: "If only one bystander is present at an emergency, he carries all of the responsibility for dealing with it; he will feel all of the guilt for not acting; he will bear all of the blame that accrues for nonintervention. If others are present, the onus of responsibility is diffused, and the finger of blame points less directly at any one person. The individual may be more likely to resolve his conflict between intervening and nonintervening in favor of the latter alternative.''[111]

If Kitty Genovese failed to receive help, it was because, being part of a large group, nobody felt responsible. For Kitty Genovese, then, there was no safety in numbers.

There is a general impression that even in nonemergency situations people often behave much less altruistically than they feel. Most people if approached by a beggar on Mexico City's Zocalo will unhesitatingly drop some pesos in his hat, and yet relatively few respond to the pleas of Caritas or the United Way. Most people, if approached by a stranger near a hospital who tells them that unless someone donates blood for him to receive a transfusion within the next fourty-eight hours he will die, would accede to that request. Yet relatively few respond to calls for blood donations. Why?

In part it is that we feel that our contribution will make no difference. What is the measurable impact of a $10 contribution to the United Way? Many charities combat this feeling of impotence by assigning wards to individual donors—then, at least, the donor feels in a position to witness the impact of his contribution. For a time the United States experimented with buying rather than soliciting blood donations. The odd result was that the number of voluntary donors dropped dramatically. What had happened? The voluntary blood donor had begun to feel superfluous. Before, he had felt that his contribution in some measure increased the probability that blood would be available to a needy person. Now that purchased blood could make up any deficit, he no longer felt his contribution would make a difference. And so that source dried up. As a result many countries have shied away from purchasing blood.[112]

Something more profound than a feeling of impotence is involved as well. Economists in recent times have come to draw a distinction between two kinds of commodities: private goods and public goods. Private goods are so called because they have the rather unremarkable property that they can only be consumed by one person at a time. The loaf of bread I eat you cannot also enjoy. The bottle of wine I empty you cannot also imbibe. Public goods are so called because they can be consumed by several people at a time. A park can be enjoyed by several visitors at the same time. So can a concert, a play, or a painting. This somewhat peculiar feature of public goods helps to account for a number of peculiar features of our economy.[113]

It accounts, for instance, for a phenomenon that has surely puzzled numerous casual observers without seeming to permit an easy solution. Many fields of endeavor, especially the arts, contain so-called superstars who command exorbitantly higher earnings than their only slightly inferior colleagues. The opera singer whose voice is only slightly more resonant than that of her closest competitor, the pianist whose performance is only slightly more accomplished than that of his most serious rival, the network's national anchorman whose manner is only slightly more urbane than that of his local counterpart will all earn several times as much as the runners-up. Why? Because they create a public good. For Arthur Rubinstein to serve another listener he only has to send him a cheaply produced copy of a performance he has already given. For Wonderbread to serve another customer, it must actually bake another loaf of bread. The result is that Wonderbread cannot, with its limited number of factories, serve the entire country. Arthur Rubenstein can! Hence other bakers can coexist with Wonderbread. But not many other pianists can coexist with Arthur Rubinstein. (Remember the old trick question: If it takes five minutes to boil one egg, how long does it take to boil two?)[114]

Some public goods, however, cannot be made available selectively. Arthur Rubinstein can exclude from his performance whoever fails to pay for a ticket or a record. The government cannot exclude from the protection of its national defense whoever fails to subsidize it. If we asked everyone to contribute an amount to national defense commensurate with the value he placed on it, everyone would have an incentive to cheat. If he fails to contribute, only slightly less will be available for setting up a system of national defense, and he will still be in a position to enjoy the benefits of such a system. If everybody did this we would not, of course, end up with any system of national defense and everybody would be worse off than if nobody had cheated.

A similar kind of problem plagues charitable contributions. We are all altruists. We all derive pleasure from seeing the poor helped. But we also realize that we can enjoy that pleasure without actually contributing ourselves. As a result, however, we end up worse than if nobody had shirked his responsibility in the first place. Taxing everyone on the presumption that they sufficiently care about a given public good, be it national defense or charitable contributions to the poor, is one way of alleviating that dilemma.

It thus turns out that we are a great deal more altruistic than our conduct at times would indicate. It's just that a number of obstacles lie in the way of our showing it. If the impression has grown that we are all egoists, that may be because biologically egoism seems a much more natural trait to possess. It seems a lot easier to explain than altruism. We are part of the animal kingdom. In the animal kingdom, it seems, you survive not through altruism and self-sacrifice but through selfishness and greed. Why should we ever have evolved into altruists? Because, explains the economist, Gary Becker, the altruism trait may actually be beneficial to its owner. The altruist is someone whose satisfaction depends on other people's satisfaction. If he finds their income (psychic or real) to be too low, he makes gifts to them until he has raised their income to some satisfactory level. Suppose a beneficiary of his largesse has an opportunity to harm the altruist, a chance to do something that would profit him $1000 but cost the altruist $5000. Will he do it? Suppose he has been receiving $2000 periodically from the altruist. What would happen if he were to stab the altruist in the back? Even if the altruist weren't vindictive, he would cut his contribution to the man's income by at least $1000, because the man now needs that much less, and probably more, because the altruist is now $5000 poorer. So it doesn't pay the beneficiary to stab the altruist in the back. The altruist has in effect protected himself against back-stabbing. The altruist will flourish, and so will the altruism trait.[115]

We saw in earlier sections how people may sometimes seem to violate a statute, though they haven't really, because they didn't act, they merely underwent something. The law acquits them. We saw in these last two sections how people may sometimes seem to violate a statute, but they haven't really, because they didn't act, they merely let something happen. The law acquits them, too. The difference between acting and omitting, however, rests on a much thinner reed than the difference between acting and undergoing. The conceptual difference between act and omission rests on the answer to a highly ambiguous counterfactual question: would a certain harmful outcome have occurred if the defendant hadn't existed? The moral difference rests on the hazy concept of personal autonomy. If we say that the expert swimmer who watches a baby drown is less culpable than the motorist who recklessly runs it over, that's because he is merely holding on to something that belongs to him, his time, whereas the motorist is appropriating something that belongs to another, a person's life. Our reluctance to infringe on the swimmer's time seems to endow personal autonomy with greater sanctity than it deserves. It's comforting to know that people are by nature more altruistic than the law requires them to be.

Crimes of the Heart

The Statute of 25 Edward III, promulgated in 1351, is a progenitor of the modern law of treason. What makes the statute so extraordinary to read today is that it made it a crime merely to "compass" the death of the king. Taken literally, a man could be punished merely for thinking homicidal thoughts about his sovereign. Of course, nobody took it literally. How could they? How could one ever enforce such a statute? "No temporal tribunal can search the heart or fathom the intention of the mind, otherwise than as they are demonstrated by outward actions," an early commentator noted.[116] He overlooked, however, the possibility of confession, not necessarily to the authorities, but perhaps in a letter to a friend. But there were more compelling reasons for not punishing mere thoughts. If criminal thoughts could be punished, observed another writer, "all mankind would be criminals."[117] Another, yet, asked: "What would a system of laws embodying a rule providing for the punishment of intentions look like? When would punishment be administered? As soon as we find out the agent's intentions? But how do we know he will not change his mind? Furthermore, isn't the series—fantasying, wishing, desiring, wanting, intending—a continuum, making it a rather hazy matter to know just when a person is intending rather than wishing?" How would the authorities distinguish between fantasying, wishing, etc.? And what about "the difficulties the individual would have in identifying the nature of his emotional and mental state. Would we not be constantly worried about the nature of our mental life?" Am I only wishing the king were dead? Perhaps I have gone further? "The resultant guilt," he concludes, "would tend to impoverish and stultify our mental life."[118] For these reasons it is now recognized as one of the fundamental principles of the criminal law that one can only be punished for acts, one cannot be punished for harboring criminal thoughts or dispositions.

Why is this a significant restriction? What we are interested in, ultimately, is to prevent harm. There is something odd about telling people not to engage in harmful conduct by telling them not even to think about engaging in harmful conduct. As one commentator puts it:

> Imagine the order "Don't intend to raise your arm!" issued by one who has made it clear that if one does intend, the person will be shot. . . . there is something strange about ordering a person not to intend to raise his arm. What is it? If one's aim is to induce a person not to intend to raise his arm, one can accomplish what one wishes by ordering him not to raise his arm. And if one's aim is to induce him not to raise his arm the natural thing is to tell him not to. But more than this, if one were to order a person not to intend to raise his arm, one would be suggesting that one wanted him to refrain from doing something other than not raising his arm, that is, one would be suggesting that it was his intending that interested one and not his raising his arm.[119]

In short, the most direct and natural way of telling people not to engage in harmful conduct, such as setting out to shoot the king, is to tell them not to shoot the king, rather than to tell them not even to think about shooting the king. So why did anybody ever feel the need to state the maxim that the criminal law should preoccupy itself with acts rather than thoughts and dispositions?

In part, because the legislature does on occasion pass laws that at least purport to punish mere thoughts. Thus phrased, a statute often seems to carry greater moral force. The Statute of Edward is but one example. Another is the Witchcraft Suppression Act. Witchcraft can, of course, be nothing more than a psychic act: a mental ritual, the silent recitation of a curse, will under certain circumstances count as witchcraft. The Witchcraft Suppression Act seems to encompass such practices. And with good reason. Just consider the case of *Olubu v. The State,* decided only recently by a Nigerian Criminal Court of Appeals.[120] The defendant Olubu one day to his alarm discovered that he was impotent. He consulted some local herbalists, but try as they might, they were unable to help him. Finally, his wife confessed to Olubu that she had bewitched him and thus brought about his impotence. She promised to cure him. Two weeks elapsed and Olubu's condition was unchanged. Finally, Olubu grew so desperate and irate that he killed his wife. It is unclear by what means Olubu's wife had tried to bewitch her husband. But even if she performed nothing more than a purely mental ritual, it was no less harmful for that. One might, of course, say the real harm only came about when she confessed what she had done to her husband. But if the British had drafted a statute reading: "No one shall engage in any witchcraft ritual involving any physical steps or confess or reveal to anyone that he has engaged in a mental act of witchcraft" that would not have carried a great deal of moral force! Nonetheless, that is almost certainly how the statute was applied. It is virtually inconceivable that anyone was ever prosecuted merely because he had revealed to the authorities reciting some malevolent spells. Here the act requirement is significant as a reminder to the authorities that, whatever the literal language of a statute suggests, a man should not be punished merely for harboring evil thoughts.

The act requirement also serves to explain one of the more puzzling doctrines of criminal law: the entrapment defense. The entrapment defense was first formally announced in a case called *United States v. Sorrells,* decided in the midst of the prohibition era.[121] One Sunday in July 1930 the defendant, Sorrells, who lived near a small town in North Carolina, received a visit of several of his friends. They brought with them a stranger named Martin, who introduced himself as a furniture dealer from Charlotte, just passing through the town. When Sorrells discovered to his great pleasure that Martin and he shared a common background—both having served in the 30th Division of the American Expeditionary Forces during World War I—the two became fast friends. Martin, Sorrells, and another friend of Sorrells's who had also served in the 30th Division then began to reminisce about their war experiences. After a little while, Martin asked Sorrells for some liquor. Sorrells apologized because he didn't have any. Some more time passed and the conversation was taking an increasingly nostalgic turn. Martin again asked Sorrells for some liquor. He explained that he was anxious to buy a half-gallon for a friend back home. Sorrells replied that he "did not fool with whiskey." As time went on Martin reiterated his request for liquor some six or seven times. Finally, Sorrells got up, excused himself for about twenty minutes, and returned with the requested half-gallon. Martin gratefully accepted and paid him five dollars. Alas, Martin turned out to be a prohibition agent posing as a tourist. Sorrells was arrested and prosecuted for the illegal sale of liquor.

The Supreme Court, however, found him innocent. The government, it thought, had illegally "entrapped" Sorrells: It was clear, the Court noted, that the defendant's crime "was instigated by the prohibition agent, that it was the creature of his purpose, that the defendant had no previous disposition to commit it but was an industrious law-abiding citizen, and that the agent lured defendant, otherwise innocent, to its commission by repeated and persistent solicitation in which he succeeded by taking advantage of the sentiment aroused by reminiscences of their experiences as companions in arms in the World War."

In later cases the Supreme Court made it clear, however, that not every governmental inducement to crime amounts to entrapment. Where the government "merely affords opportunities or facilities for the commission of the offense," where the offense is not "the product of the creative activity" of government agents, there is no entrapment defense.[122] The defense, the Court explained, was intended to protect the "unwary innocent," not the "unwary criminal."[123] Within this loophole government sting operations of monumental proportions have continued into the present day. The most recent of its kind was the so-called ABSCAM plot.

ABSCAM's purpose was to test the integrity of high government officials. To set up the operation, the FBI "hired" a known con man, Melvin Weinberg. Weinberg had made a fortune as well as landed in jail for promising various real estate firms large loans from wealthy sponsors in return for "appraisal" fees of several thousand dollars, and then disappearing from the scene. The FBI had something similar in mind. Weinberg was to let it be known that he was the business agent for Abdul Enterprises, a fictitious organization, allegedly backed by two extremely wealthy Arab sheiks looking for American investment opportunities, legal or illegal. He was first approached by Angelo Errichetti, the mayor of Camden, who "claimed to have extraordinary influence in obtaining gambling casino licenses, power over the commissioners who issued licenses, connections with organized crime, ability to deal in narcotics, . . . as well as intimate knowledge of which members of the New Jersey legislature could be bought."[124] Errichetti soon brought in several other New Jersey politicians. Through a crony of Errichetti's, an attorney named Howard Criden, the operation managed to extend its tentacles into other states as well. Weinberg told Criden, for instance, that the sheik wanted to build an elaborate hotel complex in Philadelphia, if he could "be assured of the friendship of important government officials."[125] Criden helped to arrange meetings between Weinberg and George Schwartz and Harry Jannotti, president and minority leader of the Philadelphia City Council. Both Schwartz and Jannotti welcomed the sheik's plan with circumspect enthusiasm. If the project were legitimate, they primly observed, they would gladly support it. At the end of the meeting, however, throwing caution to the wind, they accepted bribes of $30,000 and $10,000, respectively.

But ABSCAM aimed higher than at corrupt local politicians: it aimed at the United States Congress. Weinberg let it be known that the sheiks were concerned that a change in government in their homeland might force them to emigrate to the United States. To insure against any problems they might have, should the occasion arise, Weinberg indicated, the sheiks wanted to "sign up" as many congressmen and other public officials as possible. The congressmen could expect, in return, sizable investments in their districts and payments of cash to them personally. The first of those baits was, of course, entirely legitimate, it was the second only that constituted a bribe. Before the operation had run its course, five congressmen had accepted bribes from Weinberg. But ABSCAM's success was bought at a very high cost. The prodding applied to the congressmen was at times so relentless as to convert one's mild unease about government entrapment into intense discomfort. The most disturbing of the cases is that of Congressman Richard Kelly.[126] The FBI approached Kelly through another con man, Gino Ciuzio, himself a victim of the hoax. Ciuzio mentioned to Kelly the availability of large investments in his district as well as the sizable payoffs. Kelly was interested—as he should have been—in the investments, but he rejected the payoffs out of hand. A meeting was set up between Kelly and representatives of the Arab sheiks. Just before the meeting Ciuzio reiterated to Weinberg that Kelly would not accept money and that by offering money to Kelly he would only jeopardize his objectives. Nevertheless, once face-to-face with Kelly, the FBI agent offered him the money. Kelly told the agent he was interested in the investment in his district but that whatever arrangements he had about paying money for his help with immigration "he had no part in that." But the agent was not to be put off. He hinted that large investments could very well be made somewhere else in the country and brought up the illegal payments again. The congressman remained adamant. He had only come to talk about the investments in the district, he reemphasized. The conversation appeared to be going nowhere. A telephone call momentarily brought it to a halt. Another FBI agent who had been monitoring the conversations from the basement told the man upstairs to remain persistent. Kelly, he explained, was just "being cute." And so the man did persist. Finally, not too long thereafter, Kelly gave in, when $25,000 was displayed for him spread out in packets of $100 bills. He stuffed the bills into his pocket and left.

What is so disturbing about the way the government lured Kelly, or for that matter Sorrells, into crime? Why should anyone mind the use of entrapment techniques? The courts have advanced numerous reasons, each of which seems to crumble upon close scrutiny. The *Sorrells* court purported to find it "implied" in every criminal statute. It could not have been the intention of Congress, the court there reasoned, in enacting a criminal statute "that its processes of detection and enforcement should be abused by the instigation by government officials of an act on the part of persons otherwise innocent in order to lure them to its commission and to punish them."[127] "We are not forced by the letter to do violence to the spirit and purpose of the statute." But that argument was purely fictitious. There was no suggestion anywhere in the United States Code that Congress did not consider a person guilty who had been goaded into violating a statute at government behest. The court would, of course, say that we are being too literal-minded. Surely Congress could not have meant the police to go out and add unnecessarily to an already burgeoning crime culture? But is the police indeed adding crime? The crime it artificially creates hardly deserves to be counted—it is entirely harmless since it is entirely within police control and supervision. The only way in which the police may be propagating crime is by indirectly increasing the demand for crime and thus indirectly increasing the amount of crime supplied. Thus, when the government begins to buy stolen goods from fences, it may drive up the price of stolen goods and thus encourage theft. But that is a relatively minor effect. It is balanced by the fact that entrapment serves to deter many who would otherwise commit crimes and to incapacitate many who would have responded to the next opportunity had this one not come along. It is unlikely that the police would pursue entrapment activities beyond the point at which, on the margin, the two effects balance each other out.

The second reason put forth is that the entrapped defendant is fundamentally innocent. He lacks the requisite culpability for punishment. That argument too is dismissed by most as patently defective. If the defendant who yields to an insistent government agent is innocent, why not the man who yields to an insistent thug? As far as the defendant is concerned the agent is a thug. If the lure of a $100,000 payment is too great for any mortal congressman to withstand, why not acquit him regardless of whether it is the government or a genuine thug who offers it? In sum, the argument is usually given short shrift on the ground that there is no "private entrapment" defense.

But there is a private entrapment defense, although the fact is usually overlooked. True, if a criminal approaches you and offers you the sky in return for a little help on his next "hit," you cannot plead entrapment. But that is not because it was a private individual who made you the offer rather than a government agent. Rather it is because he did not seek to entrap you. He merely sought your help. The paradigm of private entrapment is illustrated by *Topolewski v. State*.[128] Mat Dolan had just been fired from his job with a meat-packing company. He owed his friend Topolewski $100, but was now hardly in a position to repay it. Topolewski proposed a deal to him. If Dolan would help him steal some meat from his former employer, that would cancel the debt. Dolan pretended to agree but then told the meat company about Topolewski's plot. The company urged Dolan to play along, because it hoped to catch Topolewski *flagrante delicto*. Topolewski's plan was quite simple. Dolan would arrange for some packages of the company's meat to be placed on their loading platform, as was customary in delivering meat to buyers. Topolewski would drive up in a truck, pretend to be a customer, load up the meat, and leave. Forewarned by Dolan, the company decided to oblige Topolewski by not only planting four barrels at the loading dock but by telling the dock attendant to turn them over to whoever should inquire after them. Topolewski's plan went without a hitch—and so did the company's. Topolewski was arrested and convicted of larceny.

But the Supreme Court of Wisconsin reversed his conviction. Its ostensible reason was that there could be no larceny since the company had agreed to Topolewski's taking of the goods. The argument is obviously disingenuous. The company had agreed to Topolewski's taking as much as the person who puts some cheese in his mousetrap has agreed to feed the mice. What the court really had in mind was something else. "To stimulate unlawful intentions for the purpose and with the motive of bringing them to maturity so the consequent crime may be punished, is a dangerous practice." After all, a "contemplated crime may never be developed into a consummated act. . . . It is safer law and sounder morals to hold, where one arranges to have a crime committed against his property or himself, and knows that an attempt is to be made to encourage others to commit the act by one acting in concert with such owner, that no crime is thus committed. The owner and his agent may wait passively for the would-be criminal to perpetrate the offense, and each and every part of it, for himself, but they must not aid, encourage, or solicit him that they may seek to punish."[129] *Topolewski* was no fluke.[130] On several more occasions, where a clever vigilante saw an opportunity to lure and trap a fellow citizen in a homemade mousetrap, courts have responded in like manner.

We dislike entrapment because it conflicts with the act requirement. If I happen to know that you, generally a very law-abiding citizen, will under some very special concatenation of circumstances commit a criminal act, and I delude you into thinking that those circumstances have come about, am I not punishing you for your disposition? As a close friend of Harry's, an FBI agent learns that he is extraordinarily devoted to his wife, Helen. One day, to test his integrity, he contrives to play a trick on him. He convinces Harry that Helen is a woman with a past: for many years, he falsely claims, she worked as a call girl. He threatens to make that fact well-known in the community unless Harry helps him bring a small cocaine shipment from Mexico into the United States. Doing so, he assures Harry, is for Harry almost riskless. He fabricates documents showing that the border patrol and high-echelon FBI officials are in collusion with him. Using Harry, who is not affiliated with the bureau, is just an extra precaution he likes to take. Harry yields. As he comes to the agent's house to receive final instructions and some money for the trip, the agent arrests him. Few would fail to find the FBI agent's actions here objectionable. He is punishing Harry for failing to be law-abiding in a hypothetical situation Harry is unlikely ever to encounter in real life. He is, I believe, punishing Harry for his disposition, not his acts. There is a story about George Bernard Shaw asking a woman: "Would you spend the night with me for a million pounds? "Yes, of course," the woman replied. "Will you spend the night with me for a hundred pounds?" he continued. The woman blustered: "What do you take me for?" "That, my dear, has already been established. Now we're just haggling over the price." The logic of the entrapper is the logic of George Bernard Shaw. The only difference is that Shaw was only aiming to expose the woman as venal not to convict her of a crime.

But why be so fastidious about the act requirement? If entrapment entails punishing somebody for his disposition, perhaps the act requirement shouldn't be so sacrosanct in the first place? The problem is that criminal dispositions of one kind or another reside within all of us.[131] Just imagine an especially ambitious sting operation that contrives to put its victim into a setting like that of Dudley and Stephens: alone in an open boat, in the middle of the ocean, in the company of but one other starving, half-dead sailor, without food and without water. The victim responds the way Dudley did: he tries to kill his companion, but he is stopped in time. If the situation were for real, he might be guilty of attempted murder. But it isn't. Is he still guilty? I don't think so. Everyone, I think, is entitled to his turn at the wheel of fortune. If he is lucky, he will never be faced with a situation in which his criminal disposition surfaces. Entrapment is a way of rigging the wheel. Perhaps, looking at Thomas Dudley, we mutter, "There, but for the grace of God, go I." That is better than: "There, but for the grace of God, the government, and moral vigilantes."

The act requirement is significant, finally, because it isn't always trivial to decide whether something is an act or a thought. Where, for instance, do words fit in? Are they acts or thoughts?

It is a relatively recent discovery of philosophers that some statements are very thoughtlike, others very actlike. On the one hand, there are simple matter-of-fact statements such as: "The cat is on the mat." Here the speaker seeks merely to describe, assert, note, constate (as philosophers like to put it) some state of affairs. On the other hand there are statements like: "Let's kill the bastard!"—as exclaimed during a lynching; "I do"—as whispered in the course of a marriage ceremony; "I name this ship the 'Queen Elizabeth' "—as declared while smashing a bottle against the stern; "I give and bequeath my watch to my brother."—as written in a will. Here the speaker is not interested in describing anything: he is seeking to do something, to perform an act, to incite, order, command, request; to marry, promise, vow, pledge; to name or baptize; to bequeath or donate. The former kind of statement, dubbed "constatives," could be true or false; the latter kind, labeled "performatives," could not really be considered true or false, but only effective or ineffective, successful or unsuccessful, happy or unhappy.[132]

Over time, this way of distinguishing constatives and performatives, though basically sound, came to be considered somewhat ill-put. After all, the speaker who utters a constative statement is also doing something: he is uttering a constative. And the speaker who utters a performative is also asserting something: he is asserting a performative. The distinction was reformulated thus: Constative statements "are supposed in some way to match an independently existing world; and to the extent that they do or fail to do that we say that they are true or false." Performative statements, by contrast, "are not supposed to match an independently existing reality but rather are supposed to bring about changes in the world so that the world matches the propositional content of the speech act; and to the extent that they do or fail to do that, we do not say that they are true or false but rather such things as that they are obeyed or disobeyed, fullfilled, complied with, kept or broken"—successful or unsuccessful, effective or ineffective, and so on. We can "mark this distinction by saying that the [constative] classes have a word-to-world direction of fit, and the [performative] classes have the world-to-word direction of fit.'' If an assertion is not true, it is the assertion ''which is at fault, not the world; if the order is disobeyed or the promise is broken it is not the order or promise which is at fault, but the world in the person of the disobeyer of the order or the breaker of the promise. Intuitively we might say the idea of direction of fit is that of responsibility for fitting. If the statement is false, it is the fault of the statement (word-to-world direction of fit). If the promise is broken, it is the fault of the promiser (world-to-word direction of fit).''[133]

The law, it seems, was on to this distinction between thoughtlike and actlike speech long before the philosophers. Whatever area of law one turns to, not just the criminal law, one finds that courts have traditionally declared themselves to be interested in actlike speech and uninterested in thoughtlike speech. The distinction is most obvious in the Supreme Court's interpretation of the free speech clause of the First Amendment. The sweep of the free speech clause is enormous, but just what are its limits? Two things have been clear throughout. Certain kinds of speech—such as dispassionate scientific discourse about abstract ideas—are protected almost without a doubt. And certain kinds of speech, without a doubt, are unprotected. ''The most stringent protection of free speech would not protect a man in falsely shouting fire in a theatre, and causing a panic,'' wrote Oliver Wendell Holmes. More generally, words advocating and inciting imminent lawless, especially violent conduct are not within the purview of the First Amendment. Whenever a case comes before the court, the more it resembles dispassionate, scientific discourse the more likely that it will be deemed protected, the more it resembles incendiary exhortation the less likely. What is the difference between these two categories of speech? One is thoughtlike, the other actlike. One has a word-to-world direction of fit (words are used to describe the world); the other has a world-to-word direction of fit (words are used to change the world).

The distinction also figures prominently in evidence law. Under the hearsay doctrine, courts categorically ban from the courtroom all out-of-court statements offered to prove the truth of the matter asserted. The idea here is that such statements are unreliable because they are not made under oath, because the jury cannot observe the declarant's demeanor as he makes them, and because the declarant usually cannot be cross-examined on them. Certain kinds of out-of-court statements do not rank as hearsay. If somebody said "I do" at a wedding, or "I agree" during a contract negotiation, or "Let's kill the bastard" during a brawl, these statements do not count as hearsay and can be freely recounted in court. They are not really statements, the courts say, they are "verbal acts." What the courts mean is that these statements have a world-to-word fit, not a word-to-world fit; verbal acts are performatives, not constatives. The declarant is not using his words to report the state of the world, but to shape it.

In labor law, when the employees of a company decide whether they want to be represented by a union, the employer is prohibited from uttering threats that if the union comes in he will close shop, refuse to raise wages, or withdraw privileges the employees now have. Such threats would interfere with a free election. The employer is permitted, however, to make sober and sincere predictions that if the union comes in economic circumstances will force him to close shop, to refuse any wage raises, or to withdraw privileges the employees now have. Such information is necessary for a sound election. What is the difference between the two kinds of statements? Threats have a world-to-word fit; they are performatives. Predictions have a word-to-world fit; they are constatives. Courts are interested only in the performative.

The same goes for the law of contracts. A surgeon tells his patient that by removing the scarred tissue from the palm of his right hand and grafting on to it some skin from the patient's chest, he can make the hand look perfectly normal again. Before the operation he says to his patient: "I will guarantee to make the hand a one hundred percent perfect hand." The operation fails—the patient's hand is still scarred, but now it is hairy as well. Has the surgeon breached a contract to the patient? Must he pay him damages? Only if his statement "I guarantee . . ." amounts to a promise rather than a prediction. The court is only interested in the former. Promises have a world-to-word fit, they are performatives. Predictions have a word-to-world fit, they are constatives. Again, courts only care for performatives.

The law of wills is another case in point. When a man's will bequeathes his fortune to his son "so that he may continue his medical research," has he made it a precondition of the bequest that his son continue his medical research or is he merely stating the motive for his bequest, without legal effect? Only preconditions interest the courts, not motives. The former have a world-to-word fit (performatives), the latter have a word-to-world fit (constatives). The courts are only concerned with performatives.

Criminal law, finally, is no exception. The act requirement here means that only actlike speech can be punished. And not all speech is actlike. If a person confesses his plan to kill the king, that's not sufficiently actlike. His statement is a constative, not a performative; it has a word-to-world fit, not a world-to-word fit. The speaker is merely *reporting,* not exhorting. Of course it won't always be easy to tell whether speech is actlike or thoughtlike, whether the speaker is reporting or exhorting. How, for instance, should one classify "We hold these truths to be self-evident, that all men are created equal . . ."?

We have seen yet a third way in which people may seem to commit a crime, yet haven't committed a criminal act, because what they did, although "criminal," was no act. But why isn't it an act, when it looks like one? Why isn't it an act when Congressman Kelly stuffs a bribe into his pocket? Why isn't it an act when someone confesses his murderous intent against the king? In a sense, these are, of course, acts. We care about them, however, not because they are themselves harmful, but because they are evidence of harmful thoughts. If we punished them, we would be punishing them not as acts, but as indicators of certain thoughts.

We have been preoccupied in this chapter with the physical half of the criminal offense, the "bad act." We concentrate next on the mental part, the "guilty mind." A crime can be perpetrated in a variety of mental states: intentionally, knowingly, recklessly, negligently, to name only the most important ones. Determining whether the defendant's mental state can properly be described by any of these terms is a tricky task. The next chapter is devoted to showing what makes it tricky.

3 Guilty Minds

Bewitched, Bothered, and Bewildered

There is more to murder than killing someone. The killing must be, depending on the statute, "intentional," "willful," "premeditated," or "with malice aforethought." Typically, it simply has to be intentional.

The following occurred in a Dinka village in the Sudan. It was 7:00 or 7:30 in the morning. Ngok Keir heard a rustle outside his house. He assumed it was a marauding monkey. He went outside and aimed a fish-spear in the direction of the noise. Alas, the noise had come from a village woman who was cutting *durra* heads on her husband's field about thirty paces away. The spear pierced her from back to breast; she died within twenty-four hours. There was no murder, the court found, because the killing was not intentional. "The evidence shows that monkeys do frequent the *durra* cultivation in that locality," the court noted, "and that the spearing of such animals is not illegal, and that, when the accused threw his spear at the deceased, he assumed she was a marauding monkey, and did not know that she was a human being."[1]

It's easy enough to see that if a person confuses a human being with a monkey he has not intentionally killed a human being. But what if he confuses a human being with a ghost? There is nothing contrived about the question, for such cases abound in the Sudan as well as elsewhere in Africa and are not unknown in North America. Here is how the court summarized the facts in one such case, *Sudan Government v. Mohamed Ahmed Mohamed Mohamedein:*[2]

> One dark night, September 11, 1947, after supper [the accused] was going from Bubha village to the village of Meki Beshir to visit his girl friend, Mastura bint Ali. The Villages are about two miles apart, and there is a local

> superstition that the path between them is haunted. The apparition (*ba'ati*) is said to be that of a man, though no one living claims to have seen it.
>
> On the way the accused was met by a figure which he described as that of a man. He certainly then thought so, for he called a greeting, but received no reply. The figure had a wrapping round his head, and appeared to have his arms folded across his chest. The accused asked who he was, but again received no reply. By this time the accused was thoroughly frightened, and, thinking that the figure might be (or possibly was) the *ba'ati* plunged his spear into it, and ran on to Meki Beshir village, where he told no-one of his adventure.
>
> The figure was that of Hamid Yahya, the deceased, a harmless old man of 60, who was killed by the accused's stab.
>
> Various reasons have been suggested as to why the deceased failed to reply to the accused's greetings. The deceased was not deaf, but he had his head wrapped up against the chill night air, and he may not have heard what the accused said. He may have been as frightened of the accused as the accused was of him. Despite his age, the deceased was on his way . . . to visit a lady friend, and he may have wished to hide his identity from anyone he met.

What was the court to make of this? "To commit homicide the accused must intend . . . to cause the death of a human being," Chief Justice Maclagan began the argument portion of his opinion. "It is no offence to kill a ghost." But the defendant had been a bit rash, the chief justice observed. "He admits that he first thought the deceased was a man. His only grounds for changing his mind were the local superstition, coupled with the fact that the deceased stood his ground and remained silent without answering his challenge. These are insufficient grounds to justify the accused thrusting his spear into what, a moment before, he had believed to be a man, and was, in fact, a man." The chief justice concluded: "The natural and probable result of such a rash and needless act was to cause death, and the accused must be held to have intended to do so."

Maclagan's decision did not sit well with subsequent courts addressing the same question. He had, it was felt, cheated by making the artificial and entirely unwarranted assumption that one intends the natural and probable consequences of one's acts. But there was no doubt that Mohamed Ahmed did not intend to kill a human being, although to any nonsuperstitious observer that was the natural and probable consequence of what he had done. The Sudanese courts had occasion to reconsider the problem some three years later. The defendant, Abdel Rahman Yacoub Daw El Bet, "mistook" a frail old cripple for an evil spirit. He first hit the man with a stone, then finished him off with two violent ax blows to the skull. The court found that the "accused honestly and reasonably believed (until after he had committed the acts of violence resulting in the old man's death) that the deceased was not a human being (but an evil spirit)." It acquitted the man.[3]

The court remained faithful to this approach in all subsequent cases.

> On March 16, 1955, in the afternoon Mirghani and Adam went to the valley (the *wadi*) for grazing their sheep. After sunset, they took their food and slept near each other. The valley is reputed to be haunted by ghosts. It was a dark night. Suddenly Mirghani felt something standing astride over his body. Frightened by this, he hoarsely said, "What is this?" Even as he spoke, the "something" fell on him. Mirghani in good faith thought that it was a ghost and stabbed it with his knife thrice. Something ran, Mirghani got up and shouted for Adam but could not find him. He ran to his father, woke him up and told him what had happened.

Adam had not responded because Mirghani had just stabbed him. The court declared, "According to the evidence . . . the *wadi* was reputed to be haunted by ghosts. It was a general superstition. The version of Mirghani is straightforward, and one only has to hear his simple tale and it impresses as an honest statement of what had happened. . . . We believe that Mirghani had stabbed an imaginary ghost."[4]

Mirghani was acquitted.

Abdullah Mukhtar Nur, a young man of twenty, had heard from his mother and other villagers, that a ghost (*afrieta*) was about.[5] One day when he was out searching for a missing cow, he saw a figure walking toward him dressed in black and carrying a stick. He spoke to the figure but got no answer. He became frightened, grew convinced the figure was a ghost, and began to club it vehemently with his stick. The man collapsed and died. The court found:

> The accused was frightened and imagined that he had met the ghost. He was no doubt influenced by the tales he heard about the ghost in the district. . . . Considering these facts we are satisfied that the accused had grounds for believing he was dealing with a ghost. . . . After the fright his behaviour was so simple that he went to the village and proudly broke the news of his victory. From this act we infer that the accused acted in good faith and in the honest belief that he killed the ghost without any intention of killing a human being. The accused found himself in danger and was driven by the instinct of self-preservation to this way. . . . He was labouring under the belief that he was fighting a ghost.
>
> . . . Accordingly, we are satisfied that the act of the accused is not an offence and he should be set at liberty.

So much for ghosts. What if the defendant thought he was killing a witch, a sorcerer, or a wizard? On June 10, 1928, Kilo Buti and a friend of his clubbed and strangled to death one Kope whom they believed to have bewitched Kilo Buti's dead son by sitting on his grave. There was nothing atypical in their suspicions or the way they reacted to them. The acting governor of the province personally wrote the chief justice concerning this case:

> I [myself] have had a regrettably large experience of such cases. . . . it matters little whether the suspected person has or has not a sinister reputation as regards sorcery. If an ordinary person unsuspected of sorcery puts a piece of ostrich meat [on] another person's land or sits on a grave, it is quite sufficient to bring down upon him the charge of sorcery in the case concerned. . . . There is no evidence of enmity between murderers and murdered man, and in such a case it is quite immaterial among these savages that there should be. I personally know of two cases in which friend killed friend solely because a question of bewitching had arisen.[6]

That did not dissuade the court from convicting the defendants.

Sudan Government v. Ngerabaya tells the story of a man who killed another man, named Tugu, because he had become convinced that Tugu had used magical spells to kill two of his brothers and his daughter.[7] In fact everyone else in his tribe thought the same. That did not stop the court from convicting him of murder and sentencing him to life imprisonment. Something very similar happened in *Sudan Government v. Tia Muni*. Tia Muni's wife had died in childbirth. He remarried and had several more children. All of these children and their mother died within two years. A diviner told Tia Muni that his first wife's father was to blame for all this because he had cast spells on his new family. The desperate Tia Muni confronted the old man and after some heated words stabbed him to death. He was convicted and sentenced to death, but his sentence was later commuted to a lighter one.[8]

What the Sudanese courts have arrived at is a very strange dichotomy. Killing a human being, believing him to be a ghost or supernatural creature, is not an offense, and yields an acquittal. Killing a human being with supernatural powers, even if he is believed to have used them to bewitch the defendant, constitutes murder, and merits the death penalty or life imprisonment. How can something as straightforward as the requirement of an intention produce such disparate results?

To be confused about whether one is killing a ghost, a witch, or a human being is to be confused about the sort of thing one is killing. More common and equally puzzling are cases where the person one kills is not the person one intended to kill. Does that amount to murder? A classic version of the problem is recounted in the old English case *The Queen v. Saunders and Archer.*[9]

> The said *John Saunders* had a wife whom he intended to kill, in order that he might marry another Woman with whom he was in Love, and he opened his Design to the said *Alexander Archer,* and desired his Assistance and Advice in the Execution of it, who advised him to put an End to her Life by Poison. With this Intent the said *Archer* bought the Poison, viz. *Arsenick* and *Roseacre,* and delivered it to the said *John Saunders* to give it to his Wife, who accordingly gave it to her, being sick, in a roasted Apple, and she eat a small Part of it, and gave the rest to the said *Eleanor Saunders,* an Infant, about three Years of Age, who was the Daughter of her and the said *John Saunders* her Husband. And the said John Saunders seeing it, blamed his Wife for it, and said that Apples were not good for such Infants; to which his Wife replied that they were better for such Infants than for herself; and the

> Daughter eat the poisoned Apple, and the said *John Saunders,* her Father, saw her eat it, and did not offer to take it from her, lest he should be suspected, and afterwards the Wife recovered, and the Daughter died of the said Poison.

The court was ill at ease with the case. As the court reporter noted, "whether or not this was Murder in *John Saunders,* the Father, was somewhat doubted, for he had no intent to poison his Daughter, nor had he any Malice against her, but on the contrary he had a great Affection for her, and he did not give her the Poison, but his Wife ignorantly gave it her." Still, the court convicted him: When a man "lays . . . Poison with an Intent to kill some reasonable Creature, and another reasonable Creature, whom he does not intend to kill, is poisoned by it, such Death shall not be dispunishable, but he who prepared the Poison shall be punished for it, because his Intent was evil." The court went even further, generalizing to similar cases: "If a Man of Malice prepense shoots an Arrow at another with an Intent to kill him, and a Person to whom he bore no Malice is killed by it, this shall be Murder in him, for when he shot the Arrow he intended to kill, and inasmuch as he directed his Instrument of Death at one, and thereby has killed another, it shall be the same Offence in him as if he had killed the Person he aimed at." And similarly, "if one lies in wait in a certain Place to kill a Person, and another comes by the Place, and he who lies in wait kills him out of Mistake, thinking that he is the very Person whom he waited for, this Offence is Murder in him, and not Homicide only, for the killing was founded upon Malice prepense."[10]

Both of the hypothetical cases contemplated by the *Saunders* court have presented themselves since then, but neither courts nor commentators have been very comfortable or confident about the *Saunders* court's dogmatic and unexplained resolution. The defendant in the American case *Bratton v. Tennessee* had tried to shoot Mr. Wilsford but inadvertently shot Mrs. Wilsford.[11] Had he intentionally killed her? "A grosser absurdity cannot be conceived," wrote the court. "The hypothesis that the killing was undesigned, concedes that the will did not concur with the act; that, in point of fact, no such specific intention existed; no such result was either contemplated or designed." Still most American courts have sided with *Saunders*.

The second of the *Saunders* court's two hypotheticals—the man who lies in wait and kills his victim "out of Mistake, thinking that he is the very Person whom he waited for"—is really quite distinct from cases of misadministered poison, misfired bullets, or other ways of bungling the execution of a crime. The problem that cases like it present is one of mistaken identity. In 1858, the lumber dealer Rosahl, citizen of the small German town of Schliepzig, owed a sizable debt to the builder Schliebe. The most convenient way to rid himself of his debts, he decided, was to kill Schliebe. He persuaded his servant Rose to do the job for him. When he heard that Schliebe was taking a walk from Schliepzig to the nearby town of Lieskau, he told Rose to ambush him on a certain lonely footpath connecting the two towns. Rose hid in the underbrush and waited for his victim. Soon he heard steps. He leapt up and fired at the man. The man groaned, but was not yet dead. Rose shot again. When the prostrate man still showed signs of life, Rose stepped out from the underbrush and proceeded to crush the man's skull with the butt of his gun. Then he threw the gun into the river and told Rosahl that he had killed Schliebe. In fact he had killed an uninvolved passerby named Harnisch. Schliebe passed by shortly thereafter, found Harnisch dead, and suspected the truth. Rosahl and Rose were charged with murder. They argued that inasmuch as they had intended to kill someone other than the person they killed, they were at most guilty of voluntary manslaughter (for recklessly killing someone) but not of murder: they did not intentionally kill Harnisch—they cared nothing for Harnisch. In a widely debated opinion the German court convicted them, nonetheless. It reasoned that even though Rose shot Harnisch mistaking him for Schliebe, still he wanted to kill the particular human being at which he was aiming. Clearly, then, he intentionally shot that human being.[12]

A common problem afflicts all of the above cases: mistake. Is a killing unintentional because the killer was mistaken about the nature of his victim (he meant to spear a ghost, not a human being), about the effect of his actions (he meant to poison the mother, not the child), or about the identity of his prey (he meant to shoot Harnisch, not Schliebe)? Each type of mistake has invited controversy. Compelling arguments can be made for diametrically opposed positions.

A good case can be made out that the Sudanese courts were right to distinguish ghost-killings from witch-killings. Glanville Williams, one of the most authoritative of criminal law commentators, has made this case. To kill someone mistaking him for a pig cannot be considered the intentional killing of a human being. But why? Because the defendant doesn't think he's killing a human being? Not quite, says Williams. Some people don't consider Irishmen human beings, but that doesn't give them license to kill Irishmen. Whether Irishmen should be classified as human beings is a *legal* question. Ignorance of how the law classifies Irishmen is no excuse for killing them. It matters little, then, that the defendant who mistakes his victim for a pig doesn't think he is killing a human being. It matters only that he mistakes his victim for a creature which the legislature wouldn't consider human. Explains Williams, "One has to inquire of the accused what are the characteristics of the class to which he believed his victim to belong, and one then has to decide whether this class, assuming it to exist, would fall within the legal definition of the class to be protected" (i.e., human beings).[13]

Using this test, Williams discusses the case of a defendant who thinks he killed a fairy:

"He may think, for example, that fairies have the magical powers of becoming invisible, casting spells, and flying through the air otherwise than in aeroplanes. [We must ask:] If such creatures truly existed, would they be classified by the law as human beings or not?"

Since one cannot clearly say they would, Williams thinks the defendant should be acquitted. Williams also explores the case of a man who kills a lunatic, who is, he thinks, possessed by the devil.

> Can we allow [the defendant] to argue that in his view a man possessed of a devil is himself a devil and no longer a man, and therefore is not within the protection of the criminal law? It is clear that the task of interpreting the words of the law is for the court, not for the accused. Here the law says that one must not intentionally kill a human being, and the court interprets this term to include a lunatic. It is not permissible for the accused to say that he for his part interprets the term "human being" as not including a lunatic. If this is so, it may be thought impossible for the accused by saying that a lunatic is a creature possessed of the devil, or is the devil, to evade criminal responsibility. The process of classification is for the court, not for the accused; the victim of the attack is in ordinary language a lunatic, and the court decides that such a creature is a human being.

The ghost-killer can be distinguished from the witch-killer like the fairy-killer from the lunatic-killer. First, Williams would say, imagine a world in which ghosts exist. Would the legislature deem them human beings? Probably not. Hence a ghost-killer is not a murderer. Next, Williams would say, imagine a world in which witches exist. Would the legislature deem *them* human beings? Probably so, although that may depend on whether the defendant thinks of witches as old women with magical powers or magical creatures in the shape of women. Hence the witch-killer is (probably) a murderer.

On the other hand, a good case can be made out against Williams's approach. What Williams asks us often is logically impossible. In effect, he asks us to imagine a world in which the defendant's false beliefs are true and to determine whether in such a world he would be a murderer. Unfortunately, an imaginary world in which the defendant's false beliefs are realized may well be logically incoherent. A person may believe that 2 plus 2 is 5. It is impossible to imagine what such a world looks like. What does a square look like in such a world? What does a cube look like in such a world? What do houses look like in such a world? How does addition work in such a world? When is a budget balanced in such a world? An imaginary world conforming to a logical falsehood makes no sense.

Even if a person believes factual, not logical, falsehoods, it may not be possible to imagine a logically coherent world in which those hold true. Sure, a person may believe that Nixon won the 1960 election or that Hitler was a famous German landscape painter. It's possible to imagine a logically coherent world in which Nixon beat Kennedy in 1960 or in which Hitler stayed with painting instead of politics. But suppose a person believes Theodore and Franklin Delano Roosevelt were the same person. How are we to imagine a world in which Theodore Roosevelt *is* Franklin Delano Roosevelt? How would the single Roosevelt look? Like Theodore? Then how can we say he is Franklin? Like Franklin? Then how can we say he is Theodore?[14]

To return to the African setting: Suppose a tribesman kills his neighbor explaining that he was "really" only a donkey. He admits that his neighbor looked like a man, talked like a man, walked like a man. He isn't arguing that the man turned into a donkey at night. And he isn't trying to be figurative either. But he steadfastly maintains, that despite his human appearance his neighbor was "really" a donkey. How do we imagine a world in which that is true? How would Williams's test apply to this case? (Such beliefs exist. The Nuer believe, for example, that a certain sacrificial cucumber used in a ritual "really" is an ox.)[15]

Williams's test has a more serious defect. It is highly ambiguous. Try, to apply it to the case of Tia Muni, who killed the father of his first wife, because he thought the man had bewitched his second wife and her children. At first it looks easy to apply. We imagine a world in which the defendant is right, in which his father-in-law did use magic to kill his family. We decide that, even if he knows magic, his father-in-law is a human being and covered by the murder statute. But have we really recreated a world that corresponds to all of Tia Muni's beliefs about his father-in-law? Tia Muni might believe that the world is full of supernatural creatures threatening people's lives. He might consider persons practicing magic halfway between a ghost and a human. If we really lived in such a world, isn't it likely that the legislature would confine the murder statute to pure humans, and would use something much less strict, something like a game law, to regulate the killing of ghosts and witches? The problem with Williams's test is that it does not tell us how many of the defendant's false beliefs to incorporate into our make-believe world. If we incorporate many, the defendant is innocent. If we incorporate few, he is guilty.[16]

The problem of mistaken consequences—misadministered poisons, misfired bullets—is equally troubling. Here, too, convincing arguments exist on both sides of the issue. American courts by-and-large say that where A intends to kill B but inadvertently kills C he has intentionally killed C. They argue: A intended to kill a human being, he killed a human being, hence he intentionally killed a human being. German courts uniformly reject this view. They argue: If A intentionally killed, whom did he intentionally kill? Not B, for B is still alive. Not C, for he never meant any harm to C. B may have been his worst enemy, and C his best friend.

The problem of mistaken identity looks least controversial. Most seem to think that, mistaken identity or not, an intentional killing took place. The argument of the German court looks pretty convincing: Even if Rose shot Harnisch mistaking him for Schliebe, he did want to kill the particular human being at which he was aiming. And yet, consider: When Rose heard that he shot Harnisch, surely he was aghast. So can we really say he intentionally shot Harnisch? Consider also: Rosahl never even laid eyes on Harnisch. He probably had no inkling Harnisch existed. So how can we say that he intentionally participated in the killing of Harnisch?

Why Ignorance Is Bliss

These exotic cases of mistake dramatize the importance of the mens rea element of an offense. Mistakes wouldn't matter if there were no mens rea requirement. Why does it matter that the defendant confused his victim with a monkey? Only because murder consists of the *intentional* killing of a human being. Why does it matter than an American soldier charged with raping a Japanese girl mistook her for a prostitute and misconstrued her protests as an invitation? Only because rape requires a belief that the woman did not consent to intercourse. Why does it matter that you mistook somebody else's umbrella for your own? Only because theft requires knowledge that you are taking somebody else's property. It is the mens rea requirement that makes mistakes relevant.

It is far from self-evident why that should be so. *Why* should mistakes be relevant? It has to do with a rather remarkable feature of our language. Take the sentence: Cain dined with Abel. Let's assume the sentence is true. Let's also assume Abel is a Russian spy. Then we also know the following sentence to be true: Cain dined with a Russian spy. I am not suggesting there is anything remarkable about *that*. Most sentences you can think of are like that: Jerome met Mark Twain. Mark Twain is Samuel Clemens. Therefore, we know: Jerome met Samuel Clemens. Joe hit Cassius Clay. Cassius Clay is Muhammad Ali. Therefore, we know: Joe hit Muhammad Ali. This very unsurprising fact about language is usually called the principle of substitutivity. If we replace one expression in a sentence with another expression referring to the same thing, the resulting sentence says the same thing. The principle is obvious almost beyond justification. Sentences are statements about things. Therefore, no matter what we call those things, the sentences should remain true.

The strange and remarkable fact is that statements containing references to people's mental states seem to violate the principle of substitutivity. Take the sentence:

Jerome thought Mark Twain a great writer.

Mark Twain is Samuel Clemens. Still, we can't conclude

Jerome thought Samuel Clemens a great writer.

Jerome, who has heard of a close friend of Ulysses S. Grant named Samuel Clemens, doesn't know that this is Mark Twain. Take the sentence:

Joe admired Muhammad Ali.

Muhammad Ali is Cassius Clay. Still, we can't conclude:

Joe admired Cassius Clay.

Joe, who has heard of the draft-resister Cassius Clay, doesn't know that that is Muhammad Ali. Take the sentence:

Cain wanted to dine with Abel.

Rudolf Abel is a Russian spy. Still, we can't conclude:

Cain wanted to dine with a Russian spy.

Cain despises Russian spies, he has no idea that Rudolf Abel is one. These sentences violate the principle of substitutivity with impunity.

Violations of this very sort explain why mistakes are important in criminal law. Ngok Keir intentionally kills something sounding like a monkey. What sounds like a monkey is in fact a woman. If the principle of substitutivity worked, it seems we could conclude: Ngok Keir intentionally killed a woman. A soldier knowingly has intercourse with a Japanese woman. The woman happens to be protesting. If the principle worked, we should be able to infer that he knowingly had intercourse with a protesting woman. You intentionally take a certain umbrella. It happens to be Maurice's umbrella. If the principle worked, we could now say: You intentionally took Maurice's umbrella. But the principle doesn't work—and so we can't.

But why doesn't it work? A century ago the German philosopher Gottlob Frege first offered a reason.[17] Consider the following two examples:

> Frankfurter's visit with the President was over. The President dismissed Frankfurter.
>
> Someone suggested that Roosevelt appoint Frankfurter to the Supreme Court. But the President dismissed Frankfurter.

The phrase "the President dismissed Frankfurter" says something different in each paragraph. Why? In the first one Roosevelt is dismissing *the man* Frankfurter, in the second he is dismissing *the thought* of Frankfurter. "Frankfurter" in the first paragraph refers to a *man*, in the second to a *thought*. (Just as a bookseller who says "We sold three Saul Bellows today." is not referring to the *man* Saul Bellow, but to his books.) The sentence in the second paragraph is really short for

> But the President dismissed *the thought* of Frankfurter.

Now consider again a sentence like

> Jerome thought about Mark Twain.

Frege would note that Mark Twain does not here refer to the real Mark Twain. It refers to a thought about (or a thought of) Mark Twain. The sentence is really short for

> Jerome thought a thought about Mark Twain.

Similarly the sentence

> Jerome thought about Samuel Clemens.

is really short for

> Jerome thought a thought about Samuel Clemens.

Now it is clear why the two sentences don't say the same thing, why Samuel Clemens cannot be substituted for Mark Twain. Mark Twain in the above sentence refers not to Mark Twain but to a thought about Mark Twain. Samuel Clemens in the above sentence refers not to Samuel Clemens but to a thought about Samuel Clemens. Evidently, a Mark Twain thought is not the same thing as a Samuel Clemens thought. Evidently, too, "Mark Twain" where it refers to a Mark Twain thought cannot be replaced with "Samuel Clemens" where it refers to a Samuel Clemens thought. We should not expect the sentence about Mark Twain to say the same thing as the one about Samuel Clemens.

Other intentional statements can be analyzed identically. The sentences involving Joe translate into

> Joe thought admiring thoughts about Cassius Clay.

and

> Joe thought admiring thoughts about Muhammad Ali.

The sentences involving Cain translate into

> Cain wantingly thought thoughts of dinner with Abel.

and

> Cain wantingly thought thoughts of having dinner with a Russian spy.

These sentences may be awkward, even ungrammatical, but they show precisely why the principle of substitutivity fails in intentional statements. Cassius Clay is Muhammad Ali, but a Cassius Clay–thought isn't a Muhammad Ali–thought. Abel is a Russian spy, but an Abel-thought isn't a Russian-spy–thought. That's why substitution doesn't work.

Two Stanford philosophers, Jon Barwise and John Perry, have offered a competing explanation.[18] They claim that, strictly speaking, substitution doesn't fail with intentional statements, it just produces misleading results. Even if Jerome has no idea that Samuel Clemens ever wrote a book, there is, strictly speaking, nothing wrong with saying that Jerome believed Samuel Clemens was a great American writer. It asserts quite properly that Jerome believes of a certain individual whom many of us know as Samuel Clemens that he is a great American writer. But why are so many people misled into calling the statement involving Samuel Clemens wrong? A statement, Barwise and Perry point out, imparts information in many different ways. Most obviously it makes an assertion—that is its primary means of informing. But a statement also indirectly imparts information about the speaker and the persons talked about. If a journalist writes in an article about Jerome Salinger that "Jerome thinks Mark Twain is a great American writer," this tells us, indirectly, that the journalist is on a first name basis with Jerome Salinger and that Jerome Salinger has read most of Mark Twain's books. We only infer these facts because we assume that Salinger and the journalist abide by certain conventions, such as not referring to someone else by his first name unless one is on a first name basis with him, or not praising a writer unless one has read most of his books. Even if these inferences turned out to be incorrect, the statement would still remain true. Similarly, it is merely a convention of our language that we do not assert that "Jerome believes Samuel Clemens to be a great writer" unless Jerome actually knows who Samuel Clemens is. If this convention is violated, it does not make the statement about Jerome false; it merely makes it misleading.

We now know why mistakes matter in criminal law. We still don't know *when* they matter. We still don't know whether a killer's mistake about the nature of his victim, the effect of his actions, or the identity of his prey should make a difference.

(The reader may feel a little nonplussed. Does what I said really explain "why mistakes matter in criminal law"? It explains, on a purely linguistic level, why mistakes prevent us from attributing the required mens rea to the defendant. It doesn't explain the larger but simpler issue of why we have a mens rea requirement in the first place—why we punish intentional killings and not just killings.)

Among the Believers

Why is it so hard to know when a mistake matters? Why is it hard to tell whether a killer who is mistaken about some aspect or other of the killing is intentionally killing a human being? The phrase "to intentionally kill a human being" seems crystal clear. If the defendant believes he is shooting a human being and if he desires to kill a human being, well, then he is intentionally shooting a human being. The problem is that, even if all the facts are known, deciding what a defendant can properly be said to believe is a surprisingly treacherous task.

If I sincerely assert something, doesn't that mean I believe it? Not at all. Paul, eight years old, can recite the formula $E = mc^2$. Does Paul really believe that E equals mc^2? If we asked him, he would probably say yes. But few people, I think, would agree with him on that score. If Paul were to actually study physics, learn about the theory of relativity and thereafter announce $E = mc^2$, then no one would hesitate any longer to ascribe to him the belief that E equals mc^2. What this example tells us is that belief requires more than the sincere assertion of some statement. It requires that the statement in question be surrounded by a variety of other statements which the believer is also willing to assert sincerely. It must be embedded, so to speak, in a whole "belief neighborhood." In short, the believer has to know "what he is talking about."[19]

Of course it is a matter of degree whether the belief neighborhood is extensive enough to warrant ascribing a belief to someone. As Paul progresses from a state of nearly complete ignorance of physics to one of expertise, at what point has he actually started to believe $E = mc^2$? At what point has he acquired sufficient background knowledge to permit us to say he believed rather than merely recited the formula? No particular point can be pinpointed because the transition from nonbelief to belief is a gradual one.

If I sincerely assert something and if I know what I am talking about, does that mean that I believe it? Not necessarily. Tom, growing up in the 1950s, repeatedly heard people talk about McCarthy. He never listened too closely and only picked up snippets of information: that McCarthy was a senator liberals felt strongly about; that he had some youthful and zealous assistants; that he constantly attacked the government, especially the army; that he was much preoccupied with America's role in Asia. Tom was apolitical, that's why he didn't learn more. Dick, growing up in the 1960s, also often heard people talk about McCarthy. He also never listened too closely and only picked up some snippets of conversation: that McCarthy was a senator liberals felt strongly about; that he had some youthful and zealous assistants; that he constantly attacked the government, especially the army; that he was much preoccupied with America's role in Asia. He, too, was apolitical; that's why he didn't learn more.[20]

Of course, Tom and Dick were hearing about two different McCarthys. Tom had heard about Joseph McCarthy, the senator from Wisconsin, the rabid anti-Communist, whom many liberals despised. His two youthful assistants were Roy Cohn and David Shine. He attacked the government and the army for allegedly harboring Communists, and he liked to talk about how the Communists in America's government had "lost" China. Dick had heard about Eugene McCarthy, the senator from Minnesota, Lyndon Johnson's bane, whom many liberals adored. His youthful assistants were the war protesters of the 1960s. He attacked the government, especially the army, for fighting the Vietnam War.

One day in the 1950s one of Tom's friends asks him what he knows about McCarthy. Tom replies: He's some kind of senator whom the liberals are always talking about, he has some young zealots supporting him, he's constantly attacking the government, especially its policies in Asia. Ten years later one of Dick's friends asks him the same question, what does he know about McCarthy. Dick replies in the same words as Tom. Question: Are the two expressing the same belief? Our strongest inclination is probably to say: No, they are talking about two entirely different individuals. They may be in the same psychological state, they may both associate the same things with the name "McCarthy," but the fact is that when they use the name McCarthy they refer to two different people. What this example shows is that whether X believes something cannot be determined solely by looking into his mind. We have to determine what objects in the outside world X's thoughts connect up with before we can decide whether he believes something. If we look into the minds of Tom and Dick we will find the same thoughts regarding McCarthy within them. Yet they are clearly thinking about two different individuals. Hence their beliefs differ.

Whether two beliefs are the same is a matter of degree. Had the two McCarthys pursued the same policies, enjoyed the support of the same groups of people, shared the same looks, displayed the same personality, they would still be distinct but not very different. We might then be more inclined to say that Tom and Dick were expressing the same belief.

If I sincerely assert something, know what I am talking about, and it is unambiguous what sorts of things I am referring to, does that mean that I believe what I say? No, it doesn't. In an old joke two men are quarrelling over who is entitled to the fruit of a certain apple tree. Unable to settle the matter, they take it to court. The first man appears before the judge: It is true, he admits that the tree is standing on the other fellow's land, but the bulk of its branches are overhanging his garden—surely he is entitled to its fruit. The judge nods: You're right. The second man appears before the judge: It is true, he says, that the branches are overhanging his neighbor's garden, but the fact is that the tree grows on his land; in fact he planted it himself. Surely the apples belong to him. The judge nods: You're right. The bailiff who has witnessed both appearances turns to the judge aghast: Judge, they can't both be right. The judge smiles: You, too, are right.[21]

The joke highlights the third attribute that a sincere assertion must possess to count as a belief: It must interact with the believer's other beliefs in a causally appropriate manner. It must cause him to draw the right inferences. We are not prepared to say the judge really believed that any of the two men were right if he was not willing to draw the inference that the other was wrong. In short, the believer must really "mean what he says," or "do as he talks." Incidentally, it does not follow from the fact that someone is sincere that he means what he says. If he is very stupid or shortsighted and hence unable to appreciate the consequences of what he is saying, he may be quite sincere and yet not really mean it.

Evidently, this, too, is a matter of degree. If the claims of the two parties were very complex, if the arguments of each were very involved and persuasive, indeed if it was not even obvious on first encounter that the two positions were inconsistent with each other, we would be much more inclined to say that the judge who listened to both of them and told each of them that he was right, genuinely believed both to be right—even though he was professing a belief in two contradictory positions.

To summarize: to say of someone that he believes something is not merely to say that he sincerely endorses it. For such a sincere endorsement to count as a belief requires the right kind of belief neighborhood, the right connection with reality, and the right sort of interaction between the belief asserted and other beliefs a person holds.

In law it is frequently important to know whether a person believes what he says. In particular it is often necessary to decide whether two people who are saying the same thing are expressing the same belief. This is an everyday problem in the law of contracts. A contract is an agreement between two people. But their agreement has to be more than verbal, it must be, as the common law phrased it, a "meeting of the minds." If you and I set our names underneath a long list of mutual promises, we seem to be in agreement. By signing the document we are, after all, both "saying" the same thing. But that isn't enough for a contract. We must agree not only in our words, but in our beliefs about what the contract entails. Only then have our minds met. Otherwise, despite appearances, no contract has been formed.

Whether people like Tom and Dick express the same belief when they talk about "McCarthy" is an everyday issue in contract law. In the classic case of *Raffles v. Wichelhaus,* decided in 1864, Raffles had contracted to sell cotton to Wichelhaus, to be shipped from Bombay to Liverpool on a boat called *Peerless*. Unbeknownst to the two parties there were two ships called *Peerless*. The first *Peerless* was expected to sail from Bombay to Liverpool in October. This was the ship Wichelhaus was counting on. The other *Peerless* was to leave Bombay in December. This was the ship on which Raffles had stored his cotton. When Raffles's cotton finally arrived, Wichelhaus refused to accept it—it had come too late, he complained. Raffles sued him for breach of contract. The court had to ask: Was there ever an agreement between Raffles and Wichelhaus. Their words agreed, but did their beliefs agree? Was there ever a meeting of their minds? The court thought there wasn't. The two parties had both said "yes" to the sale of some cotton stored on the *Peerless,* but they had not meant the same thing by that. One believed *Peerless* meant a ship sailing in October, the other believed it meant a ship sailing in December. There was no contract.[22] (The *Raffles* case, admittedly, is a little easier than the story about McCarthy. For Raffles and Wichelhaus each associated the name *Peerless* with a different sailing date. To make the case perfectly parallel one should imagine Raffles to have heard about the *Peerless* from a ticket agent who had the October ship in mind and Wichelhaus from a ticket agent who had the December ship in mind.)

The story of little Paul and $E = mc^2$ also has its contract law analogue. Courts occasionally confront the problem whether to let a party out of a contract on the ground that when he signed it he "didn't know what he was talking about." Geremia had invited Boyarsky, a carpenter, to submit bids for the carpenter's work and painting on a house he was building for himself.[23] He met with Boyarsky "in the evening of April 25th for the purpose of making their estimates, but did not complete their figures, owing to the lateness of the hour. They wrote their estimates on two separate pieces of paper, but did not add the figures." The next morning Geremia called on Boyarsky and his friends to complete the estimate. Boyarsky sat down with Geremia at the workbench, "and proceeded to add up the various items upon the two sheets. In his haste, he made an error in adding the items on the first sheet footing them up at $99.10, when the correct footing should have been $859.10. This error, being carried to the second sheet, made the apparent cost of the work $1,450.40, instead of $2,210.40." Geremia gave the contract to Boyarsky, and later the same day they executed a written contract to do the work for $1,450.40. That evening Boyarsky discovered the mistake, immediately called Geremia and offered to go forward with the work according to the actual prices in the estimate or as low as any responsible contractor would do it for, if less than that sum. But Geremia insisted that the contract be performed as written. Was there a contract? There is no denying that when Boyarsky signed the contract his belief about what the contract entailed coincided with Geremia's. But that belief was embedded in a different belief neighborhood. Hence there are grounds for saying that their beliefs about what the contract entailed were not *really* identical. Indeed the court found there to be no contract, commenting: "That a mistake through which the defendants agreed to perform the contract for a price one-third less than the total of the actual figures of their estimate was of so essential and fundamental a character that the minds of the parties never met would not seem to require discussion."

Finally, courts are sometimes asked to let a party out of a contract he signed because he "didn't really mean it," more precisely, because the terms he endorsed played a very different causal role in his belief system than in that of the other parties to the contract. A poor and unsophisticated consumer signs a boilerplate contract containing lots of small print tucked away in the corners of some translucent, hard-to-read paper. Has he actually agreed to that clause, hidden somewhere within the small print, which says that he forfeits all judicial recourse against the seller for defects in the product? Even if he scanned the phrase—did it sink in, especially if written in forbidding and cloudy legalese? Is he able to infer from the clause that if the radio he takes home falls apart the moment he sets it on his living room desk, or even explodes and injures him, he has no action, no claim of damages against the seller or producer? If he is not able to draw that inference because of the opaque way the clause is written, courts may decide he did not really "agree" to it, and void the contract.

The need to compare beliefs is ubiquitous, and so are the problems it brings with it. What does it mean to say that a person can only be convicted by a unanimous jury? It means that the jurors must be of like mind as to the defendant's guilt. What if each juror believes the defendant guilty of murder, but some think he unintentionally killed the bank president during a robbery (which would be involuntary manslaughter if it had not happened during the commission of a felony), whereas the others think the killing was cold-blooded and premeditated. Both groups "believe" the defendant guilty of murder, but that belief is embedded in a different belief neighborhood for each group. What if each juror believes the defendant guilty of theft, but some think that what he has done amounts to larceny, and some that it amounts to embezzlement. Here they all "believe" him guilty of theft, but each group is referring to something rather different when it uses the term "theft." What if a juror announces he finds the defendant guilty but still has reasonable doubts whether he "really" did it. Here the juror seems to "believe" in the defendant's guilt, but like the judge in the old joke is unwilling to follow through on this statement as we would expect him to. Should we say that he "really" means what he says?

Finally, the comparison of beliefs is a vital issue in criminal law. But whose beliefs are we comparing? The drafter of every statute has a prototype in mind. The prototype of the murder statute is the man who intentionally takes aim at another human being and, knowing perfectly well who and what he is dealing with, kills him. A person is guilty of murder only if his actions sufficiently resemble those of the prototype. Comparing the beliefs of the actual killer with those of the prototype raises all the now familiar problems of belief ascription. Interestingly enough, however, each of our three puzzles concerning "murder by mistake"—witchhunting, misfiring, and misidentification—neatly typifies one of those problems.

Why do we hesitate to call the man who kills a witch a murderer? Like the prototype he may "believe" he is killing a human being. But that belief is embedded in a very unusual belief neighborhood: a belief that the world is filled with supernatural creatures, a belief that supernatural forces pose a serious threat to human welfare, a belief that some humans are in the thrall of supernatural spirits, and so on. Saying that he knew he was killing a human may be no more accurate than saying that eight-year-old Paul knew E equals mc^2.

Why do we hesitate to call the man who misses his aim and shoots a bystander a murderer? The prototype of a murderer in this instance is someone who actually aimed at the bystander. At some level the defendant and the prototype both believed the same thing, they both believed they were killing a human being. At some level Tom and Dick both believed the same thing; they both believed certain things about "McCarthy." But "McCarthy" referred to someone different in both cases. Similarly, the phrase "human being" flashing across the minds of the actual defendant and the prototype—in a manner of speaking—refers to two different individuals.

Why might we hesitate to call the man who misidentifies his prey and shoots the wrong victim a murderer? At first he looks more like the prototype than any of the other killers. After all, he and the prototype took aim at the same human being and both unequivocally knew him to be a human being. But the belief that the man he aimed at should be killed plays a very different role in the belief system of the defendant than in that of the prototype. When the prototype inspects the corpse of the man he shot, he will, presumably, feel a sense of satisfaction. When the defendant closely inspects the man he shot he will feel, if not contrite, at least frustrated about getting the wrong man. Because, like the judge in the old joke, the defendant in some sense did not mean to kill the man he killed, we might hesitate to treat him like the prototype of a murderer.

Most courts and commentators have tended to think that the three categories of mistake should be treated uniformly, or perhaps should be further subdivided into two readily distinguishable classes, some of which would clearly merit acquittal and some of which would clearly demand conviction. German and American courts both have said all cases of misfiring should be treated identically, except that the Germans would deal with them by acquitting and the Americans by convicting the defendant.[24] German and American courts both have said that all cases of misidentification should be treated alike: by convicting the defendant. Most courts confronting cases of supernatural belief are divided into two classes: cases where the defendant believed he was dealing with a supernatural creature ("ghost" cases) and cases where he believed he was dealing with a human being with supernatural powers ("witch" cases).

These approaches now seem ill-considered. Divergence from the prototype is a matter of degree. Within each category of mistake such divergence can be slight or extreme. There are witch cases where the defendant's background beliefs are so bizarre, idyosyncratic, or downright "weird" from a Western point of view, that even if he "knew" he was killing a human being, one would not want to convict him. Conversely, one can imagine ghost cases where one might well be inclined to convict. Just think of the person who, having read Descartes, becomes convinced the world is but a dream and the creatures around him mere figments of his imagination.

There are cases of misfiring where even German courts might not resist the temptation to convict: a defendant aims to break the right window of his victim's bedroom, he ends up breaking the left one. Should he escape a charge for malicious destruction of property on that ground? Conversely, there surely are cases of misfiring where even the American courts might balk at convicting. A man puts arsenic into a roasted apple intended for his wife. The wife never eats it but throws it into a garbage can on the street. A bum walks by, fishes the apple out of the can, eats it, and dies. Has the woman's husband murdered him? I doubt it.

Finally, there surely are cases where both German and American courts might acquit the man who, for reasons of mistaken identity, perpetrates his crime on the wrong person. Consider this variation on the Rose-Rosahl case. Again, Rose, the servant, is waiting in the underbrush for Schliebe, his intended victim, to pass by. Finally, he sees a creature looking like Schliebe and fires at him. The creature collapses. Rose thinks he is dead. But he isn't, he's only wounded. Moreover, it isn't Schliebe. It's—would you believe it?—Rosahl, his master, the man who told him to get Schliebe. Both the American and the German courts would not hesitate to convict

Rose of the intentional battery of Rosahl—he intended to shoot that particular creature, and he did, they would say. But can Rosahl be convicted as Rose's accomplice? If the courts were really confident of the logic of their argument, they would have to. (They would convict him if the victim had been Harnisch.) But it is hard to believe that a sensible court would convict him for complicity in the intentional battery of himself.[25]

A Little Knowledge

Criminal statutes have resorted to a bewildering variety of adjectives to characterize the mental states required by various offenses. Murder has at different times been defined as a killing that is intentional, malicious, willful, deliberate, purposeful, calculated, premeditated, knowing, or conscious, to sample but a few of the most common ones. Manslaughter has at different times been defined as a killing that is reckless, wanton, irresponsible, negligent, or careless. Modern drafters have distilled out of this embarrassment of riches four basic mental states: intent (in the sense of purpose), knowledge, recklessness, and negligence. They have tried to simplify the criminal code by redrafting it to avoid, by and large, all but these four terms.[26]

Of the four terms, intention and knowledge are the most important. What precisely do they mean? What is the relationship between them? Does knowledge entail intention? Does intention entail knowledge? Can one do something knowingly, but not intentionally, intentionally but not knowingly? It is the first question that has elicited the most debate: Can one do something knowingly but not intentionally? Consider the facts in this well-known English case. Smith was driving a car with a trunk full of sacks of stolen scaffolding clips.[27] A constable noticed the sacks and ordered Smith to pull over to the curb. Smith began to do so, with the constable walking alongside. Then suddenly he accelerated and tried to make a getaway. The constable clung to the side of the car, although it had no running board. He held on for some 130 yards, while Smith zigzagged down the street at a high speed in an effort to shake him off. He finally succeeded. The constable fell into the path of an oncoming car, which killed him. Let us assume (although that was a central issue in the case) that Smith had acted with virtual certainty that what he did would be the death of the constable. Yet he clearly would rather have made his getaway without the constable's getting injured. Had he intended the constable's death? If one intends something to which one knows something else to be inextricably tied, is one not also intending that something else? How could it be otherwise? Suppose a doctor needs a heart to carry out a heart transplant on a dying patient. He decides to remove the heart of another patient whom he considers less worth saving than the dying one. Of course, he would like it if the patient whose heart he took were to go on living anyway. Surely, however, he killed him not merely knowingly but intentionally.

Then again, we often say that our actions have unintended but foreseen side effects. Catholic theology takes this possibility very seriously. A surgeon is permitted to remove the cancerous womb of a pregnant woman if that is necessary to save her life, even though a side effect is the death of a fetus. In this context the distinction between known and intended consequences doesn't seem so silly anymore. Moreover, when somebody intends a certain result, we feel comfortable saying that he tried to bring it about, but if he merely foresaw the result and did not like it, we would hardly say that. We might say that the doctor tried to save the mother's life, but we would not say that he tried to kill the fetus.[28]

The root of the problem is an ambiguous counterfactual question. Everybody is initially inclined to agree that the person who kills his grandmother to inherit her money has intentionally killed her. Everybody is also initially inclined to agree that the person who hurls a bomb at the queen's carriage killing both queen and bodyguard has intentionally killed the queen and knowingly, but not intentionally, killed her bodyguard. Neither the grandmother nor the bodyguard killing occurred for its own sake. The grandmother killing was a means toward an inheritance. The bodyguard killing was a by-product of a political assassination. Whether we call a killing intentional seems to hinge on whether we view it as a means or as a by-product. The difference, unfortunately, is blurry. With only slight effort, one can recharacterize most by-products as means and vice versa. The difference is blurry because we decide whether to classify event X as means or by-product by asking an inherently ambiguous counterfactual question: If the defendant had not thought event X were tied to his goal Y, would he have chosen a different course of action? If X is a means, he certainly would have. He only perpetrated X, because he thought it would get him to Y. If, on the other hand, X is a by-product, he would not have changed his course of action. On the contrary, he would have felt all the more comfortable with it, since it wouldn't have entailed the unpleasant event X.

Now try answering that counterfactual question for some concrete cases. Would Smith have speeded up if he didn't think it would result in the death of the policeman? At first glance, the answer is: Yes, he would have been delighted to get rid of the policeman without killing him. In other words, he would not have changed his course of action. That suggests the death was a by-product. At second glance, however, the answer might be: No; if he didn't think the policeman's death would result, that would have been because he thought the policeman was too firmly attached to be shaken off. But in that case he would never have tried to make a getaway. In other words, he *would* have changed his course of action. That suggests the death was a means.

Would the surgeon have operated on the mother if he didn't think that would kill the fetus? At first glance, the answer is: Yes, he would have been relieved to be able to operate on the mother without killing her child. In other words, he would not have changed his course of action. That suggests the death was a by-product. At second glance, the answer might be: No, if he didn't think operating on the mother would kill the fetus, that would have been because he thought the operation was hopeless. In that case, he would never have operated. In other words, he *would* have changed his course of action. That suggests the death was a means.[29]

In sum, there is an important difference between knowing and intentional actions. But in concrete cases, it will be awfully hard to tell—for conceptual, not evidentiary, reasons.

Much more rarely asked is the question whether it is possible to do something intentionally, but not knowingly. The answer seems obvious: of course. You may try to kill someone and not know for sure that you'll succeed. Still, if you succeed, you have killed him intentionally. Or so it seems.

If Brown hopes to throw a six in a game of dice and succeeds, we wouldn't say he threw the six intentionally. If Brown puts his last cartridge into a six-chambered revolver, spins the chamber as he aims it at Smith, his archenemy, pulls the trigger, and kills Smith, we'd say he killed him intentionally. Does that make sense? In both cases Brown hoped for a certain result, in both cases the probability of that result was the same. If Brown didn't intentionally throw a six, why did he intentionally shoot Smith?[30]

If you aren't nonplussed yet, combine the two scenarios. "Suppose that instead of an ordinary die Brown were to throw one specially constructed as a bomb designed to explode if and only if it came to rest with the six uppermost (but still properly balanced), and that Brown threw this die hoping it would explode and knowing if it did so Smith would assuredly be killed.''[31] Should we really say that Brown did not intentionally throw a six, but intentionally killed Smith—even though Smith wouldn't have died unless he threw a six?

At first one might think that what makes the gambling scenario different from the shooting scenario is the different moral quality of the two acts. In one case Brown is just trying to win a crap game, and in the other he is trying to shoot a human being. That intuition is misguided. Even if Brown were shooting at beer bottles we would call any hit intentional. And even if Brown were to use a die to explode a bomb, we wouldn't call his throwing a six intentional.[32]

The philosopher E. J. Lowe has concluded that, in fact, Brown did not shoot Smith intentionally. To do X intentionally, Lowe maintains, is to do some intermediary act Y knowing that X would certainly result. Why then do many people so firmly believe that Brown shot Smith intentionally? Because Brown didn't shoot Smith unintentionally, either. People mistakenly believe, he says, that doing something unintentionally is the opposite of doing something intentionally. It isn't. To do X unintentionally is to do some intermediary act Y, thinking that X couldn't possibly result. People don't make this mistake when they think about the gambling situation. They see that throwing a six is not unintentional but don't jump to the conclusion that the six was thrown intentionally, because that's so obviously absurd. Everyone recognizes that no one can intentionally be lucky. But Lowe's explanation flies in the face of a very solid, intuitive conviction that Brown did shoot Smith intentionally.[33]

Perhaps, suggests Kim Davies in *Analysis,* what leads to the problem is that in comparing the two seemingly symmetrical cases we are making some very asymmetrical hidden assumptions.[34] When Brown pulls the trigger of his revolver, we seem to be tacitly assuming that he has a general intention to kill Smith, if not now, then some other time. When Brown throws the die, we seem to be tacitly assuming he is not entertaining some general intention to throw a six, if not now, then later that evening. It follows from this explanation that if Brown were to fire his gun merely as a one-time lark it wouldn't be intentional, and if he were to roll the die with the intention to keep trying until he got a six it would be intentional. But suppose I see a mugger about to run his knife into a woman. I raise my gun to shoot him. The man is far away, and there is never more than a one-in-six chance that I will hit him. Here I am firing my gun as a ''one-time lark''—if I miss and the mugger kills his victim, I won't keep shooting. Yet, if I kill him, surely it will have been intentional.

I have a simpler explanation. Brown's killing of Smith requires the concurrence of two events. It requires, first, that Brown aim his gun at Smith and pull the trigger. It requires, second, that the gun fire a bullet. Brown has no control over the second event. He has complete control over the first event. That's why we call the shooting intentional. Brown's throwing a six requires only one event, that the die fall with a six face up. Brown has no control over that event. That's why we don't call his throwing a six intentional. But, you might say, strictly speaking, throwing a six also requires an event over which Brown has control: he must actually throw the die. But throwing the die is a very preliminary sort of event; it is much more remote from its end result, the roll of a six, than aiming a gun is from its end result, Smith's death.[35]

David Ross has cast this solution in the form of an elegant dialogue.[36]

> Brown invites Smith to his flat for a cup of tea and an ordinary game of dice. Brown hopes to throw a six, does so, then claims to have done it intentionally. Smith disagrees. Brown, ever testy, becomes upset. He places one live cartridge into a six-chambered revolver, spins the cylinder as he aims at Smith, and pulls the trigger. The gun fires, mortally injuring Smith.
>
> "There," says Brown to the dying Smith. "I just shot you intentionally. By parallel reasoning, I threw the six intentionally."
>
> "Bad analogy," gasps Smith.
>
> "What's the difference? My probability of success in each case was the same, and I certainly intended to roll the six just as much as I intended to shoot you."

Smith disagrees. The earmark of an intentional act, he explains, is the perpetrator's ability to have some control over the outcome. By aiming his gun at Smith, Brown had some control over whether Smith would die. Brown had no control over whether he would throw a six.

> "But," asks Brown, "doesn't the fact that I didn't have to throw the die at all evidence some control on my part?"
>
> "Your decision to throw the die only evidenced your willingness to enter into the dice game," answers Smith. "It wasn't a move *in* that game, and had no influence over the game's outcome."
>
> "Sure it did. If I hadn't thrown the die, it wouldn't have shown a six."

"When you win a chess game, do you attribute your victory to the decision to play? Obviously not; you attribute it to the moves you made."

"So an intentional act must occur—in a sense—as the outcome of a game where there is some skill involved beyond the decision to play. Then answer me this: couldn't the loading, aiming, and firing of the revolver—as with the decision to roll the die—be viewed as the entrance into a sort of 'shooting game'?"

"Certainly, with the actual shot—regardless of the ultimate destination of the bullet—corresponding to the outcome of a six on the die. But the gunshot is clearly no more intentional than the fact that the cartridge spun into just the right position for firing. Assuming that you influenced the spins of neither the die nor the cylinder, neither the six nor the gunshot was intentional."

"Then my shooting of you—how was that intentional?"

"Though your decision to play the shooting game was not a move in *that* game, it *was* one in what we might call the 'life game', the possible outcomes of which are my life and my death. Since your decision to play the shooting game was a direct factor in my imminent demise, the fact of your shooting me would have to be considered intentional."

Smith is about to say something more, but before he can finish, he expires.

Judging the Odds

Murder, rape, and larceny have to be committed intentionally, or at least knowingly. That's not required for crimes like manslaughter or battery. Here it's enough that the defendant was reckless or negligent. You may balk at this. The speeding driver who loses control of his car and hits a pedestrian didn't have "harm on his mind," no more so, it seems, than if he had done so in an unforeseen epileptic fit. He probably deeply regrets what happened. Aren't we blaming him for something that befell him rather than for something that he did? Not really. Unlike the surprised epileptic, he knew of precautions he could have taken to reduce the risk of an accident—driving more slowly, taking a nearby highway. In a way, he did have "harm on his mind," the harm of risk to others. That makes him blameworthy and deserving of punishment.

A person is negligent if he takes a substantial and unreasonable risk. He is reckless if he takes such a risk consciously. The difference is minor; I will, for the most part, say "negligent" when I really mean "reckless or negligent." What is an unreasonable risk? To decide, we have to weigh the reason for the risk against its size. Speeding along the highway at 90 m.p.h. to rush a heart attack victim to the hospital probably isn't unreasonable, but doing the same thing to win a drag race is. If the defendant is handicapped, that alone may be a good enough reason for what would otherwise be unreasonable conduct. A man who saunters lackadaisically across an intersection and blocks the way of several fire trucks and ambulances may be guilty of reckless endangerment or worse. But the cripple who finds himself in the middle of the intersection as the trucks approach and delicately hobbles to the sidewalk may move out of the way no faster, yet is hardly reckless.

The law is loath to attach too much significance to the defendant's handicaps. An erratic driver can't excuse hitting a pedestrian because of his myopia; he should wear glasses. A blind skier can't excuse crashing into a child because of his blindness; he shouldn't ski at all, except under very strict precautions. It is rarely appreciated how well many handicaps can be compensated for. Handicaps are used to explain (and excuse) human behavior more often than necessary. Many people looking at an El Greco painting have been struck by the fact that many of his figures, especially the holy ones, seem unnaturally tall and thin. Some people, ophthalmologists in particular, have undoubtedly toyed with the idea that El Greco was suffering from a defect of vision that made him see people that way. On purely logical grounds, observes the biologist Sir Peter Medawar, we know that conjecture to be wrong. Why?

"Suppose a painter's defect of vision was, as it might easily have been, diplopia—in effect, seeing everything double. If the ophthalmologist's explanation were right, then such a painter would paint his figures double; but if he did so, then when he came to inspect his handiwork, would he not see all the figures fourfold and maybe suspect that something was amiss? If a defect of vision is in question, the only figures that could seem natural (that is, representational) to the painter must seem natural to us also, even if we ourselves suffer defects of vision; if some of El Greco's figures seem unnaturally tall and thin, they appear so because this was El Greco's intention."[37]

Negligence is a troublesome concept. Calling a risk unreasonable is not like calling the sky blue. It's not a statement of fact, but of value. We call the drag racer negligent only because we prize the community's safety more than the running of drag races. The trouble is that people are often inconsistent in their value judgments. The judgments they make depend precariously on how an issue is presented to them. Recall the experiment mentioned in the preface. A group of doctors was asked the following question:

> Imagine that the U.S. is preparing for the outbreak of an unusual Asian disease, which is expected to kill 600 people. Two alternative programs to combat the disease have been proposed. Assume that the exact scientific estimate of the consequences of the programs are as follows:
>
> If program A is adopted, 200 people will be saved.
>
> If program B is adopted, there is 1/3 probability that 600 people will be saved, and 2/3 probability that no people will be saved.
>
> Which of the two programs would you favor?

The vast majority of the doctors, 72%, opted for the first program. Another group of doctors was given the same "cover story" as the first, but was asked to choose among the following alternatives:

> If program C is adopted 400 people will die.
>
> If program D is adopted there is 1/3 probability that nobody will die, and 2/3 probability that 600 people will die.
>
> Which of the two programs would you favor?

The vast majority of the doctors, 78%, opted for D. The odd thing is that C is but a different way of phrasing A, and D is but a different way of phrasing B.[38]

What explains this inconsistency? Suppose I offered you the following choice: You can either have \$100 or you can take a gamble, that when I throw a coin heads will come up. If that happens you get \$200. If not, you get nothing. The expected value of this gamble evidently is \$100. Which do you prefer? If you are like most people you prefer the certain sum. You are risk-averse with respect to gains in wealth. I now offer you a second choice: You must either pay me \$100 or you can take a gamble, that when I throw a coin heads are going to come up. If that happens, you don't have to pay me anything; if not, you must pay me \$200. The expected loss under this gamble is \$100. Which do you prefer? If you are like most people, you now prefer the gamble. You are risk-loving with respect to losses in wealth.

It isn't always clear whether something should be viewed as a gain or a loss. If I first give you $200 and then force you to participate in the choice between giving me $100 and gambling that heads come up, you may not be sure whether to think of yourself as a man who is $100 richer and has to choose among various loss alternatives or as a man who, in effect, has to choose between various profit alternatives, a certain gain of $100 and a gamble in which he could win $200. If you took the first view you would gamble; if you took the second you would not. What view you decide to take depends very much on how the question is framed. The case of the Asian epidemic illustrates that. The first formulation of the problem suggests viewing the choice as one between gains, the second as one between losses. Hence in the first formulation people opt for the safe alternative, in the second for the risky one.[39]

What this means is that it can make an enormous difference how a negligence case is presented to the jury. Suppose in anticipation of the Asian epidemic, the secretary of Health, Education, and Welfare has chosen to implement policy A. Later on, a civil suit is pressed in behalf of those who died, charging the government with negligence for not following program B. If the government's choice is described as one between saving a few lives with certainty and potentially saving many lives, the jury will probably find for the government. If the choice is described as one between letting many people die with certainty and possibly saving everyone, the jury might well find against it.

In another experiment subjects were asked to

> Consider the following two-stage game. In the first stage, there is a 75% chance to end the game without winning anything, and a 25% chance to move into the second stage. If you reach the second stage you have a choice between:
>
> C. a sure win of $30
>
> D. 80% chance to win $45
>
> Your choice must be made before the game starts, i.e., before the outcome of the first stage is known. Please indicate the option you prefer.

Three quarters of all respondents preferred C to D.

Another, similar group, was presented with the following problem:

> Which of the following options do you prefer?
>
> E. 25% chance to win $30
>
> F. 20% chance to win $45

The majority of all respondents preferred F.[40] Again, the two problems are really identical. If there is only a 25 percent chance that players will ever advance to stage 2 of the first game, then in effect they are choosing between a 25 percent chance to win $30 and a 20 percent chance to win $45. Yet, in the first problem they opted for the first alternative, in the second they didn't. Why this inconsistency? The first problem leads people to imagine themselves already at the second stage when they choose, but the second problem doesn't do that.

This has implications for everyday life. An insurance policy is more attractive if it emphasizes that it covers all fire damage, rather than that it reduces the overall probability of property loss by a specific amount. Similarly, a vaccine which cuts the risk of catching a disease in half is less attractive if it is described as effective in half the cases than if it is described as fully effective against one of two equally probable virus strains that produce identical symptoms. People value full protection against an identified virus more than probabilistic protection against the disease.

Imagine a jury asked to decide whether GM was negligent in not spending an extra $500 per car on collision-proof gas tanks. Suppose the jury is told that the $500 would have eliminated all risk of death from a gas tank explosion. They might decide GM was negligent. Suppose they are told, instead, that the $500 would have reduced the total number of collision fatalities by 5 percent—the equivalent statement. They might well decide GM wasn't negligent.

In a further experiment subjects were asked:

> Imagine that you have decided to see a play where admission is $10 per ticket. As you enter the theater you discover that you have lost a $10 bill.
>
> Would you still pay $10 for a ticket for the play?

Eighty-eight percent of all subjects said yes, 12 percent said no. Another, similar group was asked:

> Imagine that you have decided to see a play and paid the admission price of $10 per ticket. As you enter the theater you discover that you have lost the ticket. The seat was not marked and the ticket cannot be recovered.
>
> Would you pay $10 for another ticket?

Forty-six percent of all subjects said yes, 54 percent said no.

Suppose a jury is told that GM already had designs for an improved gas tank, that a fire destroyed the blueprints, and that they would have had to start all over. In the rush to get its new model on the market, GM then decided to dispense with the improvements. A sympathetic jury might well decide to acquit GM. Suppose, however, that GM had simply suffered a severe financial setback and hence decided to put out its new model without the improved gas tank. Now the jury is likely to convict.

Many more such inconsistencies exist. One group of subjects was asked:

> Imagine that you face the following pair of concurrent decisions. First examine both decisions, then indicate the options you prefer.
>
> Decision (i). Choose between:
>
> A. a sure gain of $240
>
> B. 25% chance to gain $1000, and 75% chance to gain nothing.
>
> Decision (ii). Choose between:
>
> C. a sure loss of $750.
>
> D. 75% chance to lose $1000, and 25% chance to lose nothing.

Most people, 73 percent, not surprisingly chose A and D, and only a very few, 3 percent, chose B and C. And yet everyone, when asked to

> Choose between:
>
> A & D. 25% chance to win $240, and 75% chance to lose $760
>
> B & C. 25% chance to win $250, and 75% chance to lose $750

chose B & C.[41]

A more startling inconsistency yet was revealed by the following experiment. Subjects were asked to indicate their preferences between the following kinds of gambles:

> Imagine that you are standing beside a roulette wheel and you are involved in a game involving the numbers 1–36. You are shown two possible bets.
>
> In Bet A, you will receive £4 if the ball finishes in numbers 1 through 35 (inclusive). If the number is 36, you pay £1.
>
> In Bet B, you will receive £16 if the ball finishes in numbers 1 through 11 (inclusive), and lose £1.50 if the ball ends up in numbers 13 through 36 (inclusive).
>
> Now imagine that you are told to play one of the bets. Which one would you choose?

Most subjects prefer A.

The experiment also contained a number of other tasks. Again confronting the subjects with bets like the above, it asked them to

> Imagine that you have been given tickets which give you the right to play both Bet A and Bet B. Now instead of playing the bets, you have a chance of selling them. What is the *smallest* price at which you would be prepared to sell Bet A? What is the *smallest* price at which you would be prepared to sell Bet B?

In other words, the subjects were asked to value the two bets. The startling thing was that the majority of the subjects who preferred Bet A, nevertheless put a higher value on Bet B.[42]

What is going on here? It seems to be this: When subjects are asked to choose between bets, they focus heavily on the odds involved. The more heavily one focuses on the odds, of course, the more attractive A looks relative to B. When asked to put a value on the bets, subjects focus heavily on the stakes involved. The more heavily one focuses on these stakes, the more attractive B looks relative to A. Hence the inconsistent choices.

Without too much effort one can construct scenarios in which these inconsistencies translate into inconsistent jury behavior.

The situation is reminiscent of the two monks, Theophilus and Gottlieb, who are quarreling over whether one may engage in smoking and praying at the same time. Theophilus, an unbending ascetic, says no. Gottlieb, an easy-going smoker, says why not. They meet again some weeks later. Theophilus triumphantly reports, "I took the issue to the pope. I asked him point-blank 'Is it permissible to smoke during prayer?' and he said 'Absolutely not.' " Gottlieb protests: "That's not what he said when I asked him." He smiles sheepishly. "Of course I did phrase the question a little differently. I asked him 'Is it permissible to pray while I smoke?' and he said 'Of course.' "

Maybe we shouldn't worry too much about these inconsistencies. If defense and prosecution do their job, they will let the jury know that there are different ways of looking at a negligence case. But what good will that do? When the doctors in the epidemic problem are told about the two alternative ways of looking at the problem, it's not going to become any easier for them. They will feel conflicting intuitions without an obvious way of resolving them. Jurors will be similarly at bay. What the lawyers tell them will at best make them realize that they have no firm intuitions about the issue before them; it doesn't help them decide the case.

Negligence is a troublesome concept for another reason. It requires people to estimate probabilities, and the evidence suggests that they are alarmingly poor at it.

A group of students were given the following personality sketch: "Linda is 31 years old, single, outspoken, and very bright. She majored in philosophy. As a student, she was deeply concerned with issues of discrimination and social justice, and also participated in anti-nuclear demonstrations."[43]

They were then asked which of two statements about Linda was more likely to be true: (1) Linda is a bank teller; (2) Linda is a bank teller who is active in the feminist movement. Most opted for 2. Yet they were obviously wrong. A moment's reflection will show that the probability of Linda being a bank teller *and* being active in the feminist movement is bound to be lower than the probability of her being a bank teller. The probability of event A and B occurring together is always lower than the probability of event A occurring.

Why this mistake? When people estimate the probability that object X belongs to class Y they usually ask how representative X is of class Y. Psychologists call this the "representativeness" heuristic. Linda evidently resembles more closely the creature described in 2 than the one described in 1. Applying the representativeness heuristic, most subjects concluded 2 more likely to be true than 1.

The representativeness heuristic leads to other mistakes as well. Steve strikes people as "shy and withdrawn, invariably helpful, but with little interest in people, or in the world of reality. A meek and tidy soul, he has a need for order and structure, and a passion for detail." How probable is it that Steve is a librarian? People decide this by asking themselves how closely Steve resembles the stereotype of a librarian. What if people were told that Steve is attending a large university most of whose students are pursuing careers in business or engineering, and a very small fraction of whom study library sciences. Would they change their estimates? Experiments have shown that they would not. They would remain as confident as ever that Steve was a student in the library sciences. People simply ignore base rates. All they look to is representativeness.[44]

Experimenters told a group of subjects about the results of Stanley Milgram's investigations of obedience and authority. They told them that the vast majority of participants in the Milgram study continued administering shocks to the very end. Then they presented them with a tape-recorded interview with one of the participants and asked them to predict whether he was someone who had progressed to the very end of the shock scale. Most subjects were very confident (wrongly) that he had not. They ignored the base rate, which made it very likely that he had, and simply oriented themselves by his personality, which did not seem to be a cruel one. In other words, they implicitly continued to assume that the people who had "obeyed" Milgram did so because they were inherently cruel and not because the situation tended to bring out cruelty in most people.

Most people have heard of the phenomenon of regression toward the mean. It is the statistical property that explains why very bright parents will tend to have somewhat less bright children, why students who do very well on their mid-terms will do somewhat poorer on their finals, why those who have had terrible luck in the past are likely to have somewhat better luck in the future, and so forth. We may "know" this as a statistical fact, but it conflicts with the representativeness heuristic, which suggests that bright parents should have equally bright children, superior exam writers should continue to write superior exams, and poor schnooks should remain poor schnooks. Not surprisingly, then, we forget about regression as soon as we leave our statistics class. Flying instructors have been known to tell psychologists that they had it all wrong in their theories about reward and punishment. Rewards, they claimed, are counterproductive—only punishment works. When they praised a student's splendid landing, he invariably did worse the second time around, and when they harshly criticized him for a poor landing, he invariably did better on his next landing. It did not occur to them that what they were seeing were not the effects of reward and punishment but of regression.

The representativeness heuristic is not our only rule of thumb. Psychologists read their subjects long lists of names. In some of the lists the men tended to be more famous than the women, in others the women were more famous than the men. After each reading they asked their subjects whether the list contained more men or women. When the men were more famous than the women, subjects guessed they had heard more men's names. When the women were more famous than the men, they guessed they had heard more women's names. In fact each list contained an equal number of men and women. Subjects were relying on what psychologists have dubbed the availability heuristic. We use it whenever we estimate the probability of an event by the ease with which instances of it can be brought to mind. We use it when we assess the risk of heart attack among middle-aged people by recalling such occurrences among our friends, or when we evaluate the probability that a given venture will fail by imagining various difficulties it might encounter.

Like the representativeness heuristic, it is systematically biased. Collaborators on a project or article often disagree over how much each has contributed. Each will tend to overestimate his contribution. Why? Not necessarily because he is motivated to come out with a favorable opinion about himself, but in large part because he can better remember what he did than what the other fellow did.[45]

A common technique for estimating the likelihood of a certain outcome is to picture a train of events that might lead up to it. But it is easier for us to imagine one plausible scenario than many implausible scenarios. Hence the probability of an outcome that can be produced by one plausible series of events will generally be rated higher than one which can be brought about by many unlikely series of events, even if the outcomes are equally likely.[46]

There is a third important rule of thumb. A group of subjects was asked to estimate (not calculate!) the product of

$$8 \times 7 \times 6 \times 5 \times 4 \times 3 \times 2$$

The other was asked to estimate

$$1 \times 2 \times 3 \times 4 \times 5 \times 6 \times 7 \times 8$$

Subjects in the first group consistently gave a higher estimate than subjects in the second group. They were relying on the so-called adjustment heuristic. We use it when we estimate probabilities by starting from an initial value and then adjusting it to yield the final answer. To estimate the likelihood of a fire in the house next year one might take the known probability of a flood and adjust it for the perceived greater chance of fire. The problem with the adjustment heuristic is that we generally underadjust. If we estimate the probability of a fire by starting with the probability of a flood and adjusting it upward, we will undoubtedly arrive at a much lower number than if we start with the probability of a burglary and adjust it downward.[47]

Negligence is a troublesome concept for a simpler reason yet. The process of playing and weighing the odds is wrapped up in superstition. Few persons can fully accept the fact that chance events are just that, *chance events*. We persistently behave as though we could influence such events. Remember some of the experiments cited in an earlier section showing that gamblers will roll the die softly when they want a low number and hard when they want a high one; that they are willing to bet larger amounts before the die is cast than afterwards (but before the outcome is disclosed); that they will take greater risks against diffident, shy, submissive opponents than strong and domineering ones; that they will value lottery tickets they selected themselves more highly than tickets assigned them.[48] Superstitious conduct of this kind is not the prerogative of the uneducated. Most of the experiments were conducted on university students. Legend has it that Albert Einstein once visited Niels Bohr and was surprised to notice a horseshoe on Bohr's door. Bohr apologized: "I don't believe in that superstitious stuff. But they say it brings luck even if you don't believe in it." If people find it so difficult to accept the chanciness of chance events, they are likely to attribute to others more influence over what goes wrong than they actually have. That suggests that when examining a freak accident, jurors will tend to view it as much more within the control of the participants than it really was.

An American Tragedy Retried

To understand the meaning of an offense, one has to understand more than its "guilty mind" portion and its "bad act" portion; one has to understand the relationship between the two. Murder requires not only an intent to kill and a killing, it requires that the two stand in an appropriate relationship to each other. Presumably, the one cannot come after the other, but that's the least of it. No actual case I know sheds as much light on this question as the killing in Theodore Dreiser's novel *An American Tragedy*.[49]

The novel centers on the young Clyde Griffiths, offspring of a poor family of street preachers and singers. A rich brother of his father's has secured Clyde a job as an assistant foreman in his collar factory. Here Clyde has an affair with Roberta, one of the young women working under him. Roberta becomes pregnant and, unable to obtain an abortion, insists that Clyde marry her. Clyde is aghast. He has fallen in love meanwhile with Sondra Finchley, a wealthy young woman from the circle of his rich cousin, and entertains serious hopes that she will marry him and thus improve his pitiful social position. Roberta threatens to expose him if he does not marry her. In his desperation Clyde sees but one way out: to kill Roberta. His plan is simple. He tells himself:

> Go to the lake which you visited with Sondra!
>
> . . . .
>
> Pick a boat that will upset easily—one with a round bottom, such as those you have seen here at Crum Lake and up there.

> Buy a new and different hat and leave that on the water—one that cannot be traced to you. You might even tear the lining out of it so that it cannot be traced.
>
> . . . .
>
> Tell her that you intend to marry her, but *after* you return from this outing, not before.
>
> And if necessary strike a light blow, so as to stun her—no more—so that falling in the water, she will drown the more readily.
>
> Do not fear!
>
> Do not be weak!

And afterwards:

> Walk through the woods by night, not by day—so that when seen again you will be in Three Mile Bay or Sharon—and can say that you came from Racquette or Long Lake south, or from Lycurgus north.
>
> Use a false name and alter your handwriting as much as possible.
>
> Assume that you will be successful.

But when all is ready—he and Roberta out and alone in a fragile boat—doubts assail him. He wavers, seized by a "sudden palsy of the will—of courage—of hate or rage sufficient" to commit a murder. He is in the throes of an inner "combat between fear (a chemical revulsion against death or murderous brutality that would bring death) and a harried and restless and yet self-repressed desire to do—to do—yet unbreakable here and now—a static between a powerful compulsion to do and yet not to do."

While he feels this, a strange expression comes over him, "his pupils . . . growing momentarily larger and more lurid; his face and body and hands tense and contracted." Roberta, concerned, leans forward, exclaiming, "Clyde! What is it? Whatever is the matter with you anyhow?" You look so—so strange—so—so—Why, I never saw you look like this before. What is it?" What then happens, save for the upshot, is shrouded in ambiguity by Dreiser's deliberately garbled prose. The reader sees Roberta "suddenly rising, or rather leaning forward, and by crawling along the even keel, attempting to approach [Clyde], since he looked as though he was about to fall forward into the boat—or to one side and out into the water."

Then the reader sees Clyde as he is, "instantly sensing the profoundness of his own failure, his own cowardice or inadequateness for such an occasion, as instantly yielding to a tide of submerged hate, not only for himself, but Roberta—her power—or that of life to restrain him in this way. And yet fearing to act in any way—being unwilling to—being willing only to say that never, never would he marry her—that never, even should she expose him, would he leave here with her to marry her—that he was in love with Sondra and would cling only to her—and yet not being able to say that even. But angry and confused and glowering.''

The reader next sees Roberta again ''as she drew near him, seeking to take his hand in hers and the camera from him in order to put it in the boat.''

The reader finally sees Clyde

> flinging out at her, but not even then with any intention to do other than free himself of her—her touch—her pleading—consoling sympathy—her presence forever—God!
>
> Yet (the camera still unconsciously held tight) pushing at her with so much vehemence as not only to strike her lips and nose and chin with it, but to throw her back sidewise toward the left wale which caused the boat to careen to the very water's edge. And then he, stirred by her sharp scream, (as much due to the lurch of the boat, as the cut on her nose and lip), rising and reaching half to assist or recapture her and half to apologize for the unintended blow—yet in doing so completely capsizing the boat—himself and Roberta being as instantly thrown into the water. And the left wale of the boat as it turned, striking Roberta on the head as she sank and then rose for the first time, her frantic, contorted face turned to Clyde, who by now had righted himself. For she was stunned, horror-struck, unintelligible with pain and fear—her lifelong fear of water and drowning and the blow he had so accidentally and all but unconsciously administered.
>
> ''Help! Help!
>
> ''Oh, my God, I'm drowning, I'm drowning. Help! Oh, my God!
>
> ''Clyde, Clyde!''

Clyde hesitates, wavers, delays momentarily. Then the waters close over Roberta, and soon there is nothing more he can do.

Has Clyde committed murder? That depends on how one interprets the events in the boat. At least three plausible interpretations suggest themselves.[50]

1. Intending to kill Roberta, he has rowed the boat into this forsaken spot on the lake. He is getting ready to execute his plan. When Roberta reaches out to touch him, he is still waiting for the right moment. He pushes her not so that she will fall overboard, but merely to avoid her tender touch which now that he is determined to kill her revolts him. ("And then, as she drew near him, seeking to take his hand in hers and the camera from him in order to put it in the boat, he flinging out at her, *but not even then with any intention to do other than free himself of her—her touch—her pleading*." Emphasis mine.) Thus read, the case is rather like the story about Bill who "is out driving thinking about how to kill his uncle [and whose] intention to kill his uncle makes him so nervous and excited that he accidentally runs over and kills a pedestrian who happens to be his uncle."[51] Clearly, he isn't guilty of murder, and so Clyde isn't either.

But why? Is it because, as one commentator writes, Bill's "moving and steering of the car were not done in order to give effect to his desire to kill"?[52] That explanation can't be right. For suppose Bill had been on his way to kill his uncle, then "his moving and steering" *would* have been done "to give effect to his desire to kill." Few would therefore call the killing intentional. And Clyde, of course, would not have been out on the lake except "to give effect to his desire to kill." One must distinguish, the philosopher John Searle suggests, two sorts of intentions: those intentions that are formed prior to actions and those that are not. Contrary to appearances not all intentions are prior intentions. Quite often we do things quite spontaneously or unconsciously, and yet intentionally. "For example, suppose I am sitting in a chair reflecting on a philosophical problem, and I suddenly get up and start pacing about the room. My getting up and pacing about are clearly intentional actions, but in order to do them I do not need to form an intention to do them prior to doing them. I don't in any sense have to have a plan to get up and pace about. Like many of the things one does, I just do these actions; I just act."[53] In fact even when an action *is* preceded by a prior intention it will usually comprise a number of subsidiary actions which that prior intention did not cover. "For example, suppose I have a prior intention to drive to my office, and suppose as I am carrying out this prior intention I shift from second gear to third gear. Now I formed no prior intention to shift from second to third. When I formed my intention to drive to the office I never gave it a thought. Yet my action of shifting gears was intentional." Intentions that are not prior intentions are appropriately enough called *intentions in action*.

What is amiss with the cases of Clyde and Bill now becomes evident. There was in both a *prior intention* to kill, but not an *intention in action* when the killing actually occurred.

The distinction between prior intentions and intentions in action is not foreign to the law. Many states distinguish two kinds of murder, first-degree murder, which requires premeditation, in effect a prior intention, and second-degree murder, which merely requires an intention to kill, that is, an intention in action. Drafters of criminal statutes often overlook the distinction and thus breed many thorny problems. Robbery is frequently defined simply as larceny by means of violence or intimidation.[54] The defendant, let us suppose, sees a woman strolling in the park. He decides to forcibly strip her of her purse. After he has knocked her to the ground with a hefty punch, he discovers that his victim is wearing some precious earrings. Since he knows a good "fence" who is mainly interested in jewelry, he forgets about the purse and removes, without any further use of force or violence, the woman's earrings. Has he committed robbery? He applied force to the woman with the prior intention to take the woman's purse. He committed larceny with the intention in action to take her earrings. Because the drafters didn't notice that robbery, unlike other crimes, always involves those two intentions, they failed to tell us what to do when those two intentions diverge.

In any event, under this first interpretation Clyde is innocent. *He is innocent of murder, but he may be guilty of attempted murder.*

2. When Clyde pushes at Roberta, arguably he means to kill her then and there, just as he planned, by propelling her into the water. ("And then, as she drew near him, seeking to take his hand in hers and the camera from him in order to put it in the boat, he flinging out at her, but not even then with any intention to do other than free himself of . . . *her presence forever*—God!" Emphasis mine.) But the gesture doesn't have the intended effect. The boat merely careens and Roberta merely stumbles. He, however, "stirred by her sharp scream" experiences an instantaneous change of mind, rises and reaches out "half to assist and recapture her and half to apologize for the unintended blow," but in so doing completely capsizes the boat, plunging himself and Roberta into the water.

If his original shove was strong enough to propel Roberta into the water, the case looks rather like the California case of *People v. Claborn*.[55] The defendant was being chased by a policeman. Having failed to elude the police car, he suddenly resolved on a change of strategy, turned his car around, and aimed it straight at the pursuer's car. At the last minute, it seems, he changed his mind again and tried to avoid a collision. But it was too late. The two cars collided head-on. The defendant was convicted despite his last-minute change of heart. If one intentionally performs an act to bring about certain unlawful consequences, the court said, one has consummated the crime; later unsuccessful efforts to avert those consequences cannot undo that. That's clearly right. The person who poisons his grandmother, regrets it, and hires the best doctors to save her, despite which she dies, is still guilty of murder.

But the original shove may not have been strong enough to send Roberta overboard. The immediate cause of her falling into the water was not, it seems, Clyde's push but his effort to assist her. That was what made the boat capsize. Now the case begins to look rather like *Regina v. Church*.[56] In that case the defendant in the course of a spat knocked his lover unconscious. Then, mistakenly thinking he had killed her, he panicked and threw the body into the river. It was this that really killed her. Courts have reached different verdicts in cases like this. Some have said that the defendant could be convicted of no more than attempted murder, since the actual killing was not accompanied by any intention to kill. Others have viewed the act rendering the victim unconscious and the act actually killing her as "one transaction." If the transaction was begun with an intention to kill, the defendant could be convicted of murder; if it was begun with reckless or negligent disregard of the possibility of death he could be convicted of manslaughter.[57] Rasputin's murder was similar. First, the assassins fed him poisoned cookies, to no effect. Then they shot him and threw him in the river. But the bullets hadn't killed him either, for he was found with water in his lungs. He died of drowning.[58]

As in *Regina v. Church* the act by which Clyde intended to kill Roberta did not do so. Only a later act, entirely innocent, produced that effect. What makes the case much harder than even *Regina v. Church* is that the act triggering Roberta's death was not merely noncriminal but *commendable*—it was aimed at saving Roberta's life.

The problem with cases like *Regina v. Church* is that while the death of the victim fulfills the defendant's intention to kill, the manner of death does not. A killer usually has more than an intention-to-kill. He has an intention to kill by certain means. The death occurs by other means. Obviously, it shouldn't matter if the manner of death deviates only slightly from the intended one (if the defendant shoots the victim in the heart rather than the head), but it does matter if it deviates vastly (if A shoots at B with intent to kill and misses him completely, but the shot stampedes a herd of wild pigs which trample B to death.)[59] How one should treat cases between the two extremes is a matter of line-drawing.

3. A striking feature of Dreiser's style in narrating the drowning is his exclusive reliance on sentences without predicates, sentences consisting of a subject and interminable lists of modifiers. ("And then, as she drew near him, seeking to take his hand in hers and the camera from him in order to put it in the boat, he flinging out at her, but not even then with any intention to do other than free himself of her—her touch—her pleading—consoling sympathy—her presence forever—God! Yet (the camera still unconsciously held tight) pushing at her with so much vehemence as not only to strike her lips and nose and chin with it, but to throw her back sidewise toward the left wale which caused the boat to careen to the very water's edge.") This technique serves to introduce further ambiguity into the narrative. It prevents us from telling clearly whether what happened was really Clyde's doing. The following is perfectly compatible with what the narrator tells us: Clyde sees Roberta reaching out to him. The moment has come, he decides, to free himself of her. He raises his hand to push her away and overboard. But just as he has raised his hand, an inner panic causes him to faint. The hand that is raised to kill Roberta jerks involuntarily, hits her with greater vehemence than intended, and sends her stumbling backwards, with the ultimate consequence of her drowning.

Here there is an intention in action, and it does cause the intended action, but it causes it in a very perverse way. We should, I think, be disinclined to call what happened an intentional action. Just imagine the case where "a man is unable to raise his arm because his nerves have been cut. Try as he might, he is unable to lift the arm away from his side. He keeps trying and trying without success; however, on one occasion he tries so hard that his effort makes him fall into a switch which activates a magnet in the ceiling which attracts the metal in the watch on his wrist which raises his arm. Now in such a case his intention in action caused his arm to go up, but it didn't cause it 'in the right way.' In such a case we are reluctant to say that he raised his arm intentionally or even that he raised his arm."[60]

Another example is this: "If Chopin on some occasion had intended and decided to play the piano as if nervous, and his possession of this plan so upset him so that he played nervously, he would have done exactly what he intended."[61] Yet we scarcely would then say that he had intentionally played nervously.

The problem with these cases is that the intention that caused the intended action doesn't really "explain" the action. It doesn't explain it, because the action isn't very "sensitive" to the actor's intention. Suppose the patient with the cut nerves had intended to raise his arm very slowly. The magnet would still have pulled it up at the same speed. In other words, by changing his intention, the patient would not be changing the action that it brings about. It is in this sense that the action isn't very "sensitive" to the actor's intention. Suppose Chopin had intended to play only the second movement as if nervous. The intention would still have so upset him that he would have played both first and second movement nervously. Again, by changing his intention, Chopin would not be changing the action that it brings about. Finally, suppose Clyde's real intention had been to push Roberta to the ground and then to shoot her. He would still have been seized by panic, his hand would still have jerked, Roberta would still have stumbled backwards, the boat would still have careened, and she would still have drowned. Again, by changing his intention, Clyde would not be changing the action that it brings about. Because of this, it makes more sense to say that the actor's action happens to coincide with his intention than that it fulfills it. And without such fulfillment, one would be loath to speak of an intentional action.

The mens rea, or "guilty mind," every crime requires has nothing to do with a guilty conscience. It is simply the mental state appropriate to a given offense. Mens rea matters because through it mistakes become relevant to the defendant's guilt. In a way, that's obvious. If an offense requires the defendant to have certain beliefs about what he is doing, then if he is mistaken about what he is doing he may not have those beliefs. But in a way, it's quite strange. It means that in any description of what the defendant did, certain words may not be replaced by their apparent synonyms. (George intentionally took the red umbrella. The red umbrella was Maurice's. Yet he didn't intentionally take Maurice's umbrella. How odd.) It takes a bit of philosophical finesse to explain why that is so.

It is often hard to tell, whether a mistake is relevant to a defendant's guilt or not. The seemingly esoteric panoply of cases with which this chapter opens—involving ghosts and witches, misfired bullets, and misidentified victims—brings to the fore the reasons for that. The presence of almost any mental state—intention, knowledge, recklessness—hinges on the presence of certain beliefs. A mistake is relevant if it means that the defendant lacked those beliefs. Having a belief is erroneously thought to be an all-or-nothing affair, and whether a mistake negates a certain belief is erroneously thought to be a yes-or-no question. If fact, whether a defendant has a belief is a matter of degree. It depends on the extent to which he meets a variety of criteria: Does he have the right kinds of background beliefs? Is his belief about the right kind of object? Does his belief interact in the right way with his other beliefs. The cases with which I opened are hard because there the defendant met some of these criteria, but not all of them. In a sense, those cases are not hard at all. No harder than the question whether orange is a form of red. Being red is a matter of degrees, and orange is red to a relatively small degree. Only if you insist that something either is red or isn't, does the question about orange become taxing. Unfortunately, that's what many courts have done with the cases with which we began.

There is a nearly unlimited vocabulary to describe the mental state of the defendant as he commits a criminal act. Courts have at one time or another employed almost all of them. Recently, drafters have tried to limit themselves to four basic terms: intention, knowledge, recklessness, and negligence. The meaning of these is superficially obvious. On closer inspection it becomes harder to grasp. At times, it seems that intention implies knowledge and knowledge intention. That's not so in fact, but it takes real effort to see why not. The meaning of recklessness and negligence is hard to grasp for a different reason. It hinges on our ability to evaluate risks, and we are very poor and inconsistent at that.

Having the required mens rea is more than being in the required mental state, manifesting the required intention, knowledge, recklessness, or negligence. The mens rea must fit with the actus reus in the right sort of way. The case of Clyde Griffiths shows the many reasons it might fail to fit.

We have looked so far at offenses in general, at the problems that afflict *all* offenses—the problems surrounding the "bad act" and the "guilty mind." But there are different types of offenses and each carries with it a special burden of difficulties. The next three chapters examine the three most important types: first, offenses which require that the defendant have caused certain harm (rather than merely have engaged in certain conduct, whether it produces harm or not); second, offenses that consist not of committing a crime, but of helping someone else commit one; and finally, offenses committed when a crime isn't completed, but fails along the way.

The problems of the next chapter are adumbrated in a series of cases with which the chapter opens. They are basically three. Why do we care about causation; or, why do we make punishment contingent on whether it led to harm? How do we decide whether a certain mishap would have happened if the defendant hadn't done what he did? Lastly, is every act without which a mishap would not have happened the cause of that mishap?

4 The Root of All Evil

Conundrums of Causation

Henri plans a trek through the desert. Alphonse, intending to kill Henri, puts poison into his canteen. Gaston also intends to kill Henri but has no idea what Alphonse has been up to. He punctures Henri's canteen, and Henri dies of thirst. Who has caused Henri's death? Was it Alphonse? How could it be, since Henri never swallowed the poison. Was it Gaston? How could it be, since he only deprived Henri of some poisoned water that would have killed him more swiftly even than thirst. Was it neither then? But if neither had done anything, Henri would still be alive. So who killed Henri?[1]

The defendant, police chief of a German town in 1936, applied to the Main Security Office of the Reich for permission to take three Jewish merchants into "protective custody" and subsequently to transfer them to a concentration camp. The Main Security Office granted the request. After the war the former police chief was prosecuted for the unlawful imprisonment of the three merchants. He argued that his actions could not be treated as the cause of their misfortunes. If he had not made his application, the three merchants would have been taken into custody by the Gestapo or some other government agency. And regardless of the outcome of the prosecution, they would certainly have been transferred to a concentration camp, because they were Jews. The prosecution argued that all that was quite irrelevant. The reality was that the defendant and no one else had caused the three merchants to be taken into custody and put into a concentration camp. The fact that someone else would otherwise have done so did nothing to alleviate his responsibility. Who was right?[2]

John Bush intentionally shot Annie Vanmeter with a pistol. Annie was brought to the hospital, where she contracted scarlet fever from a nurse and died of it. Did John cause Annie's death?[3]

James Vance, an old man, and Herbert Williams, his young companion, had come in from the Australian countryside to visit the town of Melbourne. As they hopped from bar to bar, they attracted the attention of a band of robbers. When they were on their way back to their hotel, the robbers decided to strike. Williams was just entering the hotel courtyard, when he was kicked in the stomach and fell down. Vance, noticing this, tried to escape into the hotel. He stumbled over the entrance, fell down, fractured his skull and died. The law provides that whoever commits a felony (such as robbery) that results in the death of a human being (intentional or not) has committed murder. Had the robbers here caused Vance's death?[4]

The inhabitants of an African village called on a witch doctor to help them find out why so many children born in recent months had died soon after birth. The witch doctor decided to organize a trial by ordeal to discover whether there were any witches in the village who might be responsible. Sixteen people voluntarily submitted to the test. The trial was a mild one as ordeals went. All that the participants were required to do was to drink a certain magic potion called *muabvi*. *Muabvi,* it was believed, would kill any witch who drank it but would not harm the innocent. The witch doctor prepared the *muabvi* and handed it out to the sixteen participants. Four of the sixteen died, several others became violently ill. A government analyst later examined the substance and found it was not poisonous; the substance was given to guinea pigs and none showed any harmful effects. The pathologist who examined the deceased found no cause of death and no trace of poison in the bodies. The closest that anyone came to an explanation was to conjecture that while *muabvi* normally was not harmful to human beings, it might prove fatal if associated with large amounts of adrenalin: a person frightened by the ordeal, and excreting a large dose of adrenalin, might thus end up "poisoning himself." Had the witch doctor murdered anyone?[5]

The next conundrum takes a bit longer to state. On 25 May 1913, the official Royal and Imperial Telegraphic News Bureau of the Austro-Hungarian monarchy reported the suicide of Colonel Alfred Redl, the long-time star of Austria-Hungary's counterespionage bureau. Redl's official position was chief of staff of the Prague Army Corps; he was rumored to be next in line for the Ministry of War. The suicide occurred while Redl was visiting Vienna, on what the report simply referred to as "official business." The report blamed the suicide on a "severe mental aberration" that had momentarily seized the hardworking and "highly talented" Redl. The funeral, the report concluded, would be attended by all high-ranking officers in the capital, by all troops off duty, and by the cadets of all military academies nearby.[6]

The same day Egon Erwin Kisch, chairman of Prague's Athletic Soccer Club, Storm, was anxiously awaiting the arrival of the soccer team's right end, the locksmith Wagner. At Sunday's game against Union-Holleschowitz, another second-string team, the championship prospects of the club would be decided. The winner stood to be promoted to the ranks of the class A clubs. But the right end, the team's strongest player, never showed up. His absence proved the team's undoing. Storm lost and Kisch was furious.

Being chairman of the soccer club was only Kisch's hobby. By profession he was a journalist, and not just any journalist, but the star reporter of one of Prague's German-language newspapers, the *Bohemia*. The next day Wagner came into Kisch's office to apologize. He had already been dressed to go, he explained, when a soldier came into his shop and said that someone had to go at once to the army corps headquarters to open some lock. Kisch didn't believe him; such a job wouldn't take more than five minutes. It took three hours, Wagner protested. First, he had to break open the lock of an apartment, then he had to stay there and open every single drawer and closet. Kisch's ears pricked up. Who were the people who wanted him to break into a stranger's apartment? Two gentlemen from Vienna, Wagner had gathered, who later were joined by the Prague Corps commander. They thought the locksmith only spoke Czech and weren't too careful about what they were saying. It seemed they were looking for Russian papers and photographs of military plans. When they found what they were looking for, they just kept exclaiming, "This is awful. God awful! Who would have dared to imagine such a thing?" Whose house was it, Kisch asked, now completely rapt. Some high officer, Wagner thought, although the apartment looked very funny, almost like a "lady's apartment"; there were innumerable cosmetics, a haircurler, perfumed letters, and photographs of young men.

Kisch put two and two together. There was no question but that the apartment was Colonel Redl's. Redl apparently was a Russian spy, and the army, having discovered it, was trying to keep it a secret. Kisch was determined to break the story. But how? The Austrian press was subject to rigid censorship. Any such announcement would result in confiscation of the paper's entire edition. Kisch hit upon a ruse. That evening the *Bohemia*'s lead story reported: "Highly placed government sources deny rumors that the chief of the General Staff of the Prague Army Corps, Colonel Alfred Redl, who committed suicide the day before yesterday in Vienna, was a Russian spy. . . . We have been assured that the special commission from Vienna which recently searched Colonel Redl's apartment and had all of its drawers and closets broken into . . . was investigating allegations of an entirely different nature." To the reader such a "denial" was entirely transparent. But the official censor would have a hard time objecting to the article, because he had to assume that the denial was an official release of the corps command or one of the ministries of Vienna. And if he checked with them about the rumor, they were bound to deny it, thus "corroborating" the *Bohemia*'s story.

The next day everyone was calling the Ministry of War. Was it true that . . . ? The ministry denied everything. But the garrison commander of Vienna felt sufficiently embarrassed to cancel all planned funeral festivities immediately. That was confirmation enough. Soon the ministry stopped denying. It seemed, they really hadn't known. The army had tried to keep the secret even from the ministry. While ministry and army lapsed into embarrassed silence, the parliament went into an uproar.

The full details of the Redl affair came to light only much later. Early in 1913, the general delivery department of Vienna's Main Post Office had received two anonymous letters, mailed in Eydtkuhnen, a town on the German-Russian border, and containing fourteen thousand crowns in Austrian currency. The letters were addressed to the general delivery of the Main Office, to be handed over to whoever presented the clerk with the code cipher "Opera Ball 13." The Secret Service had only recently made the opening of suspicious mail a routine part of its operations and its suspicion was immediately aroused. Two Secret Service men were posted in the Post Office's back rooms, and the clerk was told to summon them discreetly with a hidden bell as soon as someone requested the suspicious letters. Months went by, the police commissioner who had ordered the watch became interior minister, the clerks at the Post Office changed, but no one came to claim the letter. Then on 24 May 1913, five minutes before closing, a man came in and requested the letter with the code cipher "Opera Ball 13." The clerk rang the bell. The surprised Secret Service men ran to the delivery room, but by the time they made it they only saw the letter's recipient disappear into a cab and the cab take off. They noted the cab's number, but could do no more. They had no car with which to give chase. And the man would presumably change cabs several times before he reached his final destination.

Twenty minutes later the crestfallen detectives ran into an extraordinary piece of luck. The same cab happened to drive by. They hailed it, asked for a description of its last passenger, and had it take them to the Cafe Kaiserhof, where it had just dropped off the elegant-looking gentleman. While in the cab they found the sheath of a knife, which the man had evidently forgotten there. Another piece of luck awaited them when they got to the Cafe Kaiserhof. Yes, someone had overheard where the gentleman had directed his next cab to go: a certain hotel on the Herrengasse. Off to the hotel they rode. They asked the porter who had entered the hotel in the last couple of minutes. Just two merchants from Bulgaria, the porter replied. And before them Colonel Redl. The detectives were amused. Their spy was staying in the same hotel as the famous counterespionage man Alfred Redl! What a coincidence. Or perhaps it wasn't. Perhaps it was a feint: escape into the lion's den. Anyway, they told the porter to inquire whether any of the hotel guests had lost the sheath of his knife. The detectives were wondering whether they shouldn't go up right away and tell Redl about the spy in his own hotel. But then they saw Redl coming down the staircase. As he walked past the porter, the man asked him whether he had lost the sheath of his knife. "Yes," said Redl, took the knife out of his pocket, and slipped it on. "I've been missing it for the last fifteen minutes. Where did you find . . . ?"

Suddenly Redl remembered where he had last used the knife. He glanced about him with alarm and recognized the faces of his own former subordinates. The two detectives finally caught on. Redl hurried out of the hotel. He still hoped to make a getaway. The two detectives followed close on his heels. He headed toward the Stock Exchange Building, which he knew had three exists. On his way he tore up several documents he was carrying and scattered them behind him hoping at least one of the detectives would stop to pick them up. None of these stratagems worked. Still pursued by the two detectives Redl finally gave up and returned to the hotel.

The head of the Secret Service, Urbanski von Ostromiesc, was notified, but he refused to believe it. He had his men check the signature of the postal receipt against a handwritten copy of some reports and guidelines Redl had composed, including a list of "Rules for the Discovery of Spies both at Home and Abroad.'' The handwriting was the same. Urbanski then notified Conrad von Hoetzendorf, the head of the General Staff, the chief of chiefs. Hoetzendorf, too, was incredulous. If Redl was a spy, Russia was now in possession of Austria's mobilization plans to the last detail. Mobilization plans were not the sort of thing one could easily change. (Indeed, the affair is believed to have cost the lives of several hundred thousand Austrians during the First World War. Of course, it may have saved an equal number of Russian lives.) What would happen when the affair became public knowledge? The minister of war had been waiting for a pretext to put a tighter rein on the General Staff. Germany, the so-called ally, was already treating Austria with intolerable hubris. And the enemies, Russia, England, France, were already deriding Austria as an altogether decadent and impotent adversary. The affair had to remain secret. ''The wretch must die at once!'' Hoetzendorf decreed.

''He must? By his own hand?'' asked Urbanski.

''Precisely. No one must know anything of the causes of this death. No one!''

Some hours later a commission of high-ranking officers, headed by Urbanski, visited Redl's room. ''I know why you gentlemen have come,'' Redl murmured. ''I'm already in the midst of some farewell letters.'' Why had he become a spy, the men asked him. He was a homosexual, Redl explained; the Russians had learned about it and blackmailed him. All the evidence they needed, he said, they would find in his Prague apartment.

''Herr Redl,'' one of the officers finally asked (it was no longer *Colonel* Redl), ''do you have a weapon?''

''No.''

''You may request a weapon, Herr Redl.''

''I—humbly—request a—revolver,'' Redl managed to say. No one was carrying a gun. Urbanski himself hurried home, fetched his own Browning, and handed it to Redl. The next morning a hotel employee discovered the ''suicide.''

When, contrary to the hopes of the General Staff, the Redl affair became public, there was outrage about the fact that the General Staff had apparently ordered Redl's suicide. The General Staff defended itself on the peculiar ground that Redl was on the verge of committing suicide anyway. The question never reached a court of law. Otherwise the court would have faced a fascinating question: Is it murder to induce someone to commit suicide?

The Reasons of the Heart

Why bother with causation? John attempts to kill Annie. He shoots and, somehow or other, his shooting at her eventuates in her death. Why does it matter that in some sense his shooting at her may not be the real cause of her death? Isn't it a purely adventitious circumstance, that has no bearing on his moral guilt or innocence? Why should we even care whether Annie succumbs to or survives her bullet wounds? John's deed is no less and no more heinous whatever its consequences for Annie turn out to be.

The last question is readily answered. It's no use denying that John's deed is equally heinous whether Annie dies or survives. There is no moral difference between the assassin who attempts murder and fails and the assassin who succeeds. Yet we will want to punish the latter more harshly than the former. The reason isn't hard to see. Criminal behavior isn't what arouses our emotions, it is the harm such behavior inflicts that arouses us. Only the successful criminal has inflicted genuine harm, and only he elicits really deep emotional reactions. Only he provokes anger. His punishment serves to still that anger.[7]

But in the case of John and Annie there isn't merely criminal conduct; there is actual harm. That harm, too, will presumably arouse our emotions. So why are we less inclined to punish John than the run-of-the-mill killer? More simply, why are we less angry with John than with an ordinary murderer?

A detour into a branch of psychology called attribution theory helps to answer that question. The psychologists Stanley Schachter and Jerome Singer once invited their students in an introductory psychology course at the University of Minnesota to participate in an experiment on the effect of vitamins on vision.[8] The vitamin they were interested in, they said, was Suproxin. They persuaded 185 of their students to be injected with Suproxin and to undergo some visual experiments. In fact what they injected the students with was not Suproxin at all. Some of the students simply received a placebo. Others were injected with adrenalin. Adrenalin, of course, is the substance that our autonomic nervous system discharges in large quantities when we are emotionally aroused. Its effect is to increase our blood pressure, heart rate, respiration, cerebral blood flow, blood sugar, and lactic acid concentration. Its subjective symptoms everyone knows well: palpitations, tremors, sometimes a flushed feeling, and accelerated breathing.

The experimenters carefully explained to some of the adrenalin recipients these possible side effects of "Suproxin." Others were told nothing.

After a subject had been injected, the experimenter left the room and returned a short while later with a "stooge." The stooge, he explained, was also a subject and had also just received his shot. He asked the two to wait for about twenty minutes until the Suproxin had been absorbed into the blood stream. Then the experiment would begin.

As soon as the experimenter had gone, the stooge began to engage in all sorts of wild and exuberant behavior. He reached for a piece of paper and started doodling, remarking, "They said we could use this for scratch, didn't they?" Then he crumpled up the paper and attempted to throw it into a waste paper basket. He missed but this led him into a basketball game. He crumpled up some other sheets of paper, shot a few baskets, said, "Two points" occasionally, and did a jump shot shouting, "The old jump shot is really on today." Then he asked the other subject to join him. Finally, he stopped, saying, "This is one of my good days. I feel like a kid again. I think I'll make a plane." He folded one and threw it at the other subject. Later he tore off part of the plane, saying, "Maybe this plane can't fly but at least it's good for something." He tore the paper into little shreds, rolled them into pellets, and began to shoot them across the room with a rubber band. While shooting, he noticed a file of manila folders on a table. He stacked them into a pile and began peppering them with paper bullets from the other end of the room. The tower collapsed; he cheered. While picking up the folders, he noticed some hula hoops behind the blackboard. He tried them on. "This isn't as easy as it looks," he observed. He twirled them wildly on one hand, shouting, "Hey, look at this—this is great." Finally he sat down, with his feet on the table. The experimenter returned.[9]

What the experimenters were curious to see was to what extent the stooge's euphoria would prove infectious. Which subjects would join in this bedlam?

Euphoria wasn't all Schachter and Singer were interested in. Some subjects encountered not a euphoric but an angry stooge. In this variant, the experimenter gave both the stooge and the subject some questionnaires to fill out while they waited for the visual experiments to begin. As soon as the experimenter was gone the stooge started leafing through the questionnaire. "Boy, this is a long one," he grumbled. He got to question 7, which asked him to "List the foods that you would eat in a typical day."

The stooge exclaimed, "Oh for Pete's sake, what did I have for breakfast this morning?" Question 9 asked, "Do you ever hear bells? _____ How often? _____" The stooge turned to the other subject: "Look at question 9. How ridiculous can you get? I hear bells every time I change classes." Question 13 read, "List the childhood diseases you have had and the age at which you had them." The stooge mumbled, "I get annoyed at this childhood disease question. I can't remember what childhood diseases I had, and especially at what age. Can you?" And so it went till the very end. Question 17 asked, "What is your father's average annual income?" The stooge responded, "This really irritates me. It's none of their business what my father makes. I'm leaving that blank." Question 25 presented a long list of items such as "Does not bathe or wash regularly," "Seems to need psychiatric care," and the like, and asked the respondent to write down which of his family members that seemed to apply to. It prohibited the answer "none." The stooge said, "I'll be damned if I'll fill out number 25. 'Does not bathe or wash regularly'—that's a real insult." Question 28 asked, "How many times each week do you have sexual intercourse. 0–1 _____, 2–3 _____, 4–6 _____, 7 and over _____?" "The hell with it," he yelled. "I don't have to tell them all this." He ripped the questionnaire to shreds, shouting, "I'm not wasting any more time. I'm getting my books and leaving," and he stomped out. The questionnaire went on for eight more questions, the last one being: "With how many men (other than your father) has your mother had extramarital relationships?"

The object of this little exercise should be clear: How infectious was the stooge's anger? How many subjects would copy his behavior and attitude?

While all this was going on, the experimenters were sitting at the other side of a one-way mirror and observed their subjects. When the experiment was over, they also interviewed the subjects about their emotional reaction to the stooge's behavior and to the questionnaire. This is what they found: Subjects who had received the placebo tended to react with mild euphoria to the euphoric stooge and with mild anger to the angry stooge. Subjects who had been injected with adrenalin but not told of its effects reacted with great euphoria to the euphoric stooge and with anger to the angry stooge. The surprise was the reaction of the subjects who had been told about the effects of the drug: they remained almost entirely unaffected by the stooge's behavior. It left them "cold." They felt neither euphoric nor angry, nor did they behave that way.

How does one explain this? All subjects injected with adrenalin were experiencing the symptoms of emotional arousal. Subjects who were with a euphoric stooge attributed their arousal to euphoria. Hence they felt euphoric. Subjects who were with an angry stooge attributed their arousal to anger. Hence they felt angry. But subjects who had been told about the drug's side effects attributed their arousal to the drug and felt nothing. In fact they felt less angry and less euphoric than subjects injected with a placebo (who had not been given any instructions). The Schachter and Singer study thus unearthed an insight about our emotional life of dizzying novelty: The emotions we experience when we are physically aroused are largely determined by why we think we are aroused. More flippantly, what we feel depends on why we think we feel that way.

The study has a variety of unexpected implications, which subsequent experimenters have eagerly followed up. One such experiment was conducted on two bridges crossing the Capilano River in North Vancouver.[10] The two bridges look as though they have been designed with controlled experiments in mind. They are a study in contrasts. The first, the Capilano Canyon Suspension Bridge is 5 feet wide, 450 feet long, and consists of wooden boards attached to wire cables. It has very low handrails of wire cable, and it frequently tilts, sways, and wobbles so as to give many passersby the impression that they are about to fall off. Underneath the bridge is a 230-foot drop to rocks and shallow rapids. The second bridge, a little further upriver is a sturdy, solid structure made of heavy cedar, lined with high handrails, which does not exhibit any tilting or swaying.

On each of the bridges the experimenters stationed an attractive female interviewer, who was to approach any single males crossing the bridge and ask them to fill out a short questionnaire. The first page of the questionnaire contained some irrelevant, make-work items: age, education, prior visits to bridge, etc. The second page asked the subjects to write a brief dramatic story based upon a picture of a young woman covering her face with one hand and reaching with the other. The picture lacked any obvious sexual content. Afterwards the interviewer gave the subjects her phone number and asked them to call her if they were interested in the results of the experiment.

The experimenters were mainly curious about two things: the sexual content of the stories, and the number of subjects who decided to call their interviewer back. The group that crossed the dangerous bridge, it turned out, told stories with much more sexual content than the group crossing the safe bridge. Moreover, in the group crossing the dangerous bridge, 9 out of 18 subjects who accepted the interviewer's phone number called her back. In the group crossing the safe bridge only 2 out of 16 who accepted her phone number called her back. It seemed for some reason that the group crossing the dangerous bridge grew much more attracted to their interviewer than the other group.

The explanation is the same as in the Schachter and Singer study. Crossing the dangerous bridge, subjects tended to become anxious. They experienced arousal—a release of adrenalin into the blood stream. Then they encountered the attractive female interviewer. That led them to attribute part of their arousal to the presence of the interviewer. They interpreted their emotional arousal as sexual attraction. That's why their stories reflected so much sexual content: that's why they called the interviewer back in such large numbers. Subjects crossing the safe bridge experienced no arousal, and their attraction to the interviewer was correspondingly low.

Another surprising implication of the Schachter and Singer study was brought to light by an experiment investigating the relationship between aggression and physical exercise.[11] Subjects were invited to participate in what purported to be a "learning experiment." Each subject was asked to play the role of "teacher" and put certain questions to a "learner" (a stooge) hidden in another room. He was to punish the learner for a wrong response with an electric shock of whatever severity he thought appropriate. Before the experiment started, the experimenter saw to it that the teacher would become somewhat angry with his learner. He asked the teacher to express his opinion on a variety of controversial topics. Whenever the learner agreed with the teacher, he signalled his agreement by turning on a certain light. Whenever he disagreed, he signalled his disagreement by administering an electric shock to the teacher. He did this quite often, and most teachers were undoubtedly more than a little miffed at the learner.

With these preliminaries out of the way, the experimenter asked his subjects to participate in some exercise on a stationary bicycle in the laboratory. Later on they asked the subjects to return to their role as teachers. Some of the subjects, however, were allowed to relax a little before resuming their role. The rest were required to continue immediately with the learning experiment. What interested the experimenters was whether one of the two groups would show greater aggression toward the learner than the other. An easy measure of such aggression was the severity of the shock they administered in the course of the learning experiment. There was indeed a difference between the two groups. The group given no respite proved much less aggressive than the group permitted to rest. Oddly enough, among the rested ones, subjects who were still chafing from their exertion were much more aggressive than subjects who had recovered from it. How is one to make sense of this?

The Schachter and Singer theory works here, too. The most aroused group was the one that had just stopped exercising. But it was clear to everyone in that group why he was aroused: exercise. People who had been allowed to rest tended to attribute their arousal to the learner's irritating behavior. Thus they felt angry and behaved aggressively. Naturally, too, among people who attributed their arousal to the learner's misconduct, those who were least aroused, because they had recovered from the exercise, were much less aggressive than those who were still very aroused.

An ingenious twist to all this was added by some psychologists investigating insomnia. The people participating in this experiment were a motley group of self-selected insomniacs. All of them were given a placebo pill. One group of subjects was told the following: "This drug will increase your bodily activity. It works on the sympathetic nervous system, which is the system that arouses you and sends adrenalin through your system. The pill will increase your heart rate and it will increase your body temperature. You may feel a little like your mind is racing. In general it may arouse you."[12]

Another group of subjects was told the opposite: "This drug will lower your bodily activity. It works on the parasympathetic nervous system, which is the system that relaxes you. The pill will lower your heart rate. It will decrease your body temperature so that you will feel a little cooler. And it will calm down your mind. In general, it will relax you."[13]

Which of the two groups got to sleep faster? The group that had been told that the placebo would arouse them. Why? Whatever agitation they felt when they went to bed they attributed to the pill; they ceased worrying about their insomnia and they went to sleep.

Readers of Ann Landers are probably quite familiar with the so-called Romeo and Juliet effect. When parents disapprove of their daughter's boyfriend, it is bad strategy to interfere actively with the relationship. That will often bolster rather than undermine the relationship. The Schachter and Singer theory explains why. The daughter's conflicts with her parents arouse her emotionally. She will often misinterpret that arousal as passion for her boyfriend and feel more strongly attached to him than before.[14]

When I was in high school, a teacher would occasionally assign a book for class that I had long been meaning to read on my own. Invariably, I felt that I would have enjoyed reading the book more if it had not been assigned. I was not quite sure why that was, but the feeling was persistent. The Schachter and Singer study readily explains this sentiment. What pleasure the book gave me I tended to attribute to fulfilling an obligation, that is, my completing the assignment, rather than to the book itself. Does that sound forced or fanciful? Some psychologists who had the same conjecture put it to the test.[15] Their subjects were a class of nursery school children between forty and sixty-four months old. The experimenters divided them into several groups. They asked children in one group to draw pictures with a magic marker and promised them a reward in return: a Good Player award with a big gold star and a bright red ribbon around it. They also asked the children of another group to use the magic markers but promised them no reward. After some time had elapsed they collected the drawings and distributed the awards. Then they disappeared from the scene and left the children to do as they pleased. They were curious to see what effect the reward would have on the children's interest in drawing with magic markers when there were no rewards to be had. The results were dramatic. Children who had been promised a reward were distinctly less interested in playing with the magic markers than children who had not. Apparently they attributed their original interest in the magic markers entirely to the promise of a Good Player award. They assumed that what they had done to obtain a reward could not be enjoyable to do without one.

What the psychologists discovered had been anticipated more than a hundred years ago by none other than Mark Twain. Early in *The Adventures of Tom Sawyer,* you may remember, Aunt Polly punishes Tom by ordering him to paint the fence on a Saturday morning. Tom recruits help for this ordeal by telling his friends it is an extraordinary privilege, in which he will only let them partake for a suitable fee. The fence gets painted without any effort on Tom's part, and Tom ends up the happy owner of some invaluable trinkets. To be precise: "a kite, in good repair," "a dead rat and a string to swing it with," "twelve marbles, part of a jewsharp, a piece of blue bottle-glass to look through, a spool cannon, a key that wouldn't unlock anything, a fragment of chalk, a glass stopper of a decanter, a tin soldier, a couple of tadpoles, six fire-crackers, a kitten with only one eye, a brass doorknob, a dog collar—but no dog—the handle of a knife, four pieces of orange peel, and a dilapidated old window sash."[16]

Mark Twain concludes:

> [Tom] had discovered a great law of human action, without knowing it—namely, that in order to make a man or a boy covet a thing, it is only necessary to make the thing difficult to attain. If he had been a great and wise philosopher, like the writer of this book, he would now have comprehended that Work consists of whatever a body is *obliged* to do and that Play consists of whatever a body is not obliged to do. And this would help him to understand why constructing artificial flowers or performing on a treadmill is work, while rolling ten-pins or climbing Mont Blanc is only amusement. There are wealthy gentlemen in England who drive four-horse passenger-coaches twenty or thirty miles on a daily line, in the summer, because the privilege costs them considerable money; but if they were offered wages for the service, that would turn it into work and then they would resign.

Attribution theory—the line of experiments spawned by Schachter and Singer—helps us see why we care about causation. The defendant commits a criminal act. A death results. We are emotionally aroused. How do we feel about the death? Attribution theory tells us: It depends. If we view the defendant as the cause of our loss, we will be angry. If we view accidental circumstances as its cause, we will be sad. Only if we are angry will we clamor for a savage punishment. Causation matters to us because it determines how we feel about the loss we have experienced.

For Want of a Nail

For want of a nail the shoe was lost
For want of the shoe the horse was lost
For want of the horse the rider was lost
For want of the rider the army was lost
For want of the army the battle was lost
For want of the battle the kingdom was lost
And all for want of a horseshoe nail

George Herbert

How do we know that what A did is the cause of what B suffered? The answer seems obvious: A caused B's injury because if he hadn't done anything, B wouldn't have been injured. "But for A's act," a common law court might say, "B would still be whole." An Austrian legal theorist put it thus:

> If one attempts wholly to eliminate in thought the alleged author [of the act] . . . from the sum of the events in question and it then appears that nevertheless the sequence of intermediate causes remains the same, it is clear that the act and its consequence cannot be referred to him . . . but if it appears that, once the person in question is eliminated in thought from the scene, the consequences cannot come about, or that they can come about only in a completely different way, then one is fully justified in attributing the consequence to him and explaining it as the effect of his activity.[17]

If A shoots at B and misses him, but moments later a boiler explodes and blows B to smithereens, it's obvious why A didn't cause B's death. If A hadn't fired the shot, B would still have died.

But the test isn't always so easy to apply. Josef and his brother Paul were bicycling down a dark country road one rainy and windy evening. Neither bike was equipped with the required headlight. Josef was ducking his head to avoid the elements and thus could scarcely notice oncoming traffic. As he passed an intersection, he collided head-on with K., another bicycle rider. K. suffered a severe skull fracture and eventually died. Both Josef and Paul were charged with negligent homicide (manslaughter). The case against Josef was clear-cut, and the trial court had no trouble convicting him. The case against Paul was more complex. The prosecutor argued that Paul, like Josef, had, of course, been negligent in bicycling without a headlight. Had he had a headlight, it would have served to illuminate not only his own but also Josef's bike, K. would then have seen Josef, and the accident would never have happened. The trial court, however, did not think that Paul's negligence had caused the accident. If Paul had not been negligent, it reasoned, he would not have been out riding his bike without any headlight, in which case K. would still not have noticed the oncoming Josef, and the accident would still have happened. The appeals court, however, agreed with the prosecutor.[18]

Another case: the defendant was driving a car without a license and got involved in an accident. Driving without a license is (or rather, used to be) considered negligent per se. But was the defendant's negligence the cause of the accident? Some courts said yes, reasoning that the accident would not have happened if the unlicensed person had abstained from driving. Others said no, reasoning that even if the defendant had had a license the accident would still have happened.[19] (These are, for the most part *civil,* rather than criminal cases. The defendant, if he loses, does not go to jail, but has to pay damages. Since these cases exemplify the same problems as the criminal ones, I will freely use them where they are illuminating.)

The problem raised by these cases is epitomized by an old Jewish joke about a young Jewish boy, growing up in Lubomir, a small Eastern European shtetl. The rabbi of Lubomir was looking for a shammes, an assistant. The boy's father eagerly presented his son, but when the rabbi learned that the boy could neither read nor write he regretfully declined: "But for that, he would have done nicely." Soon thereafter, the young boy emigrated with his family to the United States, and as luck and industry would have it, twenty years later he became a tycoon, the head of a large industrial enterprise. When, in the course of events, this enterprise bought out and merged with another company, the signing ceremony became a major public affair. At the ceremony, the reporters noticed that the tycoon signed the agreement with three crosses. Asked for the reason, he frankly explained: "I never learned to read or write." "My God," exclaimed one of the reporters, "imagine what would have become of you if, in addition to everything else, you knew how to read and write." "On that point," answered the tycoon, "I can give you a precise answer: had I known how to read and write I would have become the shammes of the rabbi of Lubomir."

Conditional statements—"If A had not happened, B would not have happened"—are surrounded by an air of mystery and ambiguity. Storytellers and comedians may relish such mystery and ambiguity, judges are annoyed by it. Yet how can conditional statements be such elusive entities when we confidently and freely use them in everyday discourse without becoming entangled in any obvious inconsistencies or contradictions? The answer is that the run-of-the-mill conditional we rely on most in everyday discourse only superficially resembles the conditional in issue here. "If you are over eighteen, you are eligible to vote." "If the doctor isn't here, his answering machine will respond." These are conditional statements, too, but there isn't much mystery or ambiguity about them. That is because those conditional statements talk about the real world and are easily verified. Statements such as "If Paul had not been negligent, the accident would never have happened" or "If Germany had discovered the atom bomb by 1944, it would have used it" are of an entirely different caliber. They invite us to consider a hypothetical universe, a make-believe world, a train of events that never happened anywhere except in our mind. To see if they are true we have to investigate not the real world, but a fictional one to which we have access only through our imagination.

Why are statements about what happens in hypothetical worlds difficult to resolve? I hinted at the reason in chapter 2. It is time now to be more explicit. Why should it be difficult to imagine a world in which the antecedent of a conditional statement (e.g., Germany discovers the bomb in 1944) holds true and then investigate whether in such a world the consequent (Germany uses it) also holds true. The problem is that there are many such imaginary worlds in which the antecedent holds true. In some of these the consequent is true as well, in others it isn't. What would happen if tomorrow the United States were to throw its weapons into the sea? One might argue that if it did so all by itself there would be war, but if it did so together with all other nuclear powers there would be peace, but if they did so without sufficient precautions against polluting the world's fisheries there would be war, but if, after doing so they immediately offered generous reparations for the pollution there would be peace; but if . . . and so on.[20] In other words, what we assume about our hypothetical world in addition to the antecedent will determine whether the consequent holds true. Nevertheless, we are generally confident that a certain conditional statement is true or false. That means we must have some particular imaginary world in mind. But what world is that?

There seems to be a ready answer to that question. The world we should be looking at is one that is just like ours except that the antecedent also holds true. Unfortunately, such a world is logically impossible. Take the statement "If New York City were in Colorado, that city would be west of the Mississippi." Let us imagine a world in which the antecedent is true, that is, in which New York is located in Colorado. Can we assume everything else to be just the way it is in the real world? No, for instance, we can't continue to assume that New York has a harbor. Unless, of course, we assume that Colorado borders on the Atlantic Ocean. But that would not be like the real world either. In short, if we change one fact about the world, we have to change many others as well to make them compatible with our new counterfactual assumption.[21]

But what are the facts that we should change? If we put Colorado next to the Atlantic Ocean, then presumably New York is still west of the Mississippi and the conditional statement is false. On the other hand if we give up the idea that New York is next to the ocean, then it presumably is west of the Mississippi, and the conditional statement is true. Which is the proper thing to do?

An approach suggested by some is to treat the antecedent like a startling piece of news that is actually true. Such news would require us to revise many of our beliefs. If when we are done revising our beliefs we end up believing the consequent true, then the conditional statement is true. That is, to evaluate the statement about New York you have to ask yourself: Suppose somebody convinced me that my knowledge of geography was quite faulty: New York actually lies in Colorado. Where, relative to the Mississippi would I then place New York? I might respond: My knowledge of geography may be fouled up, but I have seen photos of New York. I know for sure it is next to the ocean. Whether or not it is located in Colorado, it thus remains east of the Mississippi.

The approach sounds sensible, but it leads to absurd results. Suppose somebody asked you: What would have happened if Oswald had not killed Kennedy? You approach the question by assuming for a moment somebody had actually convinced you that Oswald didn't kill Kennedy. In that case, you would infer that somebody else must have killed him. Hence you respond: If Oswald had not killed Kennedy, somebody else would have. And that's clearly absurd.[22]

What, then, is the right approach? To shed light on this question, one should look at the writings of the men most preoccupied with making conditional statements—the historians. Although more often than not tongue-in-cheek, historians love to ask questions such as what would have happened if the Moors in Spain had won, if Don Juan of Austria had married Mary Queen of Scots, if the Dutch had kept Nieuw Amsterdam, if Louis XVI had been more intransigent, if Napoleon had won at Waterloo, if Lee had won at Gettysburg, if Kerensky had pulled Russia out of World War I, if the attempt on Hitler's life had succeeded, and so on. One of the most elaborate attempts at "what if" history is a novel by the historian Robert Sobel entitled *For Want of a Nail.*[23]

Sobel asks what would have happened if the British had won the battle of Saratoga. That premise isn't altogether fanciful, since in the fall of 1777, when the British troops under General Burgoyne met the Continental army under General Gates, the outcome of the War of Independence hung very much in the balance. True, the rebels had scored some major victories. In 1775 they had forced General Howe to abandon Boston. On Christmas night, 1776, Washington had led a force of four thousand across the ice-strewn Delaware River for a surprise attack on the Hessian garrison at Trenton that netted one thousand prisoners. But the rebels had also suffered some humbling defeats. General Howe had expelled Washington's forces from the City of New York, and later he had taken Philadelphia, forcing the Continental Congress to flee to York. Moreover, the quality of the rebel fighting force did not compare favorably with the British: It was virtually untrained and constantly fluctuating in size as enthusiasm for the revolutionary cause waxed and waned. France had not yet decided whether to recognize and seriously assist the rebels.

The battle of Saratoga was a turning point. The British strategy in 1776 was to cut New England off from the rest of the colonies. To that purpose General John Burgoyne had been instructed to lead an army of some seven thousand regulars and many more Canadian, Tory, and Indian auxiliaries from Quebec to Albany, clearing the area of all rebel forces. Burgoyne, a bold, handsome man who went by the nickname "Gentleman Johnny" and who was regarded by many as a gambler, a dandy, and a rake, was determined to make a reputation for himself with this campaign. He took some enormous risks: He crossed the Hudson River confident of victory farther on and left himself no easy retreat. Only a few miles ahead the Continental army was massing. Before he knew it, Burgoyne found himself in the pincer of a formidable Continental fighting force. Burgoyne knew that his colleague General Clinton, was rushing an army of three thousand up the Hudson River, but he doubted that his men could hold out until Clinton arrived. His rations were running low, and he surrendered.

Saratoga was one of the Continental army's two greatest triumphs (the other was Yorktown). An entire British army had capitulated. France no longer hesitated to recognize the rebels. It prepared armies and fleets to assist the Americans and redoubled its financial support. That help was critical.

But as Sobel shows, things could easily have turned out differently. Although battered and mauled by relentless rebel attacks and running low on rations, Burgoyne holds out. He does make inquiries of the Americans about the terms of capitulation, but only to stall them. While the negotiations seesaw, Clinton continues his progress toward Saratoga. He smashes Israel Putnam's army, but Gates never learns of this. The messengers are lost in the woods. Without realizing it the nearly victorious Gates finds himself in the jaws of two British armies. By the time he understands his situation, it is too late. The tables are now turned, and after a haphazard and doomed attempt to break out, Gates's men surrender to Burgoyne.

Within months after Saratoga the rebel cause is in a shambles. France declines to come to the assistance of this weak ally. The radicals lose their control over the Continental Congress. Instead, moderates like John Dickinson and Joseph Galloway begin to set the tone. Benjamin Franklin makes peace overtures toward the British. Parliament sends the Earl of Carlisle to negotiate, and in May 1777 an armistice is signed.

The British realize that something has been amiss in their management of the American colonies, and they are eager to do better in the future. The terms of victory are generous: only the ringleaders are punished. John Adams, Sam Adams, John Hancock, Thomas Jefferson, Richard Henry Lee, Robert Treat Paine, and Roger Sherman are shipped off to London, tried, and executed. Patrick Henry and Thomas Paine, although not signatories of the Declaration of Independence, are executed as well. George Washington is sentenced to life imprisonment. Benjamin Franklin, the other prominent "radical," is spared, out of consideration for his age, scientific accomplishments, and his role in bringing about peace. He stays in London where he dies in 1781 (instead of 1790).

The British search for a modus vivendi more viable than that of prerevolutionary days. They turn America into a semi-independent protectorate, known as the Confederation of North America, overseen by a British viceroy, the first of whom is General Burgoyne, henceforth the Duke of Albany.

Not all Colonials can tolerate even such benign British rule. Nathaniel Greene, the popular former general of the Continental army assembles a caravan of five thousand malcontents, including the likes of Alexander Hamilton, James Madison, James Monroe, Benedict Arnold, and Edward Rutledge, and leads them into the American wilderness, where they can build their own rebel utopia. They settle in what we know as Texas; they call it Jefferson. Alexander Hamilton and James Monroe draft a constitution for Jefferson. In 1795, Eli Whitney invents the cotton gin and transforms Jefferson into a prosperous cotton plantation economy. There is a brief, heated debate over whether slavery should be permitted: Is it reconcilable with the sweeping language of the Declaration of Independence? Expediency carries the day, and not just the day. Slavery in Jefferson lasts until 1920.

Sobel actually traces out his "counterfactual history" into the 1970s. Some of the highlights: The French Revolution is scotched. Jefferson overruns Mexico and becomes the United States of Mexico. Karl Marx never gains more than fleeting fame, with a book called *The Anatomy of Capitalism*. Something like Marxism becomes popular through the works of one Erich Neiderhoffer, whose ideas are generally traced to the North American Rebellion, the Declaration of Independence, and Thomas Paine's *Common Sense*. In fact, it is believed by many that had the rebels succeeded in America, a Neiderhofferian society would have been born in America. The Russian Revolution results in the dissolution of Russia into many nationalities. Edison invents the airmobile, vitavision and the movies. As the world heads into the 1970s there are only two superpowers, leading a tense, potentially explosive coexistence: the Confederation of North America and the United States of Mexico.

Robert Sobel's novel is a speculative fantasy, but it does suggest the right way to understand counterfactual statements. Imagine a world in which the counterfactual's antecedent is true and which is otherwise *as close to the real world as possible*. It can't be completely like the real world, but it can come close. If in such a world the consequent holds true, the counterfactual statement is true. The philosopher David Lewis, who has developed an elaborate theory of counterfactuals along these lines, puts it thus: "*If kangaroos had no tails, they would topple over* seems to me to mean something like this: in any possible state of affairs in which kangaroos have no tails, and which resembles our actual state of affairs as much as kangaroos having no tails permits it to, the kangaroos topple over."[24]

That may sound a bit imprecise. It may suggest that counterfactual statements are by their nature speculative, like Sobel's novel. But that is not the case. Counterfactual statements can be investigated very thoroughly and proved or disproved very systematically. They are not the preserve of the novelist, but are at times employed by the most sober-minded historians.

They were so used by the economic historian Robert Fogel in his famous study *Railroads and American Economic Growth*.[25] Were railroads indispensable to American economic growth? Fogel proposed to reexamine this commonly accepted thesis through an ingeniously simple but new approach. By 1890 railroads were in their heyday. Fogel asked: How much smaller would the American gross national product have been in 1890 if there had been no railroads. He applies the technique just discussed. He imagines the American economy without railroads but otherwise as similar to the 1890 economy as we know it to the extent that it is compatible with that hypothesis.

How would goods be shipped in such an economy? Mostly by water. How much would that cost? Fogel divides the cost of shipping into two components and examines them separately. First, there is the cost of interregional shipments: the cost of getting wheat, corn, beef, and pork from Duluth, Milwaukee, Chicago, Toledo, and Detroit via the Great Lakes, from Omaha and Kansas City via the Missouri, from Minneapolis and St. Louis via the Mississippi, from Cincinnati via the Ohio River, from Peoria via the Illinois River, through various lakes, inland rivers, canals, and coastal waters to forty-three secondary markets in the East and West. The cost of a ton-mile is quickly obtained by examining the freight rates companies filed with the Interstate Commerce Commission. But then one has to take account of the fact that waterways are more circuitous. One also must figure in the greater cargo losses engendered by water transport. Fogel estimates these by looking at the insurance rates, since the average value of a loss on a given shipment should roughly equal the insurance charge on the shipment. Then, too, one must allow for the fact that waterways could not be used for about five months each year. This means that in such an economy more inventory would have to be stored. Thus if water routes were closed for 5/12 of the year, Fogel reasons, the absence of railroads should have increased inventories of agricultural commodities by roughly 5/12. Storage costs can then be estimated. One also has to calculate the amount of each product shipped from each of the centers. This can be done by looking at the reports of the produce exchanges, the boards of trade, and chambers of commerce of each of the primary market cities. Finally, one needs to estimate how much was shipped to each region. Here no ready list of figures is available—only a very roundabout method. Fogel divides the grain-importing regions into marketing areas. The area's requirement for a given commodity evidently is the difference between the area's total demand for the commodity and the amount supplied from within. Given the region's population, one can estimate, for instance, the amount of wheat needed for human consumption on the basis of what per capita consumption was then known to be in the United States. To that one adds the amount of wheat such areas export each year to other regions, based on data furnished by the Treasury Department, and subtracts from that the amount the region itself produces, found in certain documents of the Department of Agriculture.

Even more involved is the calculation of the costs of intraregional transport in such an economy, that is, the cost of getting farm products from the farm to the primary market where it was shipped off to the East. Finally, Fogel has to adjust for the fact that he has considered only a fraction of the commodities transported each year. He must also allow for the secondary effects which the building of railroads had on the economy, such as the boost to iron production. When all is said and done, Fogel finds that railroads added no more than 5 percent to our 1890 GNP, and he concludes that railroads were dispensable to American economic growth.

Critics have found fault with Fogel's argument. Whether they are right or wrong, they make one realize how tricky it is to reason properly about counterfactual statements.[26] Fogel, the critics say, has indeed shown that had there been no railroads in 1890, the GNP would only have been 5 percent lower than it was; he has also shown that in 1890 railroads were dispensable to the American economy. But why were they dispensable in 1890? Among other things, because in 1890 we already had advanced refrigeration systems for storing meat many months without rotting. What Fogel has overlooked, the critics say, is that many of the skills and technologies that would have made it easy to give up railroads in 1890 were not available in 1860. And many of them developed only as a result of the earlier introduction of the railroad. Fogel has shown that by 1890 we could have lived comfortably without the railroad; he hasn't shown that we could have lived as comfortably if it had never been built. As one writer explained, "If you step in and measure the importance of a ladder at the point where it has become possible to kick it away, you should not be surprised if it turns out to be negligible." That doesn't mean the ladder was never important.

What now of our headlightless bicyclist and our unlicensed driver? What would have happened if they had not been negligent? To answer that question we have to imagine hypothetical worlds as close to ours as possible, except that the defendants are not negligent. In the first case we have to ask: Which of two hypothetical worlds in which Paul is not negligent is closer to the real one—the world in which Paul stays home or the world in which he obtains a headlight for his bicycle? To answer that question we may need more facts. Assuming that Paul was eager to make this trip with his brother, we probably stay closer to reality if we equip him with a headlight than if we keep him at home. In such a world, the accident would not have happened. Hence we can say: If Paul had not been negligent, the accident would not have happened. In the second case we have to ask: Which world is closer to the real one—the world in which the driver carries a license or the world in which he stays off the road? Again we may need more facts to decide the issue. Let us suppose that the acquisition of a license requires demonstrable driving ability. Let us also assume that the defendant lacked such ability. Then the world in which he stays at home is closer to reality than the world in which he obtains a driver's license. Hence we can say: If the defendant had not been negligent, the accident would not have happened. But suppose that the only reason the defendant does not carry a license is that he has failed to renew it, a mere formality. Then a world in which he carries a license is closer to the real world than one in which he stays home. We can no longer say that if he had not been negligent the accident would not have happened.

We now have a clearer understanding of the conditional statement "If A had not happened, then B would not have happened," or "But for A, B would not have happened." But do we also have a clearer understanding of causation? Courts stubbornly insist that one event cannot be the cause of another unless there is a "but for" relationship between them. That flies in the face of intuition. Our intuition tells us that Gaston, who punctured Henri's canteen, caused his death, even though we cannot say that "but for" Gaston's act Henri would not have died. Our intuition tells us that the police chief caused the false imprisonment of the three Jewish merchants, even though we cannot say that "but for" his act they would not have been imprisoned. The "Austrian" formulation of the "but for" test given earlier may seem to offer a way out. It requires not merely that "but for" the defendant's act the victim's injury would not have happened, it requires that "but for" his act the victim's injury would not have happened *as it did*. "But for" Gaston's puncturing Henri's canteen, Henri would not have died as he did; he would have died of poison, not thirst. "But for" the police chief's order, the Jewish merchants would not have been arrested as they were, but by someone else at some other time. Without too much effort, however, we can dream up cases in which A's act causes B's injury, but C would have injured B in the identical way if A had not done so. Here intuition tells us that A caused B's injury. But because B's injury would have happened *just as it did* without A, the "Austrian" test tells us otherwise.[27]

Is our intuition misleading us? I don't think so. One can actually prove that a "but for" relationship is not the same thing as causation. Suppose we know that A caused B and B caused C. Then we can conclude that A caused C. Causation, logicians would say, is transitive. Now suppose we know that if A had not happened, B would not have happened, and if B had not happened, C would not have happened. Still, we cannot infer that if A had not happened C would not have happened. The "but for" relationship is not transitive and hence is not the same as causation. I won't just boldly assert that the "but for" relationship is not transitive but will prove it with a few examples. It may be true that "If Kennedy had not been president, he would not have been killed." It may also be true that "If Kennedy had not been killed, he would have been reelected." But that doesn't imply that "If Kennedy had not been president, he would have been reelected." It may be true that "If Watergate had not happened, John Doe would not have heard about it." It may also be true that "If John Doe had not heard about Watergate, he would have voted for Gerald Ford." But that doesn't imply that "If Watergate had not happened, John Doe would have voted for Gerald Ford." Without Watergate, Gerald Ford wouldn't have been the Republican nominee for president.

Here is a final example which will mean something only to aficionades of Frank Capra's movie *It's a Wonderful Life*. You may remember that at the end of that movie, some money disappears and drives the Jimmy Stewart character, George Bailey, close to suicide. It drives him to suicide because he doesn't appreciate the intransitivity of the "but for" relationship. He reasons thus: If he had never been born, that money would never have disappeared. (That's probably true.) If the money had not disappeared, a lot of people would be a lot happier, namely, his wife, his brother, his uncle, his friends, and his customers. (That, too, is probably true.) From this he incorrectly concludes that if he had never been born, a lot of people would be a lot happier. It takes Clarence, the Angel Second Class, to convince him of the fallacy of his reasoning by showing him what the world would look like if he had never been born: His wife would have become an old maid, his brother would have drowned, his uncle would have gone mad, his former employer would have gone to jail, his customers would not have gotten loans, and so on. What Clarence shows George Bailey is that the "but for" relationship is not transitive.[28]

To repeat: Because causation is transitive and the "but for" relationship is not, the two cannot be the same. Yet they clearly are intimately connected. Certainly, if "but for" A, B would not have happened, A caused B. Only the converse doesn't hold. The connection is even more intimate. If but for A, B would not have happened, and but for B, C would not have happened, then A caused C. Why? A caused B and B caused C, so A caused C. In other words, when two events are linked by a chain of intermediate events each of which would not have happened but for its predecessor, the first event in the chain caused the last event. Sometimes the last event would have happened even without the first event. Still, if there is a chain of this sort connecting first and last events then one caused the other.[29]

It has been argued quite persuasively that whenever we find a causal relationship between two events that do not stand in a "but for" relationship, it is because they are connected by such a chain. Two of our problem cases nicely bear this out. Consider the case of the three Jewish merchants. To make it a more useful example, let us embellish it. Suppose that one month after the defendant ordered the three arrested, the S.S. rounded up all the town's Jews anyway. Suppose further that if the merchants had known of their impending fate they could have made an illegal getaway across the border. Let us examine now the chain of events connecting the defendant's order to arrest the merchants with their imprisonment: (1) He orders two policemen to carry out the arrest. (2) The two policemen visit the merchants' homes. (3) They drive the merchants to the police station. (4) The merchants are put into a cell. But for 1, 2 wouldn't have occurred. But for 2, 3 wouldn't have occurred. But for 3, 4 wouldn't have occurred. You might object to the last link in the chain: Even if the policemen hadn't driven the men to the station, they would have been imprisoned sooner or later. But that's wrong. If the policemen, having arrested the merchants, had not taken them back but set them free, they would presumably have fled across the border and into safety. So the "but for" relationship between 3 and 4 indeed obtains.

We can analyze Henri's case similarly. The events of the case can be broken down into four steps: (1) Gaston punctures Henri's canteen. (2) The water runs out. (3) Henri becomes dehydrated. (4) Henri dies. If 1 hadn't occurred, 2 wouldn't have; if 2 hadn't, 3 wouldn't have; if 3 hadn't, 4 wouldn't have. Again you may object to the last link: If Henri had not become dehydrated, that could only have been because he swallowed Alphonse's poisoned water, in which case he would have died. But now you are not interpreting the conditional statement properly. "If Henri had not become dehydrated" means: "If everything had been pretty much as it was except that Henri had some water in his body." Everything being pretty much as it was surely includes Gaston's puncturing of the canteen, which precludes Henri's dying of Alphonse's poison. But if the canteen was punctured, what prevents Henri from becoming dehydrated? A number of possibilities exist: Henri's constitution might prove unusually resilient; a caravan might find him; a sudden rain might fall. If any of these events occurred, it would prevent dehydration and Henri would not die. Hence we know that if 3 hadn't occurred, 4 wouldn't have. Thus Gaston, not Alphonse, caused Henri's death. Admittedly, the question is still open whether all cases in which one cause "preempts" another cause can be analyzed and explained by this stratagem.

Causes and Conditions

I opened the last section by setting forth a certain naive theory of causation. According to the naive theory, A caused B, if B wouldn't have happened but for A. Naive or not, this is the theory many civil law countries, foremost among them Germany, have adopted.[31] The theory, as I showed, is "leaky." It lets many genuine causes (like Gaston) slip by. But by tinkering with it we were able to restate it so that not many real causes can escape its sway.

That is not the end of problems for the naive theory. In 1952, the East German scholar John Lekschas wrote a vitriolic critique of what he called the "western imperialist theory of causation," by which he meant the naive theory. In it, he reminds his readers of the recent death of the "patriot Phillip Mueller" at the hands of the West German police during a peace demonstration of German youths. Since the actions of both the police and the demonstrators were necessary preconditions for Mueller's death, he notes, the naive theory would list them both as causes of Mueller's death. "A very agreeable result for the West German reactionaries," he comments.[32] Indeed, he asks his readers with flourish, think of what the naive theory has to say about the all-important struggle between hysterical, war-mongering, western imperialists and the peace-loving, democratic, progressive forces in the world. Whatever the outcome of that struggle, whether it be war or peace, since the efforts of both groups will have been necessary to that outcome, the naive theory would call both "causes." "A very convenient result for the reactionaries of the world," he repeats. Despite the amusingly Stalinist flavor of his rhetoric and examples, Lekschas seems to be making a valid point. It flies in the face of common usage to call every necessary precondition of an event its cause. Recall the case of John, who shot Annie, who died of scarlet fever contracted from the nurse who treated her. But for what John did, she would not have died. Yet we are disinclined to call his act the cause of her death. Indeed, in many of the other cases with which I opened this chapter the same is true. We are unsure whether the men who tried to rob James Vance caused his death, even though it is clear that Vance would not have died but for the attempted robbery. We are unsure whether the witch doctor who gave his victims *muabvi* killed them even though it is clear that they would not have died but for partaking in the ordeal. We are unsure whether the men who induced Colonel Redl to commit suicide caused his death, although presumably he wouldn't have done it had they not furnished him with a weapon. So a cause is more than a necessary precondition.

It isn't just in the law that we make this distinction between causes and conditions. Suppose lightning strikes a building and sparks a fire, which consumes it. But for the presence of oxygen in the air, but for the dryness of the building, this would not have happened. Yet the cause of the fire isn't the oxygen, nor the dryness, but the lightning. A man punctures his toe with a nail and contracts lockjaw. But for the presence of his toe, but for the permeability of human skin, this would not have happened. Yet the cause of the lockjaw is not his toe or the permeability of human skin, but the nail. Those other circumstances are merely necessary conditions.

These are homely examples. They suggest that the distinction between causes and conditions doesn't much matter outside the law. But that's not so. An example is the celebrated debate between A. J. P. Taylor and Hugh Trevor-Roper over the origins of the Second World War. Taylor argued in an iconoclastic book published in 1961 that, contrary to conventional wisdom, it wasn't so much Hitler who caused the war, as the Treaty of Versailles (by which the First World War had been concluded) and the policies of the Western powers. Trevor-Roper defended the conventional wisdom. Taylor and Trevor-Roper were agreed that the Treaty of Versailles, Western policies, and Hitler's actions were all necessary links in the chain of events leading up to the Second World War. What they disagreed on was whether only Hitler should be called the cause of the war and everything else a mere necessary condition.

What kinds of arguments do they make? The historian W. H. Dray has succinctly summarized the two positions.[33] The conventional wisdom's first argument is simple: Only Hitler *wanted* war and did what he could to bring it about. Hence only he caused it. Taylor disputes the factual premise of this argument. Hitler didn't want war, he claims:

> Like most practical statesmen, he seldom made distant plans. Of course, he did have some general aims, notably the destruction of the international system created by the Treaty of Versailles, and the restoration of Germany to a dominant position in Europe once again. He was quite willing to exploit situations to those ends as opportunities arose, and even to threaten war from time to time; but that is far from saying that he actually intended to fight one. The war that came was something that, like some other statesmen of his time, Hitler blundered into. He simply lost control, and found himself involved finally in a war that he neither intended nor wanted.

Preposterous, say Taylor's critics. There can be no doubt, says Hugh Trevor-Roper, that

> Hitler meant to seize, by whatever means proved necessary, massive territories in the East some time before 1945—territories which would provide Germany with "living space" for a future population of more than 200 millions, and make possible her rise to the rank of a superpower. He also had definite, if still flexible, ideas about how this was to be accomplished. For example, he recognized the necessity of neutralizing the Western Powers before advancing on Russia—by force if diplomacy proved ineffective. And long before 1939 he had prescribed for a country like Poland only a choice between joining Germany in an offensive against the Soviets, or being invaded. Certainly he hoped to be able to take many of the initial steps toward his ultimate goal without war—for example, the annexation of Austria and Czechoslovakia, which he saw, not as an end in itself but as providing a necessary base for eastern expansion. But he never deluded himself into thinking that war would not be necessary in the end.

The dispute is somewhat clouded by the usual ambiguities surrounding the meaning of intent. Just what must Hitler have intended for us to be able to say he intended World War II? "Must he have aimed at an outbreak specifically in 1939?" "Must he have intended military operations against Britain and France as well as against Poland?" "Must the war have been envisaged antecedently as a struggle of considerable duration and ultimately global scope?" "And how long in advance would Hitler have had to form the relevant intention, whatever its actual content?" What further complicates matters is that Hitler surely did not intend war as such, but only accepted it as a necessary prerequisite to attaining his goals. He would obviously rather have gotten what he wanted without war if only the other powers would give it to him. He only *conditionally* intended war. How is his intent then different from that of Chamberlain or Roosevelt, who also did not intend war as such, but did accept it as a necessary consequence of not acceding to Hitler's demands? Conditionally they, too, intended war.

The conventional wisdom's second argument is equally simple: Only Hitler wanted a departure from the status quo; others wanted to preserve it. Hence only he caused the war. Again, Taylor disagrees. It was Hitler who wanted the status quo—as it existed before Versailles. The Western powers wanted something different. Taylor thinks that Hitler was simply doing what any statesman of a major power finding himself in Hitler's position would have done, and what Hitler's predecessors had in fact tried to do. The Treaty of Versailles had put Germany in a highly "artificial" position. Germany was left physically intact, "potentially still the most powerful nation in Europe, but denied her 'natural weight.' " Any German leader quite naturally would have striven to restore to Germany a position commensurate with its strength. Trevor-Roper, Taylor's most vehement critic, replies that Hitler went much further than that. Even the enormous gains Germany had made through the Treaty of Brest-Litovsk (with Russia in 1917) would not have satisfied him. Taylor counters that Hitler's aims did not go much further than the Treaty of Brest-Litovsk, but that in the course of the war, opportunities opened which he could not pass up. Trevor-Roper, in turn, asks why we should view Germany's position at the height of its success in World War I as a state of normalcy and its position after the Treaty of Versailles as artificial and unnatural?

However profound their disagreements, historians participating in the World War II debate agree that the mere fact that World War II would not have happened without the Treaty of Versailles and other Western policies does not make them the cause of the war. In other words, historians reject the naive theory of causation. Common law courts, like historians, do not subscribe to the naive theory either. They distinguish between "causes in fact," what we have called mere conditions, and "proximate causes," what we have simply called causes. For a defendant to be liable for a result, he must have proximately caused it. But how do courts know whether something is a condition or a cause, a mere cause in fact or a proximate cause?

Theories of Causation

Traditionally, courts have gone about the business of distinguishing causes from conditions very much the way historians have. Suppose Reckless tosses a cigarette into a bush, which catches fire. Just as the flames are dying down, Arsonist passes by, pours some gasoline on them, and burns down the forest. Courts would not say that Reckless caused the fire; he merely created a condition for it. Arsonist's act, they would say, "broke the chain of causation" between Reckless's act and the fire. But suppose that instead of Arsonist, Careless passes by. Careless inadvertently drops a box of matches into the fire. This is enough to fan the flames into a full-fledged forest fire. Now courts would say that Reckless caused the fire, although they wouldn't deny that Careless also caused it. Careless's act didn't break the chain of causation. Courts are invoking the principle that "the free, deliberate, and informed intervention of a second person, who intends to exploit the situation created by the first but is not acting in concert with him" relieves the first actor of criminal responsibility.[34] That is the very principle underlying the first argument in the World War II debate. Conventional wisdom, in effect, says that Hitler, not the Treaty of Versailles, caused the Second World War, because Hitler, like the arsonist who fanned a dying flame, freely and deliberately intervened to bring about war. A. J. P. Taylor takes issue not with the principle, but with the idea that Hitler was freely and deliberately aiming at war. Taylor would have us see Hitler, like Careless, as one who inadvertently dropped a box of matches into a burning bush.

This principle sheds light on two of the cases with which this chapter opened. Both the Vance case, about the man who tried to escape his robbers, tripped, and fractured his skull, and the Redl case, about the Austrian officer who committed suicide at the behest of his superiors, involved the intervention of another human being. Did the robbers who prompted Vance to run away cause his death? Since Vance, by running away, did not freely and deliberately aim to kill himself, the chain of causation was not broken; the robbers caused his death. Did the officers who ordered Redl to commit suicide cause his death? That's a murkier question.

Generally, courts are disinclined to say that someone who encouraged a suicide caused it. In the South African case of *R. v. Nbakwa,* the court decided that a man who commanded his mother to commit suicide had not committed murder. The defendant had lost his daughter and accused his mother of having killed her. The woman did not deny it, but promised to commit suicide. Eight days later she had still not done it. The man then came into her hut with a stout stick and a thin rope. He tied the rope to a rafter, made a noose at the other end and told the woman, "Get up and hang yourself." The woman asked for something to stand on. The man put a block of wood under the rope. He then left the hut and watched his mother get up on the block, put the noose around her neck, and kick the block away. The court held:

> The accused provided a means for causing death and he persuaded the woman to kill herself, but the actual act which caused the death of the woman was the act of the woman herself. There was, to use a common legal expression, a *novus actus interveniens* between the actions of the accused and the death of the deceased which in my view broke the chain of causation between the act of the accused and the death of the deceased. The direct cause of the death of the deceased was the act of the deceased woman in getting up onto the block of wood, putting her head in the noose and then kicking away the block of wood. The direct cause of death was not the action of the accused.[35]

Courts see the matter differently when the victim is too distraught to make a clearheaded decision. The defendant, Stephenson, had kidnapped one Madge Oberholtzer in Indianapolis and taken her on a train, where he and his companions raped her brutally. They left the train in Hammond, where they took her to a hotel room. Somehow, the desperate girl managed to get hold of some bichloride of mercury, which she swallowed in an effort to poison herself. She did not die but got very sick. The defendants did not summon a doctor but instead drove her back to Indianapolis and finally left her at home. She died a month later from the effects of her wounds and the poison. The court did not think that Madge Oberholtzer's actions were of the "free, deliberate, and informed" variety that breaks the causal chain and held the abductor liable for her death.[36]

Courts also see the matter differently when the defendant occupies a special position of authority, which he exploits to make the victim do his bidding. In *United States v. Freeman,* the captain of a ship told a weak and terrorized seaman to "go aloft to hand the mainsail."[37] The sea was heavy and the other sailors warned the captain that the man would never make it. But the captain only said, "Damn him, send him aloft"; he took a piece of rigging, beat the man with it, and repeated "Damn you, start along. I never shall be satisfied until I do see the end of you. Now, damn you, away with you aloft." The man obeyed, fell into the sea, and drowned. The court upheld the jury verdict of manslaughter.

Given Redl's state of mind and the pressures his superiors exerted on him, *Stephenson* and *Freeman* suggest that his suicide was not sufficiently "free, deliberate, and informed" to break the chain of causation.

Courts have relied on a second principle to distinguish causes from conditions. Again, suppose Reckless drops a cigarette into a bush, which catches fire. Suddenly, a hurricane comes up and blows the fire far and wide until it burns down the forest. Courts would say that Reckless did not cause the fire because an extraordinary, abnormal event intervened and broke the chain of causation. This is the principle underlying the second argument in the World War II debate. Conventional wisdom argues that Hitler's actions were of such an unusually wicked nature as to break the chain of causation between the Treaty of Versailles and the Second World War. A. J. P. Taylor counters that Hitler's aspirations weren't abnormal at all but were those which any leader of a great power would have entertained. This principle, incidentally, would take care of the case of John and Annie. Annie's contracting scarlet fever amounts to an extraordinary coincidence. Hence it breaks the chain of causation between John's act and Annie's death.

The abnormality principle has, however, an exception. When a man hits a hemophiliac, and the hemophiliac starts to bleed and dies, he has caused the hemophiliac's death, even though the hemophiliac's condition was an abnormal one. This abnormality, unlike those just discussed, predated the defendant's act. Courts have treated such abnormalities as mere conditions, rather than intervening events that break the chain of causation.

This helps to make sense of our witchcraft case. Perhaps the interaction between the *muabvi* and the adrenalin inside the victims' bodies was an abnormal coincidental event, but since the anxiety and adrenalin preceded the ingestion of the *muabvi,* they should merely be viewed as conditions rather than causes, and so do not break the chain of causation between the witch doctor's actions and the natives' death.

The traditional approach to causal problems hasn't satisfied everyone. Suppose Mrs. Green, wife of the intensely jealous Mr. Green, is committing adultery with Mr. Horner. Mr. Black, who hates Horner, hears about it. Hoping that Green will kill Horner, he tells him about his wife's affair. Green does as Black expects him to: he kills Horner. The traditional theory would deny that Black caused Horner's death, because it was Green who freely and deliberately set about killing Horner. That conflicts with the intuitions of many people who would say that Black has proximately caused Horner's death.[38]

The owner of a sporting goods store negligently sells a gun to a boy of thirteen. On his way home the boy drops the gun on his foot and injures a toe. His parents bring suit against the seller. Did the seller's negligence cause the injury? According to the traditional theory it did. Neither a voluntary act nor an abnormal event intervened to break the chain of causation. Yet many people's intuitions tell them differently. If the boy had accidentally shot himself with the gun, they would agree that the defendant's negligence had proximately caused the injury. Since he only dropped the gun on his foot, they would say it hadn't.[39]

The failure of the traditional theory to satisfactorily cope with these cases prompted courts to look for a new theory. The theory was first proposed in the legendary torts case *Palsgraf v. Long Island Railroad Company,* decided in 1928 by the equally legendary judge and later Supreme Court justice, Benjamin Cardozo. The case arose out of an accident on a railroad station platform in which a woman was hit by some collapsing scales. Mrs. Helen Palsgraf, an apartment janitor, the plaintiff in the case,

> was standing on a platform of defendant's railroad after buying a ticket to go to Rockaway Beach. A train stopped at the station, bound for another place. Two men ran forward to catch it. One of the men reached the platform of the car without mishap, though the train was already moving. The other man, carrying a package, jumped aboard the car, but seemed unsteady as if about to fall. A guard on the car, who had help the door open reached forward to help him in, and another guard on the platform pushed him from behind. In this act, the package was dislodged, and fell upon the rails. It was a package of

> small size, about fifteen inches long, and was covered by a newspaper. In fact it contained fireworks, but there was nothing in its appearance to give notice of its contents. The fireworks when they fell exploded. The shock of the explosion threw down some scales at the other end of the platform, many feet away. The scales struck the plaintiff, causing the injuries for which she sue[d].[40]

Mrs. Palsgraf was hit on the arm, hip, and thigh. The case was tried before a Brooklyn jury, which found that the railroad guards had indeed been negligent, that their negligence was the proximate cause of Mrs. Palsgraf's injuries, and they awarded her substantial damages. The railroad appealed to the New York Court of Appeals.

What struck Cardozo, who wrote the opinion for the court, was that although the railroad had been negligent, it had not been negligent toward Mrs. Palsgraf. What made the guards' behavior imprudent was the possibility that the passenger they were helping to board the moving train might be injured. But the passenger had not been injured. It is true that the railroad guards' conduct had caused Mrs. Palsgraf's injury. But causing someone an injury is not grounds for liability. The injury must have been negligently caused. And the railroad had not been negligent toward Mrs. Palsgraf. "The conduct of the defendant's guard," explained Cardozo, "if a wrong to the holder of the package, was not a wrong in its relation to the plaintiff, standing far away. Relative to her it was not negligence at all. Nothing in the situation gave notice that the falling package had in it the potency of peril to persons thus removed. Negligence is not actionable unless it involves the invasion of a legally protected interest, the violation of a right. 'Proof of negligence in the air, so to speak, will not do.' " Later commentators on this case put the point slightly differently: the defendant railroad was negligent in creating a certain unreasonable risk, the risk of injury to the boarding passenger. Mrs. Palsgraf's injury was not within that risk, hence the railroad's negligence did not proximately cause it. More generally, the theory of causation extracted from *Palsgraf* was that a negligent actor has proximately caused only those injuries the risk of which rendered his conduct negligent in the first place. The theory needn't be limited to reckless or negligent misconduct. If a negligent actor is responsible for those injuries the risk of which renders his conduct negligent, then, presumably, an intentional actor is responsible for those injuries the risk of which renders his conduct intentional. Remember again the case of the man who tries to shoot someone, misses, but accidentally stampedes a herd of wild pigs which trample the intended victim to death. According to this theory, his intentional act did not proximately cause the man's death, because that's not how he intended to bring it about.

This theory treats the case of the calculating Mr. Black and the negligent store owner just as our intuition would have it. Mr. Horner died in precisely the manner Mr. Black intended. Hence Mr. Black proximately caused his death. On the other hand, the minor with the gun did not suffer the kind of injury the risk of which makes selling guns to minors negligent. He didn't shoot himself, but dropped the gun on his foot. Hence the seller did not proximately cause the injury.

How would this theory dispose of the conundrums with which we began? John shot at Annie, but she died not at all in the manner in which he intended. Hence, no proximate causation. The witch doctor gave *muabvi* to his victims, but (arguably) they died not at all in the way he intended. Hence, again, no proximate causation. Redl's superiors handed him his gun intending that he shoot himself. That's just what happened, hence they proximately caused his death. The robbers who chased James Vance were reckless about any injury he might suffer trying to escape. That's just the kind of injury he suffered, hence they proximately caused it.

This theory hasn't satisfied everyone either. Suppose a sheep farmer contracts with a shipowner for the transport of some of his sheep. The Contagious Diseases Act requires ships to provide pens for the animals to prevent infectious diseases from spreading. The shipowner neglects to provide any pens. A storm arises and blows many of the sheep overboard. Has the shipowner's negligence proximately caused the loss of the sheep? The risk theory would say no. What makes the shipowner's actions negligent is the risk of infection, not ejection. But one remains uneasy. Sure, the pens would never have been required just to prevent sheep from being washed overboard. But if the drafters of the Contagious Diseases Act had been told that the pens would also serve that purpose, wouldn't they have exclaimed: "All the more reason to have pens." How then can we say that it is only the risk of infection that makes the lack of pens negligent?[41]

Suppose a restaurant owner places a large, unlabeled can of rat poison next to some cans of flour on a shelf near the kitchen stove. One day, while a man is making a delivery in the kitchen, the poison explodes, injuring the delivery man. Is the owner liable for the consequences of his negligence here? The risk theory would say no. What made his handling of the poison negligent was not the small risk of an explosion, but the significant risk of ingestion. Again, one remains uneasy. True, the small risk of explosion is no reason for keeping rat poison away from the stove, but if the risk of ingestion is a good enough reason for keeping it away, isn't the risk of explosion all the more reason for doing so? Almost any application of the risk theory is vulnerable to this argument.[42]

To cope with this difficulty, yet a third theory has been proposed. It is really only a variation of the risk theory. It redefines what it means to be "within the risk" of certain conduct. The theory says: An injury isn't "within the risk" of certain negligent conduct because it is the kind of injury people fear when they call the conduct negligent. It is "within the risk" if such conduct actually makes this kind of injury more probable. In many cases this "probability" theory gives the same results as the risk theory. It would not hold the sporting goods store owner liable for selling a gun to a minor, because the kind of injury the minor suffered was just as likely to occur with another heavy object. It would not hold the railroad liable for Mrs. Palsgraf's injury because the kind of freak accident she suffered was just as likely to occur outside the train station. Nevertheless, in several of the cases where the risk theory gave us trouble the probability theory yields results more in keeping with our intuitions. It would hold the shipowner liable for the sheep farmer's lost sheep, because being washed overboard is more probable without pens. It would hold the restaurant owner liable for the exploding rat poison, because an explosion is more probable near a stove.[43]

How would this theory handle our own "conundrums of causation"? It would say that John's shooting Annie did not make death by scarlet fever more probable—hence no proximate causation. It would say that the robbers' chasing James Vance made death by falling more probable—hence there was proximate causation. It would say that Urbanski's handing Redl a gun made Redl's suicide more probable—hence there was proximate causation. Finally, it is unclear what it would have to say about the case of the witch doctor. Would it say that, based on the court pathologist's investigation of *muabvi,* the witch doctor's administering of the drug made death more probable? Or would it say that, based on what was known about *muabvi* when the witch doctor gave it, *muabvi* was harmless?

Probe the probability theory a little and you'll find it too wanting. If the defendant does not act negligently, let us suppose, there is an 80 percent chance that a certain accident will result. If he is negligent, that probability rises to 88 percent. If he is negligent and an accident results, the probability theory of causation would thus say he caused it. But imagine one hundred identical defendants behaving in the identically negligent fashion. They will produce 88 accidents. Eighty of those accidents would have occurred even if they had been prudent. Their carelessness increased that number by 8. Yet the probability theory of causation would designate them the cause of all 88.

Thus, each of the preceding theories is suffering from one or another defect. Are these defects remediable? Can they be ironed out? Can we create a more perfect theory by somehow combining the best in each? I don't think so. If the theories are defective, it is because they are striving to attain an unattainable goal. The goal has never been expressly articulated; if it had been, its impossibility would have been recognized earlier.

Let me articulate that goal through an example. A certain town experiences 90 highway deaths every year, all of them involving a negligent driver. The statistics of comparable towns with few negligent drivers allow us to deduce that without negligent drivers there would only have been 70 accidents. The goal of a legal theory of causation is to hold negligent drivers liable for only 20 of the 90 deaths, since that is the number of deaths negligent driving added to the accident toll. How do we distinguish the 70 accidents for which we won't hold anyone liable from the 20 for which we will hold negligent drivers liable? Doesn't the "but for" test accomplish that? Isn't it enough to ask of every accident whether it would have happened if the driver had been careful? No, it isn't. Almost every one of the accidents wouldn't have happened if the driver hadn't been at the precise spot at which he was at the moment the accident occurred. In almost every one of the accidents, the driver wouldn't have been at that spot at that moment if he hadn't been negligent. The "but for" test would have us hold nearly all 90 drivers liable; so it won't do. What will?[44]

Why would 70 accidents happen in a town of careful drivers? Because accidents are a fact of life. Even a careful driver might suffer a sudden heart attack and kill a pedestrian. That suggests another approach. Maybe we can sort the 90 accidents into two kinds, the kind that would happen just as often in a town of careful drivers, such as the one involving a heart attack, and the kind that happens only in a town of negligent drivers, such as a speeding driver losing control of his car. There are different ways of doing the sorting. Each corresponds to a different theory of proximate causation.

The traditional theory of causation uses two principles to do the sorting. The first principle—intentional interventions break the chain of causation—tells us to set aside all accidents in which the defendant's negligent behavior resulted in an injury only because someone bent on doing harm took advantage of it. These accidents, the theory implicitly asserts, happen just as often in a town of careful drivers. If someone is hell-bent on doing certain harm, he'll just look for another, similar opportunity in case this one doesn't materialize. The second principle—abnormal events break the chain of causation—tells us to set aside all accidents in which the defendant's negligent behavior resulted in an injury only because something extraordinary, coincidental, in short, abnormal, intervened. These accidents, too, the theory implicitly asserts, happen just as often in a town of careful drivers. Abnormal events, like lightning striking a tree next to a speeding car, are as common in a town of careful as in one of negligent drivers. All other accidents, the theory assumes, are of the kind that only happens to negligent drivers.

The theory is a rough approximation of the truth, but only a very rough one. First of all, it isn't always true that someone who takes advantage of an opportunity to do certain harm would have done so even if this particular opportunity had not presented itself. Think of the negligent driver who accidentally dents another person's Cadillac without stopping. The irate Cadillac driver sets out after the escaping car. In hot pursuit, he deliberately drives through a construction pit in the middle of the road and wreaks havoc. The traditional theory would say that the pursuer's deliberate wrongdoing breaks the chain of causation—the escaping driver is not responsible for this damage. Yet it is clear that the pursuer would not have wrought such destruction if he hadn't been chasing the defendant. Second, there are accidents other than those involving the intentional intervention of another wrongdoer or some abnormal event, which are just as frequent in a town of careful as in one of negligent drivers: accidents involving sudden heart attacks, terribly slippery roads, youngsters who leap in the way of passing cars. The result is that the traditional theory could well impose liability on more or less than 20 drivers—there is no reason to suppose it will hold exactly 20 liable.

The risk theory uses just one principle to do the sorting. It asks of each accident, Is this the kind we usually associate with negligent driving? If it is, the driver is liable. Again, this theory is only a very rough approximation of the truth. Suppose certain kinds of blowouts in fact occur only at speeds above 70 mph. Since the risk of such blowout accidents is not what prompted us to call speeding negligent, we would not impose liability for them. The result is that the risk theory might impose liability for many fewer than 20 accidents.

The probability theory imposes liability for all accidents that increase in frequency as a result of the defendant's negligence. The problem is that every kind of accident may have increased in frequency. The result is that the probability theory might impose liability for all 90 accidents.

Thus none of the three most widely accepted theories of causation attains its unstated goal of holding the defendants liable for precisely the number of injuries they added to the accident toll. Can any theory? A hypothetical will show why no theory can. A corporation is looking for a site on which to build a nuclear power plant. It is closely considering two sites: one is near town A, with a population of 10,000, another near town B, with a population of 50,000. Inevitably—let us assume this *purely hypothetically*—the radioactive pollution near such a plant results in a .01 percent cancer rate of nearby populations in a twenty-year period. Let us also assume that there is no other source of cancer than radioactive fallout. Building such a plant near town A would produce 10 cases of cancer. Considering the benefits that the plant will confer on the region as a whole, let us not consider that negligent. Building such a plant near town B would produce 50 cancer cases. Considering that nearly the same benefit would have been achieved by building in a small town and considering that now 50 people will die, let us suppose building the power plant in town B is negligent. Nevertheless, the company builds in town B. In a civil suit for wrongful death or a criminal suit for manslaughter, for how many deaths will the company be liable? How many deaths has it proximately caused? Clearly it is the "but for" cause of 50 deaths. Fifty people would not have died if the company had followed the prudent course of building in town A. Each of our three theories would also find proximate cause: No coincidence or voluntary intervention occurred. Hence the traditional theory supports finding proximate causation. The cancer deaths were evidently within the risk of building such a nuclear power plant. Hence the risk theory argues for causation. The probability of cancer has been substantially increased. Hence the probability theory points to causation. But consider: If this plant had been built in town A, 10 people would have died. Our "goal" is therefore to find only 40 people's death "proximately caused" by the defendant's act. Yet no theory of causation—not the ones examined, not a hypothetical one yet to be invented—could accomplish that, because there are no principled grounds for separating the 40 from the 10.

This may look like an esoteric example, but it isn't. Typically, what negligent conduct does is to see to it that instead of one group of people being killed or injured, another, larger group is. If that group happens to be fairly homogeneous, and if it doesn't overlap with the first, we basically have the above case. It is then impossible to pinpoint any deaths or injuries as being of the kind the defendant's negligence added to the accident toll. Indeed, even if the second group happens not to be homogeneous and overlaps, or even comprehends, the second group, it may make no sense to speak of any deaths as being of the kind the defendant's negligence added to the accident toll. Suppose a car speeds, skids across a puddle, and hits a pedestrian. This sort of accident could happen even if the car is not speeding, but it is more likely when the car is speeding. In a world of speeders, there is a net increase of accidents, but there is no nonarbitrary way of ferreting out the "net increase" from the total number. Of course, for some car accidents one can say that they would not have occurred without speeding and for others one can say that they could just as easily have happened without speeding. But this accident belongs to neither of the easy categories. So even in this most commonplace of settings, a theory of proximate causation is doomed to fail in its objective of narrowing liability to the "extra" deaths or injuries the defendant's conduct brought about.

There is an analogy here to the debate surrounding the economic significance of railroads. If railroads had not been invented, but canals had been relied on instead, America would have looked very different. St. Louis, next to the Mississippi, might have prospered more, Denver, next to no major waterway less. Agriculture in the East and West would have grown more, agriculture in the Midwest less. Overall, Fogel showed, there would have been a net loss of about 5 percent of the GNP. Somebody might ask, Who then were the beneficiaries of the "net gain" brought about by the railroads? That's impossible to say. We can say that there were losers and there were winners. We can also say that the winners won much more than the losers lost; that's why there was a net gain to society. But we cannot identify a "net winner." In just the same way, we are often only able to say that the defendant's act increased the number of injured and dead people without being able to say which among them is the one whose injury or death he caused. It is impossible not because we know too little; it is impossible in principle.

Why does causation matter to us? It matters because our emotional reaction to a mishap is shaped by its causal ancestry. Unfortunately, tracing the causal ancestry of an event often is hard. It requires us to explore the make-believe world in which the defendant did not do what he did, to find out how his victim would have fared. But there isn't just one such make-believe world; there are many. Choosing between them is quite subjective. What makes things even harder is that not all necessary links in the chain of events leading to the victim's mishap qualify as "causes." Some we dismiss as mere "necessary conditions." But how tell a necessary condition from a genuine cause? Many attempts have been made to state the difference. In the end, they proved doomed, because they were in fact trying to give coherent expression to a fundamentally incoherent intuition.

The moral may be to distrust and eschew laws that make guilt dependent on consequences, and, instead, to draft prophylactic rules that impose liability so long as the defendant has behaved in certain criminal ways, regardless of the damage he wrought. In some areas, where consequences are especially hard to ascertain, the law already does that. We punish a judge for taking a case when he has a conflict of interest; we don't inquire whether the conflict caused him to render a different decision than he otherwise would have. We recognize that would be too hard. We may prohibit two large corporations from merging, if that is likely to produce anticompetitive behavior. We don't wait for such anticompetitive behavior to occur, because it would be too hard to detect. Where consequences are hard to determine, these examples are worth following. When we do, however, put causation into a statute, it should probably be the "naive," not the "proximate" kind.

5 The Company You Keep

Aid and Comfort

Who built Thebes with its seven gates
The books only name kings
Did the kings carry the boulders?

So asks the German poet and playwright Bertold Brecht, questioning the way historians like to tell history. He continues,

Young Alexander conquered India
All by himself?
Caesar vanquished the Gallians
He did not even take a cook along?
Philip of Spain cried when his fleet
Was sunk. No one else cried?[1]

What goes for history also goes for crime: much of it is teamwork. The laws of complicity and conspiracy are designed to cope with that fact. The law of complicity punishes all who aid and abet in the execution of a crime. The law of conspiracy punishes all who merely agree to commit a crime. Together these two laws see to it that courts, unlike historians, really give credit where credit is due—not merely to the ringleader, but to the ring.

But do we really need the laws of complicity and conspiracy to accomplish that? Let's worry about complicity first. (Conspiracy we cover in the next section.) It really isn't obvious why the law couldn't manage nicely without it. Suppose A persuades B to kill C. Under the law of complicity, A would be held liable as B's accomplice for helping, in fact instigating, him to kill C. In modern American jurisdictions that means

A could be punished just as severely as the actual perpetrator, B. But it seems that even without the law of complicity, we wouldn't have to let A off the hook. We could simply hold A liable for causing C's death—in short, murder. Why then do we need the law of complicity?

Perhaps, you might say, we need it because not every crime is like murder, not every crime consists of causing some harm. Take burglary, which consists of breaking and entering into a dwelling. Suppose A persuades B to burglarize C's house. Without a law of complicity, wouldn't A go unpunished? We couldn't very well say that A committed the crime of burglary, because A didn't actually break and enter. But perhaps we could: We might say that A broke and entered "using" someone else, just as we might say he broke and entered if he had used a pole to break a window, and, without actually entering, removed a painting from the interior. Admittedly, though, analogizing the use of a human being to the use of a pole may be straining things a bit. Still, it seems the law could do without the law of complicity if it just redefined crimes like burglary to include not just the act of breaking and entering but the act of causing someone else to break and enter. Why hasn't the law taken this simpler tack?

To get at the reason for the law of complicity, it pays to think about the criminal law's civil counterpart, the law of tort. Most crimes are also civil wrongs, torts. The offender faces not just a jail term at the hands of the state, but a damage suit at the hands of his victims. The tort law is quite similar to the criminal law. It also has a law of complicity, called "the law of joint tortfeasors," but its function here is more easily discerned. Suppose A, B, C, and D jointly issue some stock. As the law requires, they prepare a prospectus describing the stock, to be given to every potential purchaser. A number of people buy. Then it turns out that the prospectus contained four egregious misrepresentations, falsehoods deliberately inserted to boost the value of the stock. When the truth comes out, the stock price falls. Some injured shareholders sue A, B, C, and D. The trial reveals that each of the four defendants contributed one of the misrepresentations. A study is performed to assess the damages and it determines them to be $1,111. (The number is small to keep things simple.) The study also determines that had there only been one misrepresentation, damages would have been $1,000, had there been two they would have been $1,100, and had there been three they would have been $1,110. In other words, one misrepresentation did $1,000 worth of damage, a second added only $100 to that total, a third only $10, and a fourth only $1.

Without a law of complicity, each defendant is liable only for the damages that wouldn't have occurred without his participation. But if any of the defendants in this case had not participated, damages would only have been $1 smaller than they were. Thus each defendant would only be liable for $1, the shareholdes would only collect $4, and a $1,107 injury would remain uncompensated. Under the law of complicity, this could not happen. The defendants jointly would be liable for $1,111, which would be divided among them.

The law of complicity works the same magic in criminal law. For suppose we charged the four defendants with some form of fraud. Without a law of complicity, each could claim that because his misrepresentation contributed only marginally to the total harm ($1 out of a $1,111 total) he should either not be punished at all or only very lightly. Under the law of complicity, however, all participants are liable as accomplices in the crime of fraud and the total damage done would be looked to in assessing the punishment they merited.[2]

This explanation also helps one understand a peculiar quirk in the law of complicity. To be an accomplice, it isn't necessary that one actually bring about the commission of a crime; it's enough that one had a hand in it. Imagine that the above example had been even more extreme: it might have involved five defendants and five misrepresentations, and the fifth misrepresentation might not have added anything to the damage total. Then each defendant might argue he should not be liable for anything, since the deletion of his misrepresentation would not diminish damages by a red cent. The argument does him no good because the law of complicity only requires that he participated, not that he brought about the crime.

What makes the law of complicity necessary in the example I gave is the principle of diminishing marginal returns, familiar from economics: The last misrepresentation adds less to damages than the next-to-last misrepresentation, which adds less than the next-to-next-to-last misrepresentation, which adds less than the first misrepresentation. Most cases of group criminality are like this. Generally, when people get together to do something as a group, they are subject to the principle of diminishing marginal returns. The last person contributes less than the next-to-last person, who contributes less than the next-to-next-to-last person. That means if every group member has to answer only for the harm that wouldn't have occurred without him, there will be a lot of harm unanswered for. The law of complicity avoids that. Diminishing marginal returns is the real reason for having it.

The law of complicity is very vague as a result of all this. "Participating in a crime" is a much vaguer notion than "causing a crime." Participation only requires some general connection with the crime. Unfortunately, everyone is in some sense connected with everyone else. Stanley Milgram, the author of those classic experiments on authority, also designed an elegant experiment to show just how interconnected we are.[3] He selected people from all walks of life in Wichita, Kansas, handed them a folder and asked them to transmit the folder to a certain target person in Cambridge, Massachussets. They were only permitted, however, to hand the folder to someone they knew on a first-name basis; that person, in turn, could only hand it to someone *he* knew on a first-name basis, and so on. "Four days after the folders were sent to a group of starting persons in Kansas," reports Milgram, "an instructor at the Episcopal Theological Seminary [in Cambridge] approached our target person on the street. 'Alice,' he said, thrusting a brown folder toward her, 'this is for you.' . . . we found to our surprise that the document had started with a wheat farmer in Kansas. He had passed it on to an Episcopalian minister in his hometown, who sent it to the minister who taught in Cambridge, who gave it to the target person. Altogether the number of intermediate links between starting person and target person amounted to *two*!" Not all chains were this short. But none exceeded ten links, and the median was five. This has become known as the "small world experiment."

A famous passage by John Donne makes the same point as the "small world experiment":

> No man is an Iland, intire of it selfe; every man is a peece of the Continent, a part of the maine; if a Clod bee washed away by the Sea, Europe is the lesse, as well as if a Promontorie were, as well as if a Mannor of thy friends or of thine owne were; any mans death diminishes me, because I am involved within Mankinde; And therefore never send to know for whom the bell tolls; It tolls for thee.[4]

What is true of the Wichita farmer is true of the Wichita thug. He, too, is part of a supportive network of friends, acquaintances, and "bystanders," many of whom may well have an inkling of what he is up to. Which of them is participating in his crimes? Is the vendor who sells a gun to someone he thinks might use it on his son "participating" in the infanticide? Is the student who refers his friend to a drug dealer "participating" in the drug sale? Is the landlord who rents to prostitutes "participating" in prostitution? Is the utility which leases phones to bookmakers "participating'' in bookmaking? Does the assistance given have to be intentional, knowing, or merely reckless?[5]

Courts have struggled hard to draw a line around the notion of participation. But there is no obvious place to draw it. As a result courts have been very inconsistent. Just consider what they did in some of the more spectacular of these ''line-drawing'' cases, the war crimes trials. At the Nuremberg trial against Hitler's closest henchmen—the likes of Goering, Ribbentropp, and Streicher—several participants were acquitted. One of them, Hans Fritzsche, had been a direct subordinate of Goebbels at the Propaganda Ministry. He had been the man in charge of the German press, the author of many a Jew-baiting speech, though perhaps not aware of the mass exterminations. He was acquitted on the ground that, although his ''aim was . . . to arouse popular sentiment in support of Hitler and the German war effort,'' this support of the regime did not amount to any intention to ''incite the German people to commit atrocities on conquered peoples.''[6] Similarly, all the German generals tried in the High Commands case on the charge of participating in crimes against peace were acquitted of it. The court said that ''as long as a member of the armed forces does not participate in the preparation, planning, initiating, or waging of aggressive war on a policy level, his war activities do not fall under the definition of crimes against peace.'' At around the same time, however, another tribunal convicted the Japanese general Yamashita for atrocities committed by his troops, which he did not order and which, it seems, he did not know about.[7]

Because of its vagueness, the concept of ''participation'' is potentially all-encompassing. That makes it very dangerous. A zealous prosecutor could use it to punish whom the law never meant to punish. But the law has only found makeshift means to curb such abuse. The United States Constitution defines the crime of treason thus: ''Treason against the United States shall consist only in levying war against them, or in adhering to their enemies, giving them aid and comfort.'' The drafters apparently were aware that a broad understanding of participation (that is, of ''adhering'' and of ''giving aid and comfort'') might render every political malcontent a traitor. To frustrate that possibility, the drafters added the following proviso: ''No person shall be convicted of treason unless on the testimony of two witnesses to the same overt act, or on confession in open court.''[8] Unfortunately, that is a very imperfect way of narrowing the definition of treason. The availability of two witnesses is quite unrelated to the substantiality of the defendant's "aid and comfort." It is not even related to the probability of his guilt. Circumstantial evidence is often more reliable than direct evidence.

That is not to say that the two-witness requirement hasn't occasionally been an important check on the government's prosecution efforts. It proved the salvation, for instance, of Aaron Burr, Thomas Jefferson's first vice-president, who in 1807 was charged with treason for levying war against the United States.[9] To this day, the nature and intent of Burr's activities are somewhat obscure. Relations between the United States and Spain were tense. Burr was waiting for these tensions to erupt into war, hoping to lead an army of his own into Mexico and seize it from the Spaniards. The American government feared, and in its suit alleged, that Burr wanted more, that he hoped to sever several states west of the Appalachians from the Union and, with or without Mexico, form a separate nation. The conflict between Burr and the government came to a head when a close Burr confederate, Harman Blennerhasset, and several Burr supporters gathered on Blennerhasset Island to launch an expedition into some unsettled Western lands. The real purpose of the expedition, the government feared, was to organize an uprising of the Western territorries against the United States. It ordered Burr, Blennerhasset, and several of their co-venturers arrested. Burr was eventually charged with treason for "levying war against the United States." The problem with the government's case was that, although Burr was the driving force behind the expedition, he had not actually been present at the gathering on Blennerhasset Island, but several hundred miles away, trying to buy additional boats for the expedition. The government insisted, however, that Burr's absence did not prevent him from being a participant in the treasonous activities of the Blennerhasset group. It cited the statement of an earlier Supreme Court decision involving treason: "if war be actually levied, that is, if a body of men be actually assembled for the purpose of effecting by force a treasonable purpose, all those who perform any part, however minute, or however remote from the scene of action, and who are actually leagued in the general conspiracy, are to be considered as traitors."[10]

But if Burr's crime was that he was leagued with, more specifically, that he had procured the assembly of Blennerhasset's men, two witnesses would have to corroborate that fact. As John Marshall, the Supreme Court justice who presided over the trial, explained it: "If procurement . . . [is the treasonous act], then no presumptive evidence, no facts from which the procurement may be conjectured or inferred, can satisfy the constitution and the law. The mind is not to be led to the conclusion that the individual was present, by a train of conjectures or inferences, or of reasoning; the fact must be proved by two witnesses.''[11]

Although there was much circumstantial evidence to link Burr to Blennerhasset, there were no witnesses to testify to Burr's ''procurement'' of Blennerhasset's actions. Burr was acquitted.

Many jurisdictions have tried to distinguish between different forms of participation. But that has proved harder, even, than defining participation. The common law tried to distinguish between the ''principal'' who actually brought about the crime and the ''accessory'' who merely aided him. (Actually the breakdown was even more refined: there were principals in the first and second degree, accessories before and after the fact.) Aside from being vague, the classification bore little relationship to the respective culpability of the parties to the crime. Often the accessory who instigates a crime looks at least as culpable as the principal who executes it. So why bother with the classification?

German law tried what looked like a more promising tack. It distinguished between perpetrator and accessory on the basis of whether one played a dominant or subsidiary role in the criminal undertaking, whether the criminal act was the ''defendant's own'' rather than someone else's, whether he had an *animus auctoris* or an *animus socii*.[12] But pursued to its logical conclusion, this approach produced some strange results. The following case reached the German Reichsgericht in 1940. Two sisters had gotten pregnant out of wedlock within a short time of each other. The first sister had a miscarriage. Their father, who then learned of the pregnancy for the first time, warned both of them that he would throw them out of the house if anything like this should happen again. The second sister disguised her condition with great care and, when she gave birth to her baby, refused all assistance except that of her sister. There ensued an excited exchange about what to do next. The new mother implored her sister, who was just bathing the baby, to kill it lest their father toss them out on the street. After refusing for some time, the sister finally gave in and drowned the baby. Both were charged with murder. The court, nevertheless, found only the mother guilty of murder and convicted her sister merely as an accessory even though it was she who had actually carried out the killing. As one of the judges later explained: ''If someone can be perpetrator without raising a finger in the actual execution, I don't see why someone can't be accessory, who executes the offensive act, as long as he has put himself in the hands of another's will. If perpetration is to be defined exclusively in terms of whose will was controlling, I can see no principled difference between the two cases."[13]

A similar decision was reached by the West German Bundesgerichtshof in 1962.[14] The defendant, Stashinsky, was a Ukrainian. One late summer day in 1950 Soviet authorities found him to be riding the train without a ticket and ordered him to appear before the transportation police, then a branch of the secret service. His interrogator informed him that the anti-Soviet attitude of his family was well known to the authorities. To protect his family against reprisals, he had to prove his loyalty by rendering his country some "politically valuable" assistance. Shortly thereafter Stashinsky signed up with the secret service. He was immediately dispatched on a special assignment to Berlin, where he learned that he was to assassinate R., who lived in Munich. He was given a poison pistol, which he was assured had been used with success several times already. The pistol contained a poison which, if projected at someone a distance of 50 cm, was lethal. The assassin, however, had to take care to protect himself against the poison as well. He was to swallow an antidote in advance and carry with him a gauze-wrapped capsule containing gas, which he was to inhale immediately after shooting the pistol. Stashinsky went to Munich and waited for R. in a certain building. The two met on the staircase. Stashinsky fired his poison gun at the unsuspecting R., who staggered down the stairs. Stashinsky ran away, crushed the capsule, and inhaled the escaping gas.

Two years later Stashinsky was dispatched to observe the comings and goings of an exiled Ukrainian leader named Stefan B. He was instructed to kill B. as well. Again he was given the poison pistol, the antidote, and the gauze-wrapped capsule. He awaited B. near his office. B. had just entered the building, carrying some tomatoes. He was searching for his office key when Stashinsky approached him, offered to help him with the door, then took out the gun, fired the poison into the unsuspecting victim's face, and left. Again he inhaled the contents of the gauzed-wrapped capsule and returned to East Berlin. The next month he was received by a Soviet general, who thanked him for a job well done and awarded him the Red Banner.

The circumstances that permitted him to be brought to justice in West Germany are not recounted in the opinion. In any event, Stashinsky was not convicted of murder but merely of having been an accessory to murder. The court reasoned, "The accessory to murder as to any other crime is someone who commits an act not as his own, but as a tool or medium of another. What is decisive is his inner disposition towards the act." Stashinsky did not like to do what he did; he did it at the behest of the Soviet government. Hence he was not the perpetrator, only an accessory.

In a more recent case yet, C had agreed to join A and B in assaulting and robbing the tramp X. C, however, merely stood by as A and B began to beat and stab X. In fact he called out several times to B to stop and leave. Finally, B handed C a knife, remarking: "Don't be a coward, do your bit."[15] C did as he was told and plunged the knife into X's stomach where he left it sticking. C was charged with murder along with A and B. The court held he could only be convicted as an accessory, not a co-perpetrator. The court found that the defendant had done what he did merely to prove he was not a coward and had thus subordinated his will to that of the others. Therefore the act was not "his." He lacked the requisite *animus auctoris*.

Many American jurisdictions have given up on the idea of distinguishing different forms of participation. Indictments can now simply charge someone with participation in a crime, whether it be as accessory or perpetrator. Jurors no longer have to agree on whether the defendant's act is best classified as that of an accessory or a perpetrator. The maximum sentence of the accessory is no longer a rigid function of the maximum sentence of the perpetrator. That is not to say that it is now irrelevant whether the defendant played a dominant or subsidiary role in the execution of the crime. Judges have discretion in meting out sentences and will usually consider the defendant's role in a crime along with other kinds of variables the jury did not look at.

This uncertainty about who is an accomplice and who a mere bystander, who is a principal and who a mere accessory is unsettling but not entirely bad. It means that whoever ventures into the dim no-man's-land that lies between a clear-cut act of perpetration as a principal in the first degree and a clear-cut act of noninvolvement won't know where he is safe and where he isn't. So what? *His* uncertainty reflects *our* uncertainty about the immorality of his actions. Let him share in the agony his judges will suffer when they pass on his guilt or innocence.

Nods and Winks

When A and B agree to commit a crime, whether or not they actually go through with it, they have already committed one: conspiracy. Even when A and B agree to commit something that isn't a crime, they may be committing conspiracy: If A and B, producers of widgets, agree to charge ten cents per widget, they are guilty of conspiring to fix prices, even though charging ten cents per widget isn't a crime.

Why do we need the law of conspiracy? Why does the law punish mere agreements, rather than wait for the participants to do something substantial in the way of implementing those agreements? After all, the law doesn't usually punish someone merely for announcing he is going to commit a crime? The law proceeds on the assumption that agreements are different from such announcements. They stand a better chance of getting implemented. That's because when a group resolves to do something it is much more likely to succeed than an individual.

Is that true? Folk wisdom argues both ways. There's the saying, Too many cooks spoil the broth. And there's another saying, Two heads are better than one. But psychological evidence backs up the latter. By and large, groups do better than individuals.

For one, groups make better judgments. An experimenter once asked a class of students to estimate the room temperature. She then averaged the estimates to obtain a "group estimate." The group estimate was better than 80 percent of the student estimates. Of course, this is just a reflection of the fact that "the average of several judgments (measurements, estimates, etc.) will approximate the true value more closely than most single judgments, so long as the error of measurement is random, that is, so long as any single judgment is just as likely to be too low as it is to be too high."[16] Another experimenter asked a group of students to estimate the number of beans in a bottle. He then allowed them to confer in groups of three and asked each person individually for his "group-informed" estimate. When compared to the estimates of a group which hadn't been allowed to confer, they turned out to be much closer. The reason for this was simply that discussion permitted the individual to draw not only on his own but his neighbor's knowledge and perceptions.[17] A third experimenter first asked students to submit individually to a true-false test and then to take the same test by "majority vote." Again, the group did substantially better. The explanation in this case was that "doubtful subjects would often tend to delay their vocal or manual reactions just long enough to observe the dominant side, then would vote accordingly. It appeared, and it is in accord with studies in recognitive activity, that correct subjects were apt on the whole to respond somewhat more quickly and vigorously than incorrect subjects; so that in the long run the doubtful were more often carried in the right rather than the wrong direction.''[18] In short, for a variety of different reasons, groups tend to be better judges than individuals.

In addition, groups are better problem-solvers. In one study, 108 graduate students were asked to reassemble the letters of a word into as many new words as they could think of. The groups came up with many more words than the individuals.[19] In another study, the members of a social psychology class worked both as individuals and as groups on certain quite difficult puzzles. (Like the famous cannibalism puzzle: ''three cannibals and three missionaries must cross a river in a boat that will carry only two persons. One of the cannibals and all of the missionaries know how to row the boat. However, the crossing must be arranged so that the number of cannibals never outnumbers the missionaries—for obvious reasons!'')[20] Individuals produced 8 percent of the right answers, the group produced 53 percent.

Finally, groups learn faster than individuals. In 1926 a psychologist did a study of high school students in an algebra class. He assembled two sections of students of comparable IQ, training in algebra, and test performance. One section worked the assignments individually, the other worked them out as a group. The second section did much better on subsequent tests. In another study, subjects were asked to make certain gambles. Success at gambling depended on guessing the odds involved in the experimental game. Again, the group turned out to be much better and quicker at this than the individuals.[21]

How do we know when there is a conspiracy? Rarely do conspiratorial agreements take the form of a written contract with carefully spelled out mutual obligations. Among conspirators a wink's as good as a nod. That means the existence of such agreements must usually be proven circumstantially. Three kinds of conduct are often used as evidence for a conspiracy. I have dubbed them ''cooperation,'' ''coordination,'' and ''coalescence.'' But do cooperation, coordination, or coalescence really show there is a conspiratorial agreement? Let's examine each in turn.

Cooperation

Two accomplices are arrested. They are put into separate cells. Each knows that if he squeals and turns state's witness while his partner sits tight, he will go free, whereas his partner will get a fifteen-year sentence. The squealer will get what game theorists call the ''temptation payoff.'' His tight-lipped partner will be stuck with the ''sucker's payoff.'' Each also knows that if they both sit tight, they can only be charged with a minor offense carrying a maximum six-month sentence. Finally, each knows that if both of them squeal, they will both get ten-year sentences. Forced to change places with one of the prisoners, what would you do? You might reason as follows: If the other guy squeals, I would be a fool not to squeal myself, lest I be stuck with the sucker's payoff. If the other guy sits tight, I would do best for myself if I squealed—I would get off scot-free. So whatever my partner does, I should squeal. If both of the prisoners reason that way, both will squeal and they will both get a ten-year sentence. They would clearly have been better off both sitting tight—in short, cooperating with each other.

Situations like the prisoner's dilemma abound in the world around us. Each of us would be better off, were he free to litter the streets with his waste, whatever the others do with theirs. Yet all together we are better off if no one litters than if everyone does. Each of us would be better off not paying any taxes, whether others pay or not. Yet all together we are better if everyone pays than if no one does. Each nation might do better with tariffs on imports, whatever other nations do. Yet the world as a whole might be better off if no nation had tariffs. Each member of an industry might be better off selling his goods at a low price than at a high price, regardless of what its competitors do. Yet all of them together might be better off selling their goods at a high price.

If the prisoner's dilemma is so widespread, how is cooperation ever achieved? How is littering contained? How do taxes get paid? How do trade barriers get removed? How are cartels maintained? The prisoner's dilemma can often be surmounted by a very simple measure: an agreement to cooperate. If the two prisoners could get together and agree not to squeal, the cooperative solution—a light sentence for both of them—could easily be achieved. What makes such an agreement binding? The state, of course, will not enforce such agreements, but the underworld might. A criminal who welches on his agreements with his cronies might find it hard to do business with them in the future. Finally, there are elaborate hostage schemes that might be used to give teeth to such agreements. Each prisoner might arrange for a member of his family to be turned over to the other prisoner's family, to be executed in case the agreement is breached. An elaborate scheme of this sort is described in Mario Puzo's *Godfather.*[22] More for its own sake, than the sake of the plot line, Puzo introduces his readers to the Bocchicchio family, an old Sicilian Mafia family whose fortunes had declined drastically when it came to America—until it found a new and unique avocation. The Bocchicchios,

Puzo tells us, were basically stupid. In the competitive field of organized crime they did not stand a chance. But they had one trait that made them invaluable to the rest of the organized crime community: an impeccable sense of honor. If one of its own was killed, the family would not rest until a bloody revenge had been exacted from those responsible. Whenever an important agreement was struck between two organized crime families—for instance an agreement to meet in the open for negotiations—which needed to be backed up by assurances, the Bocchicchios would be asked to turn one of their family members over to each party to the agreement. (Needless to say, they were paid for this service.) Should one of the parties to the agreement renege, the other was entitled to kill its own Bocchicchio hostage. The Bocchicchio family could then be relied upon to make the breaching party "pay."

Our tax laws and trade agreements, like those between common market countries, and our cartel agreements, like the OPEC charter, are agreements of just this sort. They are intended to surmount the prisoner's dilemma and they are enforced by as varied a set of sanctions as those just surveyed.

Because the prisoner's dilemma is so powerful, an agreement is generally suspected whenever the parties involved are seen to cooperate in the face of it. Robert Axelrod, professor of political science and public policy at the Universtiy of Michigan, has shown that such an inference is much too hasty. Cooperation, he shows, very often comes about without express agreement even in the face of a prisoner's dilemma.[23] Axelrod ran a computer tournament in which he asked some 63 game theorists to participate. The idea of the tournament was this. Every player would play a match against every other player. The match was a series of prisoner's dilemmas. Each player would be told: If you squeal and your opponent sits tight, you get five points and your opponent gets none. If your opponent squeals and you sit tight, he will get five points and you will get none. If both of you squeal, both of you get one point. If both of you sit tight, both of you get three points. Each would decide, points would be awarded, and they would move on to the next prisoner's dilemma. The game would be broken off at some unexpected point. Again, it was in the interest of each to squeal, in the words of game theory, to defect, but in their joint interest to sit tight, in the words of game theory, to cooperate. In this game, however, the players did not merely face each other in one isolated prisoner's dilemma but had to deal with each other for the foreseeable future. The question that interested Axelrod was, What kind of player will do best, that is, accumulate the largest number of points during the entire tournament: the player who defects a lot, the player who cooperates a lot, or someone following a more devious strategy?

The players submitted a vast array of clever and elaborate strategies. One strategy, called DOWNING, for instance, makes an elaborate analysis before every move of all the past moves of its opponent, evaluates whether he has tended to retaliate for defections or not, and in light of that decides whether it is best to cooperate or defect on the next move. Another strategy, dubbed FRIEDMAN, cooperates so long as its opponent cooperates, and then defects on every move thereafter. In other words, it avenges a betrayal with permanent repudiation. Another, called TESTER, defects briefly to test whether this will induce its opponent to defect as well. If he does, it backs down and starts cooperating again. If he doesn't it continues exploiting his "softness" through continual defection. Another one, called TRANQUILIZER, tries to lull its opponent into a false sense of security by cooperating for a very long period, and then defects briefly to see if it can get way with it. The simplest strategy submitted was TIT FOR TAT. It starts out cooperating and continues to cooperate as long as its opponent cooperates. If he defects, TIT FOR TAT retaliates with a defection on the next move. But as soon as its opponent resumes cooperation, so will TIT FOR TAT.

Although far and away the most primitive strategy of the bunch, TIT FOR TAT won the computer tournament. Why? Not because it is so simple. Many other very simple programs did very poorly. To see why it did so well one has to look at some of the other programs that did very well, some nearly as well as TIT FOR TAT. All successful programs share a series of traits that set them apart from the less successful crowd. First, they are "nice." That is, they begin by cooperating and do not stop cooperating unless the other does. Second, they are "provokable"; if the other side tries to defect, they punish them with defection on the next or next several moves. Third, they are "forgiving." Even though the other side has defected, after a brief period of retaliation they are willing to let bygones be bygones and resume cooperation, provided their opponent does the same.

What makes such nice, provokable, forgiving, in short "cooperative" programs so successful? It's not that they successfully vanquish the more cutthroat strategies like DOWNING, TESTER, or TRANQUILIZER. In fact, when they play a cutthroat strategy, both they and the cutthroat strategies get very low scores. The difference is that cooperative programs get very high scores when they play with each other, whereas cutthroat strategies get low scores both with their cutthroat and their cooperative competitors.

Thus the cutthroat's overall score generally is much lower than that of the cooperator.

What does this imply about the real world? In one way or another creatures using successful strategies, whatever their field of endeavor, tend to flourish and prosper and those using unsuccessful ones fall by the wayside. In biology, the less successful ones will procreate at a lesser rate; in business, the less successful ones will tend to go bankrupt. Since cooperative strategies are successful, it is creatures who use cooperative strategies who will succeed, whether it be in nature or in the marketplace or wherever else creatures may confront each other in iterated prisoner's dilemmas. In the long run then, cooperative strategies will edge out cutthroat strategies, either because people realize that cooperative strategies help them do their best, because they imitate the strategy of people known to be successful, or because they stumble on it by trial and error, grow accustomed to it, and suddenly discover that their more cutthroat competitors have disappeared from the scene.

Cooperation without agreement can be seen to be at work in a variety of unrelated situations, many of them thoroughly hostile, where one would have expected cutthroat competition to be the order of the day. In the course of World War I, hostile regiments would often face each other in opposite trenches for long periods of time. They, too, explains Axelrod, found themselves in an iterated prisoner's dilemma.

> In a given locality, the two players can be taken to be the small units facing each other. At any time, the choices are to shoot to kill or deliberately to shoot to avoid causing damage. For both sides, weakening the enemy is an important value because it will promote survival if a major battle is ordered in the sector. Therefore, in the short run it is better to damage now whether the enemy is shooting back or not. This establishes that mutual defection is preferred to unilateral restraint . . ., and that unilateral restraint by the other side is even better than mutual cooperation. . . . In addition, the reward for mutual restraint is preferred by the local units to the outcome of mutual punishment . . ., since mutual punishment would imply that both units would suffer for little or no relative gain.

As theory would predict, cooperation developed despite the prisoner's dilemma. It began in a small way: regiments avoided bombing each other's ration supply. The rationale, as explained by one combatant, was that "It would be child's play to shell the road behind the enemy's trenches, crowded as it must be with ration wagons and water carts, into a blood-stained wilderness . . . but on the whole there is silence. After all, if you prevent your enemy from drawing his rations, his remedy is simple: he will prevent you from drawing yours."

It moved on to Christmas truces and reached the point where the regiments were periodically doing nothing but ritualistically exchanging fire, carefully aimed to avoid hitting anyone. Remarked one British soldier, "So regular were [the Germans] in their choice of targets, times of shooting, and number of rounds fired, that, after being in the line one or two days, Colonel Jones had discovered their system, and knew to a minute where the next shell would fall." And the Germans on the other side reported, "At seven it came—so regularly that you could set your watch by it. . . . It always had the same objective, its range was accurate, it never varied laterally or went beyond or fell short of the mark. . . . There were even some inquisitive fellows who crawled out . . . a little before seven, in order to see it burst." All this without a formal truce, against the express wishes of the high command. The pervasiveness of the live-and-let-live system is revealed by events in the spring and summer of 1917. At that time, part of the French army began to mutiny, to refuse to go on fighting. Although German and French trenches were only yards apart, the German soldiers apparently never became aware of these mutinies. Why not? The British historian Tony Ashworth, who has undertaken an exhaustive study of the live-and-let-live system, found a simple answer: "As far as the Germans in the trenches knew, nothing had changed: tacit truces proceeded during the mutiny, according to patterns established long before. The exchange of peace just went smoothly on."[24]

Cooperation in the face of a prisoner's dilemma is possible even without an agreement. That should give us pause. It means that cooperation is not very good evidence of an agreement. Then again, what we are really concerned about when we punish agreements is that they facilitate cooperation. If cooperation comes about even without agreements, why not punish it outright as an act of conspiracy, perhaps assimilating it to a broader understanding of the concept of agreement?

The Supreme Court came very close to doing just that in the antitrust case of *Interstate Circuit, Inc. v. United States*.[25] Interstate Circuit operated a large group of movie theaters. Like other movie exhibitors it rented its movies from a number of movie distributors. One day in 1934,

Interstate's manager, O'Donnell, sent a letter to each distributor asking him to condition the rental of films to other movie exhibitors on their charging no less than a certain minimum price. The apparent purpose of this plan was to form a movie cartel: if everybody raised the price of a movie ticket, all movie exhibitors and distributors could benefit, that is, could derive monopoly profits. The government's problem in prosecuting this case was that an agreement between an exhibitor and a distributor was not necessarily illegal. What was illegal was for members of an industry on the same level, for example, all exhibitors or all distributors, to get together and fix the price of their product. The exhibitors clearly had not gotten together. What about the distributors? It seemed they had not gotten together either. Or had they? After all, each individual distributor had agreed to O'Donnell's demands in the expectation that the other distributors would probably go along. Indeed, the court found that for practical purposes there *had* been an agreement.

> The O'Donnell letter named on its face as addressees the eight local representatives of the distributors, and so from the beginning each of the distributors knew that the proposals were under consideration by the others. Each was aware that all were in active competition and that without substantially unanimous action with respect to the restrictions for any given territory there was a risk of a substantial loss of the business and good will of the subsequent-run and independent exhibitors, but that with it there was the prospect of increased profits. There was, therefore, strong motive for concerted action, full advantage of which was taken by Interstate . . . in presenting [its] demands to all in a single document.

Apparently, however, the court could not make up its mind whether what it called the distributors' "conscious parallelism" was tantamount to an agreement or simply very strong evidence that a secret bargain had in fact been struck.

Is it a good idea to treat conscious parallelism, cooperation without formal communication, as the equivalent of an agreement and to punish it as a conspiracy? The problem with such a sweeping rule would be that it would make it very hard for the participant to tell whether he is engaging in an act of criminal cooperation. This is especially true in an antitrust case. It is easy to tell whether one is engaged in an express, prohibited price-fixing agreement. But if one is simply following a certain strategy of setting one's prices, because it seems to increase profits—perhaps simply imitating the pricing pattern of the competition out of a conviction that they know what they are doing—one may be thinking that one is doing something perfectly innocent and never realize that what one is doing is profitable because it is cooperative.

Coordination

On 30 January 1948, Nathuram Godse assassinated the Mahatma Gandhi. Eight people were eventually found guilty of conspiring to kill the Mahatma. Although one of the alleged coconspirators turned state's witness, much of the evidence linking the eight together was circumstantial. It had to do with the *coordination* of their actions just prior to the assassination. "The evidence established that [the defendants] were known to one another for a considerable time; that, more or less, they held similar political views; that they collected gun-cotton-slab, hand grenades, and pistols; that they raised a fairly large sum of money and that they suddenly set out for Delhi on or about the same day."[26] One of them made an attempt on Gandhi's life on 20 January. When that failed, Godse, ten days later, made another, successful attempt. Coordination, then, is treated as powerful evidence of an agreement.

But coordination is possible without an express agreement. "When a man loses his wife in a department store without any prior understanding on where to meet if they get separated, the chances are good that they will find each other," observes Harvard political economist Thomas Schelling. Why? Schelling explains: "Whimsy may send the man and his wife to the 'lost and found'; or logic may lead each to reflect and to expect the other to reflect on where they would have agreed to meet if they had had a prior agreement to cover the contingency."[27] And they probably will meet. To test his hypothesis that in such situations coordination is usually achieved without any communication among the parties, Schelling gave a number of teams the following sorts of tasks:

1. "Name 'heads' or 'tails.' If you and your partner name the same, you both win a prize." Result: "36 persons concerted on 'heads', . . . and only 6 chose 'tails.' "

2. "You are to meet somebody in New York City. You have not been instructed where to meet, you have no prior understanding with the person on where to meet, and you cannot communicate with each other. You are simply told that you will have to guess where to meet and that he is being told the same thing and that you will just have to try to make your guesses coincide." Result: This problem, "which may reflect the location of the

sample in New Haven, Connecticut, showed an absolute majority managing to get together at Grand Central Station (information booth), and virtually all of them succeeded in meeting at 12 noon.''

3. ''You are to divide $100 into two piles, labeled A and B. Your partner is to divide another $100 into two piles labeled A and B. If you allot the same amounts to A and B, respectively, that your partner does, each of you gets $100; if your amount differs from his, neither of you gets anything.'' Result: 36 out of 41 split the total fifty-fifty.

The moral: If we are out to do what somebody else is doing, and don't much care what that is, and if we know that the other side is trying to do the same, we are likely to achieve our objective without expressly agreeing beforehand.

Tacit coordination is a fact of everyday life. Situations abound in which we want to do something only if others are doing it too. A person will walk across the lawn if others will do the same. He will cross the street against the light if others will go along. He will double-park if others are doing it. He will bypass an orderly queue if others are ignoring it. That doesn't mean that such activities will ever be successful or that if they are, they won't fizzle. But sometimes they do succeed; they don't fizzle but have a self-sustained growth spurt. ''At the busiest intersection in Cambridge, a few nimble pedestrians cross against the light and cars keep coming; more pedestrians hesitate, ready to join any surge of people into the street but not willing to venture ahead without safety in numbers. People look left and right—not to watch the traffic but to watch the other pedestrians! At some point several appear to decide that the flow of pedestrians is large enough to be safe and they join it, enlarging it further and making it safe for a few who were still waiting and who now join. Soon, even the timid join what has become a crowd. The drivers see they no longer have any choice and stop.''[28] Coordination has occurred with not so much as a word, a nod, or a wink being exchanged.

Does this show that coordination is not really good proof that an agreement is behind the coordinated conduct? Or does it mean that we can extend the concept of agreement to cover all cases of coordinated behavior? Some judges have been so inclined. Thus in *Rex v. Leigh* it was ruled ''that an agreement to raise a tumult in a theater might be inferred from the acts of a number of people done at one time and place, and that it was not necessary that the defendants should have come together for that purpose or have previously consulted together.'' They were convicted on the charge of ''conspiring together to ruin Charles Macklin,'' in that they "unlawfully, wickedly, riotously, and tumultuously . . . made and raised a great noise, tumult, riot, and disturbance, and thereby tumultuously and turbulently prevented and hindered the said C. M. from playing and performing the part or character of Shylock."[29]

To extend the concept of an agreement in this way engenders several risks. First, it stretches the concept of an agreement out of all recognizable shape. It applies the term to situations where there has been nothing like a bargain: people may rely on each other, but they are not exchanging quid pro quos. Second, it gives the concept potentially unlimited scope. Any person failing to pay taxes in the knowledge, and perhaps because of it, that many others aren't paying them either could well be found to be conspiring with them to deprive the government of its tax revenue.

Coalescence

Sometimes the efforts of several people coalesce without any effort at coordination. They do the same thing simply because they happen to share the same objectives. Nevertheless, since they agree in their aims and they agree in their actions, can't they be said to be in agreement with each other? And doesn't that make them coconspirators?

Courts have sometimes come very close to taking that position. An example is a case brought in 1968 against Dr. Benjamin Spock and four other prominent antiwar intellectuals.[30] Aside from Dr. Spock, the well-known authority on baby care, they were: the Reverend William Sloane Coffin, Jr., chaplain at Yale University; Michael Ferber, a Harvard graduate student in English; Mitchell Goodman, a novelist and a teacher; and Marcus Raskin, a former advisor to President Kennedy and author of the widely read *Vietnam Reader,* used as a text in many Vietnam teach-ins. They were charged with conspiring to counsel American youths to violate the draft laws. The charge was based on the following events.

> In August 1967 a number of academic, clerical, and professional persons discussed the need of more vigorous opposition to governmental policies. From their eventually consolidated efforts came a document entitled "A Call to Resist Illegitimate Authority" . . . and a cover letter requesting signatures and support. The letter was signed by defendant Dr. Benjamin Spock, and defendant Rev. William Sloane Coffin, Jr., and two other persons. The Call was originally signed by them, numerous others, and eventually by hundreds. The defendant Mitchell

> Goodman had been preparing a somewhat similar statement against the war and the draft. In mid-September he learned of the Call, which he also signed. He, Coffin, Spock, [Marcus Raskin], and others spoke on October 2 at a press conference in New York City to launch the Call. It was there announced by Goodman that further activities were contemplated, including a nationwide collection of draft cards and a ceremonial surrender thereof to the Attorney General. On October 16 a draft card burning and turn-in took place at the Arlington Street Church in Boston, arranged by the defendant Michael Ferber, and participated in by Coffin. Four days afterwards all [five] defendants attended a demonstration in Washington, in the course of which an unsuccessful attempt was made to present the fruits of that collection and similar gatherings to the Attorney General.[31]

The jury convicted four of the defendants and unaccountably acquitted a fifth, Marcus Raskin.

The four convicts appealed. They argued, among other things, that there never was an agreement between them. Thus Spock argued that the "case presents no more than the publicly expressed coincidence of views on public affairs." The appeals court thought differently. The jury could find an agreement, it asserted.

> The government's claim of agreement looks basically to the Call, the cover letter, and the subsequent press conference. Spock participated in drafting the Call and, as has been stated, he and Coffin were two of the four persons who signed the cover letter. Goodman signed the Call, and was an active participant in launching the press conference which was chaired by Coffin and at which Spock appeared. . . . At the press conference, in addition to discussing the Call, Goodman advanced his own paper, signed also by Coffin, along strikingly similar lines, entitled "Civil Disobedience Against the War." . . . He announced a demonstration to be held in Washington on October 20, as an act of "direct creative resistance," at which time draft cards surrendered at turn-ins that had been planned for October 16 would be delivered to the Attorney-General. This announcement, as both conceded, was the result of prearrangement with Coffin. . . .

> The evidence disclosed more than parallel conduct . . . rather there are several instances of concerted activity from which the jury could infer an agreement.

But having said this, the court then turned around and acquitted two of the defendants, Dr. Spock and Michael Ferber. Why? Although Dr. Spock was one of the drafters of the Call to Resist Illegitimate Authority, the court said, he lacked "the necessary intent to adhere to its illegal aspects." His speeches, it said, "were limited to condemnation of the war and the draft, and lacked any words or content of counselling." He did not help plan the Washington rally, although he attended it, and even there he "contributed nothing, even by his presence to the turning in of cards." As for Michael Ferber, he "was a draft-age student. His activities were limited to assisting in the burning and surrender of draft cards. Although he made an address at the Arlington Street Church, it was not counselling draft resistance, or even the surrendering of cards. Not only did he not sign the Call, or the cover letter, or attend the press conference, but the evidence did not warrant a finding that through other statements or conduct he joined the larger conspiracy for which the other defendants were prosecuted."

It seems that, having asserted that there was an agreement involving all of the defendants, the court then suddenly reversed itself and decided that neither Dr. Spock nor Michael Ferber was a part of it. The only remaining parties to the conspiracy were the Reverend William Sloane Coffin, Jr., and Mitchell Goodman. But what did their agreement consist of? Goodman had drafted a statement parallel to the Call to Resist Illegitimate Authority. He had signed the Call to Resist Illegitimate Authority. He spoke at a press conference with Coffin and others launching the Call. He attended the Washington demonstration and the attempt to turn the collected draft cards over to the Attorney General. There is no denying that there was agreement between him and Coffin: they both hated the war, they both supported draft resistance, they both endorsed the burning of draft cards. But the fact that there was agreement between them does not mean there was *an* agreement between them. For there to be *an* agreement there must be some kind of bargain, some kind of exchange of promises, or at least mutual reliance. Nothing of the sort happened here. They merely each pursued certain ends. They would have pursued them whether or not the other shared them. Goodman was prepared to issue a call to civil disobedience, in fact did so, regardless of whether Coffin did the same. He was probably prepared to urge draft card–burning, whether or not Coffin endorsed it. The same can be said for the other defendants. As the dissenting judge in the *Spock* decision notes, it is hard to see how Spock and Ferber believed any less in draft card–burning and draft resistance than Coffin or Ferber. The proper ground for acquitting them would be that, like Goodman and Coffin, they found themselves in agreement with the others, but not in *an* agreement with them. Their views and actions just happened to coalesce.

Why not treat coalescence like an agreement? After all, what we are concerned about is group action, and coalescence means group action. But what makes the joint action of a group of *n* persons more fearsome than the individual actions of those *n* persons is the division of labor and the mutual psychological support that collaboration affords. By definition, none of these is present when the independent efforts of several similarly motivated individuals simply coalesce. That alone argues strongly against branding as conspiracy what is merely a coalescence of efforts. Worse, if coalescence counted as a conspiratorial agreement, all violators of a given law—however independent and ignorant of each other—would be coconspirators. The *Dr. Spock* case came very close to being a realization of that ominous possibility.

The law of complicity imposes liability on the person who helps someone commit a crime, rather than commit it himself. But do we really need the law of complicity for that? Often the person who helps someone commit a crime is guilty of that very crime, and if he isn't, a stroke of the drafter's pen could make it so (for example, defining burglary to include *causing someone else to break and enter*). But none of that would be enough to impose liability on every helping hand. The reason has to do with the peculiar workings of the principle of diminishing marginal returns.

The law of complicity is unusually vague, again because of diminishing marginal returns. It is hard to distinguish between participants and nonparticipants in a crime and between different kinds of participants. The vagueness has resulted in much inconsistency and many strange verdicts.

The law of conspiracy imposes liability for the mere act of agreeing to commit a crime (and sometimes for agreeing to what isn't even a crime, for example, raising one's prices). That is because an agreement between several people is more likely to lead to successful implementation than someone's unilateral announcement or resolve that he is going to commit a crime.

But when has somebody agreed to commit a crime? When is someone a coconspirator? How much less than a signed offer or acceptance of an offer will do? How tacit a form of collaboration qualifies as an agreement to participate in a crime? The different forms of collaboration arrange themselves in a natural hierarchy. Most similar to a formal contract is the informal agreement. Less similar is tacit cooperation (conscious parallelism) in the face of a prisoner's dilemma. Still, there are certain resemblances: the parties do want to collaborate, and they are giving something up in exchange for the other side's doing the same—they are giving up the chance of taking advantage of the other side. Less similar yet is tacit coordination. Again, the parties do want to collaborate, but now neither side is really giving up anything. Each is indifferent to what it is doing, so long as it is doing the same thing as the other parties. Least similar is coalescence. Here the parties don't really want to collaborate. They merely know that they are collaborating. The further down the hierarchy one moves, the less justified is the label conspiracy. But perhaps the label does not deserve to be applied to any arrangement less contractlike than an informal agreement.

6 The Crime That Never Was

A Fake Opinion in a Fake Case involving Fakes

Commonwealth v. Omeira

Supreme Court of Wessex

Before Newson, C. J., Henchard, Hardy, Farfrae, Middlebury, J.

Newson, C. J.: The defendant, Jan Omeira, is charged with attempting to export illegally "valuable artifacts of the native culture" in violation of Section 901.34(1) of the Wessex Code.

To protect our national patrimony, the Wessex legislature twenty years ago passed a law making it illegal to export native art works produced before 1920 and worth more than 100,000 pounds. This sweeping prohibition is subject to only one ill-defined exception. The Arts Council, an agency of the Interior Department, has broad discretion to grant exemptions, that is, special licenses, when it finds that "unusual circumstances so warrant." Licenses are typically granted when a work of art cannot be sold in Wessex except at a very small fraction of its world market price or when the applicant promises to secure another "native" work of comparable worth currently in foreign hands.

The defendant is a retired businessman of considerable wealth. He owns a farm in Casterbridge, Wessex, where he spends half of the year, and a rancho in Cuernavaca, Mexico, where he spends the other half. He is a zealous aficionado of the arts; indeed, since his retirement the acquisition of expensive paintings has become his chief preoccupation. He has opened art galleries both in his house in Casterbridge and in his villa in Cuernavaca, the one in Casterbridge for the public at large, the one in Cuernavaca almost exclusively for his own use and that of his guests.

The Constabulary has been aware for some time that not all native paintings Mr. Omeira is known to have acquired at public auctions in Wessex have made their appearance in his Casterbridge gallery and suspected him therefore of having illegally transported many of them to his gallery in Cuernavaca. Since few people have gained access to that gallery, no direct confirmation has been possible. For several years Mr. Omeira was systematically strip-searched on every one of his departures for Mexico. The searches turned up nothing and were discontinued.

In January of this year, the Constabulary received an anonymous tip that some time in March, Omeira would personally be smuggling a picture by the famous eighteenth-century landscape painter Ignacius Decameron out of the country. The picture, Seminole Falls, *had for several years been hanging in Omeira's Casterbridge gallery and had recently been taken down for "cleaning." When Omeira left for Mexico in March, Customs scoured his luggage. They found a false bottom in one of his trunks and inside it, tightly rolled up,* Seminole Falls.

Omeira's case was about to go to trial, when something very unusual happened. A well-known Belgian landscape painter named Flammarion remarked in an interview with the French monthly Paris Match *that he thought it "rather amusing" that a Wessex art collector was being prosecuted for smuggling a Decameron landscape when in fact the painting was a forgery. How did he know it was a forgery, the astonished journalist asked. Because, replied Flammarion, he had painted it himself.*

The government to whom Omeira had forfeited the smuggled picture immediately invited a panel of experts to test Flammarion's claim. They found that the painting's age crackle had a different structure from that of genuine eighteenth-century paintings. Moreover, the crackle seemed to have been artificially produced. They found that the dirt in the painting's crevices wasn't dirt at all. It had crept into the crevices very unevenly and had a different homogeneity from dirt. They suspected it was ink. With the help of radiographic studies they discovered a residue of a prior painting underneath the landscape, suggesting that this was an eighteenth-century canvas that had been recycled for forgery. They also noticed some of the paints used contained pigments not known in Decameron's day. Finally, one of the experts was struck by the reddish tinge of the painting's sky. He had been to Seminole Falls and he knew that tinge. But he was almost certain it was due to factory smoke and could not have been present in the eighteenth century. The group concluded that Flammarion was right: the picture was a fake.

Why had Flammarion forged a Decameron? When Flammarion was still a young, struggling painter living in Wessex, he entered into a feud with the influential art critic Arcadius Breitel. Breitel had published some scathing reviews of Flammarion's work, which had sent the painter into a fit of impotent rage. He wrote a letter to the magazine Kaleidoscope, *which Breitel edited. Breitel was a snob, he wrote, who had never yet dared to praise a painting by an unknown. His sole basis for judging a painting was its age and signature. "What a delightful prank it would be," the letter concluded, "to confront this nincompoop with a picture by an unknown in the style and name of an 'Old Master,' hear him pronounce it a masterpiece, and see him squirm when the true author is revealed." The prank, tossed in at the end of the letter more as a figure of speech than a real suggestion, captured his fancy. He resolved to give it a try.*

Flammarion bought a real eighteenth-century painting depicting the Last Supper by a mediocre and forgotten artist. He carefully ground the original painting off the canvas and now had a genuine eighteenth-century canvas to work on. He had taken care not to remove the painting's base which was cracked in many places, since he planned to use it when he began to age his own superimposed painting. He then retired to an inn near Seminole Falls, where he produced a rendition of the famous spot in the distinctive style of Ignacius Decameron. When he was done, he rolled it around in a cylinder to induce the age crackle. He covered the entire surface with India ink, letting it seep into the painting's cracks to simulate the fine dust that collects on an old canvas over time. Once it had dried, he removed the ink and added another layer of light brown varnish. He was ready to sell the picture.

He approached an art dealer–friend with an involved story about a former mistress of his, descended from an impoverished aristocratic Wessex family that now made its home in Uruguay. The family had only recently discovered the painting in its vaults, thought it might be a real Decameron, and wished to sell it without divulging their identity, since the sale of expensive works of art abroad was frowned upon by the government of Uruguay. The art dealer accepted the story unquestioningly and took the painting, as Flammarion expected, to none other than Arcadius Breitel for authentication. Breitel was known to be an expert on Decameron. In fact, Flammarion had painted the picture so as to fall in nicely with some of Breitel's pet theories about the painter.

Breitel not only authenticated the painting but pronounced it a major, if not the *major work of Decameron. He praised it as the "ultimate synthesis of the romanticist yearnings of Decameron's early years and the naturalistic sobriety of his more mature years, the sort of synthesis I argued he was on the verge of attaining when his life was so tragically cut short by that riding accident. I was wrong.* Seminole Falls *proves that he did attain it before he died." He gushed about the way "the hard facts of topography are diffused behind pearly films of colour," found the colors "purer, more prismatic" than any other of Decameron's work, and concluded that for its brilliancy and iridescence this was perhaps the finest Decameron yet.*

This was the point at which Flammarion had originally intended to step forth and expose Breitel. He didn't. A man named VanDamm had offered one million pounds for the painting. Faced with this offer and with the opportunity to see his painting forever after celebrated as a sublime example of Wessex art, he could no longer bring himself to admit the hoax. For nearly ten years the painting remained a part of the VanDamm collection. Then VanDamm, who found himself in financial straits, decided to sell it. He applied to the Arts Council for an export license so that he would be able to offer it up through Sotheby's. An expert from the Arts Council inspected the painting and concluded that it was probably a fake, worth at best 50,000 pounds. Although under the circumstances no license would have been necessary, the council issued one anyway, simply because the painting's status was still unclear.

VanDamm, however, had lost all appetite for having it sold at Sotheby's. If the painting really was a forgery, a public auction would bring that to light all too quickly. Instead, he discreetly searched for buyers among his colleagues in the business. He finally sold it to Jan Omeira for 1,200,000 pounds. Needless to say, he mentioned nothing about the paintings suspect provenance or even about the export license.

The discovery that Seminole Falls *was a forgery put the trial judge in this case in a delicate quandary. Omeira was charged with attempting illegally to export a valuable native painting. But it is perfectly legal to export a forged Decameron. How then was the defendant guilty of any wrongdoing? The trial judge chose to slight the issue. In a disturbingly desultory opinion, he simply noted that the "defendant believed he was smuggling a real Decameron. Therefore he is guilty of attempting to export a 'valuable artifact of native culture'" and sentenced the defendant to three years in prison. The defendant appealed. I believe his appeal has merit.*

A failed crime can still be a crime. That's why we have the law of attempts. The assassin who is prevented from firing a bullet by an alert bodyguard, the safecracker who is stopped short of opening the vault by an unsuspected alarm system, the rapist who is frustrated in his aim by an obstreperous victim, all have failed in completing their intended crime; yet they are guilty of a crime nonetheless, the crime of criminal attempt.

But not all failed crimes are crimes. "Suppose a man takes away an umbrella from a stand with intent to steal it, believing it not to be his own, but it turns out to be his own, could he be convicted of attempting to steal?" Baron Bramwell, who posed this hypothetical more than a century ago in a case called Regina v. Collins, *rightly considered the question purely rhetorical.*[1]

When is a failed crime not an attempt? It behooves us to make a brief foray through some of the more typical cases and to see what general principle is to be extracted from them.

In Commonwealth v. Dunaway *a man was charged with attempting to rape and engage in incestuous relations with his daughter. He had apparently advanced quite far in this undertaking when his wife called the police to arrest him. In the course of the trial it turned out that the girl was the man's stepdaughter. Wessex law makes consanguinity a prerequisite of incest. The defendant did not, of course, know that; he thought he was committing incest. He was convicted. On appeal the attempted rape conviction was upheld, the attempted incest conviction overturned. The court observed that even if the man had succeeded in his undertaking, even if he had actually completed an act of intercourse with his stepdaughter, he would only be guilty of rape, not incest. Stephen's* Digest of the Criminal Law *defines an attempt to commit a crime as "an act done with intent to commit that crime, and forming part of a series of acts which would constitute its actual commission if it were not interrupted."*[2] *The defendant's acts, even if not interrupted, would not have constituted incest. Hence, the court reasoned, he could not be guilty of the attempt to commit incest.*

The defendant in Stephens v. Abrahams *wanted to import a certain item into Victoria (Australia) without paying the duty on it.*[3] *To this end he presented the customs officer with a fake invoice for the item. Unbeknownst to him, the item was not dutiable anyway. A bill was pending in Parliament that proposed to tax such items, but it had not yet been passed.*

The Customs Office discovered the defendant's deception and charged him with attempt to "defraud the revenue contrary to the Commonwealth Customs Act." The Supreme Court acquitted him. Even "if the accused had succeeded in his object, he would not have succeeded in defrauding the revenue," it argued. Even if the defendant had managed to deceive the Customs office with his fake invoice, he would not have cheated them out of any money they were entitled to. So there could be no attempt to defraud them either.

Wilson received a check for $2.50. The upper right-hand corner of the check read: 2 50/100." The body of the check read: "two and 50/100 dollars." The top of the check read: "Ten Dollars or Less." Undaunted, Wilson inserted a "1" in front of the "2 50/100" hoping to cash the check in for $12.50. Needless to say, the pathetic ploy foundered and Wilson was charged with attempting to commit check forgery. Check forgery, however, requires an alteration of a material part of the check. The number on a check itself is immaterial. Whenever there is a discrepancy between number and words, the words control. Since Wilson had done all he meant to do and it did not amount to check forgery, how, the court asked, could he be guilty of attempted check forgery? Wilson was acquitted.[4]

In People v. Dlugash *the defendant was charged with attempted murder because he had shot a corpse.*

> *Defendant stated that, on the night of December 21, 1973, he, Bush and Geller had been out drinking. Bush had been staying at Geller's apartment and, during the course of the evening, Geller several times demanded that Bush pay $100 towards the rent on the apartment. According to defendant, Bush rejected these demands, telling Geller that "you better shut up or you're going to get a bullet." All three returned to Geller's apartment at approximately midnight, took seats in the bedroom, and continued to drink until sometime between 3:00 and 3:30 in the morning. When Geller again pressed his demand for rent money, Bush drew his .38 caliber pistol, aimed it at Geller and fired three times. Geller fell to the floor.*[5]

Then, to confuse the police and to buy the defendant's silence, Bush ordered him to fire some extra bullets into Geller's body. The somewhat frightened defendant did just that, believing that Geller was still alive. The autopsy, however, revealed that Geller was almost certainly already dead. In an arcanely reasoned opinion, the New York Court of Appeals somehow reached the conclusion that the defendant could indeed be found guilty of attempted murder. Few courts, I venture to say, would accept that conclusion. Lord Reid in Haughton v. Smith *some years ago contemplated just such a case and gave what I think is the definitive answer: "A man lies dead. His enemy comes along and thinks he is asleep, so he stabs the corpse. The theory [advanced by some] inevitably requires us to hold that the enemy has attempted to murder the dead man. The law may sometimes be an ass but it cannot be so asinine as that."*[6]

The defendant in People v. Jaffe *had bought what he thought were stolen goods from some undercover policemen.*[7] *He could not be charged with buying stolen goods since the goods weren't stolen. Instead, he was charged with attempting to buy stolen goods. The courts acquitted him: "If all which an accused person intends to do would if done constitute no crime it cannot be a crime to attempt to do with the same purpose a part of the thing intended."*

In State v. Clarissa *the defendant, a black slave, was charged with attempting to murder two white men by feeding them a substance called Jamestown weed, which she believed to be poisonous.*[8] *The prosecution failed to allege or prove that it was. The Supreme Court of Alabama reversed the conviction, explaining:*

> *[The] administration of a substance not poisonous, or calculated to cause death, though believed to be so by the person administering it, will not be an attempt to poison, within the meaning of the [murder] statute. From this analysis of the statute, it follows, that the indictment should allege, that the substance administered was a deadly poison, or calculated to destroy human life, as it is necessary that every indictment should warrant the judgment that is rendered upon it. Yet every allegation in this indictment may have been proved, and the life of the persons against whom the supposed attempt to poison was made, never have been in jeopardy; as it cannot be known as a matter of law, that the seed of the Jamestown weed is a deadly poison. The moral guilt, it is true, is as great in the one case as in the other, but that is not the offense which the law intended to punish; but the actual attempt to poison, by means calculated to accomplish it.*

A notable curiosity occurred in our own jurisdiction only very recently in Commonwealth v. Jejune.[9] *The defendant and his wife were Haitian immigrants. The defendant's wife had grown very sick shortly after coming to this country. At the behest of a neighbor a doctor visited her. She told him that she could not be helped because her husband had cast a spell over her. Two days earlier she had found in his shaving cabinet a doll bearing her likeness with pins in it. The doctor ordered her taken to the hospital, where she quickly recovered. No organic cause for her illness was ever discovered. The woman's husband did not deny having tried to kill her by magic. He was charged with attempted murder. The trial court rightly dismissed the charge and acquitted the man. It observed, "To try to kill someone by sticking pins in a doll is to try the impossible. Even if the man had continued sticking pins in the doll for the rest of his life he could not have killed his wife. How then can we brand such an inherently innocent activity attempted murder?"*

These cases establish a simple yet powerful principle. An act which, unless interrupted, constitutes a crime is a criminal attempt. But an act which, even if completed, wouldn't be a crime, is not.

The defendant in all of these cases is morally heinous. But why is he morally heinous? Because of what he did? No, because of what he thought he did. In that case to convict him "would be to convict him not for what he did but simply because he had a guilty intention." It is a fundamental tenet of our criminal law that a man cannot be convicted for his thoughts, only for his acts.

My disposition of Omeira's case should now be clear. Even if Jan Omeira had succeeded in smuggling his painting across the border, he would not have violated the export ban, since Seminole Falls *is a forgery. If the completed act was no crime, the attempt could not possibly be one either. The trial court's verdict should be reversed.*

Henchard, J.: I disagree sharply with the reasoning of Justice Newson. He would have us endorse what I think is a rather strange principle: that an "act which, although intended to be a crime, would not have amounted to one, even if it had not been interrupted, is not a criminal attempt." Taken seriously, this principle would have absurd implications. Justice Newson concedes that the assassin who is overpowered by a bodyguard, the safecracker who is caught by an unsuspected alarm system, the rapist who is stymied by a resistant victim all are guilty of a criminal attempt. But suppose that given the way the assassin aimed his gun, he would have missed his target anyway. Justice Newson's principle would have the man acquitted. Suppose the gold bars in the vault were too heavy for the safecracker to move, even if he had gotten to them. Justice Newson's principle would have the man acquitted. Suppose the rapist was impotent and could not have achieved an erection. Justice Newson's principle would have the man acquitted. I do not see how Justice Newson can propose a principle with such consequences.

Nor can I approve of many of the decisions that seem to have endorsed this principle. If the defendant in Jaffe *thought he was buying stolen goods, he was attempting to buy stolen goods. If the defendant in* Jejune *thought what he did would tend to kill his wife, he was attempting murder. By contrast, the decision of the* Dlugash *court was exactly right: If the defendant in* Dlugash *thought he was shooting a human being, he was attempting murder. In each of these cases, what the defendants were attempting was impossible only because of some unforeseen contingency. That makes them no different from the assassin, the safecracker, the rapist. They, too, failed because some unforeseen contingency stopped them in their tracks.*

Justice Newson contends that to punish the defendants in cases like Dlugash, Jaffe, *and* Jejune *is to punish evil thoughts, not evil acts. But that's not so. We punish the defendants there not because they wanted to commit an evil act but because they took what they thought were substantial steps toward putting those thoughts into practice. I think I can pinpoint the source of Justice Newson's confusion. He thinks that when but for the defendant's evil thought he would not be punished we are punishing him for the evil thought. That's a mistaken idea. We would not convict a murderer but for the fact that he intended to kill a human being. Yet it can hardly be said that we are punishing him only for his evil thoughts.*

I do not think, therefore, that Jan Omeira is innocent of a criminal attempt to violate the export ban on art merely because what he took to be a real Decameron turned out to be a forgery. But I think there are other reasons for acquitting him.

Suppose two men furtively engage in homosexual intercourse thinking that it is illegal. In fact, state law has nothing against mutually consented-to homosexual intercourse. Are they guilty of a criminal attempt? Evidently not. You cannot invent the law against yourself. Just because you think something is illegal and then attempt to do it, you haven't yet done anything illegal. The crime you attempt is, we might say, "legally impossible" because there isn't such a crime. This is very different from the case where what you are attempting to do isn't really criminal because the facts, not the law, are different from what you took them to be: because the man you attempt to shoot is already dead, because the goods you attempt to buy are not really stolen, because the method you adopt for killing someone won't really work. We might call these cases of "factual impossibility." In sum, attempting the legally impossible is not a crime, attempting the factually impossible is. *In a way, this is a corollary to the principle that ignorance of law is no excuse. Just as thinking something is legal when it isn't won't get a defendant out of a bind, thinking it is illegal when it isn't won't get him into one.*

This principle, rather than the one endorsed by Justice Newson, serves to make sense of the three cases cited in his opinion with which I agree. I agree that the defendant in Dunaway *who thought he was committing incest should have been acquitted of the charge of attempting incest. What he attempted was legally impossible. The law does not make intercourse with one's stepdaughter part of incest. Thinking that the law does cannot make the defendant guilty of attempted incest.*

I also agree that the defendant in Stephens v. Abrahams *who thought he was smuggling a dutiable item past customs should have been acquitted of the charge of attempting to "defraud the revenue." He, too, attempted the legally impossible, since Victoria did not make the item he smuggled dutiable. Thinking that it did could not have made the defendant guilty of attempted smuggling.*

Finally, I agree that the defendant in State v. Wilson *who thought he was forging a check when he altered its numerals should have been acquitted of the charge of attempting check forgery. He thought that what he did was forgery. The law happens to define forgery differently. Thus, he, too, attempted the legally impossible. Thinking that the law prohibited what he did as forgery did not make him guilty of attempted forgery.*

When the Decameron was still in Mr. VanDamm's possession, he applied for an export license to the Arts Council. The Arts Council granted him the license. In effect, they amended the export law so as to exempt this particular painting from its sway. Thus what Mr. Omeira attempted to do was to smuggle out of the country a painting under the mistaken belief that the law prohibited him from exporting it. In fact, the law specifically exempted that painting. What he was attempting to do was not merely factually impossible (because he was dealing with a forgery) but legally impossible (because the painting had been exempted from the export ban). The case is thus on all fours with Dunaway, Stephens, *and* Wilson. *It is for that reason that I too would acquit Mr. Omeira, not-*

withstanding my wholehearted disagreement with the reasoning of Justice Newson's opinion.

Farfrae, J., with whom Hardy, J., concurs: I agree in spirit with Justice Newson's approach. I agree with him that many of the so-called impossible attempt cases should be resolved in the defendant's favor. I disagree with the particulars of his argument, for many of the reasons given in Justice Henchard's opinion. And I disagree with his resolution of this case.

I disagree both in spirit and substance with Justice Henchard's approach, and, of course, with his resolution of this case in particular. The approach hinges on a distinction that strikes me as both obscure and unimportant, that between law and fact, legal impossibility and factual impossibility.

The distinction between "law" and "fact" has proved obscure wherever it is employed. For instance, the common law used to require that a plaintiff's complaint in a civil action only state the "facts" of his case, not any "legal conclusions." Unfortunately, no one has ever been able to tell whether the allegation that "on November 9, the defendant negligently ran over the plaintiff with his car at the intersection of State Street and Chestnut Street" is a statement of fact or a legal conclusion. In fact, the distinction between law and fact is just the legal version of the philosophical distinction between "empirical" and "analytical" statements, a distinction on whose existence philosophers have been unable to agree to this day.

The distinction is as unimportant as it is obscure. It distinguishes between cases that are really alike. [Here Justice Farfrae retells the story of Mr. Law and Mr. Fact, which the reader already encountered in chap. 1.] The present case shows neatly just how unimportant it is. The defendant Omeira made two mistakes. First, he mistakenly thought the picture was authentic. Second, he mistakenly thought it hadn't been licensed for export. Under Justice Henchard's rule, the first mistake fails to exonerate him, but the second mistake does. The first is a mistake of fact, the second a mistake of law. Yet I fail to see any profound difference between the two kinds of mistake. If Omeira's ignorance of the painting's authenticity doesn't exonerate him, then neither should his ignorance of the export license.

The proper way to approach cases like the present is to ask two questions. Let me ask them in turn, explain why they are important, show how one goes about answering them, and answer them for the present case. The first question is this: Did the defendant really attempt something criminal?

An attempt is often mistakenly thought of as the fragment of a completed offense. Of course, that isn't so. The driver who hurtles down a slippery road at breakneck speed may be inviting a deadly accident that would qualify as involuntary manslaughter if it occurred. Nevertheless, he is not attempting to commit the crime of involuntary manslaughter. To attempt something one must not merely be on one's way to committing it, one must intend to commit it. The reckless driver clearly is not.

This obvious point has subtle implications. It means that a defendant may be thinking he is committing a crime, without actually attempting to commit it. He knows the bomb he plans to hurl into the queen's carriage will kill not only the queen, but her bodyguard, but he is only attempting to kill the queen, not the bodyguard. Killing the bodyguard is an unintended by-product of killing the queen. Of course, determining whether somebody is actually attempting something or merely engaging in conduct which he thinks will bring it about, often is hard. It depends on whether the commission of the crime is his desired end or a means toward such an end (in which case we have an attempt) or whether it is rather a by-product of bringing about some desired end. To find out which it is, one has to ask whether the defendant would change his course of conduct if he thought the commission of the crime was not tied to the achievement of his desired end.[10]

If we apply this analysis, we will see that many defendants charged with impossible attempts are not in fact attempting the crime they are charged with attempting. They merely think they are committing a crime. The rapist in Commonwealth v. Dunaway *is not guilty of attempted incest, because he was not intending to commit incest. He only thought he was committing incest. Had he been told that incest requires consanguinity, he would have been relieved. He would certainly not have desisted from his actions. The "smuggler" in* Stephens v. Abrahams *is not guilty of attempted smuggling because he was not intending to smuggle. He merely thought he was smuggling. Had he been told that the items he was importing weren't dutiable, he would have been relieved. He would certainly not have abstained from importing them. The "killer" in* People v. Dlugash *is not guilty of attempting murder, because he was not intending to kill the already-dead man. He merely thought he was killing him. Had he been told that he was shooting a corpse, he would have been relieved. He would certainly not have avoided shooting it. The "fence" in* People

v. Jaffe *is not guilty of attempting to buy stolen goods because he was not intending to buy stolen goods. He merely thought he was buying stolen goods. Had he been told that the goods were not stolen, he would have been relieved. He would certainly not have eschewed buying them.*

What now of this case? Was the defendant intending to export an authentic Decameron? Or was he merely thinking he was exporting an authentic Decameron? That depends: Had he been told that the Decameron was fake, would he have cared? Would he have changed his course of conduct? Would he not have exported it? The defendant will, of course, argue that although he thought the painting was a genuine Decameron, that was not the reason he wanted to export it. He will argue that he liked the painting for its artistic merits, not its provenance, and that he would still have wanted to take it to Cuernavaca, even if it was a forgery. That's a tough argument to reckon with.

The record indicates that the defendant liked to keep his most exclusive and prized possessions in his Cuernavaca gallery. It also indicates that the defendant did not collect art as an investment. Very few paintings he acquired he ever resold. He collected them purely and simply for the aesthetic pleasure they afforded. Asking whether the defendant would have tried to export a forged Decameron to Cuernavaca amounts to asking whether his aesthetic enjoyment of the painting would have been diminished by his discovery that it was a fake. Should it have been? Is it rational to enjoy a painting as long as you think it is a Decameron and on learning it is a mere Flammarion-imitating-Decameron cease to do so?

Some decades ago it was discovered that a widely hailed Vermeer depicting Christ and the Disciples at Emmaus, *exhibited for many years at Rotterdam's Boymans Museum, was a forgery by a twentieth-century painter named van Meegeren. Hundreds of thousands of visitors, many of them connoisseurs and critics, had enjoyed the painting. When the fraud was discovered, the picture was immediately removed from view. Was that rational? The philosopher Alfred Lessing argues that it wasn't:*

> *What is the difference between a genuine Vermeer and a van Meegeren forgery? It is of little use to maintain that one need but look to see the difference. The fact that* The Disciples *is a forgery (if indeed it is) cannot, so to speak, be read off from its surface, but can finally be proved or disproved only by means of extensive scientific investigations and analyses. Nor are the results of such scientific investigations of any help in answering our question, since*

> *they deal exclusively with nonaesthetic elements of the picture, such as its chemical composition, its hardness, its crackle, and so on. . . .*
>
> *The plain fact is that aesthetically it makes no difference whether a work of art is authentic or a forgery, and, instead of being embarassed at having praised a forgery, critics should have the courage of their convictions and take pride in having praised a work of beauty. . . .*
>
> *The fact that a work of art is a forgery is an item of information about it on a level with such information as the age of the artist when he created it, the political situation in the time and place of its creation, the price it originally fetched, the kind of materials used in it, the stylistic influences discernible in it, the psychological state of the artist, his purpose in painting it, and so on. All such information belongs to areas of interest peripheral at best to the work of art as aesthetic object, areas such as biography, history of art, sociology, and psychology. I do not deny that such areas of interest may be important and that their study may even help us become better art appreciators. But I do deny that the information which they provide is of the essence of the work of art or of the aesthetic experience which it engenders.*
>
> *It would be merely foolish to assert that it is of no interest whatever to know that* The Disciples *is a forgery. But to the man who has never heard of either Vermeer or van Meegeren and who stands in front of the* Disciples *admiring it, it can make no difference whether he is told that it is a seventeenth-century Vermeer or a twentieth-century van Meegeren in the style of Vermeer. And when some deny this and argue vehemently that, indeed, it does make a great deal of difference, they are only admitting that* they *do know something about Vermeer and van Meegeren and the history of art and the value and reputation of certain masters. They are only admitting that* they *do not judge a work of art on purely aesthetic grounds but also take into account when it was created, by whom, and how great a reputation it or its creator has.*[11]

Is Lessing right to suggest that we are being snobbish and irrational if we permit our pleasure in a painting to be decisively influenced by its identity? I will offer two examples to show that he is not. (To be sure, a bit of irrational self-suggestion is *involved. The art critic takes to a famous signature like many a patient to a placebo. He will find virtues in the painting that really aren't there. This doesn't prove that all virtues in all paintings are the invention of the art critics, just as the reaction of the patient doesn't prove that the real medicine is superfluous. For unlike the forgery and the placebo, the real painting and the real medicine do their job without suggestion—which is why the medicine works for many not susceptible to the placebo's suggestive power.)*

My first example is the plot of a film made some time ago by the American director Martin Ritt, written by Walter Bernstein and starring Woody Allen. It was called The Front. *The story takes place sometime in the 1950s. Howard Prince, a man in his late twenties or early thirties, works as a cashier in a diner. He is a bright college dropout and sometime bum. One day Al Miller, a childhood pal who has become a well-known TV scriptwriter, drops in. The man is depressed. He had been ordered to appear before the House Committee on Un-American Activities, had taken the Fifth Amendment, and had been blacklisted as a result. On seeing Howard he hits upon a ruse for salvaging something of his dwindling livelihood. He proposes that Howard (Woody Allen) submit his manuscripts for him, representing himself to be their author. In return, he promises Howard 10 percent of the proceeds. Howard is delighted. He is pleased to help. Besides he likes the adventure, the money, and the glamor of holding himself up as a television scriptwriter. The first, second, and third scripts are accepted without much questioning and with much acclaim. But the charade doesn't always go smoothly. Howard is not very well read and therefore hard-pressed to make conversation on literary subjects. Nor is he much good at explaining and "selling" his own scripts. Finally, disaster threatens when the director asks him to rewrite a scene on the spot. Howard finesses all of these obstacles, and so successful is the scheme that several more blacklisted authors are brought in to take advantage of Howard's ability as a front. Howard Prince soon becomes known as one of the most prolific TV scriptwriters around.*

On the set Howard meets a young directorial assistant named Florence Barret, a tall, pretty, young woman with long, brunette hair and soulful eyes. Florence is involved with a stockbroker but cannot resist the charms of this outwardly rather clumsy but yet so clever and creative writer. She is a friendly, warmhearted, open-minded person, but it is clear that Howard Prince would not have had a chance with her but for his new persona—but for his reputation as an immensely talented, prolific new writer.

Months later Howard confesses his real identity to Florence. She is shocked and angry, she feels duped, and she wonders whether she really knows him. But she doesn't break with Howard. As things stand when the movie ends the two are likely to be married soon.

Why does Florence love Howard? He doesn't have the attributes she was looking for in a man. He only seemed, at some point, to have those attributes. Why does she not discard him when she discovers he doesn't? Because she has grown to love him. But why has she grown to love him? Because of attributes he doesn't have. In other words, she continues to love him for no other reason than that he is identical with the person she loved in the past. Even if a man came along who genuinely epitomized the attributes she had been looking for in a man, she would not abandon Howard for him. Do we consider her snobbish or irrational for placing such emphasis not on Howard's real attributes but the fact that he happens to be identical with someone she loved in the past? Not in the least. We might consider her snobbish if she did otherwise. Identity then is a crucial concern not only to the snob.

Evidently it doesn't much matter that the person we love possess certain attributes making him suitable for loving, but only that he be identical with a person we once considered suitable for such loving.

My second example: ABC corporation, a car-manufacturing company, is being prosecuted for negligent homicide. One of its buses has caused the death of thirty school children. The bus model, the state's attorney argues, was thrown on the market quite recklessly with only a modicum of testing. As a result, its tendency to explode readily after a head-on collision with another vehicle was never discovered and corrected. Before the indictment is officially announced, the company is reorganized top to bottom. Almost all of the management and personnel involved in the production of the fatal model are fired. Two-thirds of the board of directors, the real culprits, are tossed out. The fired and dismissed managers, employees, and board members coalesce into a new corporation of their own, called the XYZ company and also begin to produce cars. Which of the two companies will be liable for the misdeeds of the ABC corporation? Why, clearly the ABC corporation. Evidently, we don't punish the entity because we think it particularly deserving of punishment, but because it happens to be identical with an entity which sometime in the past was particularly deserving of punishment.

Why then should we only admire a Decameron painting for the aesthetic qualities it now possesses rather than because it is identical with the work of a man whose work we have come to admire? I don't think there is anything snobbish about such an attitude. A man is not irrational or unreasonable for behaving in this fashion. And I don't feel we are imputing any irrational, unreasonable or implausible trait to Mr. Omeira when we assume that he cared very much that his picture be a real Decameron rather than merely "another pretty picture."

We have established that the defendant really attempted to export an authentic Decameron. But that is not enough to show that he is guilty of a criminal attempt. Before finding him liable for that, we need to answer a second question: Did the defendant really create an unreasonable risk of a crime being committed? Why do I think this question needs to be asked?

Before we convict someone for recklessly or negligently causing harm, we require that his conduct be "unreasonable," that it be the sort a reasonable man would take exception to. In a sense, that introduces an element of luck into the law. The defendant may think that what he is doing creates an unreasonable risk, but if in fact it does not, he will not be convicted. The law does not want to trouble itself with conduct that wouldn't bother a reasonable man.

We should impose the same requirement of unreasonableness before we convict someone for intentionally or knowingly causing harm. Indeed, I think we already do. It's just that, typically, when a defendant intentionally brings about harm, there is no doubt that his conduct was such as would have bothered a reasonable man. If it wouldn't have bothered a reasonable man, the prosecutor usually decides not to press charges. That has the unfortunate effect of making us overlook this potentially important point.

Let me elucidate with an example. Suppose a father wants to kill his five-year-old son. He decides to do so by sending him to summer camp, not, as he did in past years, by train, but by plane instead. He is under the mistaken impression that plane crashes are a lot more frequent than train crashes. He hopes such a crash will occur. And indeed it does. Clearly, the father has intentionally caused his son's death. (He intended his son to die in just the manner he did, and the son wouldn't have died, if he hadn't been on that plane.) But should we convict him of murder? I don't think so. Why? Because the father did nothing a reasonable man would object to: It was not unreasonably risky to send the boy to summer camp by airplane.

Suppose the plane never crashed. But the police learn of the father's evil intentions and charge him with attempted murder. Should we convict him? I don't think so. Why? Because the father did nothing a reasonable man would object to: To repeat, it is not unreasonably risky to send the boy to summer camp by airplane.

The same analysis applies to many cases of impossible attempts. The man who tried to kill his wife by witchcraft was engaging in conduct a reasonable man would not object to. It is not unreasonably risky to stick pins into someone's likeness. Hence the defendant should be acquitted. Whether the slave who tried to kill someone with the harmless Jamestown weed created an unreasonable risk depends on the facts of that case. From what I know of the case, I cannot say. In any event, the decision is one for the jury. Whether Wilson, who tried to forge a check with ludicrous ineptitude, created an unreasonable risk is a close call.

In the present case, did the defendant Omeira create an unreasonable risk that valuable artifacts of the native culture would be exported? Would a reasonable man have objected to his conduct? I believe so. The forgery was near-perfect. A reasonable man would certainly have been worried that what Omeira was trying to export was a real Decameron. Of course, if the forgery were terribly crude, so crude that any reasonable man could detect it, the answer would be different.

I conclude that the defendant's conviction should be affirmed.

The court being evenly divided, Justice Middlebury will cast the deciding vote. I leave it to the reader to make Justice Middlebury's decision for him. But first read on.

A Possible Explanation of the Impossible Problem of Impossible Attempts

The three opinions in the *Omeira* case present two views of impossibility—two, not three, because the third opinion is really a refined version of the first. The first represents the "English" approach, the second the "American" approach. The third is designed to show that the English approach, properly argued, isn't as silly or incoherent as its critics often claim. Which of these perspectives is the right one?

Why do we hesitate to punish impossible attempts? Why do we have such a thing as an "impossibility defense"? It seems to make the defendant's guilt dependent on luck. Everyone who attempts a crime intends to succeed. Some fail because of impossibility. They seem no less evil than those who succeed. Why do we acquit them on grounds of impossibility? To sharpen the issue: We punish attempts to reduce the role of luck in the criminal law—to treat all would-be assassins alike, whether their bullet happens to hit or miss its mark. Why do we reintroduce luck by allowing the impossibility defense?

Some practical reasons have been offered for the impossibility defense: First, it is said that if we allowed the law to punish someone for attempting something he thinks is a crime, even though it isn't (e.g., homosexual intercourse when it isn't forbidden), we would be violating the "principle of legality: *nulla poena sine lege,* "no punishment without law." (Glanville Williams writes: "If the legislature has not seen fit to prohibit the consummated act, a mere approach to consummation should *a fortiori* be guiltless. Any other view would offend against the principle of legality; in effect the law of attempt would be used to manufacture a new crime, when the legislature has left the situation outside the ambit of the law.")[12] Second, it is said that if we allowed the law to punish someone whenever he mistakenly thought he was committing a crime, we would be making it very easy for a malicious prosecutor to convict the innocent. After all, he only needs to fabricate some evidence suggesting that certain innocent conduct in fact served some sinister purpose.

The real reason for the impossibility defense, I believe, is more fundamental, less pragmatic. It is for logical reasons impossible to design a system of criminal law that doesn't have some kind of impossibility defense. To be sure, one can give the defense a broad or a narrow scope, but one cannot wipe it out. It is an inevitable by-product of the inherent vagueness of rules.

Why are rules inherently vague? They are vague because all of language is vague. Language is vague because it rests on human perception and human perception is of limited acuity. The word "red" is vague because we can't distinguish close shades of color. There is a substantial range of colors in the color spectrum of whose redness we are unsure. It might seem that we could eliminate this vagueness by using scientific instruments with potentially unlimited perceptual acuity, but a human has to read those instruments. The point is neatly made by the philosopher Michael Polanyi:

> The award of the winner's place in a horse race in England used to be a highly skilled performance entrusted to the stewards of the Jockey Club, until the advent of the photofinish camera which seemed to render the de-

> cision altogether obvious. However, some years ago, the late A. M. Turing showed me the print of a photo finish where one horse's nose is seen a fraction of an inch ahead of another's, but the second horse's nose extends forward by six inches or so well ahead of that of its rival by virtue of the projection of a thick thread of saliva. Since such a situation was not foreseen by the rules, the case had to be referred to the stewards and the award made on the grounds of their personal judgment. Turing gave me this as an example for the ultimate vagueness of even the most objective methods of observation.[13]

How does vagueness lead to the impossibility defense? Vagueness means that for any rule there are numerous cases in which the applicability of the rule is uncertain. Now suppose we wanted to implant in the criminal law an "anti-impossibility" rule, a rule designed to eradicate the impossibility defense. Such a rule would have to say something like this: Whenever the defendant is certain that he is committing a crime, rightly or wrongly, he is at least guilty of a criminal attempt. This anti-impossibility rule is itself vague. There are cases in which its applicability is uncertain. Consider such a case. The defendant is uncertain whether, under the anti-impossibility rule, he is committing a crime. Since he is not certain that he is committing a crime, under the rule he is not committing a crime. But that contradicts the original assumption that it is uncertain whether he is committing a crime. Nor can the rule be rewritten to avoid this difficulty. You might think that adding a provision stating that the rule should not be applied to itself, might resolve the problem. But it doesn't, because that provision too is inherently vague. What this means is that an anti-impossibility rule, if rigorously applied, is self-contradictory.

The argument is rather analogous to that used by Bertrand Russell to show that the notion of certain sets is conceptually incoherent. He asked us to imagine the set of all sets that don't have themselves as a member. It seems like a perfectly coherent notion, at first. The set would comprise most sets we are familiar with, like the set of numbers and the set of desks, and would exclude certain others, like the set of mathematical objects. But would the set have itself as a member? If it does, then it doesn't. If it doesn't, then it does. The idea of such a set turns out to be self-contradictory.

Interestingly, there is a principle related to the impossibility defense which can be rationalized in an analogous manner, the principle that ignorance of the law is no defense. The principle is usually justified by saying that permitting ignorance to be a defense would encourage willful ignorance of the law. But again the reason lies deeper. Ignorance of the law is no defense because we couldn't draft a rule that would always make it a defense. Suppose we had a rule that said: When a person is uncertain whether something is illegal, he is innocent of any crime. This rule, too, is unavoidably vague. There are cases in which its applicability is uncertain. Consider such a case. The defendant thinks that he may or may not be committing a crime. Thus, according to the rule, he is innocent. But that contradicts the assumption that it is uncertain whether the rule applies. What this means is that an "ignorance rule," if rigorously applied, is self-contradictory.

So the impossibility defense cannot be rooted out. As noted, however, it can be given a small or a large role to play. Which of these one prefers depends on what role one thinks luck should play in the law of attempt.

The American approach assigns luck a small role. It takes its cue from the principle that ignorance of the law is no defense. Whether a defendant who doesn't think he is doing anything wrong has violated the law depends on whether he was lucky enough to be correct. The American approach assigns luck a similar role in the law of attempt. Whether a defendant who thinks he is doing something wrong has violated the law should depend on whether he is lucky enough to be incorrect.

The English approach assigns luck a larger role. It takes its cue from negligence law. Whether a defendant who thinks he has done something negligent has violated the law depends on whether he was unlucky enough, first, actually to have caused some harm and, second, actually to have created an unreasonable risk. The English approach thinks luck should play a similar role in the law of attempt. To begin with, in cases other than attempts, in the narrowest, truest sense, it would impose no liability except for the completed crime. Even in genuine attempts, it would impose no liability unless an unreasonable risk was created.

Which approach is right? Neither strikes me as wrong. I think both are legitimate. The choice between them belongs to Justice Middlebury.

A Real Story about Real Fakes

The *Omeira* case may seem contrived. In chapter 1, I explained why that's not a serious grievance. As it happens, though, *Omeira* is loosely based on a real case—the story of Han van Meegeren, the "master forger."[14] Van Meegeren was a Dutch painter, born at the end of the last century. He was fond of the Old Masters (Rembrandt, Hals, de Hoogh, Vermeer), spurned his "modern" contemporaries (the Impressionists and Post-Impressionists), and painted in a very traditional style. His technical virtuousity brought him some early recognition: as an architecture student at the Delft Institute of Technology, he won a coveted medal the school's art department awarded to the best painting by a student every five years—and he hadn't even studied in the art department. He set up as a professional painter and was moderately successful. His first exhibitions won him applause, but his success was short-lived. His later work was dismissed as out-of-touch with modern currents. Unable to earn a living from his artistic efforts, he turned to painting Christmas cards, posters, and commissioned portraits, although he remained eager for artistic success and resentful of his critics.

He had always been a prankster. As a youth he stole the local church's wine and hid the only key to the neighborhood police station. After he had sold his prize-winning painting for one hundred guilders, he tried to sell a copy of it as the original to someone else. Frustrated and impoverished by his artistic career, he resolved on the ultimate prank: the forgery of an Old Master. His original plan was to have the picture submitted for authentication to the doyen of Dutch art critics, Dr. Abraham Bredius, and then embarass Bredius by exposing the hoax. Things turned out differently.

Van Meegeren obtained an old canvas, *Raising of Lazarus,* aged it much in the manner of Flammarion, and imposed on it a biblical painting in the distinct style of Jan Vermeer, the esteemed seventeenth-century Dutch painter. Its name: *Christ at Emmaus*. The choice of painter and subject matter alone was ingenious. Only a few Vermeers were known to exist. Because Vermeer's pictures were not really appreciated until more than two hundred years after his death, many had been destroyed, many forgotten. Critics were expecting more Vermeers to surface. The typical Vermeer subject was quotidian. Vermeer had produced only one biblical painting, *Martha and Mary,* authenticated by none other than Dr. Abraham Bredius. Bredius had his own theories about Vermeer. He had speculated that Vermeer had traveled to Italy and been influenced by Caravaggio; he also suspected that there were more biblical Vermeers and was eagerly on the lookout for them. Just such a Vermeer was what van Meegeren offered him. Moreover, he chose a subject that Caravaggio had painted no less than three times. Finally, he gave the face of Christ a distinct affinity with the Christ in *Martha and Mary.*

When he was done, he handed the picture to a friend with an involved story about its provenance and had him take it to Bredius for authentication. Bredius was delighted. The biblical Vermeer corroborated all his theories. He certified it as authentic: "This glorious work of Vermeer, the great Vermeer of Delft, has emerged—thank God!—from the darkness where it lay for many years, undefiled and just as it left the artist's studio. Its subject is almost unique in his *oeuvre;* a depth of feeling springs from it such as is found in no other work of his. I found it hard to contain my emotions when this masterpiece was first shown to me and many will feel the same who have the privilege of beholding it. Composition, expression, colour—all combine to form an unity of the highest art, the highest beauty."[15]

In a later article he described it as "*the* masterpiece of Vermeer of Delft." The Boymans Museum in Rotterdam eventually acquired the painting for an astounding half million guilders. It was displayed there as one of the museum's finest treasures and drew the largest crowds the museum had known. Van Meegeren himself once visited there and was amused no end when a uniformed attendant sternly reprimanded him for leaning over a rope barrier to examine it. As a lark, he would argue with colleagues whether the picture was authentic. After all, he said, Vermeer's typical subjects are not biblical; there haven't been scientific tests; the composition looks undistinguished; and so on. Finally, he would magnanimously let them convince him that it was genuine.

Van Meegeren's original plan had been to expose the critics as ignorant, venal snobs. But his handsome profits from the sale dissuaded him. Instead he kept producing more forgeries: some more Vermeers, de Hooghs, and Halses. His execution became more slapdash, but he was never found out. He incurred perhaps the least suspicion with his subsequent Vermeers. Critics tended to authenticate them by comparing them to Vermeer's best-known work, the *Emmaus*. Not surprisingly, they found both pictures had been done by the same hand.

In the course of time, van Meegeren sold seven more forgeries, all of them for royal sums. He became a wealthy man, able to sustain a luxurious and dissolute life-style even in the most austere years of the Second World War. Perhaps his greatest, if unintended, coup came during the war. He had just created another Vermeer, *Christ and the Adulteress*. When van Meegeren's agent began showing the picture around, it came to the attention of Hermann Goering, who had been plundering masterpieces all over Europe. He offered to buy it in exchange for two hundred other (authentic) Dutch paintings. Van Meegeren didn't like dealing with Goering, but he didn't have much of a choice. The sale went through.

When, after the war, the allies ransacked Goering's possessions for stolen art, they were most surprised to come across yet another unknown Vermeer. They hardly suspected it could be a forgery; instead they were eager to find out what collaborator had passed the picture to the Nazis. Retracing the picture's provenance, they finally arrived at van Meegeren's doorstep. They asked him how he had obtained the painting. Van Meegeren was evasive; he gave them his usual obscure story about an Italian family wishing to remain anonymous. Just now that was not a good story to tell. It made the Dutch police even more suspicious. Had van Meegeren also had dealings with Italian fascists? They kept pressing him for the name of the Italian owner. Van Meegeren refused. They arrested and interrogated him for six weeks. Finally, he could stand it no longer. "Fools," he shouted at them, "you are fools like the rest of them! I sold no Vermeer to the Germans! I sold no treasure! I painted the picture myself! It is a valueless van Meegeren for which Goering paid this fortune. And for eight years I have deceived others—just as he was deceived."[16] And then he proudly told them about the *Emmaus* and all the other forgeries.

At first they wouldn't believe him, but he gave them proof. X-ray the *Adulteress,* he told them, and you will find an underpainting. They did and found the underpainting van Meegeren had described. Check my Nice villa, he said, and you will find a strip of canvas cut from the famous *Emmaus*. Again, they found he was right. And if you'd like, he said, taking up a suggestion the police had made perhaps half in jest, I'll produce a Vermeer forgery right before your eyes, which he began to do. "He paints for his life" one newspaper headline read. Eventually a commission was set up to investigate van Meegeren's claims. Many of its members were the very people who had praised the Vermeer fakes to the sky. They tested the crackle, dust, paint composition, underground, and with van Meegeren's solicitous help, finally concluded that they were indeed dealing with fakes. Van Meegeren was poorly rewarded for his help. The collaboration charges were dropped; but he was convicted of criminal fraud instead. It was unlikely, though, he would ever go to jail. Opinion polls showed him the second most popular man in Holland, second only to the prime minister. A pardon by the queen was soon arranged. Before the pardon reached him, however, his dissolute life-style finally took its toll. His reputation as the greatest forger of all time secure, he died.

7 Epilogue: Final Reckoning

Criminal law is important for its own sake, but not only. It is important not merely as the body of rules which determines whom we brand an outcast, whom we throw into the dungeon. It is important for much broader reasons.

Criminal law puts to the test the judgments of everyday life. Many a fondly treasured piety has had to be abandoned when a man's conviction was the price for continued adherence to it. Lip service to the absolute sanctity of human life is easy enough. But are we willing to pronounce guilty the spelunkers who kill one of their own to survive? Some may still be tempted to give a facile "yes." Of them we ask: How would you advise the trolley driver whose brakes have failed, if he has the choice between letting his car run over five workmen or veering it onto a side spur where it would kill only one pedestrian. Is it really better he let five die than kill even one?

More generally, criminal law puts to the test the *concepts* of everyday life. "Depend upon it, sir," said Dr. Johnson, "when a man knows he is to be hanged in a fortnight, it concentrates his mind wonderfully." The prospect of someone else's hanging can do the same. In other words, when a man's conviction hinges on the correct understanding of an everyday concept like intention or cause, we are liable to investigate it with special care. Herein really lies the broader significance of the criminal law. It makes us think hard about concepts and ideas to which we frequently give the back of the hand.

The concepts of everyday life aren't just the concepts of everyday life. They are the concepts on which the practitioners of many academic disciplines draw: the literary critic, the psychologist, the historian, the philosopher. What we learn about these concepts, as we think about a hard criminal case, has implications for everyone who uses them–including the critic, the psychologist, the historian, and the philosopher. The best way to demonstrate the broader significance of the criminal law is to trace out some of these implications.

Literature and the Meaning of Rules

The literary critic faces a perennial quandary. He is in the business of constructing elaborate and ingenious theories to explain the meaning of arcane works of art. But the suspicion continues to gnaw at him, or at least at his readers, is this really what the author had in mind? Sometimes a malicious author will simply pull the rug from under the critic by announcing point-blank: "Silly you, that's not at all what I meant. Such a thought never crossed my mind." And if he doesn't want to bite the hand that strokes him, he may say euphemistically: "How cleverly that critic penetrated into my unconscious. I never knew these meanings existed in my work." Does that prove the critic's work is illegitimate? Is the meaning of a work of art necessarily present in the author's mind?

Perhaps not. We faced a similar quandary in construing the meaning of a rule. Is the meaning of a rule necessarily what's in the minds of the persons who draft it? Not necessarily, I argued. I explored this quandary by examining an exotic piece of legislation called the Witchcraft Suppression Act, and a case decided under it, *Regina v. Puna*. Puna, you may recall, had been charged with calling someone a witch. To determine the meaning of the rule, as it applied to Puna, we looked far beyond the thoughts of the drafters. Puna, we decided, should not be acquitted simply because the legislature thought witchcraft consisted of sorcery or the throwing of bones. (We likened the drafter to the man who asks his wife to talk to the man in the corner wearing a Brooks Brothers suit, an Yves St. Laurent tie, and Gucci shoes, when in fact the suit is from Marshall Fields, the tie from Pierre Cardin, and the shoes from Florsheim. His order can be followed all the same.) What goes for legal rules may go for works of art: their meaning, too, may be only partially determined by what is in the artist's head. Not surprisingly, then, critics are able to discover meanings in a work of art that are news to their creator.

Chesterton already observed that it is possible for an "author to tell a truth without seeing it himself." "I was once talking to a highly intelligent lady about Thackeray's *Newcomes*," he recalled.

> We were speaking of the character of Mrs. Mackenzie, the Campaigner, and in the middle of the conversation

> the lady leaned across to me and said in a low, hoarse, but emphatic voice, "She drank. Thackeray didn't know it; but she drank." And it is really astonishing what a shaft of white light this sheds on the Campaigner, on her terrible temperament, on her agonised abusiveness and her almost more agonised urbanity, on her clamour which is nevertheless not open or explicable, on her temper which is not so much bad temper as insatiable, bloodthirsty, man-eating temper. How far can a writer thus indicate by accident a truth of which he is himself ignorant?[1]

Psychology and the Guilty Mind

We considered at length some bizarre cases, involving the killing of ghosts and witches, misfired bullets, and misidentified victims. The puzzling issue these cases raised was: Does the defendant who kills a "witch," a "ghost," an unlucky bystander, a misidentified passerby, *intentionally* kill his victim? We felt the pull of competing intuitions and kept wondering which of those intuitions was right. Ultimately, it turned out, we were misguided in our conviction that intention is always either present or absent. What someone intends hinges on what he believes. What he believes is a matter of degree. It depends on the extent to which his background beliefs resemble the beliefs of the prototype credited with such a belief, the extent to which what he is referring to resembles what the prototype believer is referring to, and the extent to which the causal-behavioral consequences of his belief resemble those of the prototype. If in describing those bizarre killings, we feel the pull of competing intuitions, it's because we can't decide whether the defendant "believed" he was killing his victim. He meets some of the criteria of belief ascription completely and others very poorly.

Notions like intention and belief are central to the psychologist's vocabulary. Our criminal cases suggest he should be wary of them. They may not be adequate to the task of sensibly stating the laws of human behavior. The imprecision of these notions is only part of the problem. It does mean, of course, that any psychological explanation that employs them automatically incorporates all of the imprecision they carry with them. The more serious part of the problem is this: Whether a certain person can be said to believe something depends on the extent to which he resembles a certain prototype of whom it might quite clearly be said that he has that belief. (Whether the killer can be said to have shot his victim intentionally depends on the extent to which he resembles the prototype who knows he is killing something human, is not mistaken about whom he is aiming at, and in fact succeeds in shooting that very person.) But for some people no such prototype exists, and any effort to describe them in language that presupposes such a prototype is doomed to sound either mysterious or silly.

In fact, we encountered several instances of this problem already. Remember the attribution experiments carried out with little children. The children were divided into two groups. Both groups were given some crayons to draw with, but one group was promised a reward if they actually used them. After the rewards had been distributed, the psychologists discovered that the group that had been given rewards was much less interested in playing with the crayons than its counterpart. The psychologists' explanation was that the rewarded group, in effect, believed that if an activity is rewarded, it can't be inherently enjoyable. In a way that explanation is plausible, but in a way it sounds absurd. It surely is impossible that any of those children articulated any such thought. Again, we feel the pull of competing intuitions: to say those children believed that what is rewarded isn't enjoyable both fits and doesn't fit. The reason for this imperfect fit is that the children evince the causal-behavioral consequences of such a belief but quite evidently lack the network of concepts and background beliefs that usually goes with it. In sum, the word "belief" isn't very good at capturing the important psychological phenomena illustrated by the experiment.

Another example: Recall the insomniacs who were given a placebo. Some were told the placebo would arouse them, others that it would relax them. It turned out, paradoxically, that the former were more likely to go to sleep than the latter. The psychologists' explanation was that the first category of patients thought, "I'm wide-awake, but I needn't worry about that; it's because of the pill." That made the patients stop worrying and allowed them to go to sleep. The latter category of patients believed, "I'm wide-awake despite the pill. I must really be upset." Their worrying intensified, and they couldn't get to sleep. Again, the explanation is plausible, but in a way it, too, is absurd. When the patients were interviewed, they denied ever entertaining such thoughts. Again, we feel the pull of conflicting intuitions. To say the patients had these beliefs both fits and doesn't fit. The patients manifested many of the causal-behavioral consequences of holding such a belief, but they had none of the background beliefs that usually go with it. The word "belief" just isn't very good at capturing what went on here.

The problem with words like "belief" is that they depend on our being able to liken the mental processes of the person being described to those of some "normal" prototype, a run-of-the-mill adult member of Western civilization. That makes it unsuitable for all branches of psychology investigating deviations from the norm, such as developmental psychology, which deals with children, clinical psychology, which is concerned with abnormal behavior, and comparative psychology, which is preoccupied with other cultures. In short, it makes it unsuitable for most of what psychologists are interested in.[2]

History and Causation

Problems of causation are as dear to the historian as to the lawyer. Think only of the number of historical works that are titled "The Causes of. . . ." But the historian tends to be much more sanguine and confident in his handling of these problems than the lawyer, unfortunately, without good reason. What our study of causation in the criminal law has taught us is that many causal claims, especially those of the historian, are very fragile. Let us examine a few of the more typical causal claims historians are apt to advance.

Historians are apt to say "Event X was important because without it Y would never have happened." Such a claim is difficult to substantiate, not just because we don't know all the facts. It would be difficult, even if we had all the facts we wished to have. It requires us to make a counterfactual judgment, to explore a make-believe world in which X didn't happen to find out whether Y nevertheless happened. Unfortunately, there is an infinite number of such make-believe worlds. In some Y happened, in some it didn't. The trick is to pick the make-believe world most similar to our own. But here there are many candidates too; there are no hard-and-fast, objective rules for deciding which is closest. The historian's claim that without X, Y would not have happened may not be so much more solid than the art critic's claim that something is a masterpiece.

Historians are apt to blame past generations for the travails of their own. That claim, too, proves more tenuous than first appears. What historians often overlook when they make such a claim is a fact on which we dwelt at some length: just because event X caused event Y doesn't mean that but for X, Y would not have happened. Watergate probably caused Gerald Ford to lose the 1976 election to Jimmy Carter. Yet we can't say: But for Watergate Ford would have won. Without Watergate, it is unlikely Ford would ever have been the Republican nominee in 1976. We can generalize the example. Suppose two hundred years from now a historian denounces our generation for having used up a disproportionate share of the earth's oil. Let us suppose that his generation is in fact experiencing a much lower standard of living than ours because it has to make do without oil. Undoubtedly we "caused" their misery. What the historian cannot say, however, is that if we hadn't binged on oil, he and his people would now be better off. Why not? Think about it for a moment. If we pursued a different energy policy, many things would be different. Innumerable lives would be affected. In particular, many persons would be married to different spouses. They would sire different children. In other words, the generation after us would contain many people who would not otherwise be around and lack many people who would. As these people mate with others, they will give birth to yet another generation, an even larger fraction of which would not have existed but for our different energy policy. And so on down the line. Two hundred years from now very few, if any, people will be alive who would have been alive without such a policy. The complaining historian would never have been born. He cannot say therefore that but for our energy policy he and his generation would experience a higher standard of living. He and his generation would not be living at all. To be sure, the historian's claim isn't downright false or meaningless. There are probably ways of construing his reproach that make it look valid. But the claim is much more delicate than first appears and requires a somewhat unconventional interpretation before it can stand up.[3]

Finally, historians are apt to distinguish emphatically between causes and conditions, between circumstances that cause a certain consequence and circumstance that are merely necessary to its occurrence. What they have in mind, it seems, is the historical counterpart to the lawyer's distinction between causes in fact and proximate causes. It is impossible, however, to articulate a set of principles that expresses the lawyer's distinction in a consistent and intuitively satisfying manner. The distinction is based on certain fundamentally incoherent intuitions. That makes one suspect that the historian's distinction is just as misguided. This may explain why many of the historical debates over causes, such as the celebrated one between Hugh Trevor-Roper and A. J. P. Taylor over the origins of World War II, have proved inconclusive.

Philosophy and the Unity of Criminal Law

Philosophy has been my most steadfast helpmate in analyzing the problems of the criminal law. But the relationship is far from one-sided. Criminal law gives a healthy workout to many facile assertions in the philosophy of language, of mind, and of morals. More important, it brings out the often unfathomable potency of certain philosophical ideas. The reader has probably sensed the seeming recurrence of certain modes of argument from chapter to chapter, often in seemingly unrelated contexts. What he was sensing is the underlying unity behind the diverse problems of criminal law, the common philosophical ancestry of superficially unrelated issues. Philosophy gets the chance to demonstrate its power by revealing the nature of that unity.

The manifold conundrums of the criminal law boil down to a much smaller number of philosophical conundrums. A large number of the criminal law problems I have considered are manifestations of but two philosophical problems dubbed by philosophers "the problem of intentionality" and "the problem of possible worlds." "Intentionality" stands for the peculiar property that bedevils certain sentences: the failure of substitutivity. (Cain wants to dine with Abel. Abel is a Russian spy. Yet Cain does not want to dine with a Russian spy.) "Possible worlds" stands for those make-believe constructs that underlie our counterfactual assertions—the worlds of the "what if." The "problem of intentionality" and the "problem of possible worlds" stand for that vast range of knotty questions associated with those two concepts.

Let's take intentionality first. If we were puzzled about the meaning of certain misdrafted rules, such as the Witchcraft Suppression Act, that was a manifestation of the problem of intentionality. The legislature meant to forbid witchcraft. Among the Shona, witchcraft refers to practices the legislature didn't know existed. So can we conclude the legislature meant to forbid those practices? It's not immediately clear—the failure of substitution at work again. If we were puzzled by those spectacular cases of mistake (involving ghosts and witches, misfired bullets, and misidentified victims), that too was a facet of the problem of intentionality. Without the intentionality of certain verbs like "intend," "believe," "think," or "know," mistakes would never matter in criminal law. If we were puzzled about whom to hold liable for aiding a crime, that again was a result of the intentionality of words like "aid" and "abet." We may know that the defendant aided X. We may know that X is a thief. But we aren't sure whether that means that the defendant aided a thief. Finally, if we are puzzled by attempts, that's a reflection of the intentionality of the word "attempt." The defendant attempts to export a Decameron. The Decameron is forged. Yet we can't conclude, X attempted to export a forged Decameron.

Many other questions that concerned us were manifestations of the problem of possible worlds. Our inability to always tell acts from omissions reflected the vagueness and ambiguity inherent in counterfactual assertions. Our dissatisfaction with one seemingly simple solution to the problem of ghost- and witch-killings—which required us to imagine a world in which the defendant's false beliefs are realized—was another consequence of that vagueness and ambiguity. Our difficulty distinguishing intention from knowledge was a further upshot. Our befuddlement with questions of factual causation—"what would have happened but for"—was yet another instance of it. Finally, our incapacity to formulate a theory of proximate causation—a set of principles to distinguish causes from conditions—resulted directly from the impossibility of making certain comparisons between the actual world and a hypothetical "possible world."

The law is often called a seamless web because everything here seems connected with everything else. What is remarkable is how few the threads are that compose the web.

Notes

1. Necessity, the Mother of Invention

1. This story is a slightly altered version of Lon Fuller's classic, "The Case of the Speluncean Explorers," *Harvard Law Review* 62 (1949): 616. I have changed the facts in minor ways either to throw into relief a problem suggested but not raised by the original version or to add dramatic color.
2. *The William Gray,* 29 Fed. Cas. 1300, 1302 (No. 17, 694) (Circuit Court, D. New York, 1810).
3. *State v. Jackson,* 53 A. 1020, 1023–24 (New Hamp., 1902).
4. *Woods v. State,* 121 S.W. 2d 604 (Ct. of Crim. App. of Tex., 1938).
5. Ibid. 605.
6. *United States v. Ashton,* 24 Fed. Cas. 873 (No. 14470) (Circuit Court, D. Mass., 1834).
7. Sanford H. Kadish and Monrad G. Paulsen, *Criminal Law and Its Processes,* 3d ed. (Boston: Little, Brown, & Co., 1975), 367.
8. Christian Morgenstern, *The Gallows Song,* trans. Max Knight (Berkeley: University of California Press, 1966), 93.
9. *United States v. Holmes,* 1 Wall Jr. 1, 226 Fed. Cas. 360 (No. 15, 383) (3d Cir., 1842). I have gleaned additional facts from Frederick C. Hicks, *Human Jettison* (St. Paul: West Publishing Co., 1927), and A. W. Brian Simpson, *Cannibalism and the Common Law* (Chicago: University of Chicago Press, 1984).
10. Hicks, *Human Jettison,* 31.
11. Ibid. 37.
12. Ibid. 42–43.
13. Ibid. 64.
14. Simpson, *Cannibalism,* 174.
15. Hicks, *Human Jettison,* 64–65.
16. Ibid. 66
17. Simpson, *Cannibalism,* 168.

18. Hicks, *Human Jettison,* 67.
19. Ibid.
20. Ibid. 69.
21. Simpson, *Cannibalism,* 170.
22. Hicks, *Human Jettison,* 102–3.
23. Ibid. 106–7.
24. Ibid. 107.
25. Ibid. 132.
26. Ibid. 134.
27. Ibid. 200.
28. Ibid. 229.
29. Ibid. 239.
30. Ibid. 243.
31. *The Queen v. Dudley and Stephens,* 14 Q.B.D. 273 (1884). I have gleaned additional facts from Donald McCormick, *Blood on the Sea* (London: Frederick Muller, 1962); Simpson, *Cannibalism*; and Simpson, "Cannibalism and the Common Law," *Law School Record* 27 (Fall 1981): 1.
32. McCormick, *Blood,* 64.
33. Ibid. 70–81, but cf. Simpson, *Cannibalism,* 70.
34. Simpson, "Cannibalism," 4.
35. McCormick, *Blood,* 81.
36. *The Queen v. Dudley and Stephens,* 14 Q.B.D. 279.
37. Ibid. 287.
38. Ibid.
39. Simpson, "Cannibalism," 10.
40. Fuller, "Speluncean Explorers," 619.
41. Ibid. 642.
42. Joel Feinberg, "The Expressive Function of Punishment," *Doing and Deserving* (Princeton: Princeton University Press, 1970), 95–118.
43. Ibid. 97.
44. Ibid. 98.
45. For a brief summary of facts, see Peter A. French, *Collective and Corporate Responsibility* (New York: Columbia University Press, 1984), 31.
46. "John Thomas Scopes," in Brandt Aymor and Edward Sagarin, *A Pictorial History of the World's Great Trials* (New York: Bonanza Books, 1984), 247–55, esp. 247.
47. Harper Lee, *To Kill a Mockingbird* (Philadelphia: Lippincott, 1960).
48. Feinberg, "Expressive Function," 102–3.
49. Quoted in H. L. A. Hart, "Punishment and the Elimination of Responsibility," *Punishment and Responsibility* (New York: Oxford University Press, 1968), 158–85, esp. 161.
50. Feinberg, "Expressive Function," 118.

51. Ibid. 106.
52. H. L. A. Hart, "Prolegomenon to the Principles of Punishment," *Punishment,* 1–27, esp. 13 n. 16.
53. Fred Harwell, *A True Deliverance* (New York: Alfred A. Knopf, 1980).
54. Based on *Courvoisier v. Raymond,* 47 P. 284 (Colo., 1896) and George P. Fletcher, *Rethinking Criminal Law* (Boston: Little, Brown, & Co., 1978), 763.
55. Fuller, "Speluncean Explorers," 620.
56. Ibid. 621.
57. Ibid. 626.
58. P. T. Geach, *Reason and Argument* (Berkeley and Los Angeles: University of California Press, 1976), 39–40.
59. Oberlandesgericht Bamberg, Süddeutsche Juristen-Zeitung 5 (1950): 207. An excellent recent discussion of the natural law controversy is found in Jeffrie G. Murphy and Jules L. Coleman, *The Philosophy of Law* (Totowa, N.J.: Rowman & Allanheld, 1984), 7–68, which also offers a good bibliography of the primary literature.
60. H. L. A. Hart, "Separation of Law and Morals," *Harvard Law Review* 71 (1958): 593, 619–20.
61. Benjamin Cardozo, *Law and Literature* (New York: Harcourt, Brace, & Co., 1931), 113.
62. Edmund Cahn, *The Moral Decision: Right and Wrong in the Light of American Law* (Bloomington: Indiana University Press, 1955), 71.
63. Anthony Kenny, *Freewill and Responsibility* (London: Routledge & Kegan Paul, 1978), 38.
64. Judith Jarvis Thompson, "The Trolley Problem," *Rights, Restitution, and Risk* (Cambridge, Mass.: Harvard University Press, 1986), 94–116.

You might object that even if Edward lets the trolley run he is *killing* five people, not just letting them die. After all he is the driver of the trolley. If you feel that way, suppose instead that Edward is just a passenger (the only passenger!) on the trolley. The trolley's brakes fail and the driver has a heart attack. Edward could do nothing, in which case five men die, or he could step in and turn the trolley, in which case one man dies. Most people think it's all right for him to turn the trolley.

65. Jonathan Glover, *Causing Death and Saving Lives* (Harmondsworth: Penguin, 1977), 102.
66. See Judith Jarvis Thompson, "Killing, Letting Die, and the Trolley Problem," *Rights, Restitution, and Risk,* 78–93, esp. 78.
67. Model Penal Code, Sec. 3.02 (1)(a).
68. This hypothetical, too, is from Thompson, "Trolley Problem."
69. For a detailed account of this case, see Herbert J. Stern, *Judgment in Berlin* (New York: Universe Books, 1984).

70. Ibid. 327.
71. Robert Nozick, *Philosophical Explanations* (Cambridge, Mass.: Belknap Press of Harvard University Press, 1981), 483–84.
72. *City of Chicago v. Mayer,* 308 N.E. 2d 601 (Ill., 1974).
73. McKinney's Consolidated Laws of New York Annotated, 39 Sec. 35.05. A more subjectivist reading of the statute is, however, possible. Arguably, something could be necessary now, even though in tomorrow's retrospect it turns out to have been superfluous. See also Model Penal Code, Sec. 3.02(2).
74. *Pange and Matini v. The Queen,* High Court of Southern Rhodesia, Bulawayo Criminal Session, 25 September 1961; Federal Supreme Court, Judgment 142/61 and 143/61, summarized in Emmett V. Mittlebeeler, *African Custom and Western Law* (New York: Africana Publishing Co., 1976), 175.
75. Ibid. 175–76.
76. Ibid. 176–77.
77. Cf. Alan Donagan, *The Theory of Morality* (Chicago: University of Chicago Press, 1977).
78. Jon Elster, *Ulysses and the Sirens,* rev. ed. (Cambridge: Cambridge University Press, 1984), 85–86.
79. *Butterfield v. Texas,* 317 S.W. 2d 943 (Ct. of Crim. App. of Tex., 1958).
80. *Sansom v. Texas,* 390 S.W. 2d 279 (Ct. of Crim. App. of Tex., 1965).
81. Ibid. 280.
82. Herman Wouk, *The Caine Mutiny,* 1st ed. (Garden City, N.Y.: Doubleday, 1951).
83. Mary Douglas and Aaron Wildavsky, *Risk and Culture* (Berkeley: University of California Press, 1982), 16–21.
84. Cf. Paul H. Robinson, "Causing the Conditions of One's Own Defense: A Study in the Limits of Theory in Criminal Law Theory," *Virginia Law Review* 71 (1985): 1. The case law and statutes, however, tend to follow a tack like the one outlined earlier in the section.
85. Glover, *Causing Death,* 182–202; Richard Sherlock, "For Everything There Is a Season: The Right to Die in the United States," *Brigham Young University Law Review,* 1982, 545; Glanville Williams, *The Sanctity of Life and the Criminal Law* (New York: Alfred A. Knopf, 1957), chap. 8.
86. *State v. Kroncke,* 459 F. 2d 697, 698 (8th Cir., 1972).
87. Ibid. 699–700.
88. *State v. Dorsey,* 395 A. 2d 855 (New Hamp., 1978).
89. Mortimer R. Kadish and Sanford H. Kadish, *Discretion to Disobey* (Stanford: Stanford University Press, 1973), 42.
90. Ibid. 45.
91. See Harry Kalven and Hans Zeisel, *The American Jury* (Boston: Little, Brown, & Co., 1966). For a survey of the literature since the Kalven and Zeisel

classic, see Valerie P. Hans and Neil Vidmar, *Judging the Jury* (New York: Plenum Press, 1986).

92. *United States v. Dougherty,* 473 F. 2d 1113 (D.C. Cir., 1972).
93. Ibid. 1134.
94. The preceding analysis of discretion, necessity, and the jury is based on Kadish and Kadish, *Discretion.*
95. Herbert Simon, *Administrative Behavior,* 3d ed. (New York: Free Press, 1976), 82.
96. Michael Polanyi, *Personal Knowledge* (Chicago: University of Chicago Press, 1962).
97. Oliver E. Williamson, *The Economic Institutions of Capitalism* (New York: Free Press, 1985); idem, *Markets and Hierarchies: Analysis and Antitrust Implications* (New York: Free Press, 1975).
98. Model Penal Code, Sec. 3.02(1)(c). The Model Penal Code also contains a related provision, Sec. 3.02(1)(b), requiring that "neither the Code nor other law defining the offense provides exceptions or defenses dealing with the specific situation involved."
99. The three allocation mechanisms and their principal virtues and vices and a wealth of examples (on which I draw freely) are set forth in Guido Calabresi and Phil Bobbit, *Tragic Choices* (New York: W. W. Norton & Co., 1978). I have expanded that discussion in a number of ways, most important, by bringing to bear the "control literature," the concept of common knowledge (through the puzzle of the forty logicians), and the efficient market hypothesis. A somewhat different approach to the question of choice mechanisms, focusing mostly on nontragic situations, is to be found in Michael Walzer, *Spheres of Justice* (New York: Basic Books, 1983). A Rawlsian approach to tragic choices is offered in Gerald R. Winslow, *Triage and Justice* (Berkeley: University of California Press, 1982).
100. David C. Glass, Bruce Reim, and Jerome E. Singer, "Behavioral Consequences of Adaptation to Controllable and Uncontrollable Noise," *Journal of Experimental Social Psychology* 7 (1971): 244–57.

    For a recent survey and bibliography, see Suzanne M. Miller, "Controllability and Human Stress: Method, Evidence and Theory," *Behavior Research and Therapy* 17 (1979): 287–304; Susan Menka and Robert Wittendersen, "Controllability and Predictability in Acquired Motivation," *Annual Review of Psychology* 36 (1985): 495–529.
101. Hans Eysenck and Michael Eysenck, *Mindwatching* (London: Michael Joseph, 1983), 127.
102. Ellen J. Langer, "The Illusion of Control," in Daniel Kahneman, Paul Slovic, and Amos Tversky, eds., *Judgment under Uncertainty: Heuristics and Biases* (Cambridge: Cambridge University Press, 1982), 231–38.

103. Shana Alexander, "They Decide Who Lives, Who Dies," *Life,* 9 Nov. 1962.
104. Ibid.
105. I learned this puzzle from Richard Kimmel in 1973.
106. Many illustrations of this kind of phenomenon are to be found in Erving Goffman, *The Presentation of Self in Everyday Life* (Woodstock, N.Y.: Overlook Press, 1975).
107. Kenneth Boulding, "The Population Trap," *The Meaning of the Twentieth Century* (New York: Harper & Row, 1964), 121–36, esp. 135–36.
108. Irving Wallace, David Wallechinsky, and Amy Wallace, "Significa," *Parade Magazine,* 23 Oct. 1983, p. 32. See also Calabresi and Bobbit, *Tragic Choices,* 159–60.
109. I learned this from Donald McCloskey in 1978.
110. For general introductions to the efficient market hypothesis, see Richard A. Brealey, *An Introduction to Risk and Return from Common Stock,* 2d ed. (Cambridge, Mass.: MIT Press, 1983), and Burton G. Malkiel, *A Random Walk Down Wall Street,* 4th ed. (New York: W. W. Norton, 1983).
111. Charles Fried, "The Value of Life," *Harvard Law Review* 82 (1969): 1415.
112. Willard Van Orman Quine, "On a Supposed Antinomy," *The Ways of Paradox* (New York: Random House, 1966), 21–23.
113. *Lynch v. Director of Public Prosecutions of Northern Ireland* [1975] 1 All ER 913.
114. Ibid. 656.
115. *United States v. Olsen,* 20 C.M.R. 461 (1955).
116. Ibid. 462.
117. Robert Cialdini, *Influence: The New Psychology of Persuasion* (New York: William Morrow, 1984), 76.
118. Ibid. 77.
119. *United States v. Olsen,* 20 C.M.R. 462.
120. Ibid.
121. *Lynch v. D.P.P.,* [1975] 1 All ER 917.
122. Model Penal Code, Sec. 2.09(1).
123. See George P. Fletcher, *Rethinking,* chap. 10. See also, Hart, "Prolegomenon"; Paul H. Robinson, *Criminal Law Defenses,* 2 vols. (St. Paul, Minn.: West Publishing Co., 1984), chap. 2.
124. The ambiguous character of mistakes is noted in Kent Greenawalt, "The Perplexing Borders of Justification and Excuse," *Columbia Law Review* 84 (1984): 1894, and Joshua Dressler, "New Thoughts about the Concept of Justification in the Criminal Law: A Critique of Fletcher's Thinking and Rethinking," *U.C.L.A. Law Review* 32 (1984): 61.
125. *Abbot v. The Queen,* [1976] 3 All ER 140 (Privy Council). See also V. S. Naipaul, "The Killings in Trinidad," *The Return of Eva Peron* (New York: Alfred A. Knopf, 1980).

126. *Abbot v. The Queen,* [1976] 3 All ER 141–42.

127. Some of the *Abbot* judges insisted there was a major difference between Abbot's direct and Lynch's indirect participation in the killing. But what, other judges countered, amounts to direct participation? Consider the old Canadian case *Rex v. Farduto,* (1912) 10 D.L.R. 669, in which a "big Italian named Pardillo" had asked the defendant for his razor in order to kill a man several paces away. Was *Farduto* a case of direct or indirect participation? Should the simple fact that Pardillo had asked Farduto to hand him a razor rather than hold the victim make the difference between Farduto's going free or ending up on the gallows? And what about the Australian case *Regina v. Brown,* [1968] SASR 467? Brown was a guest in Mrs. Legget's boardinghouse. Morley, another tenant, intended to kill her and abscond with her possessions. Brown and Morley became casual acquaintances, and Morley told Brown of his plan to kill the landlady. Brown at one point tried to call the police, but Morley's threats stopped him. Morley then asked Brown, whose room was adjacent to Mrs. Legget's, to emit a loud cough so as to cover up Morley's footsteps when he approached her room. He threatened to kill Brown's family otherwise. Brown did as he was told. Is this a case of direct or indirect participation? And why does the classification really matter? As one of the judges observed: "The difficulty about adopting a distinction between [direct] and [indirect participation] as a rule of law is that the contribution of the [indirect participant] to the death may be no less significant than that of the [direct participant]." *Abbot v. The Queen,* [1976] 3 All ER 149.

128. *Abbot v. The Queen,* [1976] 3 All ER 146.

129. Anthony Kenny, "Duress *Per Minas* as a Defense to Crime," *The Ivory Tower* (London: Basil Blackwell, 1985), 31–38, 37–38.

130. The point is made, for instance, in Kadish and Paulsen, *Criminal Law,* 570–71, and Hyman Gross, *A Theory of Criminal Law* (New York: Oxford University Press, 1979), 290.

131. The Model Penal Code commentators offer this somewhat cryptic explanation. In case of a human threat "the basic interests of the law may be satisfied by prosecution of the agent of unlawful force." In the case of a natural event "if the actor is excused, no one is subject to the law's application." *Model Penal Code and Commentaries* (Philadelphia: American Law Institute, 1985), Sec. 2.09, 279.

132. Arie W. Kruglanski and Yoel Yinon, "Evaluating an Immoral Act under Threat versus Temptation: An Illustration of the Achievement Principle in Moral Judgment," *Journal of Moral Education* 3 (1974): 167–75.

133. On this question, see generally J. Roland Pennock and John W. Chapman, eds., *Coercion* (Chicago: Aldine-Atherton, 1972).

134. The commentators of the Model Penal Code have pointed out that their version of the duress defense can, skillfully applied, probably accom-

modate at least some cases of brainwashing, although many other statutes can't even do that.

135. Stanley Milgram, *Obedience to Authority* (New York: Harper & Row, 1974).

136. W. F. Dukes and W. Bevan, "Accentuation and Response Variability in the Perception of Personally Revelant Objects," *Journal of Personality* 20 (1952): 457–65.

137. Anthony N. Doob and Alan E. Gross, "Status of Frustrator as an Inhibitor of Horn-Honking Responses," *Journal of Social Psychology* 76 (1968): 213–18.

138. Cialdini, *Influence,* 213–14.

139. Solomon E. Asch, "Effects of Group Pressure upon Modification and Distortion of Judgments," in Dorwin Cartwright and Alvin Zander, eds., *Group Dynamics: Research and Theory* (Evanston, Ill.: Row, Peterson, & Co., 1953), 151–62.

140. Kalven and Zeisel, *American Jury,* 488.

141. Elizabeth Noelle-Neumann, *The Spiral of Silence* (Chicago: University of Chicago Press, 1984), 1–8.

142. Cialdini, *Influence,* 142–50; David P. Phillips, "Airplane Accidents, Murder, and the Mass Media: Towards a Theory of Imitation and Suggestion," *Social Forces* 58 (1980): 1001–24.

143. Charles Mackay, *Extraordinary Popular Delusions and the Madness of Crowds* (1841; New York: Harmony Books, 1980), xix–xx.

144. Jonathan L. Freedman and Scott C. Fraser, "Compliance with Pressure: The Foot-in-the-Door Technique," *Journal of Personality and Social Psychology* 4, no. 2 (1966): 195–202.

145. Cialdini, *Influence,* 80–81.

146. On the paradox of the heaps, see Max Black, "Reasoning with Loose Concepts," *Margins of Precision* (Ithaca: Cornell University Press, 1970), 1–13; Michael Dummett, "Wang's Paradox," *Truth and Other Enigmas,* (Cambridge, Mass.: Harvard University Press, 1978), 248–68; Derek Parfit, *Reasons and Persons* (Oxford: Clarendon Press, 1984), chap. 3; Hilary Putnam, "Vagueness and Alternative Logic," *Realism and Reason* (Cambridge: Cambridge University Press, 1983), 271–86.

147. Black, *Margins,* 1.

148. Martin Shubik, *Game Theory in the Social Sciences* (Cambridge, Mass.: MIT Press, 1982), 291.

149. Howard Raiffa, *The Art and Science of Negotiation* (Cambridge, Mass.: Belknap Press of Harvard University Press, 1982), 85–86.

150. Malkiel, *A Random Walk,* 348.

151. Edgar H. Schein, "The Chinese Indoctrination Program for Prisoners of War," *Psychiatry* 19 (1956): 149–72.

152. Ibid. 153.

153. Cialdini, *Influence,* 77.
154. Schein, "Chinese Indoctrination," 158.
155. Cialdini, *Influence,* 96–106.
156. For an exhaustive, encyclopedic overview of all defenses, see Robinson, *Defenses.* For a psychological study of rationalizations that mask as excuses, see C. R. Snyder, Raymond L. Higgins, and Rita J. Stucky, *Excuses* (New York: John Wiley & Sons, 1983).

2. Bad Acts

1. R. Howman, "Witchcraft and the Law," *Nada* 25 (1948): 7.
2. Ibid.
3. Reprinted in J. R. Crawford, *Witchcraft and Sorcery in Rhodesia* (London: Oxford University Press, 1967), 297.
4. Emmet V. Mittlebeeler, *African Custom and Western Law* (New York: Africana Publishing Co., 1976), 135–62.
5. See Hilary Putnam, "The Meaning of Meaning," *Mind, Language, and Reality* (Cambridge: Cambridge University Press, 1975), 215–71, esp. 215–22.
6. This is based on the argument advocates of the so-called theory of direct reference have made against their predecessors. The arguments are neatly summarized in Nathan Salmon, *Reference and Essence* (Princeton: Princeton University Press, 1981), 23–31, 59–61. The arguments Salmon is summarizing originate with Saul A. Kripke, *Naming and Necessity* (Cambridge, Mass.: Harvard University Press, 1980), and Putnam, "Meaning." For a critical discussion of these arguments, see also Leonard Linsky, *Names and Descriptions* (Chicago: University of Chicago Press, 1977). Michael S. Moore has built an entire theory of statutory interpretation around these ideas. See Moore, "A Natural Law Theory of Interpretation," *Southern California Law Review* 58 (1985): 279.
7. Hilary Putnam, "Explanation and Reference," *Mind, Language, and Reality,* 196–214.
8. See Keith Donellan, "Reference and Definite Descriptions," *Philosophical Review* 75 (1966): 281–304.
9. The causal theory of reference is discussed in the sources cited in note 6.
10. Jesse Dukeminier and Stanley M. Johanson, *Family Wealth Transactions,* 2d ed. (Boston: Little, Brown, & Co., 1978), 357–70.
11. *Roth v. United States,* 354 U.S. 476, 489 (1957).
12. *Mishkin v. New York,* 383 U.S. 502 (1966).
13. Mittlebeeler, *African Custom,* 157–58.
14. Ibid. 158.
15. Howman, "Witchcraft."
16. Ludwig Wittgenstein, *Philosophical Investigations,* 3d ed., trans. G. E. M. Anscombe (New York: Macmillan Publishing Co., 1958), 31–32.

17. Wayne R. LaFave and Austin W. Scott, *Criminal Law* (St. Paul: West Publishing Co., 1972), 622, 644, 655.
18. *Commonwealth v. O'Malley,* 97 Mass. 584–85 (1867).
19. LaFave and Scott, *Criminal Law,* 677.
20. Grant Gilmore, *The Ages of American Law* (New Haven: Yale University Press, 1977), 95–96.
21. Securities Act of 1933, Sec. 11(b).
22. Ibid., Rule 176.
23. Uniform Commercial Code, Sec. 102(19).
24. Federal Rules of Evidence, Rule 401.
25. Securities Act of 1933, Sec. 2.
26. Uniform Commercial Code, Sec. 102.
27. Saul A. Kripke, *Wittgenstein on Rules and Private Language* (Cambridge, Mass.: Harvard University Press, 1982), 8–9; quoting Kripke.
28. A fiery attack on this view is to be found in G. P. Baker and P. M. S. Hacker, *Scepticism, Rules, and Language* (Oxford: Basil Blackwell, 1984). A more moderate challenge is to be found in Simon Blackburn, *Spreading the Word* (Oxford: Clarendon Press—Oxford University Press, 1984), 39–107.
29. Hans Juergen Eysenck, *Sense and Nonsense in Psychology* (Harmondsworth: Penguin Books, 1957), 201.
30. The cases have, in fact, "rewritten" the statutory duress definition to avoid this mishap. For a description of this phenomenon, see Comment, "Implied Fortitude: California's Defense of Duress," *Pepperdine Law Review* 6 (1978): 171.
31. See Myles Brand, *Intending and Acting* (Cambridge, Mass.: MIT Press, 1984), 51–83. For further background in this area, see also Alvin I. Goldman, *A Theory of Action* (Princeton: Princeton University Press, 1970), Donald Davidson, *Essays on Actions and Events* (Oxford: Clarendon Press, 1980), Michael S. Moore, *Law and Psychiatry: Rethinking the Relationship* (New York: Cambridge University Press, 1984), Irving Thalberg, *Enigmas of Agency* (New York: Humanities Press, 1972), idem, *Perception, Emotion, and Action* (New Haven: Yale University Press, 1977).
32. Jorge Luis Borges, "Pierre Menard, Author of Don Quixote," *Ficciones* (New York: Grove Press, 1962), 45–55. See also, Arthur C. Danto, *The Transfiguration of the Commonplace* (Cambridge, Mass.: Harvard University Press, 1981).
33. Peter T. Geach, *Reference and Generality: An Examination of Some Medieval and Modern Theories,* 3d ed. (Ithaca: Cornell University Press, 1980), 215–18.
34. *Blockburger v. United States,* 284 U.S. 299 (1932).
35. Ibid. 300 n. 2.

36. Ibid. 304.
37. *Sudan Government v. Fatma Hussein El Bakheit* (1966) S.L.J.R. 75, in Krishna Vasdev, *The Law of Homicide in the Sudan* (London: Butterworths, 1978), 20–21.
38. Bernard Williams, "The Self and the Future," in Jonathan Glover, ed., *The Philosophy of Mind* (Oxford: Oxford University Press, 1976), 126–41, esp. 128–29.
39. These experiments are recounted in Thomas Nagel, "Brain Bisection and the Unity of Consciousness," in Glover, *Mind,* 111–25; Julian Jaynes, *The Origin of Consciousness in the Breakdown of the Bicameral Mind* (Boston: Houghton Mifflin, 1976), 100–125; Hans Eysenck and Michael Eysenck, *Mindwatching* (London: Michael Joseph, 1983), 111–19; Charles E. Marks, *Commissurotomy, Consciousness, and Unity of Mind* (Cambridge, Mass.: MIT Press, 1981). The last also contains an extensive bibliography of the primary sources.
40. This argument is developed in Nagel, "Brain Bisection."
41. John Locke, *An Essay concerning Human Understanding,* bk 2, chap. 27, Secs. 10, 19, 20.
42. Thomas Reid, *Essays on the Intellectual Powers of Man* (Cambridge, Mass.: MIT Press, 1969), 357–58. He lived from 1710 to 1796, whereas Locke lived from 1632 to 1704.
43. William James, *The Principles of Psychology* (Cambridge, Mass.: Harvard University Press, 1981), 359–63.
44. James Hilton, *Random Harvest* (Boston: Little, Brown, & Co., 1942).
45. Robert E. Conot, *Justice at Nuremberg* (New York: Harper & Row, 1983), 44–49.
46. The argument, originally Bernard Williams's, is presented in Derek Parfit, *Reasons and Persons* (Oxford: Oxford University Press, 1984), 229–30.
47. Cf. Parfit, *Reasons,* 199–347.
48. Endel Tulving, *Elements of Episodic Memory* (Oxford: Clarendon Press, 1983).
49. Cf. Parfit, *Reasons,* 324.
50. Ludwig Wittgenstein, quoted in Godfrey Vesey, *Personal Identity* (Ithaca, N.Y.: Cornell University Press, 1977), 104–5.
51. "Amnesia as Affecting Capacity to Commit Crime or Stand Trial," 46 A.L.R. 3d 544 (1973).
52. *R. v. Luka Matengula* 5 L.R.N.R. 148 (1952).
53. *Fain v. Commonwealth,* 78 Ky. 183, 183–91 (1879).
54. Norval Morris, "Ghosts, Spiders, and North Korea" (1951), quoted in Alexander D. Brooks, *Law, Psychiatry, and the Mental Health System* (Boston: Little, Brown, & Co., 1974), 233–34.
55. *People v. Newton,* 87 Cal. Rptr. 394 (Ct. of App., 1970).
56. Ibid. 402–3. The facts as I present them are, of course, just the testimony of a witness. Newton's account differs.

57. John Kaplan and Jon R. Waltz, *The Trial of Jack Ruby* (New York: Macmillan, 1965), 3, 135, 150.
58. Thalberg, "Can We Hold People Strictly Liable for Their Deeds?" in Thalberg, *Enigmas,* 171–85, esp. 176.
59. Michael Polanyi, "The Logic of Tacit Inference," *Knowing and Being* (Chicago: University of Chicago Press, 1969), 138–58.
60. J. Greenspoon, "The Reinforcing Effect of Two Spoken Sounds on the Frequency of Two Responses," *American Journal of Psychology* 68 (1955): 409–24.
61. W. Lambert Gardiner, *Psychology: A Story of a Search* (Belmont, Calif.: Brooks/Cole, 1970), 76.
62. B. F. Skinner, *A Matter of Consequences* (New York: Alfred A. Knopf, 1983), 150–51.
63. Norman P. F. Maier, "Reasoning in Humans, II: The Solution of a Problem and Its Appearance in Consciousness," *Journal of Comparative Psychology* 12 (1931): 181.
64. Jaynes, *Origins of Consciousness.*
65. Paul M. Churchland, *Matter and Consciousness* (Cambridge, Mass.: MIT Press, 1984), 73–81; Phillip N. Laird-Johnson, *Mental Models* (Cambridge, Mass.: Harvard University Press, 1983), 396–477.
66. Churchland, *Matter,* 143.
67. Ibid. 77.
68. Raymond Smullyan, *The Lady or the Tiger* (New York: Alfred A. Knopf, 1982), 29–31.
69. *Martin v. State,* 17 So. 2d 427 (Ct. of App. of Ala., 1944).
70. Norval Morris, "An Australian Letter," [1955] *Criminal Law Review* 290, 295.
71. D. Lanham, "Larsonneur Revisited," [1976] *Criminal Law Review* 276 (summarizing view of Rupert Cross).
72. *Robinson v. California,* 370 U.S. 660, 666 (1962).
73. *Powell v. Texas,* 392 U.S. 514, 517 (1968).
74. Ibid. 548–50.
75. H. L. A. Hart, "Acts of Will and Responsibility," *Punishment,* 90–112, esp. 101–2.
76. Hans Welzel, *Das deutsche Strafrecht,* 10th ed. (Berlin: Walter De Gruyter, 1967), 30–39, 124–25.
77. Joel Feinberg, "Action and Responsibility," *Doing and Deserving* (Princeton, N.J.: Princeton University Press, 1970), 119–51, esp. 134.

I advisedly say that it is only *generally speaking* true that the bringing about of any consequences by an act I perform is also an act. It isn't always true. One consequence of my act of going to vacation in Europe is that I am not saving lives in Africa. But my failure to save lives is not an act—it's an omission. Why is that? A later section of this chapter, Crimes of Omission, seeks to answer that question.

78. Donald Davidson, "Agency," *Essays on Actions and Events* (New York: Oxford University Press, 1980), 43–61.

The parenthetical qualification about farfetched or remote redescriptions is important. Since one consequence of my going to vacation in Europe is that I am not saving lives in Africa, my vacationing in Europe could, arguably, be "redescribed" as failing to save lives in Africa. But failing to save lives in Africa isn't an act. It's an omission. The redescription here is too farfetched and remote. If "farfetched and remote" sounds too vague, Crimes of Omission will make it concrete.

79. John Searle, *Intentionality* (New York: Cambridge University Press, 1983), 79–111.

80. I am overstating things a little when I refer to what I am offering as a definition. It is really only a set of conditions distinguishing acts from happenings. The definition of an act cannot be said to be reasonably complete until I have done what I do in the rest of the chapter: distinguish acts from omissions and distinguish punishing acts from punishing thoughts.

81. Paul J. Reiter, *Antisocial or Criminal Acts and Hypnosis: A Case Study* (Copenhagen: Ejnar Munksgaard, 1958), 55–56.

82. Ibid. 60–62.

83. Ibid., passim.

84. Robert Nozick, *Philosophical Explanations* (Cambridge, Mass.: Harvard University Press, 1981), 48–49.

85. Model Penal Code, Sec. 2.01.

86. Abraham M. Rosenthal, *Thirty-eight Witnesses* (New York: McGraw-Hill, 1964), 33, 36, 53–54.

87. Glazebrook, "Criminal Omissions: The Duty Requirement in Offenses against the Person," *Law Quarterly Review* 76 (1960): 386, 388–89.

88. *Self's Case,* 1 East P.C. 226.

89. Glazebrook, "Criminal Omissions," 390, quoting a contemporary commentator stating the position of the courts in these matters. The quote is *not* from the judicial opinion.

90. T. Macauley, *Notes on the Indian Penal Code,* quoted in Jonathan Glover, *Causing Death and Saving Lives* (Harmondsworth: Penguin, 1977), 107.

91. *People v. Beardsley,* 113 N.W. 1128–29, 1131 (Mich., 1907).

92. LaFave and Scott, *Criminal Law,* 185.

93. *Anderson v. State,* 11 S.W. 33 (Ct. of App. of Tex., 1889).

94. *King v. Commonwealth,* 148 S.W. 2d 1044 (Ct. of App. of Ky., 1941).

95. *Immigration and Naturalization Service v. Chadha,* 462 U.S. 919 (1983).

96. Jonathan Bennet, "Whatever the Consequences," *Analysis* 26, no. 3 (1965): 83.

97. P. J. Fitzgerald, "Acting and Refraining," *Analysis* 27, no. 3 (1967): 133.

98. D. Diniello, "On Killing and Letting Die," *Analysis* 31, no. 3 (1971): 84–85.

99. Nicholas Rescher, *Hypothetical Reasoning* (Amsterdam: North-Holland Publishing Co., 1964).

100. Wallace M. Rudolph, "The Duty to Act: A Proposed Rule," in J. M. Ratcliffe, ed., *The Good Samaritan and the Law* (Gloucester, Mass.: Peter Smith, 1966), 243–78, esp. 243–44.
101. Richard A. Posner, *Economic Analysis of Law,* 3d ed. (Boston: Little, Brown, & Co., 1986), 174.
102. Douglas N. Walton, *On Defining Death: An Analytic Study of the Concept of Death in Philosophy and Medical Ethics* (Montreal: McGill-Queen's University Press, 1979).
103. Cf. Joel Feinberg, *Harm to Others* (Oxford: Oxford University Press, 1984), 165–71.
104. B. Darley and J. M. Latane, *The Unresponsive Bystander: Why Doesn't He Help?* (New York: Appleton-Century-Crofts, 1970), 1–2.
105. Ibid. 7–17.
106. Ibid. 4.
107. Ibid. 46.
108. Ibid. 57–58.
109. Ibid. 42.
110. Ibid. 95–96.
111. Ibid. 90.
112. D. A. Collard, *Altruism and Economy: A Study in Unselfish Economics* (New York: Oxford University Press, 1978); Richard M. Titmuss, *The Gift Relationship* (London: Allen & Unwin, 1970).
113. Paul A. Samuelson, "Diagrammatic Exposition of a Theory of Public Expenditure," in William Breit and Harold M. Hochman, eds., *Readings in Microeconomics* (Hinsdale, Ill.: Dryden Press, 1971), 538–46.
114. Sherwin Rosen, "The Economics of Superstars," *American Economic Review* 71 (1981): 845.
115. Gary Becker, "Altruism, Egoism, and Genetic Fitness: Economics and Sociobiology," *The Economic Approach to Human Behavior* (Chicago: University of Chicago Press, 1976), 282.
116. Blackstone, quoted in Sanford H. Kadish and Monrad G. Paulsen, *Criminal Law and Its Processes,* 3d ed. (Boston: Little, Brown, & Co., 1975), 81.
117. James Fitzgerald Stephen, *History of the Criminal Law of England* (London: Macmillan & Co., 1883), 78.
118. Gerald Dworkin and G. Blumenfeld, "Punishment for Intentions," *Mind* 75 (1966): 396–401.
119. Herbert Morris, "Punishment for Thoughts," *On Guilt and Innocence* (Berkeley: University of California Press, 1976), 1–30, esp. 22–23.
120. *Olubu v. The State,* 1980 (1) NCR 309.
121. *Sorrells v. United States,* 287 U.S. 435, 440–41 (1932).
122. Ibid. 441, 451. Emphatically quoted in *United States v. Sherman,* 356 U.S. 369, 372 (1958).

123. *United States v. Sherman,* 356 U.S. 372.
124. *United States v. Myers,* 527 F. Supp. 1206, 1210 (E.D. N.Y., 1981). See Comment, "Abscam, the Judiciary, and the Ethics of Entrapment," *Yale Law Journal* 91 (1982): 1565.
125. "Abscam," 1574.
126. *United States v. Kelly,* 539 F. Supp. 363, 370 (D.C. D.C., 1982).
127. *Sorrells v. United States,* 287 U.S. 448.
128. *Topolewski v. State,* 109 N.W. 1037 (Wis., 1906).
129. Ibid. 1040.
130. See *Edmondson v. State,* 89 S.E. 189 (Ct. of App. of Ga., 1916); *People v. Rollino,* 233 N.Y.S. 2d 580 (S.Ct., 1962).
131. Gwynn Nettler, *Lying, Cheating, Stealing* (Cincinnati, Ohio: Anderson Publishing Co., 1982), 21.
132. John L. Austin, *How to Do Things with Words* (Cambridge, Mass.: Harvard University Press, 1962).
133. Searle, *Intentionality,* 7.

3. Guilty Minds

1. *Sudan Government v. Ngok Keir* (1953) AC CP 108 53; KDN Maj. Ct. 28 53, unrep., in Krishna Vasdev, *The Law of Homicide in the Sudan* (London: Butterworths, 1978), 130–31. The defendant was in fact convicted of "culpable homicide not amounting to murder," i.e., manslaughter.
2. *Sudan Government v. Mohamed Ahmed Mohamed Mohamedein* (1948) AC CP 17 48; DP Maj. Ct. 41 .C 3 48, unrep., ibid. 134–35.
3. *Sudan Government v. Abdel Rahman Yacoub Daw El Bet* (1951) AC CP 165 51; DP Maj. Ct. 41 .C 27 51, unrep., ibid. 135.
4. *Sudan Government v. Mirghani El Tahir* (1955) AC CP 271 55; KDN Maj. Ct. 39 55, unrep., ibid. 136.
5. *Sudan Government v. Abdullah Mukhtar Nur* (1959) SLJR 1, ibid. 137.
6. *Sudan Government v. Kilo Buti and another* (1928) AC CP 224 28; NP Maj. Ct. 41 .C 14 28, unrep., ibid. 144–45.
7. *Sudan Government v. Ngerabaya* (1936) AC CP 253 36, unrep., ibid. 147–48.
8. *Sudan Government v. Tia Muni* (1939) AC CP 95 39; KDN Maj. Ct. 30 39, unrep., ibid. 148.
9. *The Queen v. Saunders and Archer,* 2 Plowd. 474a, 75 Eng. Reprt. 706, 1 Hale, P.C. 466 (1576).
10. Ibid. 474a.
11. *Bratton v. Tennessee,* 10 Humph. (Tenn.) 103, 108 (1849).
12. *Fall Rose-Rosahl* (1858). See *Goltdammer Archive* 7 at 332.
13. Glanville Williams, "Homicide and the Supernatural," *Law Quarterly Review* 65 (1949): 496–97.

14. See, e.g., Leonard Linsky, *Oblique Contexts* (Chicago: University of Chicago Press, 1983), chap. 5.
15. Stephen P. Stich, *From Folk Psychology to Cognitive Science: The Case against Belief* (Cambridge, Mass.: MIT Press, 1983), 98.
16. See Nicholas Rescher, *Hypothetical Reasoning* (Amsterdam: North-Holland Publishing Co., 1964).
17. Gottlob Frege, "On Sense and Meaning," in A. P. Martinich, ed., *The Philosophy of Language* (New York: Oxford University Press, 1985), 200–212. See also Leonard Linsky, *Referring* (London: Routledge & Keagan Paul, 1967), and Simon Blackburn, *Spreading the Word* (New York: Clarendon Press—Oxford University Press, 1984), 328–33.
18. Jon Barwise and John Perry, *Situations and Attitudes* (Cambridge, Mass.: MIT Press, 1983), 263–64.
19. See Stich, *Folk Psychology,* 57–58.
20. Ibid. 60–63.
21. Ibid. 66–72.
22. *Raffles v. Wichelhaus,* 2 Hurl. & C. 906, 159 Eng. Rep. 375 (Ex., 1864).
23. *Geremia v. Boyarsky,* 140 A. 749, 749 (S.Ct. of Errors of Conn., 1928).
24. Hans-Heinrich Jeschek, *Lehrbuch des Strafrechts* (Berlin: Duncker & Humblot, 1978), 249; Wayne R. LaFave and Austin W. Scott, *Criminal Law* (St. Paul, Minn.: West Publishing Co., 1972), 243. A detailed exposition of this and related problems in German law is found in Thomas Hillenkamp, *Die Bedeutung von Vorsatzkonkretisierungen bei abweichendem Tatverlauf* (Göttingen: O. Schwartz, 1971). Even in German law the defendant might, of course, be found liable for attempted murder or negligent homicide.
25. An actual case with a faintly similar fact pattern is *People v. Antick,* 539 P. 2d 43 (Cal. 1975).
26. Model Penal Code, Sec. 2.02.
27. *D.P.P. v. Smith* [1961] A.C. 290.
28. Cf. H. L. A. Hart, "Intention and Punishment," *Punishment and Responsibility* (New York: Oxford University Press, 1968), 113–35, esp. 122–25.
29. The question whether the defendant would have done the same thing if he didn't think event X tied to goal Y is even more ambiguous than the text lets on. Even if we know precisely what the defendant would have done if he didn't think X tied to Y, we may be unsure whether to call what he is doing under such changed circumstances the "same thing." Suppose the doctor doesn't think removing the womb of a cancerous woman will kill the fetus. If he removes the womb, thinking this, can we coherently say that in some sense he is doing the "same thing" as if he had removed the womb thinking this would kill the fetus? Isn't that like asking: If

Socrates had been of average intelligence, would he have lived the same kind of life? Is Socrates with average intelligence still Socrates? This problem of transworld identity is nicely captured in an old tale: Ivan asks, "Is it true that Popov won a million rubles in the lottery?" And Dmitri answers, "Generally speaking, yes. Except it wasn't a million, only a thousand. It wasn't the lottery, just a poker game. It wasn't Popov, but Pavlov. And he didn't win it, he lost it."

30. R. J. Butler, "Report on Analysis Problem No. 16," *Analysis* 38 (June 1978): 113–14.
31. E. J. Lowe, "Peacocke and Kraemer on Butler's Problem," *Analysis* 40 (June 1980): 113–18.
32. Butler, "Report," 113.
33. E. J. Lowe, "Neither Intentional nor Unintentional," *Analysis* 38 (1978): 117.
34. K. Davies, "Killing People Intentionally, by Chance," *Analysis* 41 (June 1981): 156–59.
35. See also Christopher Peacocke, *Holistic Explanations* (Oxford: Oxford University Press, 1979), 74.
36. D. Ross, "He Loads the Gun, Not the Dice," *Analysis* 38 (1978): 114–15.
37. B. Medawar, *Advice to a Young Scientist* (New York: Harper & Row, 1979), 9.
38. Amos Tversky and Daniel Kahneman, "The Framing of Decisions and the Psychology of Choice," *Science* 211 (30 Jan. 1981): 453.
39. Kahneman and Tversky, "Prospect Theory: An Analysis of Decisions under Risk," *Econometrica* 47 (March 1979): 263–91.
40. Tversky and Kahneman, "The Framing of Decisions," 455–57.
41. Ibid. 454.
42. Robin Hogarth, *Judgment and Choice* (New York: John Wiley & Sons, 1980), 70–71.
43. A. Tversky and D. Kahneman, "Judgments of and by Representativeness," in D. Kahneman, P. Slovic, and A. Tversky, eds., *Judgment under Uncertainty* (Cambridge: Cambridge University Press, 1982), 84–98, esp. 92–93.
44. Tversky and Kahneman, "Judgment under Uncertainty: Heuristics and Biases," ibid. 3–20, esp. 4, 10, 11.
45. Michael Ross and Fiore Sicoly, "Egocentric Biases and Attribution," ibid. 179–89.
46. Tversky and Kahneman, "Causal Schemas in Judgments under Uncertainty," ibid. 117–28.
47. "Judgment under Uncertainty," ibid. 14–15.
48. Langer, "Illusion of Control," ibid. 231–38, esp. 231–32.
49. Theodore Dreiser, *An American Tragedy* (New York: New American Library, 1981), 471–72, 491–93.

50. I put aside the question whether it was murder for him not to save Roberta. Assuming he owed her such a duty, even though she was not his wife, the question boils down to a factual one: Could he have saved her had he tried?
51. John Searle, *Intentionality* (New York: Cambridge University Press, 1983), 82.
52. Russell, quoted in Wayne R. LaFave and Austin W. Scott, Jr., *Handbook on Criminal Law* (St. Paul, Minn.: West Publishing Co., 1972), 239.
53. Searle, *Intentionality,* 84–85.
54. LaFave and Scott, *Criminal Law,* 692.
55. *People v. Claborn,* 36 Cal. Rptr. 132 (Ct. of App., 1964).
56. *Regina v. Church* [1965] 2 W.L.R. 1220.
57. See, e.g., LaFave and Scott, *Criminal Law,* 241–42.
58. Alex de Jonge, *The Life and Times of Grigorii Rasputin* (New York: Coward, McCann, & Geoghegan, 1982), 332. There is some dispute about the facts.
59. Searle, *Intentionality,* 83.
60. Ibid. 136.
61. Peacocke, *Holistic Explanations,* 56–57.

4. The Root of All Evil

1. Based on J. A. McLaughlin, "Proximate Cause," *Harvard Law Review* 39 (1925–26): 149, 155, n. 25, and Martin Bunzl, "Causal Overdetermination," *Journal of Philosophy* 76 (1979): 134–50.
2. BGH St (Entscheidungen des Bundesgerichtshof in Strafsachen) 2 (1951), 20.
3. *Bush v. The Commonwealth,* 78 Ky. 268 (1880).
4. *Regina v. Dowdle and others,* 26 V.L.R. 637 (1900); under the name *Regina v. O'Shannessy,* 7 Arg. L.R. 10.
5. *Nyuzi and Kudemera v. Republic* (1966–68) African Law Reports 249.
6. See Egon Erwin Kisch, "Wie ich erfuhr dass Redl ein Spion war," *Marktplatz der Sensationen,* in *Gesammelte Werke,* 7 (Berlin: Aufbau-Verlag, 1979), 271–89. English version available in Kisch, "A Lost Football Game and the Mystery of Colonel Redl," *Sensation Fair,* trans. Guy Endore (New York: Modern Age Books, 1941), 299–320. Some aspects of Kisch's account have been challenged in Georg Markus, *Der Fall Redl* (Vienna: Amalthea Verlag, 1984), and Michael Horowitz, "Enthüllungen einer Enthüllung: Der Fall des Oberst Redl," in Michael Horowitz, ed., *Ein Leben für die Zeitung* (Vienna: Verlag ORAC, 1985) 32–36.
7. But see Bernard Williams, "Moral Luck," *Moral Luck* (Cambridge: Cambridge University Press, 1981), 204–39, and Thomas Nagel, "Moral Luck," *Mortal Questions* (Cambridge: Cambridge University Press, 1979), 24–38.
8. Stanley Schachter and Jerome E. Singer, "Cognitive, Social, and Physiological Determinants of Emotional State," *Psychological Review* 69, no. 5 (1962):

379–99. There have been challenges to some aspects of this classic experiment. See, e.g., G. D. Marshall and P. G. Zimbardo, "Affective Consequences of Inadequately Explained Physiological Arousal," *Journal of Personality and Social Psychology* 37 (1979): 970–88.

9. Schachter and Singer, "Cognitive, Social, and Physiological Determinants," 384–85.

10. D. G. Dutton and A. P. Aron, "Some Evidence for Heightened Sexual Attraction under Conditions of High Anxiety," *Journal of Personality and Social Psychology* 30 (1974): 510–17. Alternative explanations of what happened are clearly possible. See, e.g., Hans Eysenck and Michael Eysenck, *Mindwatching* (London: Michael Joseph, 1981), 125.

11. D. Zillman, R. C. Johnson, K. D. Day, "Attribution of Apparent Arousal and Proficiency of Recovery from Sympathetic Activation Affecting Excitation Transfer to Aggressive Behavior," *Journal of Experimental Social Psychology* 10 (1974): 503.

12. M. D. Storms and R. E. Nisbett, "Insomnia and the Attribution Process," *Journal of Personality and Social Psychology* 16, no. 21 (1970): 319–28, esp. 321. There have been challenges to these findings: Frank D. Fincham, "Clinical Applications of Attribution Theory: Problems and Prospects," in Miles Hewstone, ed., *Attribution Theory: Social and Functional Extensions* (Oxford: Basil Blackwell, 1983), 187–203, esp. 189. Some would confine the term "attribution theory" to the work of H. H. Kelley and refer to Schachter and Singer's work as the theory of cognitive labelling. A more recent and suggestive usage calls both attribution theory.

13. Storms and Nisbett, "Insomnia," 322.

14. Eysenck and Eysenck, *Mindwatching,* 121.

15. Mark R. Lepper, David Greene, and Richard G. Nisbett, "Undermining Children's Intrinsic Interest with Extrinsic Rewards: A Test of the 'Overjustification Hypothesis,' " *Journal of Personality and Social Psychology* 28 (1973): 129–37.

16. Mark Twain, *The Adventures of Tom Sawyer,* in John C. Gerber, Paul Baender, Terry Firkins, eds., *The Works of Mark Twain* (Berkeley: University of California Press, 1980), 49–50.

17. Glaser, *Abhandlungen aus dem oesterreichischen Strafrechte* (1858), quoted in H. L. A. Hart and A. M. Honore, *Causation in the Law* (Oxford: Oxford University Press, 1959), 391–92.

18. RG St. (Entscheidungen des Reichsgerichts in Strafsachen) 63 (1930), 392. Nonetheless, it affirmed the acquittal on the ground that Paul had no duty to illuminate Josef's bicycle.

19. See Hart and Honore, *Causation,* 193.

20. David Lewis, *Counterfactuals* (Cambridge, Mass.: Harvard University Press, 1973), 10.

21. See Nicholas Rescher, *Hypothetical Reasoning* (Amsterdam: North-Holland Publishing Co., 1964).
22. Lewis, *Counterfactuals,* 71.
23. Robert Sobel, *For Want of a Nail* (New York: Macmillan, 1973).
24. See, generally, Lewis, *Counterfactuals,* 1.
25. Robert Fogel, *Railroads and American Economic Growth: Essays in Econometric History* (Baltimore: Johns Hopkins Press, 1964).
26. Jon Elster, *Logic and Society: Contradictions and Possible Worlds* (London: John Wiley & Sons, 1978), chap. 6, p. 208.
27. The reader may wonder: Doesn't the fact that C rather than A brought about B's injury mean that B's injury came about in a different way? Under a very extreme version of the Austrian test one could make this argument. But the extreme version of the test quickly generates intolerable absurdities: The nurse turns off the light in a room in which a man happens to be dying. According to the extreme version, she has caused the man's death, because if she hadn't done what she did, he would have died in a different way than he did—he would have died with the lights on rather than off.
28. See Lewis, *Counterfactuals,* 31–36.
29. David Lewis, "Causation," in Ernest Sosa, ed., *Causation and Conditionals* (Oxford: Oxford University Press, 1975), 180–91.
30. This analysis deals with cases of preemption, but not the related problem of overdetermination, i.e., the case where two fires simultaneously converge on a house and burn it down. The law has tended to cope with the problem of overdetermination by creating a special doctrine to deal with the area where it is most prominent—group activities. More on that in the next chapter.

    An alternative treatment of factual causation is found in Richard W. Wright, "Causation in Tort Law," *California Law Review* 73 (1985): 1737.
31. Usually they have, however, reserved it for the criminal context. See Hart and Honore, *Causation,* 393–94.
32. John Lekschas, *Die Kausalitaet bei der verbrecherischen Handlung* (Berlin: VEB Deutscher Zentralverlag, 1952), 43.
33. W. H. Dray, "Concepts of Causation in A. J. P. Taylor's Account of the Origins of the Second World War," *History and Theory* 17 (1978): 159–74, esp. 152–55, 160–61. Here as in the next few paragraphs, what is being quoted is Dray's excellent summary of the various adversaries' positions. The key primary source is, of course, A. J. P. Taylor, *The Origins of the Second World War,* 2d ed. (New York: Atheneum, 1983). The first edition was published in 1961. Adversary positions are collected in E. M. Robertson, ed., *The Origins of the Second World War* (London: Macmillan, 1971). Necessarily, my sketch of this grand debate is a gross simplification.

I should also note that historians distinguish causes and conditions in two quite different contexts, which Hart and Honore have called the "explanatory" and the "attributive." The cause-condition distinction in these contexts is drawn along similar but not identical lines. Obviously, the attributive context is closest to the legal one. The World War II debate switched back and forth between these two contexts. I have here focused on the debate's attributive aspect. Dray focuses on its explanatory aspect.

34. Hart and Honore, *Causation,* 326.
35. *R. v. Nbakwa,* (2) S.A. 55 (S.R.) (1956), 558–59.
36. *Stephenson v. State,* 179 N.E. 633 (Ind., 1932).
37. *United States v. Freeman,* 25 Fed. Cas. 1208 (Circuit Court, D. Mass., 1827).
38. Feinberg, "Causing Voluntary Actions," *Doing and Deserving* (Princeton, N.J.: Princeton University Press, 1970), 152–86, esp. 157.
39. Cf. Restatement (Second) of Torts §281, illustration 3.
40. *Palsgraf v. Long Island R. Co.,* 162 N.E. 99 (N.Y. Ct. of App., 1928). For background on this case, see John T. Noonan, "The Passengers of Palsgraf," in *Persons and Masks of the Law* (New York: Farrar, Straus, & Giroux, 1976), 111. For further development of the theory of causation adumbrated in this case, see Robert Keeton, *Legal Cause in the Law of Torts* (Columbus: Ohio State University Press, 1963).
41. Cf. *Gorris v. Scott* (1874) L.R. 9 Exch. 125.
42. See Keeton, *Legal Cause in the Law of Torts,* 3–11.
43. See, e.g., Jeschek, *Lehrbuch,* 229–30 (discussion of German adequacy theory); Hart and Honore, *Causation,* chap. 17 (discussion of same). Variations of the adequacy theory have been proposed in the economic analysis of law: Guido Calabresi, "Concerning Cause and the Law of Torts: An Essay for Harry Kalven, Jr.," *University of Chicago Law Review* 43 (1975): 69; Steven Shavell, "An Analysis of Causation and the Scope of Liability in the Law of Torts," *Journal of Legal Studies* 9 (1980): 463; William M. Landes and Richard A. Posner, "Causation in Tort Law: An Economic Approach," *Journal of Legal Studies* 12 (1983): 109.
44. There are ways of applying the "but for" test in such cases that would in fact narrow the scope of liability considerably before we even get to the question of proximate causation. Take the case of the speeding driver who kills a child that suddenly leaps in his way. One way of applying the "but for" test leads us to reason that if he hadn't speeded, the driver wouldn't have been at the spot where the child leaped into the street at the moment it leaped into the street and therefore he wouldn't have killed it. But another way of applying the "but for" test leads us to reason that if he hadn't speeded, but been at the very same spot where the child leaped into the street at the moment it leaped into the street, he would still have killed it.

This kind of approach would not, of course, eliminate our need for proximate causation, but it would make it somewhat less pressing.

5. The Company You Keep

1. Bertolt Brecht, "Fragen eines lesenden Arbeiters" [Questions of a worker who reads (translation mine)], *Gesammelte Werke* (Frankfurt: Suhrkamp Verlag, 1967), 9:656.
2. For an alternative explanation of complicity, see Sanford H. Kadish, "Complicity, Cause, and Blame: A Study in the Interpretation of Doctrine," *California Law Review* 73 (1985): 323. See also Joshua Dressler, "Reassessing the Theoretical Underpinnings of Accomplice Liability: New Solutions to an Old Problem," *Hastings Law Journal* 37 (1985): 91.
3. Stanley Milgram, "The Small World Problem," *Psychology Today* 1 (1967): 60–67, esp. 64–65.
4. Joseph Vining, *Legal Identity* (New Haven: Yale University Press, 1978), 32, note. Vining quotes Donne to illustrate a related form of interconnectedness he calls the "Donne effect."
5. Cf. Model Penal Code Sec. 2.06, Comment, 316.
6. Sanford Levinson, "Responsibility for Crimes of War," in Marshall Cohen, Thomas Nagel, and Thomas Scanlon, eds., *War and Moral Responsibility* (Princeton, N.J.: Princeton University Press, 1974), 104–33, esp. 117.
7. *In re Yamashita,* 327 U.S. 1 (1945).
8. United States Constitution, Art. III, Sec. 3.
9. See generally, Milton Lomask, *Aaron Burr: The Conspiracy and Years of Exile* (New York: Farrar, Straus, & Giroux, 1982).
10. *Ex parte Bollman and Swartwout,* 8 U.S. 74, 125–26 (1807).
11. *United States v. Aaron Burr,* 8 U.S. 470, 517 (U.S. Circuit Court, District of Virginia, 1807).
12. Jeschek, *Lehrbuch,* 529–30.
13. Fritz Hartung, "Der Badewannenunfall," *Juristenzeitung* (1954): 430–31.
14. BGH (Bundesgerichtshof), NJW (Neue Juristische Wochenschrift), 355–56 (1963).
15. BGH (Bundesgerichtshof) Dallinger MDR (Monatsschrift für deutsches Recht) 547 (1974).
16. Marvin E. Shaw, *Group Dynamics: The Psychology of Small Group Behavior,* 3d ed. (New York: McGraw-Hill Book Co., 1981), 58.
17. A. Jenness, "The Role of Discussion in Changing Opinion Regarding a Matter of Fact," *Journal of Abnormal and Social Psychology* 27 (1932): 279–96.
18. H. Gurnee, "A Comparison of Collective and Individual Judgments of Fact," *Journal of Experimental Psychology* 21, no. 1 (1937): 106–12, at 110.
19. G. B. Watson, "Do Groups Think More Efficiently than Individuals?" *Journal of Abnormal and Social Psychology* 23 (1928): 328–36.

20. Shaw, *Group Dynamics,* 61.
21. Ibid. 64–66.
22. Mario Puzo, *The Godfather* (New York: G. P. Putnam's Sons, 1969).
23. Robert Axelrod, *The Evolution of Cooperation* (New York: Basic Books, 1984), 27, 75, 79, 86.
24. Tony Ashworth, *Trench Warfare, 1914–1918: The Live and Let Live System* (New York: Holmes & Meier, 1980), 224.
25. *Interstate Circuit, Inc. v. United States,* 306 U.S. 208 (1939).
26. Topan Ghosh, *The Ghandi Murder Trial* (New York: Asia Publishing House, 1975), 132.
27. Thomas C. Schelling, *The Strategy of Conflict* (Cambridge, Mass.: Harvard University Press, 1980; originally published 1960), 54–57.
28. Thomas C. Schelling, *Micromotives and Macrobehavior* (New York: W. W. Norton & Co., 1978), 92–93.
29. *Rex v. Leigh* (1775) 1 C. & K. 28 n; 174 E.R. 697 n; 2 Camp. 372; 170 E.R. 1188n, discussed in Gerald Orchard, " 'Agreement' in Criminal Conspiracy—1," [1974] *Criminal Law Review* 297, 300.
30. *United States v. Spock,* 416 F.2d 165 (1st Cir., 1969). See also Jessica Mitford, *The Trial of Dr. Spock* (New York: Alfred A. Knopf, 1969).
31. *United States v. Spock,* 416 F.2d 168, 174–79. Final note: Although I have described an agreement as sufficient for a conspiracy, many modern conspiracy statutes add to this a relatively inconsequential overt act requirement.

6. The Crime That Never Was

1. *Regina v. Collins,* 9 Cox C.C. 497, 498 (1864).
2. Stephens, *Digest of Criminal Law,* 5th ed. (1894), art. 50, quoted in *Haughton v. Smith,* [1975] A.C. 476, 491.
3. *Stephens v. Abrahams,* 27 V.L.R. 753, 768 (1902).
4. *State v. Wilson,* 38 So. 46 (Mississippi, 1905).
5. *People v. Dlugash,* 363 N.E. 2d 1155, 1157 (Ct. of App. of N.Y., 1977).
6. *Haughton v. Smith,* [1975] A.C. 500.
7. *People v. Jaffe,* 78 N.E. 169–70 (N.Y. Ct. of App., 1906).
8. *State v. Clarissa,* 11 Ala. 57, 60 (Ala., 1847).
9. Invented case.
10. Although I develop it here as an outgrowth of my earlier analysis of the distinction between intention and knowledge, the test here proposed is in effect the "rational motivation" test set forth in Fletcher, *Rethinking Criminal Law* (Boston: Little, Brown, & Co., 1978), 131–97.
11. Alfred Lessing, "What Is Wrong with a Forgery," in D. Dutton, ed., *The Forger's Art* (Berkeley: University of California Press, 1983), 58–59, 62–64.

12. Glanville Williams, *Criminal Law: The General Part* (London: Stevens & Sons, 1961), 633–34.
13. Michael Polanyi, *Personal Knowledge* (Chicago: University of Chicago Press, 1962), 20 n. 1.
14. Hope Verness, "Han Van Meegeren Fecit," in Dutton, ed., *The Forger's Art*; Lord Kilbracken, *Van Meegeren* (1967); John Godley (Lord Kilbracken), *The Master Forger* (1951).
15. Kilbracken, *Van Meegeren,* 62–63.
16. Godley, *Master Forger,* 190.

7. Epilogue: Final Reckoning

1. G. K. Chesterton, "Introduction" to Charles Dickens, *The Old Curiosity Shop* (London: Everyman's Library, 1966), xi.
2. That is not to say that these notions are adequate for describing the mental processes of normal people. Just remember the two-string experiment, where people were asked to find a way of getting hold of two strings far apart from each other. The trick was to hold on to one string and attach a heavy object to the other string that would permit it to swing. People who couldn't find the solution on their own hit upon it when the experimenter "inadvertently" brushed past one of the strings and caused it to sway slightly. But they would sincerely deny having gotten a clue from the experimenter's conduct. So did they or did they not believe that what the experimenter did would help them solve their problem? They behaved as though they believed it. Yet they possessed none of the background beliefs that go along with such a belief—e.g., the belief that that's what they believed.

The thesis that problems like the above make the mental vocabulary of everyday life unsuitable for psychology is developed is great detail in Stephen Stich, *From Folk Psychology to Cognitive Science: The Case against Belief* (Cambridge, Mass.: MIT Press, 1983).

3. This problem is explored in great detail in Derek Parfit, *Reasons and Persons* (Oxford: Oxford University Press, 1984).

Index